E L E A N O R   C O O K

* * * * *

Poetry, Word-Play, and Word-War

in Wallace Stevens

*

PRINCETON

UNIVERSITY PRESS

Published by Princeton University Press, 41 William Street,
Princeton, New Jersey 08540
In the United Kingdom: Princeton University Press, Guildford, Surrey

This book has been composed in Linotron Aldus

Clothbound editions of Princeton University Press books
are printed on acid-free paper, and binding materials are
chosen for strength and durability. Paperbacks, although satisfactory
for personal collections, are not usually suitable for library rebinding

Printed in the United States of America by Princeton University Press,
Princeton, New Jersey

Designed by Laury A. Egan

Library of Congress Cataloging-in-Publication Data

Cook, Eleanor.
Poetry, word-play, and word-war in Wallace Stevens / Eleanor Cook.
p.   cm.   Includes index.
ISBN 0-691-06747-3 (alk. paper)
1. Stevens, Wallace, 1879–1955—Criticism and interpretation. 2. Play
on words. I. Title.
PS3537.T4753Z6229 1988   811'.52—dc19   88–4817   CIP

FOR RAMSAY

Poetry, Word-Play, and Word-War
in Wallace Stevens

We enjoy the ithy oonts and long-haired
Plomets, as the Herr Gott
Enjoys his comets.

The danger is in the neatness of identifications.
(Beckett, "Dante . . . Bruno. Vico . . Joyce")

Contents

Preface

THIS IS A STUDY of the poetry of Wallace Stevens, with special attention to his word-play. It offers a full reading of his work, from his earliest to his latest poems, together with some mapping of his word-play. It also comments on his methods, especially in relation to current critical concerns.

By "word-play," I do not mean simply punning in the narrow sense of the word, though there are sufficient puns to satisfy the "true Carthaginian" or "Homo Pun-icus," as Swift and Coleridge called such an addict. I mean, generally speaking, the play of rhetoric and dialectic against each other (of which, more later). This is word-play that is essential, not ornamental, for Stevens' poetry. There has been much interest lately in rethinking the divisions between conceptual and playful, logical and a-logical uses of language. I hope this book will contribute to such thinking through its study of the essential word-play of Stevens' poetry, without which it is impossible to read him well.

Studies of word-play in a narrow sense run two risks. One is the risk of lapsing into miscellany, unless they are centered on some larger structure or decorum. Yet centering word-play on a larger structure can also be a risk. Too often, word-play is made subordinate to theme or plot or argument, a pleasing but inessential ornament that illustrates what is already there. My sense of Stevens' word-play is that it says what cannot be said in other ways. It is not necessarily subordinate or superior to theme or plot or argument. It may be either, or neither. And Stevens often plays with precisely those larger structures (of belief, ideas, conventions; of grammar, dialectic, rhetoric). Not that his word-play simply "subverts" (our all-too-fashionable verb) or always eludes argument.

I have addressed this book to the common reader of poetry, as well as the specialist and the theorist. I hope the theorist will take pleasure in some close readings, which I have tried to keep lively and clear without sacrificing critical acumen. Some of these readings are of poems virtually unread before. I hope the common reader will take pleasure in a few theoretical arguments, such as those about the metaphor poems. Often with Stevens, theory takes on the pleasure that we associate with practice, while practice takes on the rigor we associate with theory. There is a combination of pleasure and rigor that is Stevens' own, and no one else's.

The book is arranged chronologically, with each chapter concentrating on a major poem or group of poems. This arrangement has the advantage of showing change and development in Stevens' thinking and imagination as well as in his skills. Each chapter may be read as an essay in itself, speaking about a text and one or more aspects of word-play appropriate to that text. Some chapters could be expanded into separate studies, so that in a sense this is several books in one. The book is also cumulative; the close reading of *Notes toward a Supreme Fiction*, for example, will be a little clearer for someone who has followed terms and arguments presented earlier. With such a wide definition of word-play, I have had to speak of some types of word-play rather than others. Among types of word-play, I have had to choose areas of concentration. The play of allusiveness has been mapped in some detail, while other areas such as Stevens' play against synecdoche, have been located and outlined. I have raised more questions than I can answer about metaphor and about the sublime, but I think they are useful questions. One of the pleasures of reading Stevens' poetry is that it teaches us to read contemporary poetry, and I occasionally show this by inserting a line from, say, Geoffrey Hill or John Ashbery. One of the pleasures of reading Stevens' poetry is that it also teaches us to read backwards in a fresh way, and I occasionally show this too.

My reading of Stevens as poet builds on the work of his two best readers, Helen Vendler and Harold Bloom. Stevens' word-play makes us think again about Vendler's idea of his "qualified assertions"—about precisely how the assertions are qualified, and to what effect. Our very ways of qualifying seem to me to be questioned by Stevens, and then relocated, so to speak. Vendler's recent remark about Stevens' art of deflecting words from their denotative meaning (of which more below) points toward the area that interests me. Stevens' word-play also made me want to look at particulars in a way that Bloom sometimes does not. It is Bloom's work that initiated our current interest in the play of allusiveness, especially in metaleptic play. Stevens' work in this area is extraordinary in ways we have not heard. More even than Joyce, he can make us hear the words we have inherited in a new way. Some of the echoes in Stevens' work confirm Bloom's sense of Stevens as heir to a Whitman-Emerson tradition. Others widen that inheritance to include Shakespeare and Milton and the English Bible. Stevens' echoes offer a powerful, intricate rewriting of the English Bible, as mediated through a

Milton-Wordsworth line or a Milton-Keats-Whitman line. They work against mediation through a Dante-Eliot line, and they conduct an on-going battle with Eliot. I am, of course, indebted to other readings of Stevens, as well as general and particular studies of word-play, for example, in the area of allegory, and in Shakespeare and Joyce and biblical literature.

Acknowledgments

THE SPIRIT OF THIS BOOK is especially indebted to two people: to Northrop Frye for a half-hour of concentrated conversation and for much more; and to John Hollander for teaching of the highest order and for much more. Friends and colleagues cleared up vexing small problems, read earlier versions of some chapters, and offered encouragement when things were tangled. Among many, I should like to thank Jay Macpherson, and also James Carscallen, Denton Fox and Ruth Harvey, Heather and J. R. de J. Jackson, Eli and Ann Mandel, Jane and Michael Millgate, Mary Nyquist and Julian Patrick, Patricia Parker, Magdalen Redekop, and David Shaw. Students asked stimulating questions, and one graduate class provided a surprise meal out of Stevens' poetry, observing that Eliot would have confined them to ham and a peach; my thanks herewith. I am grateful to Holly Stevens for her generosity in all matters connected with her father's work.

Victoria College and the Department of English at the University of Toronto have been true places for scholarly and poetic work, as have the university and college libraries; I cannot speak too highly of the librarians of the E. J. Pratt Library. The Huntington Library, that earthly paradise of scholars, provided every possible support. Unpublished material is used with their permission, and the permission of the University of Chicago Library, Dartmouth College Library, the Houghton Library at Harvard University, as well as of Holly Stevens. Quotations from the published work of Wallace Stevens are reprinted by permission of Alfred A. Knopf, Faber and Faber, and Holly Stevens. Permission to quote from unpublished writing by Marianne Moore was granted by Clive E. Driver, Literary Executor of the estate of Marianne C. Moore. I have adapted a few pages of my "Riddles, Charms and Fictions in Wallace Stevens," from *Centre and Labyrinth: Essays in Honour of Northrop Frye*, edited by Eleanor Cook et al., published in 1983 by the University of Toronto Press. In Chapter 12, I have adapted a few pages of my "Directions in Reading Wallace Stevens: Up, Down, Across," from *Lyric Poetry: Beyond New Criticism*, edited by Chaviva Hosek and Patricia Parker (copyright © 1985 by Cornell University Press; used by permission of the publisher). This book was completed with the help of a Leave Fellowship from the Social Sciences and Humanities Research Council of Canada.

ACKNOWLEDGMENTS

The editors of Princeton University Press, Robert E. Brown, as well as Gretchen Oberfranc, and my copyeditor, Eve Pearson, have been exemplary in their good sense and consideration. I am very grateful to Jefferey Donaldson for help with the index.

To my family, I owe more than I can easily say: to Mark, whose wordplay is quicker than mine; to Maggie, who has all French poetry in her head; and above all, to the dedicatee, clearest of spirits.

Poetry, Word-Play, and Word-War
in Wallace Stevens

Introduction

I NEED to say a number of things all at once, because readers come to word-play with such different assumptions. So I shall say them briefly, then speak in a general way about word-play, before proceeding to an outline of this book, and then to some specialized matters. First, the simple and important point that Stevens liked word-play because it is often wonderfully funny. We sometimes read him a shade solemnly. Second, Stevens "words are almost always deflected from their common denotation," to quote Helen Vendler.[1] ("Personally I like words to sound wrong," he once wrote apropos of a translation of his work.[2]) We sometimes read him as if we were reading Wordsworth. Third, all language may be thought of as functioning through the interplay of dialectic and grammar and rhetoric, to go back to the old trivium. Word-play points to relations already there in language; it is not just added on. Fourth, though word-play may indeed be trivial (our usual view of it), it may also come as close as words can to some of our most vital concerns. Nor are its sportings always gaily comic; my contrary, "word-war," is meant to imply that word-play can also be mental war.

One way of reading poetry is to start with argument or theme, that is, in the general area of dialectic. (I use the term "dialectic" throughout in the old-fashioned sense of "debate" or "discussion." No Hegelian process is implied.) Certainly, Stevens' arguments must always be pursued to their logical conclusions. Their kind and degree, their "If this, then that," must be worked out. Some of his poems have minimal argument. Others debate with the rigor of a good lawyer, and the rigor and economy of a good poet. Sometimes the arguments are concealed. We might suppose that the title, *God Is Good. It Is a Beautiful Night*, is perfectly straightforward. It is not. (See Chapter 9.) Stevens is almost always thinking about methods of argument, and the implications of a line of argument, even as he is working them out. That is what some of his word-play points toward. And he often pays his readers the compliment of assuming they have thought through the common arguments about a

---

[1] *New York Review of Books* (November 20, 1986), 47.

[2] *Letters of Wallace Stevens*, ed. Holly Stevens (New York: Knopf, 1966), p. 340, June 1, 1939; hereafter cited in the text as *L*.

subject that interests them. Hence the occasional explicit invitation to the reader to fill in the boring blanks.

Yet to start with matters of dialectic can be frustrating or hazardous in reading Stevens. Often a poem seems to resist or deflect inquiries about its argument or theme. As Stevens says in a much-quoted sentence, "The poem must resist the intelligence / Almost successfully."[3] We do not always give enough emphasis to the word "almost." (As if Stevens ever supposed the intelligence did not have a vital role in reading poetry.) Nor do we give enough thought to the word "intelligence." For it is not the intelligence alone that gives meaning to poems, any more than the intelligence alone gives meaning in general, as Oliver Sacks shows most movingly in his book, *The Man Who Mistook His Wife for a Hat, and Other Clinical Tales*. (I am adapting the term "intelligence" in making this comparison.) Increasingly, we are coming to realize how often we ask the wrong questions of Stevens' poems. We ask questions as if we were reading Wordsworth, and Stevens simply cannot be read that way. This is Helen Vendler's point, and it is essential:

> Wordsworth almost always uses words in their common denotative meaning, and he uses syntax for the normal purposes of syntax— momentum and organizing. Stevens's words are almost always deflected from their common denotation, and his syntax serves to delay and to disarticulate. . . . The appearance of "telling" is superficially maintained . . . but one gets nowhere reading Stevens in a Wordsworthian spirit. . . . [This] is not conservative discursive writing. . . . Stevens's art is always about to refresh itself at the well of nonsense.[4]

One way of describing this book is to say it is about that process of deflection in Stevens' language, about his trips to the "well of nonsense." I have tried to locate precisely Stevens' angles and points of deflection, and to consider the implications of such deflecting. I have tried to follow his trips to the "well of nonsense" (though the term "nonsense" is problematic, and I have avoided it).

Where to begin, then, if dialectic is not taking us very far? Sometimes with obvious questions, which are often the ones that do not get asked, and should be. Always with the dictionary, or rather several dictionaries.

[3] *The Collected Poems of Wallace Stevens* (New York: Knopf, 1954), p. 350. Unless otherwise noted, poems are quoted from this edition. Where useful, I include page numbers of this volume, hereafter abbreviated in the text as *CP*. Cf. "Poetry must resist the intelligence almost successfully," in Stevens' "Adagia," *Opus Posthumous*, ed. Samuel French Morse (New York: Knopf, 1957), p. 171; hereafter abbreviated in the text as *OP*.

[4] *New York Review of Books* (November 20, 1986), 47.

Often with the rule of thumb: what did I expect to hear? It is not enough to observe the fact of word-play and word-war. We need to go on, pressing Stevens' text, which so often responds to the right pressure. We should also remember that Stevens quickly became wary of any simple reversal, that easiest of dialectical and rhetorical traps. Time and again, he tests and rejects our easy reversals. Or tests and retains them, as seems appropriate. One witty little example is the last poem of *Ideas of Order, Delightful Evening*, on which see Chapter 6.

My general working definition of word-play is the play of rhetoric and dialectic against each other (occasionally rhetoric and grammar against each other). This is, I think, a new definition, and I have found it useful. Such play may be on a scale of small to large, quiet to loud, background to foreground. Rhetoric may dance around or lead dialectic, dialectic may move toward or work with certain kinds of rhetoric rather than others. To put it in Aristotle's terms, rhetoric and dialectic speak to each other like lines of strophe and antistrophe in Greek poetry. (By "rhetoric," he means the art of persuasion. By "rhetoric," I mean throughout a system of figuration, for example, of tropes and schemes.) As we read Stevens' poems, we gradually come to hear certain terms or pairs of terms or triads of terms, and the center or axis or triangle that such terms set up. We hear how such centers or axes or triangles help locate and define our thinking and imagining. We hear how they shut out or push away other centers or axes or triangles. We consider alternatives; we consider how to keep ourselves from being trapped in such patterns, or trapped in mere randomness. This is not just play with language that we already own and work with, which will then settle down again to sober, sensible use after we have been briefly diverted. Once we have heard what Stevens does with some language, we cannot use it in the same way again.

Of course, word-play is not necessarily trivial. On the contrary, it can be the best way of approximating in words some of the most vital and mysterious parts of our lives. Centuries ago, the paradoxes of word-play offered ways of voicing the mysteries of Christ's Incarnation. Augustine and other church fathers are fine expositors of word-play, as are some rabbinical, biblical, and medieval scholars. The Renaissance understood the importance of word-play. Ruth Wallerstein observes that "wordplay was one of the recognized devices of ornamentation of poetry from the beginning of the re-creation of style in the Renaissance. But even in Lyly . . . though wordplay owed so much to the tradition of pure scheme of sound, it threw into prominence the underlying dialectic of thought." We might quarrel with the implicit metaphor in "underlying" and still rightly say that Wallerstein's 1950 account of word-play remains one of the best short introductions to it.[5] We might also listen to James Merrill on this subject in our own day:

> The next generation's problem [after Valéry and Joyce] was to create works whose resonance lasted more than a season. A culture without Greek or Latin or Anglo-Saxon goes off the gold standard. How to draw upon the treasure? At once representing and parodying our vital wealth, the lightweight crackle of wordplay would retain no little transactional power in the right hands. . . . Even today, how many poets choose the holy poverty of some secondhand diction, pure dull content in translation from a never-to-be-known original. "There is no wing like meaning," said Stevens. Two are needed to get off the ground.[6]

Word-play also offers, among other things, a way of writing about the Einsteinian world in which we all live (even if we often live in a Newtonian world for practical purposes and a Ptolemaic world for personal purposes). And it offers a way of writing about what Stevens called the "supreme fiction."

IF WE HAD to name the subject of Stevens' poetry in one phrase, that phrase would be his own: a poetry "of the earth."("The great poems of heaven and hell have been written and the great poem of the earth remains to be written."[7]) If we had to expand this phrase, we might divide it as follows: the poetry of nature, or better, of place, especially American place; the poetry of eros; the poetry of belief, later of a supreme fiction. The three subjects are, of course, related. Stevens began by speaking of his interest in the interaction between "reality" and the "imagination." (The unhelpful terms are his own; each is best defined on a sliding scale.) Later he subordinated this interaction to the question of a supreme fiction. ("[My] work suggests the possibility of a supreme fiction, recognized as a fiction, in which men could propose to themselves a fulfilment. . . . There are many poems relating to the interactions between reality and the imagination, which are to be regarded as marginal to this central theme" [L 820, 1954].) At the time of *Harmonium* in 1923, Stevens was chiefly interested in the first two subjects, though the second, eros, had become problematic. The third subject was chiefly a matter of polemics.

---

[5] *Studies in Seventeenth-Century Poetic* (Madison: University of Wisconsin Press, 1950), p. 169, and see pp. 169–80.

[6] *Recitative: Prose by James Merrill* (San Francisco: North Point Press, 1986), p. 112.

[7] *The Necessary Angel: Essays on Reality and the Imagination* (New York: Knopf, 1951), p. 142 (1948); hereafter cited in the text as *NA*.

In the late twenties and the thirties, Stevens' center of interest slowly changed.

To open *Harmonium*, Stevens took an early poem, *Domination of Black* (1916), and paired it with a poem written five years later, *The Snow Man*. In front of this powerful pair, he placed six slighter poems, written between 1916 and 1921. Stevens usually arranges his work in approximate chronological order (cf. *L* 766), but not here. I read the first six poems as I think Stevens meant us to read them—as lessons in approaching his work. Without them, we might allow a mimetic reading to dominate our sense of the seventh and eighth poems. Thematically, these eight poems treat American place, and they show Stevens' passionate desire for a poetic place that is a true home. They also show ways of beginning a volume of poetry in 1923; that is, they map a rhetoric of beginning and they map it in a remarkably fresh way, which is very much a result of Stevens' word-play.

Stevens uses different kinds of word-play in the first six poems. These include grammatical play (with prepositions), a play he will continue all his life. (I note later his continued play with prepositions, with verbal conjugation, and so on. An entire study could be made of Stevens' poetics of grammar.) Word-play also includes riddling effects, and the pure riddle poem. (For terms, see Part III of this Introduction.) Again, this is a continued play in Stevens. Word-play also includes etymological play. Always, we need to go to the dictionary when reading Stevens, or rather not the dictionary (the indispensable Oxford English Dictionary) but dictionaries in the plural: dictionaries of United States usage, French dictionaries ("a good many words come to me from French origins" [*L* 699, 1950]), German dictionaries ("After all, I read German well enough . . . and used to read it freely" [*L* 576, 1948]), Spanish dictionaries ("In MUD MASTER, the word *pickanines* is correct. In this form it seems to me, for no good reason, to reflect its Spanish origin."[8]), the Lewis and Short Latin dictionary (see *L* 275), and more. And we must read dictionaries remembering that they are compiled by lexicographers and include errors; that their definitions are themselves plots; that false etymologies are as useful to a poet as true ones.[9] Stevens' sophistication in etymological word-play and word-war is extraordinary. So is his multilingual punning. When I argue for a pun on Homer's Greek in *An Ordinary Evening in New Haven* (v), I trust my readers to accept the possibility of such punning. It may help to know that Stevens copied Greek passages

[8] To R. L. Latimer, May 27, 1935, University of Chicago Library. Quoted by permission of Holly Stevens and the University of Chicago Library.

[9] Cf. K. K. Ruthven, "The Poet as Etymologist," *Critical Quarterly* 11 (1969), 9–37.

into his notebook,[10] but it helps more to listen to the words of Stevens' poems.

The most useful rule of thumb in reading these poems, as in reading much of Stevens, is to ask this question: what do we expect to hear? That is, what would we ordinarily say? If the answer helps, then we should go on, always watching Stevens' guidelines, and our own habit of sliding back into familiar ways of thinking and imagining.

The remarkable poem, *Domination of Black* makes us look again at the word "topos" in a full sense, including the sense of actual place, the places of argument (classical topos), thematic places (postclassical topos), the places of voice. I suggest we think of topos as a memory-place. Stevens' poem presents a possible image of topos, with an appropriate and terrible genius loci. His echoing of Wordsworth shows Stevens' great intelligence about the difficulties of a beginning poet. It also shows how he hears Wordsworth echoing and revising Milton. (Stevens will himself echo and revise both poets in his later work, and even make us hear Milton *through* Wordsworth.) *The Snow Man* may also usefully be thought of as a poem of topos, whose word-play is with paradox.

Stevens' early word-play functions to displace us slightly as we look about us or read—to disrupt a little our ordinary sense of a native place in nature and in language. The effect of this is not so much to leave us merely displaced as to concentrate our attention on just how and why we feel at home in the first place. It awakens us. In the later poetry, Stevens' word-play functions quite differently. It allows us to possess both a foreign and a native sense of words and place at one and the same time.

Chapter 2, on the Venus poems, introduces Stevens' second subject, the erotic, and expands our sense of "place" to include the places of love. I have chosen to draw together Stevens' love poems and his Southern poems, notably the Florida poems. The love poems, which gradually develop an unhappy plot, include one great poem, *Le Monocle de Mon Oncle*. It is not an easy poem, and I try to elucidate it, extending some of the methods developed in Chapter 1. The places of love proved a troubled subject for Stevens. He was more at ease with the second group of poems, the Florida poems, where he could write poetry of the earth as beloved body. But after a time, these poems also lose their sense of ease and become equivocal. In some ways, Stevens remained an erotic poet even after his ritual farewell to his erotic muse in the 1936 *Farewell to Florida*. But the erotic force is much submerged and dispersed. I have not pursued biographical criticism here or elsewhere, though I contribute to such crit-

---

[10] Cf. Joan Richardson, *Wallace Stevens: A Biography*, vol. 1, *The Early Years, 1879–1923* (New York: Beech Tree Books, 1986), p. 241.

icism in passing. Readers interested in biographical criticism should make use of Milton Bates's *Wallace Stevens: A Mythology of Self*, George S. Lensing's *Wallace Stevens: A Poet's Growth*, and Joan Richardson's *Wallace Stevens: A Biography*.[11]

Most readers of Stevens, asked to name a poem of word-play, would say at once, *The Comedian as the Letter C*. This also is a poem of place, and in its original form it was connected with Venus. As it stands, it is a problem poem, and reading some of its unheard word-play helps only a little. Among the interesting questions this poem raises is the question of the limits of word-play. Stevens eventually abandoned the crowded and wearyingly elusive style of much of *The Comedian*. In so doing, he said no to deconstructionist polysemy, and refused the role of the perpetual trickster who evades all statement and definition.

As with word-play in general, so with the matter of allusiveness. Readers have such different assumptions about allusion and echo that it is hard to know where to begin. We have lost the habit of hearing words inside our head as living voices of the dead, lost the habit of cherishing words that best catch the reality of our lives (reality in the sense of "that which is real" as distinct from "actuality"). It is quite wrong to think of allusion as the use of a mental card catalogue. It is quite wrong to think of a necessary opposition between allusion and reality—or rather, language that refers to reality. If writing of reality is powerful enough for us, then we remember it. Why should we expunge our memory with each new encounter with reality? Chapter 4 sets out terms I use throughout in the area of allusiveness. Some of Stevens' work is saturated with echoing effects, though there is little of Eliot's imperative use of quotation and allusion. Helen Vendler noted, some years ago, Stevens' "concealed allusiveness,"[12] and we are just beginning to comprehend his work in this area. I consider two remarkable examples: *The Emperor of Ice-Cream* and *The Man Whose Pharynx Was Bad*. Both poems include one allusive echo of a Shakespearean play; both also include diffused echoing of a second Shakespearean play, whose echoes rebound against the first and stronger echo. The poems have to do with death, and the death of one's own voice, both of which are most appropriate areas for the play of allusion. They are also appropriate for Stevens at this stage in his work, as he approached a period of crisis in his writing.

The *Harmonium* chapters end with Stevens' third subject and his most

[11] *Wallace Stevens: A Mythology of Self* (Berkeley and London: University of California Press, 1985). *Wallace Stevens: A Poet's Growth*, (Baton Rouge and London: Louisiana State University Press, 1986).

[12] Vendler, *On Extended Wings: Wallace Stevens' Longer Poems* (Cambridge, Mass.: Harvard University Press, 1969), p. 274.

familiar poem, *Sunday Morning*. It is worth considering Stevens as a poet of endings, both thematic endings (mortal and eschatological matters) and formal endings (matters of closure). We may hear him desiring a Virgilian pattern of endings rather than a Miltonic pattern, and in this he is like the Romantic poet most congenial to him, Keats. As I began with a rhetoric of beginning, and the opening poems of *Harmonium*, so I end this section with endings. These include the two short closing poems of this collection, and I show why the little poem *Tea* is placed where it is. Stevens ordered his volume so that it came to rest on a sense of poetic home. The closing poems, of place, of eros, of the sublime, provide a sense of felicity. Dialectic and rhetoric are more and more in harmony, and there is little sense of displacement. But Stevens was approaching a dry time in his poetic work.

The second section, on *Ideas of Order, The Man with the Blue Guitar*, and *Parts of a World*, treats a transitional period in Stevens' work. The first volume looks at ideas of order in a very full sense of that phrase, as Stevens works toward a fresh beginning. I consider his rhetoric of beginning again, as seen in poems of immense intelligence about this most difficult and necessary step. Many poems show Stevens working against simple reversals in argument or in rhetoric. *Autumn Refrain* shows his developing skill in allusiveness, and the title poem *The Idea of Order at Key West* is a triumph over old ghosts, both of eros and of place.

Stevens' renewed poetic energy became focused in *The Man with the Blue Guitar*, a crucial, pivotal poem. Its language of covenant at the end signals a rededication to poetry, and the poem as a whole marks the first step toward a subject that will engage Stevens more than any other until the end of his life, the search for a supreme fiction. We are watching a shift of relation in the three subjects of place, eros, and belief. And we are seeing an enlargement of the ample sense of word-play and word-war in Stevens' earlier work.

If *Ideas of Order* looks at orders, then *Parts of a World* looks at the contrary, at the language of particulars. *Parts of a World* is a book of parts in many ways, with various relations of parts to wholes, and parts to other parts. Throughout, Stevens is wary of themes that commonly give a sense of unity, whether war and nation, old ideas of light and space, home or heaven or the quest for either. He is equally wary of rhetorical patterns that commonly give a sense of unity or wholeness: synecdoche, metaphor, symbol, closure. And so I have titled this chapter, "Against Synecdoche," where of course "against" does not mean a simple reversal any more than it means mere randomness. The first three poems, including *Poems of Our Climate*, may be read as working against synecdoche. This last poem also shows Stevens moving away from his first general interest, the interactions of reality and the imagination, and reaching toward his final interest, the supreme fiction.

Stevens' growing interest in a possible supreme fiction leads him to consider things that are communal, or might truly be so. In 1935, Stevens remarked of his early heroic figure, Hoon, that Hoon "found all form and order in solitude" (CP 121, 65). If Stevens wanted to write, or point the way toward writing, a supreme fiction that might some day have something of the authority Christianity once had, then he had to consider what things may truly be held in common by a people. Stevens' complex of *cum-* words, in *Poems of Our Climate* and later, speak to this growing concern. It is explicit in *An Ordinary Evening in New Haven*: "a recent imagining of reality . . . A larger poem for a larger audience . . . A mythological form, a festival sphere" (CP 465–66). It is also explicit in a letter of 1943: "As I see the subject [of the supreme fiction], it could occupy a school of rabbis for the next few generations. In trying to create something as valid as the idea of God has been, and for that matter remains, the first necessity seems to be breadth" (L 435). Then, with his fine sense of humor and logic and metaphor, and of Dante's *punto* (point), Stevens adds: "It is true that the thing would never amount to much until there is no breadth or, rather, until it has all come to a point." Perhaps such a thing will never come, but Stevens hears "edgings and inchings of final form" by (and in) the end of his poem (CP 488).

Stevens' poetry from *Transport to Summer* to the end of his life is a rich body of work. I begin with his play with the figure of metaphor, a play suggested by the title of his best volume, on which Marianne Moore commented. Stevens' poems on metaphor are more precise than we have supposed about types of metaphor (archetypal, anagogic, juxtaposing, etc.). They are also suggestive for various theories of metaphor. For example, Stevens wrote an essay on "Effects of Analogy," and I think his little poem, *Les Plus Belles Pages*, which he glossed, is talking about metaphor as analogy. I touch on some remarks by philosophers and literary critics on metaphor in relation to Stevens' cryptic statements in his poetry and prose. We have hardly begun to read Stevens' thinking in this area.

The rest of the book until the closing chapter is taken up with readings of three of Stevens' major sequences, *Esthétique du Mal*, *Notes toward a Supreme Fiction*, and *An Ordinary Evening in New Haven*. *Esthétique du Mal* began with a soldier's letter, and it is a war poem, addressing itself to questions of evil and to theories of the sublime. Stevens' all-important strategy is to make us think of evil in a different way from the usual evil-versus-divine-good axis. He wants us to think of evil as against the normal—the normal good things of this earth. One great challenge to a poetry of the earth is the force of a poetry of hell, especially in wartime. Stevens answers that challenge here. In so doing, he also speaks throughout to theories of the sublime: the transcendental sublime, the natural sublime, the psychological sublime, and even a political sublime. The poem includes some of his richest and his most outrageous word-play, as he listens in turn to his old, great poets, to thoughts of human love, to easy wartime rhetoric. This is full-dress word-play and word-war at once.

With *Notes toward a Supreme Fiction*, we come to Stevens' major poem on questions of belief, on our sacred or supreme texts, written or unwritten, if we have any sacred or supreme texts. As so often, he clears the ground by reexamining his own heritage. For example, I hear an undoing of the "I am" of Coleridge and the very different "I am" of Descartes in cantos iii and iv. (Coleridge's "I am" is essentially the biblical "I am" and part of his well-known definition of the imagination. Descartes's "I am" comes in his *cogito, ergo sum*.) Stevens begins with a mentor and a student, having observed how many "supreme fictions" (including Genesis) begin this way. The student is a type and includes that future writer, that "virile poet" (*NA* 37), who may one day write our new supreme fiction.

Stevens knew as well as Paul de Man that metaphors are harder to get rid of than ideas.[13] Part II of *Notes* shows the persistent tropes of supreme fictions in action. The cantos are like nine one-act plays, and some are exceedingly funny. The series ends with a "translation" canto (ix), then the tenth "transformation" canto, where a poet much like Stevens envisions the whole sequence in a park much like his favorite Elizabeth Park in Hartford. Part III is the most challenging part, as Stevens turns to the difficult subject of proper pleasure in a new supreme fiction. This section builds toward the Canon Aspirin cantos, where Stevens gives full due to an inheritance he loved in his way and also fought: the biblical inheritance that is also Milton's and Coleridge's and Browning's. Stevens' early antipietism cannot touch the strength of such an inheritance, and here he allows it all he can in the figure of Canon Aspirin. Yet it remains untrue for him, and he must turn away from it. In the eighth canto, Stevens makes us hear Milton, then Milton through Wordsworth, and so tells a story of literary history and the history of belief. His last canto encloses the whole sequence in a Genesis-to-Revelation pattern.

An Ordinary Evening in New Haven is a poem of place in a special way. It began with a phrase from Gerard Manley Hopkins, "heaven-

---

[13] *Allegories of Reading: Figural Language in Rousseau, Nietzsche, Rilke, and Proust* (New Haven and London: Yale University Press, 1979), p. 4.

haven." At least, so I surmise. Stevens copied the phrase in the course of copying part of a review. Next came the title, in a long list of wonderfully suggestive titles. Stevens was remembering a poem he had written some thirty years earlier, a poem of earth, written against St. John's apocalyptic text, "I saw a new heaven and a new earth." Now he considers St. John's "new heaven" in conjunction with Connecticut's New Haven. What is left of this old vision of the earth, and what vision may we now have? The thirty-one-canto poem begins with older visions of a new heaven and a new earth, as for example those of the original settlers of New Haven, or those of Dante and his modern disciple, Eliot. It moves through the meditations of a Professor Eucalyptus, so called because of the rich punning on "apocalypse." And it closes on a vision of Stevens' own loved earthly paradise, together with a view of this earth that accords with a modern sense of reality. Stevens was considering an "ordinary evening" in an ordinary place, and how a man just turning seventy might best speak of this. Sometimes bleak, sometimes angry, sometimes tender, the poem sums up over Stevens' longtime concerns. It looks forward and also says farewell. For it is Stevens' last long poem in the remarkable series of long poems from 1942 through 1949. He would now turn back to shorter forms in the extraordinary late lyrics. The word-play in this poem asks to be read with special care, for Stevens is a subtle and forceful examiner of our sometimes overeasy language of apocalypse and revelation.

We have hardly found a language in which to speak of Stevens' late poems, and their sense of place. Stevens is so much the master, so much at ease in his play with and through words. At the same time, many of these poems are fierce and loving poems, as Stevens looks back over a lifetime, and looks forward against death. They are poems of place in the sense that they are of the earth that Stevens loved and did not want to leave. They are poems of place that include the places of love and the places of a supreme fiction. They have a wisdom of their own. Here Stevens' language achieves the seemingly impossible. It looks through and at language at the same time, as it holds in tension the reality and the imagination of a place Stevens now fully possessed.

A WORD about terms. "Dialectic," as I noted above, is used generally in the old-fashioned sense of "debate" or "discussion." I am following the threefold division of the old trivium, and so use the term in the wide sense. I do not distinguish puns from word-play but include them within word-play.[14] I do not distinguish, except in passing, kinds of puns, those

---

[14] It is possible to distinguish logical plays on words from capricious puns, on which see

kinds much older than the word "pun" itself. ("Paronomasia" is the best known, and it functions as a synonym for "punning," though it is strictly only one type of punning. Nowadays, "syllepsis" is making a comeback. Leo Spitzer wrote a generation ago about how the comparatively recent term, "pun," includes a series of older rhetorical categories.[15]) By rhetoric, I mean a system of figuration, for example, of tropes and schemes, a trope being a figure of thought in which meaning is changed (metaphor, synecdoche), and a scheme being a figure of speech in which meaning is not overtly changed (alliteration, chiasmus). My terms in the area of allusiveness are discussed in Chapter 4; I touch on definitions of topos and of metaphor in Chapters 1 and 9. Only occasionally do I use the word "game," which is not synonymous with play, having set rules and set, direct consequences. Some kinds of play I have mentioned only in passing, for example, play of acoustic sound.

I have used the term "sense of place" throughout in passing. This is a more difficult sense to define than we may realize. Santayana spoke of Virgil's sense of place, and Dame Helen Gardner has spoken of T. S. Eliot's. If a sense of place comes only in writing mimetically, then Frank Kermode is right, and Stevens has little sense of actual place.[16] Yet we have all been in art galleries where a man looks at a Picasso painting, and asks the standard question: "Did you ever see anyone who looked like that?" The trouble is that eventually all Picasso's viewers start to look like this or that painting. We learn to read the idiom. So also with place in Stevens' poems. One of my developing arguments is that Stevens has a profound sense of place, historical, sensual, physical, and so on. Another ongoing argument is that Stevens is sometimes a poet of place in the sense of writing accurate descriptive lines quite realistically. (See Chapter 2, on *Floral Decorations for Bananas*.) It is a particular pleasure to demonstrate this. I have not contributed, except in passing, to the discussions of Stevens in relation to local poetry, or in relation to such poets of place as Williams.

There seems to be an interesting relation between word-play and a sense of place. Walter Redfern writes that "the pun is a sixth sense."[17] I

Walter Redfern, *Puns* (Oxford and New York: Blackwell, 1984), p. 7. Cf. the outline of Wurth's divisions, where true word-play combines sound-play and sense-play, in Herbert A. Ellis, *Shakespeare's Lusty Punning in "Love's Labour's Lost"* (The Hague and Paris: Mouton, 1973), p. 18n.

[15] Cf. Leo Spitzer, "Puns," *Journal of English and German Philology* 49 (1950), 952–54. The most common division is between homonymic and semantic puns; Stephen Booth has a useful category of "ideational pun" in his *Shakespeare's Sonnets* (New Haven and London: Yale University Press, 1977), p. 465.

[16] See below, Chapter 2, n. 18.

[17] *Puns*, p. 6.

wonder if it is not a slight disruption of the sixth sense. Suppose we take the term "sixth sense," not as an undefined intuitive sense added to our familiar five. Suppose we take it in a precise neurological sense as the proprioception. This is what locates us in space; it enables us to place ourselves. So also, by analogy, one way that we place ourselves is by language; we also place ourselves within language. We are at ease with our native language, our mother tongue. (The common metaphors are those of being at home.) At least, we are at home until the sixth sense that has always helped to locate us, without our being much aware of it, is disrupted by a pun or other word-play.

Stevens is so riddling a poet that it is possible to speak of much of his work as "riddle," and go on to solve what we can. If we do use the word "riddle" in a general way, we should watch our loose terminology. Formally, a riddle poem asks a question, usually "What am I?" Or it describes or defines something without naming that something. I am talking about a "pure" riddle, or what folklorists call descriptive riddles. Other kinds of riddles, like puzzles or parody riddles, are rarely literary forms, and the didactic riddle seems to me to belong properly with wisdom literature. I use the term "riddle" in the sense of "pure riddle" when speaking of poems or passages by Stevens. For other effects, I prefer the term "riddling." *Solitaire under the Oaks* (OP 111) is a riddle poem proper, whose implicit question is: what solitaire? The answer is found in a witty word-play on cards and Descartes and the card game of solitaire.[18] The phrase "bronze rain" from *Invective against Swans* is a riddling phrase but not a riddle proper.

Sometimes riddles point toward an object and away from riddler and riddlee. But sometimes the answer to the riddle is "you," as in the children's game of "Adam and Eve and Pinch Me." Here the riddle sets up a recognition scene of which the formula is *de te fabula*. Baudelaire's *hypocrite lecteur* is a well-known modern example, and Nathan's story concluding "Thou art the man" is an Old Testament prototype. Here the self is seen, rather than being an observer; recognition is usually unhappy. The literary form is related to the "neck-riddle" in myth and folklore, where one's life depends on answering a riddle. Does Stevens practice this kind of riddle? I think so. *Oak Leaves Are Hands* sounds like a riddle poem whose answer is "my one-time muse." Stevens' enigmatic moon-writing in an enclosed room, and his echoes of Belshazzar's

---

[18] See my "Riddles, Charms, and Fictions in Wallace Stevens," in *Centre and Labyrinth: Essays in Honour of Northrop Frye*, ed. Eleanor Cook et al. (Toronto: University of Toronto Press, 1983), pp. 227–28.

feast, make riddle-settings where the answer to the riddle is, somehow, himself.

The poetics of the literary riddle or enigma is a large and fascinating subject. One point is worth making here, and that is Stevens' precision and sophistication in this as in other generic areas. Here, for example, are some remarks about enigma (*CP* 472):

> The enigmatical
> Beauty of each beautiful enigma
>
> Becomes amassed in a total double-thing.
> We do not know what is real and what is not.

Stevens begins with what sounds like a cliché, "enigmatical / Beauty" (though the cliché is actually "enigmatical beauty" with no line-break suggesting the mystery of enigma). The reversal to "beautiful enigma" can sound like mere cleverness until we listen to Stevens' chiasmus and consider it in relation to enigma. St. Paul's enigma is a form of allegory which is resolved, which opens out into revelation, in his well-known text in 1 Corinthians 13:12: "For now we see as through a glass darkly." (Both New Testament Greek and the Vulgate's Latin use a form of the word, "enigma," translated as "darkly" in the King James version.) St. Paul's enigma is Eliot's kind of enigma in *East Coker* IV: "The sharp compassion of the healer's art / *Resolving* the enigma of the fever chart" (my italics). But chiasmus is a self-enclosed figure, a "total double-thing," as Stevens says. Enigma that is chiastic becomes self-contained and antiapocalyptic, and it does not resolve. We shall see why in *An Ordinary Evening in New Haven*.

Northrop Frye has mapped riddles and their contrary, charms, very finely.[19] A riddle presents a "verbal trap" or a "verbal spider-web," where "guessing is an integral part of the poetic experience involved." They may be called "generic seeds or kernels, possibilities of expression sprouting and exfoliating into new literary phenomena."[20] Charm poetry is "dissociative and incantatory," uses repetitive devices such as "refrain, rhyme, alliteration, assonance, pun, antithesis," and seeks to "break down and confuse the conscious will." (When Auden says, "Or find a charm in syllables that rhyme," he is speaking both generally and particularly of "charm.") Riddles tend to be visual and conceptual, charms

---

[19] "Charms and Riddles," in his *Spiritus Mundi: Essays on Literature, Myth and Society* (Bloomington: University of Indiana Press, 1976), pp. 123–47.

[20] Ibid., p. 123. Alastair Fowler reminds us that the old and popular forms of charm and riddle are themselves complex, not simple, genres (*Kinds of Literature: An Introduction to the Theory of Genres and Modes* [Cambridge, Mass.: Harvard University Press, 1982], p. 151).

tend to be aural and hypnotic. Both riddles and charms may influence action if they are of the efficacious kind. Both riddles and charms may influence action for better or for worse. Or, at the other end of the efficacy scale, both may become trivial games. In this polarity, where too much or too little seems to depend on them, riddles and charms resemble word-play in general.

Stevens uses charm poetry throughout his work, and I speak in passing of some charm effects, notably some early Tennysonian effects. Stevens stayed deeply suspicious of his own gift for charm poetry, as for euphony. His fluency poems (see Chapter 1) sometimes make use of charm effects and any refrain tends to do so. The broken refrains of *Autumn Refrain* have the effect of a charm, remembered and set aside. The guitar lines from Stevens' late letter, quoted in connection with *The Man with the Blue Guitar*, have a charm effect. Stevens' suspicion of charm effects is partly personal and partly historical. Personally, he became exceedingly wary of what he called the "spirit's own seduction" (*L* 438, January 28, 1943). Personally and historically, he began to write at a time of transition from charm poetry to riddle poetry, from incantatory late-Victorian poetry to modern, riddling poetry. Delmore Schwartz thought that both John Crowe Ransom and Stevens were caught in the move from high-style to colloquial diction at the turn of the century. Hence the play of one diction against the other in their poetry.[21] Frye widens the change from simply a change in diction. Charm poetry "dominated taste until about 1915, after which a mental attitude more closely related to the riddle began to supersede it."[22] Stevens does not seem to me to be caught by anything. Like Joyce, he exploits the possibilites of both kinds of diction and verse.

Riddles and charms, like game and dream, or like nonsense and magic (Elizabeth Sewell's contraries), are usually two distinct kinds of writing and speaking. "Magic would disrupt Nonsense," says Sewell.[23] But the two may converge, as they do in Joyce and often in Stevens. "The game or the dream, logic or irrationality, may lead us to the same point in the end."[24] For "charms and riddles . . . are psychologically very close together, as the unguessed or unguessable riddle is or may be a charm."[25] *Solitaire under the Oaks* is a pure riddle poem, but the Arabian's hoobla-hoobla-hoobla-how (*CP* 383) is a riddle whose repetitions have the incantatory effect of a charm.

[21] "Instructed of Much Morality," *Sewanee Review* 54 (1946), 439–49.
[22] Frye, "Charms and Riddles," p. 142.
[23] *The Field of Nonsense* (London: Chatto & Windus, 1952), p. 40.
[24] Ibid., p. 43.
[25] Frye, "Charms and Riddles," pp. 137–38.

After some thought, I have avoided the term "nonsense" in my discussion. Reading the commentaries on Lewis Carroll's Alice books persuaded me that "nonsense" is too often a catchall term for strange effects. Into this capacious bin, we toss all manner of different things. We might usefully note what is not nonsense, though it is sometimes called that. Imitative words or phonetic conventions or new phonetic equivalents are not nonsense. "No rou-cou, / No rou-cou-cou," from *Depression before Spring*, is not a nonsense sound any more than the cock's onomatopoeic "ki-ki-ri-ki" (*CP* 63). *Roucouler* is the imitative French verb, "to coo," usually of a dove. "I heard their rou-cou-cou," Stevens wrote of some pigeons in 1907[26] and of his dove in 1952 (*CP* 519). Joyce prefers the anglicized form, "roocoocooed."[27] As for phonetic conventions, readers who accept without a blink Eliot's "jug jug" will balk at Stevens' onomatopoeic "tink-tonk" (*CP* 475) for the sound of a raindrop, or his jazz sounds, "tink and tunk and tunk-a-tunk-tunk" (*CP* 59). Or his use of the common phrase "tum-ti-tum" (*CP* 20). What we hear sometimes through these phrases is a "principle of discontinuity," a principle that J. Hillis Miller finds most typical of Stevens.[28] It is their break with decorum that makes them sound like nonsense. In some folk tale or some story by Mark Twain, they would not sound nonsensical. Some are local idioms, and readers from other countries should test any irritated response against their own local idioms. Conventions, like humor, may not travel easily.

Seeming nonsense is sometimes actually parody. As Eliot puts it, "His [Lear's] non-sense is not vacuity of sense; it is a parody of sense, and that is the sense of it."[29] And parody can certainly have an affective function, though nonsense is sometimes defined as having no such function.[30] To my ear, Stevens' "nonsense" is sometimes deeply affecting or

[26] Holly Stevens, *Souvenirs and Prophecies: The Young Wallace Stevens* (New York: Knopf, 1977), p. 175; hereafter abbreviated in the text as *SP*.

[27] Joyce, *Ulysses* (New York: Vintage, 1961), p. 228.

[28] *The Linguistic Moment: From Wordsworth to Stevens* (Princeton: Princeton University Press, 1985), p. 14.

[29] "The Music of Poetry," in *Selected Prose*, ed. John Hayward (London: Penguin, 1953), p. 56.

[30] See John M. Munro, *Princeton Encyclopedia of Poetry and Poetics*, ed. Alex Preminger (Princeton: Princeton University Press, 1974), "Nonsense Verse." I am arguing in part against Hugh Kenner, in his "Seraphic Glitter: Stevens' Nonsense," *Parnassus: Poetry in Review* 5 (1976), 153–59, and *A Homemade World: The American Modernist Writers* (New York: William Morrow, 1975), pp. 50–57. On Stevens' nonsense, see also James Rother, "Wallace Stevens as a Nonsense Poet," *Tennessee Studies in Literature* 21 (1976), 80–90; "American Nonsense and the Style of Wallace Stevens," *Bucknell Review* 23 (1977), 164–86; Irvin Ehrenpreis, "Strange Relation: Stevens' Nonsense," in *Wallace Stevens: A Celebration*, ed. Frank Doggett and Robert Buttel (Princeton: Princeton University

uncanny, as is Lear's. The Arabian's "hoobla-hoobla-hoobla-how" in
Notes toward a Supreme Fiction I.iii is one such example. The "mic-mac
of mocking birds" (*CP* 486) is another, the two affective functions being
very different. A comic erotic example from *Transport to Summer* is:
"Unsnack your snood, madanna" (*CP* 349). We hear "madonna" playing
against "madanna," and so must logically try "unsnock" against "un-
snack," which thereby becomes quite clear. Not an outright imperative,
like "Unsmock, madam," or "Unwrap your snood, madam," but an im-
perative invitation pretending there is a snack-snood or a snood-unsnood
verb. Or as if a snood held a snack or as if snood were a past participle of
which the present imperative form might be snack. (For sexual implica-
tions of the word "snood," see Joyce's notes to *Exiles*. As with *Le Mo-
nocle de Mon Oncle*, we are reminded of an older language for hair.) This
is a "nonsense" effect that works by transposing letters, the same process
used in the Arabian's riddle in *Notes* I.iii.

Another example from *Transport to Summer* (*CP* 349) functions dif-
ferently again. Stevens' "ithy oonts" in the following lines reads to me
like Lewis Carroll.

> We enjoy the ithy oonts and long-haired
> Plomets, as the Herr Gott
> Enjoys his comets.

"Ithy" is not any one truncated word but potentially several different
ones with two "i" values (pithy? slithy?). The phrase sounds vaguely
portentous, and the vowel sounds may be reversed with even more por-
tentous effect. The play on hair is clear to anyone who has looked at
comets, whether in the sky or in the dictionary. I hear Stevens truly
enjoying as well as smiling at the "plomets" of language, as of comets.
As with Stevens' word-play in general, so with these various examples
that we label "nonsense": along with enjoyment, there can be "serious-
ness in Stevens' apparent nonsense."[31]

It is possible to think of riddles along another axis than a riddle-charm
axis. We may think of proverbs or aphorisms as the contrary to riddles.
Again, the proverb is a very old form of writing and speaking, and it too
would qualify as a "generic seed or kernel." Proverbs turn riddles inside
out. In contrast to riddles, the answer is given before the question is

---

Press, 1980), pp. 219–34; and Alan Golding, "The 'Community of Elements' in Wallace
Stevens and Louis Zukofsky," in *Wallace Stevens: The Poetics of Modernism*, ed. Albert
Gelpi (Cambridge: Cambridge University Press, 1985), pp. 121–38.

[31] Golding, "The 'Community of Elements' in Wallace Stevens and Louis Zukofsky," in
Wallace Stevens, ed. Gelpi, p. 128. Golding demonstrates how Stevens' "nonsense" and
his imitative effects spoke to Objectivist poets.

asked. Or the answer is given without raising the possibility of a question. Proverbs enlighten or confirm rather than block the reader. Wisdom is offered rather than withheld. Proverbs comfort; whatever the situation, a proverb will offer support. (Look before you leap. He who hesitates is lost.) Proverbs belong to the category of wisdom literature, and riddles usually do not. This is a form very congenial to Stevens.[32] If he is suspicious of charm effects, he is much less so of proverbs and aphorisms. He loved wisdom literature. (We might note that the Bible has a Book of Proverbs [one of Stevens' favorites], but its riddles are scant, as if this teasing genre was not well favored among its literary forms.) Proverbs and aphorisms usually give a sense of stability and decorum. As we consider the principle of discontinuity so typical of Stevens' work, we should not forget this contrary instinct—all the more congenial to someone who likes to break with our expectations.

The OED defines "word-play" in a way that underlines the nineteenth-century view of such frivolities. The definition of "pun" seems to have been written by another hand altogether.

> PLAY: 7b, play of words: a playing or trifling with words; the use of words merely or mainly for the purpose of producing a rhetorical or fantastic effect. *Play on* or *upon words*: a sportive use of words so as to convey a double meaning, or produce a fantastic or humorous effect by similarity of sound with difference of meaning, a pun.
>
> PUN: the use of a word in such a way as to suggest two or more meanings or different associations, or the use of two or more words of the same or nearly the same sound with different meanings so as to produce a humorous effect; a play on words.

To read this small drama of definition is to see in little a longstanding state of war. And indeed, word-play all too often has to defend itself. The usual charges are triviality or frivolity, or being self-enclosed and cut off from the real world, or engaging in an endless play of signifiers. Against the first charge, we may show how word-play supports a theme, but I have not chosen such a defense. Word-play may indeed embody or inform or illustrate an argument, but argument or theme or dialectic is only one form of the meaning. I hear a play or speaking back and forth between the areas of rhetoric and dialectic. What a pun does is to dramatize this process by revealing unexpected directions or connections or paradoxes.

The second charge seems to me mostly polemical, and not a genuine

[32] Cf. Beverley Coyle, *A Thought To Be Rehearsed: Aphorism in Wallace Stevens' Poetry* (Ann Arbor: UMI Research Press, 1983).

literary problem. Of course, word-play may by choice give the effect of being self-enclosed and cut off from the real world—that is, from language referring to what we take as the real world. It is always useful to keep in mind Francis Sparshott's timely warning: "Discussions of referentiality have been bedeviled by a tendency to treat the issue as one of ontology, rather than as one of the functioning of symbol systems."[33]

The third charge is a possible but wrong charge against Stevens. Deconstructionists like to speak of the endless deferral of meaning, and the continuous play of signifiers as they evade univocal meaning. The poets were there before them, and I mention in passing some of Stevens' similar play. And Stevens sometimes outdoes the deconstructionists through his larger, more intelligent sense of play. In *The Comedian as the Letter C*, he approaches the limits of word-play, evading firm closure, plot, theme, structure, allusion, genre. Of this poem, we might indeed say that Stevens endlessly defers meaning; that is his very subject. Later word-play works differently. And Stevens' supreme fiction is a notion that deconstructionists have not yet seriously considered.

Sometimes we speak of the "terms and territories" of word-play, as if it were a peaceful country over which we could quietly ramble. Sometimes we speak of words that "warble and chuckle to themselves (e.g. pun or alliterate)," to quote Stanley Cavell.[34] But puns and alliteration may growl or shriek. Some a-logical associations are sad or sinister or aggressive or even visionary. Words may not just be *in* a territory. They may try to occupy some territory or space in our minds. Perhaps they are only following nature and filling a vacuum, but perhaps they are warring with other words. "Nor is it easy to fix the frontiers of word-play," as M. M. Mahood says.[35] This, I think, is because word-play is better troped as a frontier-crosser or a boundary-breaker than as a territory or a state. Word-play crosses borders unexpectedly or finds unexpected borders, and this break with expectations is always worth watching.

For some time, I thought an anatomy of word-play would grow out of this essay, but I have concluded that such a thing is not possible. Word-play seems to me like the topics to Walter Ong,[36] a phenomenon seemingly impossible to map, though some areas may be mapped. Here I need to come back to my working definition of word-play, a definition that is very general yet very useful: the play of rhetoric against dialectic (less

---

[33] *The Theory of the Arts* (Princeton: Princeton University Press, 1982), p. 76.

[34] Stanley Cavell, *The Senses of Walden* (New York: Viking, 1972), p. 40.

[35] M. M. Mahood, *Shakespeare's Wordplay* (London: Methuen, 1957), p. 164.

[36] Walter Ong, in the Introduction to Joan Marie Lechner, *Renaissance Concepts of the Commonplaces* (Westport, Conn.: Greenwood, 1962, 1974).

often, against grammar). Such a definition sees word-play as a crosser of boundaries. Such a definition helps explain why word-play is so difficult to map. It may happen in any area.

Against the usual charges of triviality and frivolity, word-play hardly needs to defend itself to readers of poetry. Readers of poetry know something about "knowledge / of the kind / that . . . brings only hunch and gaiety for proof," to quote Richard Wilbur.[37] Many centuries ago, Wisdom was said to play before God at the time of creation, and creation always seems to have an element of play. Such a sense of play needs no defense. The question rather becomes why theme and argument cannot play.

[37] Wilbur, *New Yorker*, July 4, 1985.

I

* * *

Harmonium

* * * * *

CHAPTER ONE

Places, Common and Other:

A Rhetoric of Beginning

> Place: space, extension in two (or three) directions;
> a particular part of space, the position of a body in
> space; a residence, dwelling, house; a particular
> part, page, or other point in a book or writing; a
> topic (OED 2, 3a & b, 5b, 7, 7c).

STEVENS is such a master of openings that we expect the first poems of *Harmonium* to entice us, and we are a little baffled when they do not. Stevens selected these poems to open *Harmonium*, choosing from work written between 1916 and 1921; he saw no reason to alter the order in 1931 for a second edition or in 1954 for his *Collected Poems*. They are the entrance into his work and I propose to begin with the first six. Slight, pleasing poems, they lead into the powerful pair, *Domination of Black* and *The Snow Man*, but have themselves attracted little attention. Yet to read these poems well is to begin to learn how to read all of Stevens' poetry. And of the opening poem, *Earthy Anecdote*, Stevens remarked cryptically, "There's a good deal of theory about it" (*L* 204, February 20, 1918), a gloss no one has attempted to explain, for a less likely theoretical poem, on the face of it, would be hard to find.

At first glance, the six poems appear to be a miscellany, and Stevens did in fact break up earlier pairings that encourage ready classifying. Some arrangement by contrast seems at work, before we come to the two poems that are contraries proper, *Domination of Black* and *The Snow Man*. We may attempt a thematic reading. It is not difficult to map themes of old versus new, American-and-desirable versus European-

and-undesirable, a progression of earth-heaven-earth-sea, elemental fire-earth-air-water, and so on.[1] The most interesting result of this is the extent to which these are poems of againstness, and not just againstness between poems but within poems; the extent to which each poem is built on contraries, sometimes opposites. Almost as interesting is how often some blocking agent is present and must be resisted or overcome. Sometimes, as in the opening poem, both blocking agent and resister seem necessary for some kind of vitality—a thesis and antithesis set of contraries. Sometimes, as in the second and fourth poems, the blocking agent seems seasonal or generational, an old order that must pass away. Only with the sixth poem, *Infanta Marina*, do we come to the end of struggle between contraries.

One common experience new readers of Stevens' poems share is a sense of being blocked, and even experienced readers may have that sense here at the beginning of Stevens' volume. Of his poems, we sometimes say what D. H. Lawrence said of the Australian landscape: "You feel you can't *see*—as if your eyes hadn't the vision in them to correspond with the outside landscape." If these opening poems are both about blocking and themselves block, then it looks as though our sense of bafflement over them is very much to the point.

One difficulty is that outside place and the figures which inhabit it are not stable. Neither are the order of words and the figures which inhabit that realm. Stevens' word-play functions to keep this so, and the interest lies in mapping the kind and degree of dislocation. For the figures who inhabit these first poems are singularly difficult to locate; they appear to live in a world that is neither properly realistic nor legendary nor allegorical. They tend to be moving figures, and in their motions we may see the act of crossing from place to words and back again—in short, of reading. The culmination of place, words, and figures comes in the two powerful poems, *Domination of Black* and *The Snow Man*, for here figure either becomes one huge encroaching figure or else the figure of the self as nonfigure. Instead of landscapes inhabited and perceived, the self becomes inhabited or else gives up the notion of habitation altogether. The first six poems offer us a series of possible genii loci: bucks and firecat, swans or geese or crows, Venus as alma or aspic, a new if paltry Venus, the giant and the three Graces, the Infanta Marina. The infanta

---

[1] Cf. Louis L. Martz, " 'From the Journal of Crispin': An Early Version of 'The Comedian as the Letter C,' " in *Wallace Stevens: A Celebration*, ed. Frank Doggett and Robert Buttel (Princeton: Princeton University Press, 1980), p. 20, on poems of earth and sea, and the effect of "oscillation, undulation, or contrast." Robert Buttel suggested the idea of approaching *Harmonium* through its opening poems in his "Teasing the Reader into *Harmonium*," *Wallace Stevens Journal* 6 (1982), 79–86.

comes closest to a conventional genius loci, as if Stevens were working toward some such figure through these six poems. In *Domination of Black*, the mind is threatened by a terrible genius loci; in *The Snow Man*, the mind tries to become the genius loci itself. In thematic terms, it is possible to say that these poems show new versus old, and so on, but I should say that these first poems show Stevens' desire for a place that is a poetic home.

Paul de Man says that Proust "dramatizes tropes by means of landscapes or descriptions of objects."[2] Stevens does not so much dramatize tropes as dramatize ways of reading by means of landscapes or the actions of figures. His opening poems act out various ways of opening a volume of poetry in 1923. It is as if Stevens were not only doing it, and implicitly showing us what he is doing, but also finding the appropriate tropes for doing and showing.[3] See, I swerve, he might be saying in *Earthy Anecdote*, but not randomly or forever; the energy of my swerve is formed, thus, and this is an anecdote of my new beginning (like Oklahoma's), both its energy and its shaping. Or, see, I inveigh in *Invective* against old ways, both encoding them and breaking with them. Or: see how, in *In the Carolinas*, I empty American spring of its Whitmanian associations and its Lucretian associations also, the breast of mother earth being sweet but utterly untrustworthy as nourishment. Or: here overtly is my new American muse in *The Paltry Nude*, both understated as paltry and overstated as pomp, both high as cloud and high-style diction and low as sea and words like "spick." Or: here in *The Plot against the Giant* is Polyphemus or a giant earth figure, virile but crude, and this energy will be seduced and civilized by sensuous delicacy (and if you listen well, you may hear my challenge to Whitman). Or, finally: here is the least revision, or it may be the most, a collective ghost-as-genius-loci, the loveliest

---

[2] *Allegories of Reading: Figural Language in Rousseau, Nietzsche, Rilke, and Proust* (New Haven and London: Yale University Press, 1979), p. 13.

[3] That is, he is finding tropes for revisionary methods. Our most schematic revisionary map is Harold Bloom's, and Stevens' first four poems map quite neatly as his first four ratios (clinamen, tessera, kenosis, and daemonization). The fifth mocks askesis and uses allegory rather than metaphor. The sixth is no more metonymic than the other poems, and I hear no apophrades. In terms of the revisionary ratios, this is as far as Stevens will go with askesis and apophrades, perhaps because he is saving an extraordinary poem of askesis, *The Snow Man*, and an extraordinary poem fearful of apophrades, *Domination of Black*. All this suggests that Stevens is still working chiefly with the negative side of revision. Bloom's ratios follow a crisis pattern; I am not sure that revision always does. See his *Anxiety of Influence: A Theory of Poetry* (New York: Oxford University Press, 1973); *A Map of Misreading* (New York: Oxford University Press, 1975); and *Poetry and Repression: Revisionism from Blake to Stevens* (New Haven and London: Yale University Press, 1976).

and least problematic of my female figures, in a flowing that is perhaps too fluid or fluent.

But it is time to look at these first six poems. My interest is to find precisely where each poem breaks with our expectations, and to consider the kind and degree of these breaks. I use the word "break" though I might also use the word "play." Both tropes imply ordinary "working" norms of poetry.

Earthy Anecdote blocks the reader in more ways than one: it blocks ready paraphrase, ready generic classifying, and especially ready answers to the question, what is the point of this poem? We might begin with an obvious question. How can bucks go clattering *over* Oklahoma any more than I can place a jar *in* Tennessee?[4] One possible answer is generic: if we read the poem as a tall tale, then of course bucks can go clattering over Oklahoma. (I surmise that Stevens once thought of it that way, for he paired it with an obvious tall-tale poem, *The Jack-Rabbit.*) Or we may attempt a legendary reading, with Oklahoma seen from an overview or heard from beneath, as if it were a giant body. Yet as either tall tale or legend, this seems a tale of meager plot or point. Nor does it invite an allegorical reading; we may attach an allegory but someone else may attach quite another; no allegory will adhere. Stevens himself remarked that there was "no symbolism in the 'Earthy Anecdote.' There's a good deal of theory about it, however" (*L* 204, February 20, 1918). He offered no further explanation. Five months later, he commented wryly of Pach's illustration for the poem: it "is just the opposite of my idea. I intended something quite concrete: actual animals, not original chaos" (*L* 209, July 10, 1918). Here is the poem:

> Every time the bucks went clattering
> Over Oklahoma
> A firecat bristled in the way.
>
> Wherever they went,
> They went clattering,
> Until they swerved
> In a swift, circular line
> To the right,
> Because of the firecat.
>
> Or until they swerved
> In a swift, circular line

---

[4] For all its obviousness, this question usually does not get asked. Harold Bloom and George Steiner are two exceptions. See Bloom, *Kabbalah and Criticism* (New York: Seabury, 1975), p. 110, and George Steiner, *On Difficulty and Other Essays* (New York and Oxford: Oxford University Press, 1978), pp. 38–40.

To the left,
Because of the firecat.

The bucks clattered.
The firecat went leaping,
To the right, to the left,
And
Bristled in the way.

Later, the firecat closed his bright eyes
And slept.

We note that when the bucks swerve, "In a swift, circular line," their metrical feet do just that, for the line describes itself—an anapest back-to-back with a dactyl, the swerve coming over the comma. The reader's eye in the ordinary experience of reading an English text moves in a swift circular line to the right, then to the left (a moving circle along the line, then a hairpin turn). When the firecat closes his bright eyes and sleeps, the poem stops and so does the reader's eye. And some memory of the firecat's leaping is in the -lept of "slept," the closing word, as the memory of the whole poem is enfolded in the moment of closure.

We might move here to speak of this poem as Hugh Kenner speaks of Pound's poems. We might say that poetry is made of the rushing energy of feet and lines, but also made by directing that energy, shaping it, and ending it too. The firecat, bristling as if against aimless chatter (one meaning of "clatter"), gives order to words that grow out of the first two consonants of the word "Oklahoma" (kl: bucks clattering). If Oklahoma is America in its raw state (and it became a state only eleven years before this poem was written), then at the threshold of his volume Stevens has placed a poem about the ordering of the energies of a state, or rather of one form of energy combating another—whether the state is outer Oklahoma or this poem or the reading of this poem. What the "ground" of our seeing and hearing is: that is what this small poem, this "earthy anecdote," makes us think about.

This seems an unexceptionable allegorical reading, yet it still seems an insufficient answer to my first question: how can bucks go clattering *over* Oklahoma any more than I can place a jar *in* Tennessee? What would we ordinarily say? Something like: in Oklahoma, every time the bucks went clattering over the ground. . . . (We customarily say "in Oklahoma" or "in Tennessee" or "in the Carolinas" without giving the preposition further thought.) Or we might say: "all over" Oklahoma, as Stevens did in 1917, in the opening poem of *Primordia* (*OP* 7): "All over Minnesota, / Cerise sopranos, / Walking in the snow. . . ." *All* over? Well, frequently, in Minnesota, etc. *In* Minnesota? Well, within the boundaries of, on or

29

extending above the ground for a considerable distance, beyond which it would seem inappropriate to say "over" Minnesota or Oklahoma. Not to belabor the point, Stevens seems to me to be introducing here his play with the buried tropes of words that appear to have purely grammatical functions. Stevens' play with prepositions acts to dislocate slightly the logic of referential language, to displace slightly the language of place. Both lawyers and poets have to think about the implications of seemingly neutral words, as Stevens well knows. "As a lawyer might say it, 'In, on or about the words,' " he once remarked, apropos of the sounds of another poem (*L* 352, January 12, 1940). Roman Jakobson speaks of "words endowed with purely grammatical functions, like conjunctions, prepositions, pronouns, and articles,"[5] but such words do not always function this way. And we know how Shakespeare plays with prepositions.[6] This little word-play tells us to watch out for Stevens' prepositions, and to watch out for our own.

Yvor Winters calls this poem "willful nonsense,[7] and at first it may seem to have affinities with nonsense verse. Yet the more we stay with it, the more it reads as a spirited troping of one complex of tropes for beginning something. Though slight (anecdotal), it is also a secret history (anecdote).

In *Harmonium* and the *Collected Poems*, Stevens follows *Earthy Anecdote* with a quite contrary poem, *Invective against Swans*. The effect is to make very pointed the breaking of convention in the first poem and the limits of convention in the second. Before this, *Earthy Anecdote* had appeared twice in print, each time paired with a different and lesser poem whose presence tended to undercut its force. It first appeared in 1918, along with what we now know as *The Jack-Rabbit* (*CP* 50). This tall-tale poem with its caroling Brer Rabbit, akin to the Remus of *Ploughing on Sunday*, comes with a flourish of puns:

---

[5] *Selected Writings*, vol. 2, *Word and Language* (The Hague and Paris: Mouton, 1971), "Two Aspects of Language and Two Types of Aphasic Disturbance," p. 251. Of course, Jakobson is not considering the poetics of grammar here.

[6] On Shakespeare's play with prepositions, see among others, Stephen Booth, *An Essay on Shakespeare's Sonnets* (New Haven and London: Yale University Press, 1969), p. 22; William Empson, *Seven Types of Ambiguity*, 3d ed. (New York: Penguin, 1961), p. 117; and N. F. Blake, *Shakespeare's Language: An Introduction* (London: Macmillan, 1983), pp. 111–12. Alastair Fowler notes how grammatical play may "replace" or "supplement" ordinary usage (*Kinds of Literature: An Introduction to the Theory of Genres and Modes* [Cambridge, Mass.: Harvard University Press, 1982], p. 22). I hear Stevens' play questioning rather than supplementing ordinary usage, yet without replacing it.

[7] Yvor Winters, "Wallace Stevens or the Hedonist's Progress," in *Wallace Stevens: A Critical Anthology*, ed. Irvin Ehrenpreis (London: Penguin, 1972), p. 133.

In the morning,
The jack-rabbit sang to the Arkansaw.
He carolled in caracoles
On the feat sandbars.

"Feet," "bars," "carolled"? Those sandbars belong also on a sheet of music, where the bass clef resembles the seashell called the caracole. The rabbit could carol in mere car-ols, but caracoles are much better: a shell as variant on the standard Romantic reechoing shell;[8] a word extending the schematic echo of ack-Arka-car-car-ac. The sound effects and exuberant punning together with the unlikely rabbit (but then, jack-rabbits are unlikely per se) are a delight. Yet for all its fun, *The Jack-Rabbit* tends to undercut *Earthy Anecdote* by its stronger humor, its Midwest locale, its obvious generic placing. In a different way, so does *Life Is Motion*, which Stevens paired with *Earthy Anecdote* in the July 1919 number of *Others*. It pulls our reading toward ordinary mimesis. Stevens' opening arrangement demonstrates that he does not want his poems dominated by such a reading.

Earthy Anecdote is an emptied poem. By contrast, *Invective against Swans* is overfull, a crammed Old World park of tropes. It demonstrates how *Earthy Anecdote* does not work: regular iambic pentameter, much rhyme, no questions about where "over" is, no Amerindian place names, imitative Shakespearean syntax ("which that time endures"—which disrupts the tone). Stevens is challenging his readers: if you do not like my little anecdote as a beginning, try your hand on this "old-style" poem; let me test your knowledge of old tropes and old legends in a variation of the riddle poem, the chief riddle being the absence of swans.

For of course, not one swan appears in this *Invective against Swans*, only well-apostrophized ganders. As the poem offers ample invective against ganders, surely Robert Buttel's tentative suggestion is exactly right.[9] The poem takes as its unspoken premise the invective aphorism, "All your swans are geese." Variations abound, including one that Stevens was likely to remember, his father's, when writing to congratulate him on his election to Harvard's Signet Club: "a Cygnet on it—to distinguish you from commoner geese" (*L* 26, May 21, 1899). I see no good reason for pointing to Yeats's swans here. Stevens' ironic revisions of standard tropes suggest a different, more general context. For example, if he had not written "A bronze rain from the sun descending" but instead "A gold rain from the sun descending," we would recognize at once

---

[8] Cf. John Hollander, *Images of Voice: Music and Sound in Romantic Poetry* (Cambridge: Heffer, 1970), pp. 14–25.

[9] Buttel, "Teasing the Reader," p. 81.

the legend of Zeus visiting Danae in a shower of gold—"that gold snow Jove rained on Rhodes," as Browning has it (*The Ring and the Book* I.490). "A bronze rain" is the autumnal version of the impregnating shower of gold, the rain of a weakening sun and dying summer, old gods and old conventions. Their potency gone, their amorous descents on mortals are no longer golden and fruitful. This standard trope for poetic inspiration is itself aging.

At the end of Stevens' invective, the soul flies off beyond the trajectory of such vehicles as chariots. What is this "soul," a word we never encounter again in Stevens' poetry? Surely it is what the soul has always been in legend: Psyche, envied by Venus, loved by Eros, taken up to heaven in an apotheosis, and here the poetic self as the new Venus. The end represents Psyche's triumph over the old Venus, whose swans appear in the phrase "chilly chariot." (Swans are also birds of Venus, though less familiar than her doves.) Camoens, whom Stevens knew, gave his Venus a memorable team of swans to draw her chariot: "The snowy swans of love's celestial queen / Now land her chariot on the shore of green."[10] Stevens' "chilly chariot" is a witty and pointed revision of old tropes like "snowy chariot" or "snow-white chariot." Such old tropes leave him cold.

Yet though wittily built, *Invective* falters, and Stevens cut it from the opening eight poems of the Faber *Selected Poems* (1953). My guess is that *Invective* is related to *The Comedian as the Letter C* and suffers similar problems. Stevens' crammed lines are like those of *The Comedian*, and the apotheosis at the end resembles the apotheosis at the end of *From the Journal of Crispin*, the early version of *The Comedian*. Given the place of Venus in the *Journal* and the c-sounds in Psyche, I wonder if Stevens once considered a role for Psyche in that poem. Stevens' problem here is both logical and formal. Logical because seasonal change seems to bring in new turning or troping as a matter of course; that last flight seems effortless. Formal because Stevens is divided between invective and romance, the romance of a fresh poetic. La Fontaine is wiser than Stevens in the ways of invective when he limits Psyche's story to crisp low comedy. As an introduction to ways of reading—to riddle poems, adages, parodies of old tropes—the poem belongs here. But for a nonsatiric poem to embody flaws, as well as talk about them, is hazardous.

[10] *The Lusiad or The Discovery of India*, trans. William Mickle (London: George Bell, 1907), p. 269. Camoens is mentioned in *From the Journal of Crispin*, in *Wallace Stevens: A Celebration*, ed. Doggett and Buttel (hereafter in the text as *Journal of Crispin*), p. 43.

In the Carolinas is a virtuoso performance in nine lines, for all its seeming lightness:

> The lilacs wither in the Carolinas.
> Already the butterflies flutter above the cabins.
> Already the new-born children interpret love
> In the voices of mothers.
>
> Timeless mother,
> How is it that your aspic nipples
> For once vent honey?
>
> *The pine-tree sweetens my body*
> *The white iris beautifies me.*

This seems a more comfortable text than the preceding two poems, asking as it does for a customary mimetic reading. The challenge seems minimal: it lies in single words, in that odd word "vent" and especially in the adjective "aspic," a choice of genius and an early example of Stevens' formidable gifts of word-play. The poem turns on the contrast between honey and aspic; aspic is usual and this honey of late spring is exceptional, as the chilling little phrase, "for once," tells us. These are the foods of mother earth, seen in her late-spring Carolinas manifestation. Since she provides honey through her nipples, where human mothers provide milk, she is at once a mother-land and a promised land, as in the original Old Testament trope of the land of milk and honey. Or "for once" fulfilling her promise, anyway. Her body is sweet and beautiful; she testifies that sweetness and beauty come from pine-tree and white iris, but what she says is not sweet. "How is it that your aspic nipples / For once vent honey?" And the answer is to both senses of this question, "By what means do you . . . ?" and "Why do you . . . ?" The means are the pine-tree and the iris, and the reason is also the pine-tree and the iris. That is, the sweetening and beautifying of the spring season is an occasion for the timeless mother to vent honey. It is not the other way around; no principle of sweetness or beauty or life-sustenance can be deduced from the spring. This mother nature is no natural law, and this poem of Stevens is anti-Lucretian, for what is profoundly absent is an alma mater figure. In the first two poems, the reader might conceive of the energy and renewing of earth (and tropes) as part of nature and so part of us. Stevens blocks such a reading here. The parallel of human children and mothers, time-bound and not timeless, is pointed. And even for human children, Stevens will allow no more than interpreting, an act of reading and inferring in this first essential bonding. The poem then invites us to interpret what we will in the voice of our "timeless mother."

33

What sense can we make of an aspic-nippled mother? Cleopatra is the first association, "Cleopatra regal-drest / With the aspics at her breast," as Keats has it, writing on the theme of "fair and foul I love together."[11] But Stevens is not following the Milton-Gray-Keats theme of the pleasures of vicissitude. The structural principle of this poem is the taking over of an alma mater by an aspic mater. The opposite of sweetness is bitterness, and the opposite of honey is gall. If the English language had taken over not only the famous "alma mater" of Lucretius, but also some opposite, what would that opposite be? An "amara mater" is one answer, and there are fine poems working from a bitter-love pun in *amare*.[12] But an "aspera mater" would do equally well. The Latin adjective *asperus* survives in "asperity"; the English adjective "asper" had only a short life. In both English and Latin, "asper" means rough or pungent or sour; it is used of sounds, of taste, of feelings (bitter, cruel), and of climate. Caxton makes use of it ("aspre tormentes") in *The Golden Legend*, which Stevens knew. The mother earth of *In the Carolinas*, though now sweet and beautiful, is essentially asper in all the ways listed above. If she were essentially generative, then the poetic voice might accommodate her destructive side as part of the order of things, as Whitman could do—and not just accommodate but celebrate—in his lilac poem. Stevens can do this elsewhere but not here.

And here we need to pause and ask if an American poet could open a 1917 poem with the line, "The lilacs wither in the Carolinas," and not expect his readers to recall Whitman. Probably not (and the dooryard in *The Comedian* alludes to the same poem). But Whitman can turn the bitterness of death into song by the end of his poem. His nature replies through thrush-song in a "Come, sweet death" theme, which is a forerunner to his own returning strength in song. Stevens' poem ends with nature's reply, and no poet's song follows. I would even hazard a guess that the word "Carolinas" is used here as a trope for the place of caroling, and that Stevens does this to make the poem more anti-Whitman, for Whitman uses the word "carol" three times of his magnificent singer. (Stevens' two other carolers are hardly Whitmanian either; one is the "mechanical optimist" of a weak 1937 poem of that title; the other is the caroling jack-rabbit, who is warned "Look out, O caroller" for the reality principle in the form of a buzzard's rattling stomach.)

11 *John Keats: The Complete Poems*, ed. Jack Stillinger (Cambridge, Mass. and London: Harvard University Press, Belknap, 1978), "Welcome joy, and welcome sorrow," p. 171. All quotations from Keats's poetry are from this edition.

12 Punning on *amare* (to love) and *amare* (bitterly) is common. Cf. *Auctor ad Herennium* 4.14.20, and, in English, Lewis Carroll (*A Lesson in Love*) and Anthony Hecht in *The Short End* (*The Venetian Vespers* [New York: Atheneum, 1980], p. 18).

"Aspic," then, through the contrast with honey and through its first three letters, draws the reader toward the obsolete latinate adjective, "asper," suggesting a gap in our language of nature, the gap which should be filled by the aspera mater. But "aspic" first comes with snaky and poisonous associations, which the verb "vent" reinforces. The body does vent substances, usually air, and we figuratively vent or give vent to emotions. The breasts do not normally vent, though a mouth might. Those aspic nipples carry an uneasy sense of snake-mouths, with the sought-after place of nourishment transmuted into a poisonous and gulping place of destruction. (There is a similar effect in Tennyson's *Lucretius*, where the breasts of Helen shoot out fire rather than milk.) Places where the body of mother earth "vents" are likely to be fearsome—geysers, volcanoes, or cleft rocks that are "hell's vent-holes" (Pater, *Marius the Epicurean*, chap. 5). The missing term in this transmutation is the meaning of aspic as food, that is, as jelly.

In this one adjective, Stevens has concentrated the displacing effect of this short poem. He seems about to offer the reader a mother earth and mother tongue, both alma, but turns against our assumptions that "honey and milk are under thy lips" (Song of Solomon 4:11). My reading of this adjective is supported by Stevens' use of "aspic" and "bitter" twenty-seven years later in *Esthétique du Mal*. Here, he drops both the serpentine and maternal associations. Aspic reads chiefly as a form of food: "Life is a bitter aspic . . . A man of bitter appetite despises / A well-made scene . . ." (*CP* 322–23). In *Esthétique du Mal* Stevens distinguishes different kinds of sweetness as he does not in *In the Carolinas*. He also sees the intricate desires of a "bitter appetite."

As with Stevens' play with prepositions or with the riddle poem or with old tropes, this play with asp- words in 1917 is an early example of etymological and echoic effects he will develop later. We note also that we are now starting to see a pattern in these early lessons in reading. For each of these poems, the most useful rule of thumb is to ask ourselves what we would ordinarily say or what we expect to hear.

Stevens' high-spirited fourth poem, *The Paltry Nude Starts on a Spring Voyage*, offers another Venus. I hear Stevens replying not only to Pater and his Venus but also to Henry Adams and his: "in America neither Venus nor Virgin ever had value as force—at most as sentiment. No American had ever been truly afraid of either" (*The Education of Henry Adams*, chap. 25). Stevens knew what it was to be afraid of Venus: he had already written *Le Monocle de Mon Oncle*. And his nude is a force by virtue of being nude, at least by one test of Adams ("when she was a true force, she was ignorant of fig-leaves"). "An American Venus would never dare exist," Adams wrote, having just quoted the opening lines of Lucretius, to which "not one of Adams's many schools of education had ever drawn his attention." If I am right that *In the Carolinas* was written in full awareness of the Lucretian Venus, then Stevens might have felt a little oddly about this remark.

"This is meagre play," says this poem of the quite unmeager circles it cuts from low to high in landscape and diction. ("Meagre" like "paltry" is part of a modesty topos.) At first we are apt to be too busy conjuring and then dismissing Botticelli to notice the slight and funny play on the preposition "on" ("on a spring voyage / But not on a shell she starts"). The word-play on "pomp" is simply of modern against archaic (or English against French), pomposity against procession. This lady does not "process"; she "scuds the glitters," and pomp comes later. Pomp as procession we are likely to know from Milton's lines, "Not unattended, for on her as Queen / A pomp of winning Graces waited still."[13] But Campion is even more to the point. ("I like Dr. Campion," said Stevens in 1908 [*L* 110, December 7].) "What faire pompe have I spide of glittering Ladies": so begins his exquisite song. Generations of Venuses, like generations of words, may retrieve from the past some old freshness for us. Or so we casually conclude.

But of course this is not what the theme is telling us, if the diction is. Stevens' playfulness is paradoxical. For majesty we need to retrieve old meanings, though for this American Venus-cum-muse we need a new figure. The poem itself closes on paradox, the paradox of an "irretrievable way," and of a later Venus as queen and Cinderella both. As "scullion of fate," she may clean up fate or clean for fate. The muse may alter things or they may alter her. Cleansing, at any rate, is essential. Stevens plays with the semantic, phonetic, and tropic possibilities of a family of Germanic words, including the Dutch words of his ancestors. Semantically, many are words for cleaning; phonetically, they are sk- or scr- words. Harold Bloom, in the best commentary on the poem, hears the resonances of these words for a Pennsylvania Dutchman.[14] I would add only some remarks on cleansing. For the sea itself is cleansing, and it can be troped as cleansing its own figures, tropes and Venuses both. Stevens avoids (or submerges) the most obvious sc-, cleansing, marine word, which is "scour." Ships routinely "scour" the sea, and insofar as this nude is a figurehead (which is not very far) she does too. Geoffrey Hill

---

[13] *Paradise Lost* VIII.60–61, in *Complete Poems and Major Prose*, ed. Merritt Y. Hughes (Indianapolis: Bobbs-Merrill, 1957). All quotations from Milton are from this edition; hereafter, *Paradise Lost* is abbreviated in the text as *PL*.

[14] Harold Bloom, *Wallace Stevens: The Poems of Our Climate* (Ithaca: Cornell University Press, 1977), pp. 25–26, whence also the phrase "raffish humor."

hears what Stevens is doing, and goes on from there in his *Re-birth of Venus*: "And now the sea-scoured temptress . . ."

As a beginning, this is, for once, what we expect: the new American muse answering Adams's challenge, spring anticipating summer, the cleansing of tropes with firm Dutch scouring. Stevens does not see it quite so simply, but his paradoxes are a matter of "later reason" (*CP* 401). The poem's "raffish humor" carries it and us.

Any trope of renewal or progress satisfies the decorum of beginnings, and *The Plot against the Giant* is no exception. We look forward to the civilizing of that maundering giant by the three running girls (so our first reading goes) and the "rendering of half-formed into fully formed speech." I take the phrase from Marie Borroff's fine analysis of the acoustic and articulatory sound symbolism at the end of Stevens' poem: "the change from guttural to labial and apical sounds is like the finishing off of articulation, the rendering of half-formed into fully formed speech. And this . . . is like the relationship between natural sound and language itself. The former is vast, the latter limited; the former is crude, the latter 'civil' in the root-sense of that word."[15] Borroff is the best guide to the sounds of the poem, though I would argue that the guttural giant also belongs in fully formed language; that we are seeing contraries as well as a progression; that we may read more than one allegory here. (Poets can do remarkable things with gutturals: consider what Aristophanes can do for the thundering giant Aeschylus and against the smooth-tongued Euripides.) And we should not forget odor and color, that is, the first and second girls.

The poem does encourage allegorical reading: it declares itself a "plot" (loosely, not necessarily, fairy tale), and its dialogue does suggest a narrative and linguistic plot. But clear signs of one allegory are not present. We might also read the poem as a poem of the three Graces or Persuasion against the giant, of a female form of Ulysses against Polyphemus, of any subtle beauty against a bumbler (Pecksniff, Peter Quince). The most interesting question is implicit in the preposition of the title. What kind of "againstness"? Civilizing as against the primitive? Female as against the male? There is no resolution to this plot, no hint of a best answer, no giant's perspective. As always, it is important to watch where Stevens ceases to tell us how to read—and to watch our habit of going on from there. This poem is also a plot against the maundering giant within all readers. "I shall run before him," say Stevens' girls and Stevens' lines at once. Stevens' own delight in the graces personified by the girls makes

---

[15] Marie Borroff, "Sound Symbolism as Drama in the Poetry of Wallace Stevens," *ELH* 48 (1981), 915–21.

us associate them with him, but we must not forget how suspicious he
could be of euphony.

Any reading must take account of the unnoticed echoes of Whitman
in this poem, especially in the third speech:

> Oh, la . . . le pauvre!
> I shall run before him,
> With a curious puffing.
> He will bend his ear then.
> I shall whisper
> Heavenly labials in a world of gutturals.
> It will undo him.

In *Song of Myself* (xi), personified female desire plays like wind over the
bodies of twenty-eight young men. "They do not know who puffs and
declines with pendant and bending arch." (The second girl's "arching
cloths" also owes something to Whitman's line.) And "whisper / Heav-
enly labials" is elided Whitman: "whispers of heavenly death murmur'd
I hear, / Labial gossip. . . ."[16] I do not hear Stevens' "I shall run before
him" as a verbal echo of Whitman, though this forerunning does read
like a recollection of Whitman's memorable closure to *Song of Myself*,
where "I stop somewhere waiting for you." All this means that we want
to be as cautious of Stevens' irony in his maundering giant, whetting his
hacker, as of Whitman's in his barbaric yawp. I read Stevens' poem as at
once a tribute to Whitman as the chief American forerunner, and a chal-
lenge to Whitman and to himself—placing Whitman as forerunner, re-
vising his language, stressing "againstness," so that in the end the girls
remain dominant after all and we anticipate the giant's undoing. It is as
if Stevens were saying: if Whitman were merely this barbaric giant, I
could check, abash, and undo him by reusing some of his own language.
But even as I use that language, I know Whitman is no maundering
giant. Still, this is one way of beginning, one possible plot against the
giant.

Stevens echoes other writers in work written before *Plot against the
Giant*. But Whitman dominates as forerunner to his volume, and so he
ought, for he is uniquely a beginning figure for any American poet.[17]
How powerful a figure he is, we may hear by returning to those verbal

---

[16] *Whispers of Heavenly Death*, ll. 1–2. Unless otherwise noted, quotations from Whit-
man's work are from *Leaves of Grass*, ed. Sculley Bradley and Harold Blodgett (New York:
Norton, 1973).

[17] Whitman and Dickinson dominate nineteenth-century United States poetry, but I say
"uniquely" because Whitman works extensively with the rhetoric and dialectic of begin-
ning.

echoes and recalling that, in Whitman's poetry, they are about secret longing and about voice. Insofar as these are Stevens' words, they function as I have described. But insofar as they remain Whitman's words, they transform that maundering giant into a persona of Stevens himself, and it is Whitman who has waited ahead to undo him. We go on asking who is whom, as plot and giant change identities. Stevens knows very well the strange plots—stories, secret schemes, or conspiracies—of verbal echo. Playful as it is, this is a profound fable of beginnings. It is also a warning against overeasy biographical readings of Stevens' poems. He playfully signed himself the "Giant" in some correspondence.[18] Not until we have read well the giant of this poem should we attempt to read the play of that signature.

We rightly think of Stevens as a poet of "wit and turn" rather than a poet of "an open sincerity of sentiment flowing in a plain expression," to use James Thomson's terms.[19] But *Infanta Marina* seems just such a "flowing" poem, or what I prefer to call a "fluency" poem, one of those playing on the motions and sounds of flowing language and flowing water, usually rivers. We know very well the standard couplets of Denham in English, but the play is an old one. Stevens quotes Horace's variation in 1904.[20] His own earliest example of a fluency poem is *Indian River* (1917), the latest is *The River of Rivers in Connecticut* (1953). Between comes a remarkable series of poems working with the concept and trope of flowing or fluency, modifying both concept and trope, and telling us something about the functions of euphony and charm poetry as well.

Infanta Marina, where both sea and evening "flowed around / And uttered their subsiding sound," is the first fluency poem we meet in Stevens' volume. Such argument as there is harmonizes with grammar and rhetoric in the usual way of fluency poems. We do not ask how ordinary language would work because there is little extraordinary language. The reader's desire for unity, which deconstructionists have taught us to mistrust, is here fulfilled. (In *Frogs Eat Butterflies. Snakes Eat Frogs. Hogs Eat Snakes. Men Eat Hogs*, it is overfilled in a parody of the usual fluency tropes and a lesson in unities.) There are no obvious problems in

[18] See Joan Richardson, *Wallace Stevens: A Biography* (New York: Beech Tree Books, 1986), vol. 1, p. 335.

[19] James Thomson, *The Seasons*, Preface to "Spring."

[20] "Oh, could I flow like thee, and make thy stream / My great example, as it is my theme! / Though deep yet clear, though gentle yet not dull; / Strong without rage, without o'erflowing full" (*Cooper's Hill*). Horace: "fons Bandusiae, splendidor vitro," in Holly Stevens, *Souvenirs and Prophecies: The Young Wallace Stevens* (New York: Knopf, 1977), p. 143.

Infanta Marina, at least once Stevens has explained that his phrase "sleights of sail" is a variation on "sleights of hand" (*L* 785, June 29, 1953). "Sleights of sail" is itself sleight of hand in the sense of word-play. It is referential in depicting sails in the distance, as Stevens says, and in depicting ghosts. It puns on the slightness of the optical effect and the verbal effect, and it works a slight change on usual ghost figures. For the infanta is ghostly; she merges into fanlike leaves and glimpses of sail in a "twilight" or doubleness of reading and of light. But she is a benign ghost and she fulfills the functions of a genius loci in this American shore poem. Stevens seems to have found here a place of marriage, the marriage of his own poetic genius with a genius of place, to follow Geoffrey Hartman's formulation.[21] It is right that this poem should have no againstness, the first of the introductory poems so designed.

Yet we want to look again at this little poem, especially at the second of the two puns at work. The first pun on the "fan" in "infanta" is not hard to read, and we smile at the aptness of an infanta as genius loci for fanlike palms; and for a man who liked the look and motion of a fan in a female hand. Ten years earlier, Stevens had compared his own writing to fan-painting (*L* 171, August 6, 1911). Courtly fan-language and *évanteil* poems also connect fans and words.[22] This pun is not disruptive but corroborative; the elusive, graceful, magical motions of sails and palms are pleasingly embodied in such a "creature of the evening." The pun also functions in a second way: it alerts us to the possibility of word-play and hence to another pun.

One of Stevens' best readers, Helen Vendler, hears this second pun,[23] whose presence seems all the more likely because Eliot's *Gerontion* was published a year earlier and was read by Stevens (*L* 216–17, March 4, 1920). In *Gerontion*, Eliot repeats the old word-play on the infant Christ as the Word who is also *infans* or unable to speak, "The word within a word, unable to speak a word." Given Stevens' delight in the standard large Latin dictionary of Lewis and Short,[24] and also in word-play, I read the "fan" within his "infanta" also as "the word within a word *able* to speak a word." (Lewis and Short list one *fans atque infans* paradox, from

---

[21] Geoffrey H. Hartman, "Romantic Poetry and the Genius Loci," in his *Beyond Formalism* (New Haven and London: Yale University Press, 1970), pp. 319, 322, 333.

[22] I am indebted to John Hollander for these suggestions.

[23] "Called a Spanish 'infanta' because she is speechless—*infans*—and because we are in that Florida which is the Spanish *tierra florida*," in her *Wallace Stevens: Words Chosen Out of Desire* (Knoxville: University of Tennessee Press, 1984), p. 63.

[24] "I hope that its occasional use will give you as much delight as it has given me." (Stevens to Robert Frost, on making him a present of the dictionary; letter of July 16, 1935, Dartmouth College Library; quoted by permission of Holly Stevens and the Dartmouth College Library; cf. *L* 275, March 4, 1935.)

Plautus, *Pers.* II.i.7.) The infanta may be "infans" in one way: even the most powerful genius loci needs a poet to do the uttering in human speech (the sea and evening are uttering *their* subsiding sound). Yet as a muse figure, she seems to have within her the power of *fans* (Latin, not English). This undivine "creature of the evening" can make us think about human words as much as Gerontion's infant Christ. Without disrupting its poem, this word-play keeps the unity from becoming too easy and keeps in play questions about the conventions of human speech. It also keeps us from reading too passively the visual resemblance of fans, palms, and sails. I do not hear this pun clearly at work in other of Stevens' fans. But I do hear it in some, if not all, of his infants: "Infant, it is enough in life / To speak of what you see," 1946 (*CP* 365); "It is the infant A standing on infant legs," 1949 (*CP* 469); "an infancy of blue snow," 1950 (*OP* 95).

"Subsiding sound": these are the last words we hear before the sounds of *Domination of Black.* We expect the hushed evening closure of the lovely infanta's poem to call forth a poetic voice, as the evening anticipates the dawn. And so she does, in one way: the first "I" of the volume appears. But this is a threatened "I," an unwilling "host"[25] for memory and a spirit of night. We move from fluency to radical disjunction.

Domination of Black was written earlier than any of the six opening poems. What they do for it is to discourage an easy mimetic reading. For at first, *Domination of Black* sounds like a fluency poem, especially after *Infanta Marina*—a partaking poem in which the outside world will flow around and utter a subsiding sound, and easily consent to be turned into tropes, in which any presiding muse or genius loci will be benevolent and sustaining, in which tropes will happily play with topoi in the multiple senses of "turning" that Stevens' poem slowly develops. The conventional associations of the fireside as a place of pleasant musing support such expectations.

> At night, by the fire,
> The colors of the bushes
> And of the fallen leaves,
> Repeating themselves,
> Turned in the room,
> Like the leaves themselves
> Turning in the wind.

---

[25] This suggestive term is adapted from J. Hillis Miller, "The Critic as Host," in *Deconstruction and Criticism*, Bloom et al. (New York: Seabury, 1979), pp. 217–53, an essay on the paradoxes of reader and text as host and parasite.

Yes: but the color of the heavy hemlocks
Came striding.
And I remembered the cry of the peacocks.

The play on the word "turning" is extraordinary: a mimesis of moving colors in a firelit room, a recollection of leaves turning color in the fall, any possible troping of leaves, past tropings of leaves, the turning of the leaves of a book and the colors of rhetoric, turnings over the end of the line as we read, and, later in the poem, the turning of our planet that brings on night, and the turning of the stars. In the first few lines, we must guess among several grammatical functions for the words before one is confirmed as dominant in the slow unfolding of the poem, the others retaining only a ghostly possibility. Our syntactic turnings revise earlier readings as we turn the ends of lines, and these syntactic turnings are emblematic of the entire poem, which keeps turning back retrospectively and revising itself, as it moves forward, repeating. A whole system of conjunctive effects, as at the end of *Infanta Marina*, works to lull us until the unaccountable breaks at the end of each stanza. The verse sounds like a kind of hypnosis against which the poem's breaks or disjunctions awaken us—awaken us to a sense that they have always been there in some form, as they have, from the moment of the title and the first line.

For the title points forward to the extinguishing or damping down of fire. Stevens breaks only three lines in this flowing poem, and only line 1 with the unobtrusive comma. But after the title, that comma is meant to give us pause. Even in such small breaks, we can see in retrospect a potential opposition: "Domination of Black. At night, by the fire. . . ." The title acts to divide line 1 at the caesura so that one phrase will come to dominate the other, for all the flow of the lines. And so it happens at the end, when night is no longer governed by a preposition in a casual phrase, but itself "came / Came striding." This is the moment Stevens remembered twelve years later when he consented to correct one interpretation of the poem. It is not the firelit room but the heavens full of color and sounds, the climactic *timor noctis*. "I am sorry that a poem of this sort has to contain any ideas at all, because its sole purpose is to fill the mind with the images & sounds that it contains. A mind that examines such a poem for its prose contents gets absolutely nothing from it. You are supposed to get heavens full of the colors and full of sounds, and you are supposed to feel as you would feel if you actually got all this" (*L* 251, March 31, 1928). Stevens' comments on his work are sometimes more interesting for what they do not say than for what they do. What Stevens does not say here is that the feeling one is "supposed" to feel is

42

fear. He recorded the thought of a similar fear in 1904: "I thought, on the train, how utterly we have forsaken the Earth, in the sense of excluding it from our thoughts. There are but few who consider its physical hugeness, its rough enormity. . . . It still dwarfs + terrifies + crushes. . . . Man is an affair of cities. . . . Somehow, however, he has managed to shut out the face of the giant from his windows. But the giant is there, nevertheless" (*L* 73, Journal 1904).

Domination of Black treats the topos of fallen leaves, though the topos never points overtly to its own history or to specific arguments about mortality or indeed to any argument at all. Stevens keeps such argument as there is implicit. The poem circles and recircles around its topos, with the incantatory circles broken, then resumed, broken, then resumed around the break, then finally broken.

Or rather, not its topos but its topoi, for I want to argue for the presence of another topos. The more important topos of the fallen leaves has been finely read.[26] But before we come to the topos of the leaves, we come to something else. We come to the fireplace, in Stevens' first indoor setting in *Harmonium* and his first use of what will become a repeated and important phrase, "in the room." We come, that is, to a human dwelling place, as we also come to the first "I" in Stevens' volume. The title begins by sounding painterly; the text begins by sounding domestic. We may call the fire a setting or a light to read or muse by (and Stevens' preposition "by" has more than one sense). We may think of the fire as a mimetic starting point, since we begin with a visual effect of flickering colors in a firelit room. But we may more usefully consider it as a topos, remembering how it functions as a symbol for home so often (in Russian fairy tales, in the poem by du Bellay that Stevens loved where its smoke is seen from afar,[27] in Hawthorne). It is conventionally not only the center of a home but also a place where one remembers, a memory-place, a place for ghost stories and old romances. It is a fit place also for recognition scenes, where memory confronts new knowledge (thus Isabel in James's *Portrait of a Lady*, chap. 42). It naturally makes for a circle around it, whether of people or of light or even of odor (as in Proust's *cercle magique* of firewood aroma).[28]

Fireside memories tend to divide into beneficent or threatening. Browning maps this polarity nicely in his two "By the Fireside" poems, and Stevens may have had in mind stanza i of the better-known *By the*

---

[26] Bloom, *Wallace Stevens*, pp. 375–79; John Hollander, *The Figure of Echo: A Mode of Allusion in Milton and After* (Berkeley, Los Angeles, London: University of California Press, 1981), pp. 121–22.

[27] "Heureux qui comme Ulysse . . ." (cf. *L* 150–51).

[28] *A la recherche du temps perdu* (Paris: Gallimard, 1954), vol. 6, *La Prisonnière*, p. 28.

Fireside when he wrote *Domination of Black*, with its fire and wind and leaves and turnings. He seems to be moving toward such beneficent reverie until the turn of line 8, which does not turn with, like the flowing appositive turns of lines 1 through 7, but against: "Yes: but."

I want to take one more step. I want to suggest that the fireplace is not only a topos but also itself an image of a topos. Not a storehouse or hunting-region or mine—not those places where memory stores arguments like objects or hunts arguments like animals or quarries arguments like metals, as in Aristotle and Cicero and Quintilian.[29] But a memory-place where memory sees old arguments or assertions by a certain light, or hears old arguments or assertions in a certain sound. Older images for topoi treat arguments like objects that may be retrieved or captured by someone in charge—appropriate images for topoi developed for judicial or political oratory. For Curtius's kind of topic or commonplace, or for Renaissance sententiae, as for topos as a place of voice,[30] the fireside is an excellent image: a "common place" around which we gather for ordinary heat and light, around which ordinary, cosy memories may be evoked (to follow Larzer Ziff's argument about nineteenth-century United States hearths).[31] Yet a place whose powerful focus may also, in proportion to its comforting power, become a fearful power. If the topos of the fallen leaves raises thoughts of mortality, whether physical or spiritual or verbal, the topos of the fireplace raises thoughts about home. But not just domestic home. When Stevens suddenly changes perspec-

[29] For a stimulating discussion of spatial thinking about the topoi or places, see Walter J. Ong, *Remus, Method and the Decay of Dialogue* (New York: Octagon, 1974), "The Loci or Places: Woods and Boxes," pp. 116–21.

[30] Ernst Robert Curtius, *European Literature and the Latin Middle Ages*, trans. Willard R. Trask (Princeton: Princeton University Press, Bollingen Series, 1953), pp. 79–105 and *passim*. For Renaissance sententiae, see Joan Marie Lechner, *Renaissance Concepts of the Commonplaces* (Westport, Conn.: Greenwood, 1962, 1974). On the classical topoi, see generally, George A. Kennedy, *Classical Rhetoric and Its Christian and Secular Tradition from Ancient to Modern Times* (Chapel Hill: University of North Carolina Press, 1980), *passim*. The word "topoi" is properly "topoi koinoi" (Latin, "loci communes"), that is, the "common places." Aristotle's four common or universal arguments are those applicable to various arts or sciences. (They are arguments by degree, by possible and impossible, by past and future, by amplification and depreciation.) The word "topos" is also used of specific arguments, as in Cicero and Quintilian, and of the place in the memory where such things are to be sought, and, one hopes, found. Postclassical topoi expand into themes and formulas, as used in all kinds of literature, not just judicial or political oratory, to follow Curtius's definition ("a somewhat special meaning," Ong says in the Introduction to Lechner's *Commonplaces*). We retrieve literary topoi through memorable treatments, as, for example, of the topos of the leaves of a tree as the dead. It is in this sense, I take it, that a topos may be a place of voice, on which see Bloom, *Wallace Stevens*, pp. 389–400.

[31] Larzer Ziff, *Literary Democracy: The Declaration of Cultural Independence in America* (New York: Penguin, 1981), pp. 53–4.

44

tive in the last stanza, the context becomes cosmic. It becomes a question of being at home in the universe, under those planets that should also turn, like so much else in this poem. Yes, but they do not turn. Instead, they "gather."

If a topos or locus communis may have a genius loci—and why not?—what genius of place presides here? A genius or spirit of hunting would work for Quintilian's "places" and a genius of safekeeping for Aristotle's. Here we should have a god or goddess of hearths, a Vesta. Or even possibly Vulcan, patron of craftsmen, if his fearful forges could be domesticated. But the most powerful spirit in the poem is antithetical to human fire, and to the fiery colors of North American fallen leaves, and to the colors of rhetoric, or the colors that books made for Stevens. (Books are "like so many fantastic lights filling plain darkness with strange colors" [L 123, 1909].) In the end, it is a spirit of black that prevails, and it comes from Wordsworth. The colors of the fallen leaves recall, without echoing, Shelley's apocalyptic leaves in the *Ode to the West Wind*, a poem that Stevens echoes many times. The striding hemlock-color and striding night recall, and also echo, Wordsworth's memorable haunting in Book I of *The Prelude*. The metaphoric use of "stride" marks the echo, which is strong enough to my ear to be allusive. Even the placement in the line is similar, each example working with enjambment or "striding-over":

> a huge peak, black and huge,
> As if with voluntary power instinct
> Upreared its head. I struck and struck again,
> And growing still in stature the grim shape
> Towered up between me and the stars, and still,
> For so it seemed, with purpose of its own
> And measured motion like a living thing,
> Strode after me. With trembling oars I turned . . .
> . . . o'er my thoughts
> There hung a darkness, call it solitude
> Or blank desertion. No familiar shapes
> Remained, no pleasant images of trees,
> Of sea or sky, no colours of green fields;
> But huge and mighty forms. . . .[32]

Wordsworth has Milton in mind here, though I see no direct evidence that Stevens has. (His extraordinary echoing of Milton *through* Words-

[32] 1850 *Prelude* I.378–98, in *The Prelude, 1799, 1805, 1850*, ed. Jonathan Wordsworth, M. H. Abrams, Stephen Gill (New York and London: Norton, 1979). All quotations from *The Prelude* are from the 1850 version and from this edition.

worth will come later.) Yet it is Stevens who makes us notice the word "stride" and inquire what Milton did with the word, and where. The answer is startling, when we read the following lines of "black night," "came" with "strides," "strode," and "fear," and then think of Wordsworth's lines. Edmund Burke singled out the first eight lines as "dark, uncertain, confused, terrible, and sublime to the last degree," and Wordsworth read and admired Burke.[33]

> The other shape,
> If shape it might be call'd that shape had none
> Distinguishable in member, joint, or limb,
> Or substance might be call'd that shadow seem'd,
> For each seem'd either; black it stood as Night,
> Fierce as ten Furies, terrible as Hell,
> And shook a dreadful Dart; what seem'd his head
> The likeness of a Kingly Crown had on.
> *Satan* was now at hand, and from his seat
> The Monster moving onward came as fast,
> With horrid strides; Hell trembled as he strode.
> Th' undaunted Fiend what this might be admir'd,
> Admir'd, not fear'd; God and his Son except,
> Created thing naught valu'd he nor shunn'd.[34]

It is important that Wordsworth *does* fear some created things, as the lines framing this episode in *The Prelude* make clear. Such fear is part of his training as a poet. Wordsworth records that he found a later comfort from his boyhood fear ("purifying . . . And sanctifying, by such discipline, / Both pain and fear" [1.410–13]). And Stevens? If he also has Coleridge in mind at the end of *Domination of Black*,[35] then the question is whether his fear is Wordsworth's kind of fear or Coleridge's, that is,

---

[33] Andrew Wilton, *Turner and the Sublime* (London: British Museum Publications, 1980), p. 101. See J. T. Boulton's argument about the influence of Burke on Wordsworth, in his edition of Burke's *Philosophical Enquiry into the Origin of our Ideas of the Sublime and the Beautiful* (London: Routledge & Kegan Paul, 1958), p. ci. On Wordsworth's fear as "an important element in the poet's formative experience," see Stillinger's note to *Prelude* 1.302ff., in his *William Wordsworth: Selected Poems and Prefaces* (Boston: Houghton Mifflin, 1965), p. 542. Students from British Columbia confirm that hemlocks can induce a sense of fear. Students from northern Ontario confirm that flickering firelight in a cabin in the bush can make a dark night appear to be coming in at you. Perhaps Stevens is drawing on memories of his camping trip to British Columbia in 1903 (*L* 64–67).

[34] *Paradise Lost* II.666[!]–79. My exclamation mark notes the coincidence of Milton's line number with the number of the Beast in the Apocalypse, a coincidence not noted in standard Milton editions.

[35] Cf. Bloom, *Wallace Stevens*, pp. 378–79.

46

fear that is useful and even necessary for the poet's vocation, or fear that is debilitating and finally silencing. The question is all-important, but Stevens cannot in honesty answer it in 1916. He closes without an answer, only a memory of voice, and that not of a human cry but of a peacock's. We may not hear Stevens' echoing until we return to Wordsworth, but, once heard, it tells us what this powerful 1916 poem is doing at the beginning of Stevens' volume. It too has to do with the forming of a poet's mind, and with a poet who is not yet at ease in the places of his imagination. It has to do with the possible domination of black— black night, the "black" of Milton and Wordsworth and Coleridge, the black of spooky North American hemlocks, and the ugly black of the beautiful peacock's feet against which it cries out.

The Snow Man, Stevens' 1921 companion poem to his 1916 *Domination of Black*, is not a domination of white but a poem written against domination, the strategy being as pure a verbal "nothing" as possible. Stevens' poem is an exercise in sensation explicitly dissociated from feeling. He practices rather than mourns "dissociation of sensibility." (Eliot's essay, "The Metaphysical Poets," appeared in the same month as *The Snow Man*.) *Domination of Black* is invaded by memory, *The Snow Man* purged of it as far as possible, and hence Graham Hough's sense that the poem "seems to owe nothing to inherited poetic property."[36] The two poems make a fine study in contrast: black versus white, night versus day, fire versus ice, "I" versus "one," past tense versus present. What they have in common are leaves and wind and boughs, the sensations of seeing and hearing, places that are full of sounds, and referential words that gradually take on literary significance like the history of the words themselves. ("Turning" becomes trope, "place" becomes topos.)

Stevens' poem owes something to Eliot's *Rhapsody on a Windy Night*, as does *Domination of Black*. Stevens is too strong an ironist to write Eliot's *Rhapsody*, though he remembered its strange new "music" many years later, and misquoted it, presumably from memory (*NA* 124–25). Both *Domination of Black* and *The Snow Man* are meditative, nondramatic, and far from dramatized. Stevens' poems are unlike Eliot's in another way. Eliot's poem deals with "twisted" things and places, Stevens' with turned things and common or bare places. Eliot's diction includes words like "fatalistic," "madman," an eye "like a crooked pin," "skeleton," "washed-out smallpox," "female smells," "rancid butter." ("I have been churning . . . a very rancid butter," said Stevens of *From the Journal of Crispin*, a very different poem [*L* 224, December 21, 1921].) Deliberately antinormal, Eliot's fragmentation is effective within

[36] Graham Hough, "The Poetry of Wallace Stevens," *Critical Quarterly* 2 (1960), 205.

the conventions of dramatic monologue. Stevens' disjunctions, like Wordsworth's, have a wider range.

Domination of Black openly turns away from the expected development of a commonplace: "Yes: but," "against, against, against." *The Snow Man* breaks implicitly with topoi in the older sense of kinds of argument. When Stevens changes Emerson's "bare common" to "the same bare *place*," he knows very well what he is doing. (I do not mean that he must have known the history of the topoi, simply that he is aware of the history of the words "common" and "place." He was a dictionary addict, like any good poet.) He is moving against the community and the commonalty of the topoi or commonplaces, and back to a "bare place," no longer common. Usual cheerful-northerner or hard-primitive arguments run as follows: one must have a stout heart to look at a gray sky and not to think of any misery, etc. Or (Emerson's variation): one may be visited by a kind of grace, a self-begotten "exhilaration," even when crossing "a bare common, in snow puddles, at twilight, under a clouded sky, without having in my thoughts any occurrence of special good fortune." If Emerson had a "mind of winter" like Stevens' snow man, he would accept or enjoy his bare scene, and there would be nothing special in the place of his experience, or in himself for experiencing it there. Why does Stevens say "misery" after such a pretty-winter picture? The logic calls for an "also": and *also* not to think of any misery in the sound of the wind, the sound of a few leaves, at some other time and in some other place. (Those are dead, deciduous leaves, not evergreen needles as in the pines, junipers, and spruce of stanzas i and ii.) But the poem circles back, saying that it is this same, now bare place that paradoxically is "full" of this same sound (in which one must not think of misery), full for all its bareness. *The Snow Man* is a poem climaxing on paradox, but if we pay attention, it is paradoxical from the middle point on, not just at the end.

> One must have a mind of winter
> To regard the frost and the boughs
> Of the pine-trees crusted with snow;
>
> And have been cold a long time
> To behold the junipers shagged with ice,
> The spruces rough in the distant glitter
>
> Of the January sun; and not to think
> Of any misery in the sound of the wind,
> In the sound of a few leaves,

Which is the sound of the land
Full of the same wind
That is blowing in the same bare place

For the listener, who listens in the snow,
And, nothing himself, beholds
Nothing that is not there and the nothing that is.

Word-play in this poem is intertwined with the play of paradox, especially the paradox of being and nothingness on which the poem closes. Or rather, not being and nothingness, but "is" and "nothing." We should beware of changing "a" or even "the nothing" to "nothingness," a word which comes with portentous metaphysical associations. (Consider the effects of le néant or das Nichtige.) Discussions of the "nothingness" of The Snow Man by definition weigh the poem's paradoxes on the existential side—that being one kind of paradox about nothing, as we know from Pascal. But Stevens' paradoxes function in other ways, not least of which is the play of paradox itself, whether rhetorical, logical, or epistemological. Paradox plays with, and thereby criticizes, the limits of things by being a self-contradiction. Like puns, it turns inside out, then outside in, and so alters our sense of what is outside and what inside.[37] So also a snow man who tries to be one with winter, that is, to be a snowman.

We are conscious today of paradoxes inherent in the act of writing, or of making traces on the page. One "nothing that is" is obviously the word "nothing" as it appears on "the same bare place" that is the place of listening and beholding for the reader. Letters on the page give the lie to the last two lines as simple description though not as paradox or trope. This paradox is an old one, inherent also in the mathematical concept of zero and in the letter O (whence the play on O and the word "nothing" in King Lear or The Waste Land). In Shakespeare, the metaphysical "nothing" of the rhetorical paradoxists, the psychological sense of not-being, and the "nothing" of comic bawdy play may all be found. And we should not forget the acoustic sounds of O, and its visual shape, since a snowman is made of three O's. (The letter and number and shape of O seem to go to extremes, for its other associations are just the opposite of nothing; they are of plenitude.[38])

[37] Cf. Stephen Booth, Shakespeare's Sonnets (New Haven and London: Yale University Press, 1977), s.v. "nothing." I have drawn on Rosalie Colie's Paradoxia Epidemica: The Renaissance Tradition of Paradox; see especially the Introduction, and ch. 7, " 'Nothing is but what is not': Solutions to the Problem of Nothing," pp. 219–51.

[38] For an example of O as perfection and plenitude, see the frontispiece to Terence Cave,

One paradox about the poem is that snowmen are not cold; they just are. (Creatures like polar bears, who feel misery in summer, are comfortably warm in winter.) That is, Stevens' poem is not so much about a pure snowman as about what native northerners call a transformation figure. Inuit and Amerindian legends abound with humans who get transformed into appropriate creatures, and works of art representing such legends usually depict the moment of transformation.[39] So also Stevens here. It is, as he says, a question of "identity" (so is paradox). "I shall explain The Snow Man as an example of the necessity of identifying oneself with reality in order to understand and enjoy it" (L 464, April 18, 1944).

Stevens does not work here with echo or allusion, unless of the faintest kind. We may hear a faint echo of the first quatrain of Shakespeare's sonnet 73, a sonnet to which Stevens will return again and again:

> That time of year thou mayst in me behold
> When yellow leaves, or none, or few, do hang
> Upon those boughs which shake against the cold,
> Bare ruin'd choirs where late the sweet birds sang.

Stevens diffuses the words of this sonnet through his poem (behold, leaves, few, boughs, cold, bare), and he may be faintly echoing Shakespeare in the phrase "few leaves." For the snow man, there are no bare choirs (a lost place of voice), not even finally Emerson's bare common, but just a bare place. The snow man tries to change himself into an Emersonian transparent eye and I, so that "That time of year thou mayst through me behold." But Emerson lies when he says, "I am nothing." He is a transparency, and a transparency is not nothing.

This is the first poem in *Harmonium* in which Stevens plays with compacted argument, and, in this way if no other, it prepares us for *Le Monocle de Mon Oncle*, the eleventh poem. In its play with logic, it makes a riddle poem (in contrast to *Domination of Black*, which is a charm poem). The text poses a question which the title answers, either in standard form or in truncated form: Who am I? A snow man. Am I? No man.

After the first eight poems of *Harmonium*, we are well instructed in ways of reading Stevens. Acting out what they describe, finding lan-

---

The Cornucopian Text: Problems of Writing in the French Renaissance (Oxford: Clarendon, 1979).

[39] See Jean Blodgett, *The Coming and Going of the Shaman: Eskimo Shamanism and Art* (Winnipeg: Winnipeg Art Gallery, 1978), ch. 5, "Transformation," pp. 75–88. Joseph Campbell, *The Way of Animal Powers* (San Francisco: Alfred van der Marck Editions, Harper & Row, 1983), passim.

guage for a poem's process, playing with grammar and etymology and echoes and standard tropes, witty or flowing by turn—these are fine poems, all the more because of the unobtrusiveness of some effects. *Domination of Black* and *The Snow Man* are extraordinary in what they do with topoi and with paradox. They are also extraordinary in what they do with the theme of desire for a poetic home. Stevens' effects of displacing in these first eight poems make us aware of our language of place, and our perceptions of place. We play back and forth between outside and inside, and find pleasure in the play. We undo the metaphor of outside and inside; we walk around the places of our own words. The effect is enlivening, especially in the powerful seventh and eighth poems.

Throughout my discussion, I have been listening to the ways in which dialectic and rhetoric talk back and forth to each other. Or, to change the metaphor, how dialectic and rhetoric play against each other. It is some such sense of the play of words that offers, for me, one of the best methods for reading Stevens. And such a sense is not different in kind from the narrow sense of word-play. For word-play in the narrow sense of punning is, in miniature, a play between dialectic (as semantic meaning) and rhetoric (as schematic echoing).

✳   ✳   ✳   ✳   ✳

CHAPTER TWO

The Play and War of Venus:

Love Poems and Florida Poems

> The artist . . . is *un amoureux perpétuel* of the
> world that he contemplates (*NA* 30, 1942).

> A poet looks at the world as a man looks at a woman
> (*OP* 165).

Tʜᴇ ʏᴏᴜɴɢ Sᴛᴇᴠᴇɴs was a love poet, who wrote verses of paralyzing dullness to his future wife. He read erotic poetry when he "was young and reading left and right" (*L* 381): Ovid's *Ars Amatoria* (*L* 65), Paulus Silentiarius from Mackail's *Greek Anthology* (*SP* 183–84), Campion, and so on. When the miraculous year 1915 came, and Stevens inexplicably began to write major poetry, it was not surprising that one of his subjects was erotic love. The poem itself is surprising. It is *Peter Quince at the Clavier*, a variation on the Apocryphal story of Susannah and the Elders. Stevens anticipated it in a struggling poem called *Dolls* (1914),[1] which treats sexual guilt with strained humor and the alleviations of escapist fantasy. In *Harmonium*, Stevens placed *Peter Quince* near the end of the volume. *The Ordinary Women* (1922) appears as the ninth poem; it warns of the unsatisfactory allure of escapism. *Le Monocle de Mon Oncle* (1918), the eleventh poem, bursts into the volume, joking in its title, swearing in its opening lines, the first poem of any length, the most difficult in argument so far, the one great love poem that Stevens wrote.

---

[1] Robert Buttel, *The Making of "Harmonium"* (Princeton: Princeton University Press, 1967), p. 186.

Here we find, not a development of Stevens' very ordinary verses to Elsie Moll, but rather a development of his playful fantastic letters to her. Yet the poem is different from the letters in one crucial way. The playful letters are fantastic in a charming but hazardous way, as Stevens' biographers make clear. The letters have little to do with the actuality of love. *Le Monocle de Mon Oncle* does. Read chronologically, Stevens' love poems into the thirties have a painful plot. He finally stopped writing poetry of erotic love (some bitter, unpolished work from the thirties was left uncollected), and we lost in him a rarity, a poet of middle-aged eros.

The subject of eros proved a troubled one for Stevens, and the love poems in *Harmonium* are difficult to read. Stevens' accessible love poems are not written to a woman but to a state, to Florida. Venus is quite as much a presiding figure for the Southern poems as for the love poems, and so I have drawn together these two types of poetry. To map the places of the natural world is one thing; to map the places of love is another. Some poets are at ease with the topography of a woman's body as beloved ground, and a beloved part of earth as woman's body. Stevens regularly practices the latter kind of writing but virtually never the former. He maps the seductive landscape of Florida like a lover mapping a woman's body. One poem even asks her to restrain herself and be a little more heavenly, which is the reverse of mon oncle's plea, but then Stevens is not avuncular with Florida. He also sometimes tropes on the male body in a comic way.

Do the Venus poems displace us slightly, moving us away from ordinary mimesis as the opening poems did? Though the language of the Florida poems is sometimes unusual, it is grounded in ordinary mimesis. The love poems are very different. They show rapid, elusive play and war between and by dialectic and rhetoric. Each stanza of *Le Monocle de Mon Oncle*, for example, offers a field of argument and some familiar battlelines; offers the usual troping for such arguments; offers a generic placing; and offers a judgment on all these proceedings. In a sense, it is argument that Stevens plays with in these stanzas. He pays his readers the compliment of supposing they have thought through certain arguments. And so he works with a kind of shorthand, not so much using argument in poetry as making poetry out of the places of argument. If the topoi or commonplaces of love could be troped, what would arguments, themes, and tropes look like? Could the various places of love be laid out this way, as if the love poet were building a memory-place similar to the classical or Renaissance memory-places? To play and war with language in this way would be to offer an anatomy of the "origin and course / Of love." And indeed, one could write a small handbook on the writing of love poetry from this packed poem.

But first, *The Ordinary Women*, a useful introduction to *Le Monocle de Mon Oncle*, if chronologically an unhappy postlude. This is a poem caught within the terms of its two specular halves, its "catarrh" and "guitar" worlds.[2] Cattarhs are colds, and Stevens plays on coldness throughout the poem, and outside it too: it is placed between *The Snow Man* and the warm river-movement of *The Load of Sugar-Cane*. There is much glitter in this escapist fantasy but no fire. "Wickless halls" tells us that the girandoles have dead candles; the moonlight "fubs" them by making them look fiery. The word "wickless" itself fubs the reader: "cried quittance to the wick-" seems to cry out for the word "wicked" as if the women were the Muses fleeing Pyreneus over the end of the line. But no Muses they, nor any menace in this one-line plot. These ordinary women oscillate between an ordinary or tedious everyday life and a fantastic night-time moonlit-palace life, or what Stevens later calls "minor wish-fulfillments" (*NA* 139). He judges their reading of the heavens thus: 'they leaned and looked / From the window-sills at the alphabets, / At beta b and gamma g." We have allegorized these lines most ingeniously, but they are first and foremost standard astronomical nomenclature for stars. Stevens is telling us that the women see no stars of alpha or first magnitude; their stars, like their abortive erotic fantasies, are of the second or third order. (If we ask whether men as well as women are subject to such fantasies, Stevens' answer is yes, on the testimony of a Polish aunt [*CP* 84, 1919].) Between *The Ordinary Women* and *Le Monocle* comes the slight *Load of Sugar-Cane*, a fluency poem implicitly commenting on *The Ordinary Women*: warmth against cold, flowing against vacillation, mostly ordinary against much precious diction, work against fantasy—in short, "ordinary" work and nature and beauty at their ordinary best. It is with these varying senses of how the "ordinary" or "common" may work that we turn to Stevens' great poem.

Mon oncle is a persona of Stevens himself, and thus, of course, a Dutch uncle as well as a French uncle. One of Stevens' selves, as he very well knows, is an all-too-willing pedagogue, that self he calls "the Devil of sermons, within me" in 1909 (*L* 124), smiles at in the opening canto of *Notes toward a Supreme Fiction*, and metamorphoses into Canon Aspirin and Professor Eucalyptus. Mon oncle begins with word-war:

> "Mother of heaven, regina of the clouds,
> O sceptre of the sun, crown of the moon,
> There is not nothing, no, no, never nothing,
> Like the clashed edges of two words that kill."

[2] A. Walton Litz notes how the second half mirrors the first; see *Introspective Voyager: The Poetic Development of Wallace Stevens* (New York: Oxford University Press, 1972), pp. 110–11.

This is detached dialogue from a preceding dispute, as Stevens' next line makes clear: "And so I mocked her in magnificent measure." The opening apostrophes are swearing, as Stevens says they are (*L* 251, March 31, 1928), and lines 3 and 4 are surely a hyperbolic negative in Shakespearean style and not a logical positive.[3] We infer that the woman has said that there *are* two words that kill, though we are not told what these sword-words are. Stevens directs us away from the particulars of the quarrel, which functions as a starting point for this great meditation on changing love. Any nomination for Stevens' "two words" must suggest some logical dialogue that comes before this opening mockery, and I wonder if the two nominations so far proposed can do so.[4] This invitation to the reader to fill in omitted argument is a technique Stevens will use repeatedly.

The tone changes sharply after the mocked mockery turns back against its speaker:

> And so I mocked her in magnificent measure.
> Or was it that I mocked myself alone?
> I wish that I might be a thinking stone.
> The sea of spuming thought foists up again
> The radiant bubble that she was. And then
> A deep up-pouring from some saltier well
> Within me, bursts its watery syllable.

Stanza i is prologue to the poem proper, which goes on to work out this stanza's succeeding reactions of speech and silence, attack and self-wounding, present versus various pasts, willed and unwilled memory (what Proust calls *mémoire volontaire* and *mémoire involontaire*). Between stanzas i and ii comes a decision to turn "her" into "you," which is to say, to write this poem as address. The entire poem is a passionate desire to answer "no" to the last word of line 6 ("alone"), a desire to make it a dramatic monologue with an addressee, and not a soliloquy. We may map the poem's progression by its personal pronouns: I and her (i), I and you (ii–v), third person except for a universal "us" (vi–vii), I and we (viii), I and you (ix), I (x), we (xi), I (xii).

---

[3] Cf. Craig Raine, *Times Literary Supplement*, December 6, 1974.

[4] The words proposed are "nothing," by Richard Ellmann, in "Wallace Stevens' Ice-Cream," *Kenyon Review* 19 (1957), 98; and "no, no," by Harold Bloom, *Wallace Stevens: The Poems of Our Climate* (Ithaca: Cornell University Press, 1977), p. 38. If it is easier to enter the poem by speculating on words that kill, my guess would be based on a poem by Emily Dickinson, with a sword-word and some syllables: "There is a word / Which bears a sword / Can pierce an arméd man—/ It hurls its barbed syllables / And is mute again." Dickinson's word is "forgot," and my nomination for the two words that kill would be "I forgot" or "you forgot," from which we can work out the usual recriminations.

Commentators are generally aware of Wordsworth's informing presence, but I shall argue that a specific troping *against* Wordsworth's *Immortality Ode* lies at the threshold of Stevens' poem. "Saltier" is usually read allegorically, but I am unable to read the last two lines of stanza i without agreeing with Frank Doggett's passing (and ignored) suggestion that "saltier well / Within me" refers quite simply to the speaker's tears.[5] Here is Stevens, writing to his wife in 1911: "Such nights are like wells of sweet water in the salt sea (to repeat an ancient fancy)" (*L* 170, August 6, 1911). A fresh-water well would be a figure of hope, but welling tears are saltier than thought's salt sea. "Its" in the phrase "its watery syllable" is ambiguous, as Stevens' pronouns often are: the up-pouring well may burst its own watery syllable or (more likely) burst the watery syllable of that radiant bubble or (most likely) both, in a bursting and a bursting forth of the bubble-syllable. We burst into tears quite as much as we burst into song. The memory of Venus does not vanish into thin air with the bursting of that radiant bubble; rather, bubble is metamorphosed through logic and image into a teardrop and through near-rhyme into "syllable." Again, the syllable may be burst open like a bubble (Stevens returns to this remarkable trope late in his life [*CP* 515–16]), so that we come to the end of sound and speech, as we come to the end of this stanza—itself strongly encapsulated, like all the stanzas of *Le Monocle*.[6] This double possibility in the reading of "its" and "bursts" and "bubble, syllable" is typical of Stevens' rhetoric throughout the poem. It is by turns intensely reticent and expressive. A sense of fit private and public utterance affects the poem's rhetoric as it does that of *Peter Quince at the Clavier*. Stevens' language is reticent in its exceedingly compact argument and troping, yet expressive in its occasional bursting forth, and a peculiar tension is generated by such different rhetorical impulses.

In *Ode: Intimations of Immortality*, Wordsworth too is suffering a crisis of loss; "glory" is his repeated word for what has gone, though the word "radiance" is used once. ("What though the radiance which was once so bright / Be now for ever taken from my sight?") Wordsworth ends thus:

> Thanks to the human heart by which we live,
> Thanks to its tenderness, its joys, and fears,

[5] Frank Doggett, *Stevens' Poetry of Thought* (Baltimore: The Johns Hopkins Press, 1966), p. 25.

[6] Isabel MacCaffre makes the point in "The Ways of Truth in 'Le Monocle de Mon Oncle,'" in *Wallace Stevens: A Celebration*, ed. Frank Doggett and Robert Buttel (Princeton: Princeton University Press, 1980), pp. 196, 208.

> To me the meanest flower that blows can give
> Thoughts that do often lie too deep for tears.

In Stevens' poem, it is tears that lie deep, deeper than spuming thought. Wordsworth's great reconciling closure cannot speak to the loss of erotic radiance, because it is precisely the desire for intimations of immortality that threatens to destroy mon oncle's love. Stevens must begin where Wordsworth ends.

The rest of the poem is a lesson in mortality, or "shade," the word on which the poem quietly closes. The barrier between speaker and beloved is not the power of two words that kill but the killing power of fanciful illusion, especially the illusion that love ("true love" is the usual way of putting it) does not change. Stevens may be struggling quite as much against something in himself as in the woman: "Elsie—you will never grow old, will you? You must always have pink cheeks and golden hair. To be young is all there is in the world. The rest is nonsense—and cant. . . . The point is to be young—and to be a little in love, or very much— and to desire carnations and creations—and to be glad when Spring comes" (L 97–98 and cf. 100, 127, 1907–1909). In any case, we should observe that the poem is not centered on the male speaker's egotistical sublime nor is it recentered on a new radiant Venus. For all its early harshness, its anger, queries, and imperatives, it is not a rejection but a plea. What rhetoric is appropriate to address a beloved woman, apparently bound by conventional romantic fictions, fictions whose remnants remain in the lover himself? This is the poem's problem.

Mon oncle's farewell to birdsong in stanza ii takes leave of one of Stevens' early memories. We may well ask if "any strong poet [has] ever disliked birdsong as much as Stevens did,"[7] but not of very early or very late Stevens. "But to fly! Gli uccelli hanno le ali—that's why they're not here. Whenever I think of these things I can see, + do see, a bird somewhere in a mass of flowers and leaves, perched on a spray in dazzling light, and pouring out arpeggios of enchanting sounds" (L 48, November 10, 1900). Stevens' early letters and journal regularly note various birds, especially their songs and flight. He writes of the "immense satisfaction in studying the lyrics of song-sparrows, catbirds, wrens and the like," a memory he will use forty-three years later (L 30, July 26, 1899; CP 393–94). And birdsong is still part of the earthly paradise in 1915 in *Sunday Morning*. But after 1918, Stevens stopped himself from using the beautiful tropes of liquidity for birdsong, the "avia . . . liquidis vocibus" of Lucretius (II.145–46). Only birds that sound dry-throated are allowed,

---

[7] Bloom, *Wallace Stevens*, p. 195.

grackles who crack their throats of bone. Or the tropes of liquidity are punned on with heavy irony. In 1932, Stevens turned sharply on his memory of 1900, and on *Le Monocle*, in the phrase, "arpeggi of celestial souvenirs" (*OP* 35). Birds and birdsong are harshly treated in the thirties, for the most part. (One exception is the 1935 *Meditation Celestial and Terrestrial*, where Stevens allows the word "radiant" to reappear.) Only in the forties do we hear some detachment, and only at the end of his life does Stevens rediscover a way of writing about birdsong. Stanza ii of *Le Monocle* begins thus:

> A red bird flies across the golden floor.
> It is a red bird that seeks out his choir
> Among the choirs of wind and wet and wing.
> A torrent will fall from him when he finds.
> Shall I uncrumple this much-crumpled thing?

"Wind and wet and wing": it makes a fine student exercise to hunt for tropes of birdsong that are *not* liquid, blowing, or flying. We conventionally say that a bird pours forth torrents of song, and so expect to hear, "A torrent will fall from him when he sings," rather than "when he finds." Given the numerous tropes of song pouring forth or the wings of song or song that breathes, a choir of "wind and wet and wing" sounds like a brisk, almost impatient summing-up of three histories of troping. A red bird sums up in a different way, taking his color partly from symbol and partly from nature. (Red is the color of love, and red birds are striking in the northern temperate zone, as we have only two, cardinals and scarlet tanagers.) Colors, direction, quest, harmony—all are now inappropriate for mon oncle.

Like "wind and wet and wing," Stevens' word "uncrumple" sums up a whole family of tropes, not so much for singing as for penning. Stevens is pointing toward a favorite group of punnable words for reading and writing: explicate, explicit, implicit, infolded, unfold, braided, and so on—all the Latinate variations on *plicare* and Germanic synonyms for the word. "Uncrumple" suggests "explication," as with Bishop Blougram: "the great bishop rolled him out a mind / Long crumpled, till creased consciousness lay smooth" (Browning, *Bishop Blougram's Apology*, 978–79). The figure is an old one. "Uncrumple" is also a personal memory from Stevens' courtship.[8]

Stanza iii is worth pausing over as an example of exceedingly difficult

---

[8] Joan Richardson, *Wallace Stevens: A Biography* (New York: Beech Tree Books, 1986), vol. 1, p. 333.

argument—a tight or braided argument, we might say; the troping, appropriately, is of hair. (We might compare John Ashbery: "To speak the plaits of argument / Loosened" [*Fragment*].) The theme of mutability is at work, and Richard Ellmann and J. V. Cunningham rightly see the thought of death informing all the tropes of hair.[9] The stanza ends before the lady has put up her hair; it urges her to reflect on why and how she does so. The mirror imagery, the verb "studied out" (where we expect "combed out"), the word "studious," and the adjective "all-speaking" (e-voking heightened to something like pan-voking)—all these suggest that the lady reflect, study, listen. But to what conclusion? The closing lines are a notorious puzzle.

> Is it for nothing, then, that old Chinese
> Sat tittivating by their mountain pools
> Or in the Yangtse studied out their beards?
> I shall not play the flat historic scale.
> You know how Utamaro's beauties sought
> The end of love in their all-speaking braids.
> You know the mountainous coiffures of Bath.
> Alas! Have all the barbers lived in vain
> That not one curl in nature has survived?
> Why, without pity on these studious ghosts,
> Do you come dripping in your hair from sleep?

Venus figures appear and disappear in this poem—the Botticelli Venus; his unknown original, the Venus Anadyomene; and the Venus of Arles with a mirror in one hand and an apple in the other. (Apples are sacred to Venus, not just fatal to Eve, as we should remember for the next stanza.) The question about barbers is mostly rhetorical, and I side with a "yes-and-no" rather than any "yes-or-no" party of interpreters.[10] In fact, this seems to me the chief point of the question: to move the debate from an either-or to a both-and. Yes-or-no answers say: yes, it all comes down to the proverbial six feet. Barbers are justified only if they bring eternal and unchanging curls, or at least point toward such curls. (Barber as poet is not an arbitrary analogy, as curling is a common enough figure for troping or for revising. Barber as lover is not an arbitrary analogy,

[9] Ellmann, "Wallace Stevens' Ice-Cream," 98–99; on Nashe, see J. V. Cunningham, "The Poetry of Wallace Stevens," in *Wallace Stevens: A Critical Anthology*, ed. Irvin Ehrenpreis (London: Penguin, 1972), p. 185.

[10] Cf. John Hollander, "Poems That Talk to Themselves: Some Figuration of Modes of Discourse," I, "Questions of Poetry," *Shenandoah* 34.3 (1983), 16.

given the subject of this poem and the use of hair in erotic poetry.)[11] This answer leads to an all-or-nothing alternative, and so does its opposite.

But the question may be turned back on itself. *Though* not one curl in nature has survived, barbers (poets, lovers) have not lived (curled, written, loved) in vain. Barbers, etc., make different curls at different times, hair or beard styles vary according to time or place. Witness the famous hair styles of ancient China, eighteenth-century Japan, eighteenth-century England. Hair styles also vary according to different times in one individual life. A current reader needs to remember the conventions for female hair in 1918: hair was worn loosely tied by schoolgirls, and one rite of passage into womanhood was putting up one's hair, after which a woman was not seen with her hair down except by intimates.[12] This lady's own progression in years has been marked by changing hair styles. It is only after "studying out" the "all-speaking braids" of this argument that we are ready for the next question. What matters here is very much a poetics of the question that itself questions the way we ask questions, just as the first stanza mocks and then turns to mock the mockery.

If something in us protests, against the first question, that combing and curling (and writing and going on loving) are not in vain just because "in nature" they do not survive unchanged, something protests much more vehemently at this second question. The two immediate answers are poles apart, and it is this very polarity that is interesting. The first answer seems impossibly savage. (Look in the terrible mirror at this parody of your former self. Or in Eliot's words: why don't you "make yourself a bit smart"?) The second answer seems impossibly idealizing, a reinforcing of the "starry connaissance" that Stevens has just fought. (Look: you are still more powerful than any ghost.) I wonder if Stevens' strategy is not to shock us, and the lady, into mapping these two answers in order to fight against an either-or polarity. (Despair: I am nothing but a parody of my old self, and love is dead. Pride: I am still my old self, and love is still the same starry bliss, or should be.) A good lawyer might pursue just such a strategy in order to move past an impasse. For the space between stanzas iii and iv, we might invent the following conversation:

[11] Cf. Elisabeth J. Gitter, "The Power of Women's Hair in the Victorian Imagination," *PMLA* 99 (1984), 936–54. Ovid's *Ars Amatoria*, which Stevens read, talks at some length of ways of arranging women's hair.

[12] I am indebted to Michael Laine for a reference to Ford Madox Ford in *The Good Soldier*, on Nancy Rufford, who "had only just put her hair up" (New York: Vintage, 1927, 1983), p. 127; Ford began writing the novel in 1913. See also Max Beerbohm: "And now she was sixteen years old. Her hair, tied back at the nape of her neck, would very soon be 'up' " (*Zuleika Dobson*, 1911, ch. 14).

She: Why do I come dripping in my hair from sleep? Because I always take my hair down at night, and this is how it looks "in nature." Did you expect to see it always combed and curled?

He: No, no, though I admit to Apollo's delight in the arrangements of hair. ("Spectat inornatas collo pendere capillos et 'quid, si comantur?' ait.") I also wanted to provoke you. Otherwise you will turn from belief in a starry connaissance to some quite "fictitious doom" and against that I can do nothing.[13]

She: Well then, here's another answer. I come dripping in my hair from sleep because you don't dislike my hair down. (I too know about the Venus Anadyomene.) I know that from the way you put the question, and I also observe that your strongest feelings come at the end of your stanzas.

He: Ah, yes.

She: I also come dripping in my hair from sleep because that's the time and place for hair to be down. Now I'll go to my mirror and put it up, since I too am a barber of sorts. In a way, curls do survive in nature since I keep on making them.

He: That's just it. Think, think. Here you don't live by all or nothing— eternal hair forever as it was, or else hair wild and disheveled and abandoned because it can't be one way forever. Hair, like love, takes different styles for different ages. And not just for you, but for men too. (And to show this, I shall write in stanza vi, "when amorists grow bald.") People study their hair, as you do yours, and also their love. Take pity on these "studious ghosts"—and on my studious self too, for, as you know, I am a "dull scholar." Studying out, combing out: our two activities may lead to the same reflections. Ah but, with you, I studied all the Venuses, and also Eve—and—

This luscious and impeccable fruit of life. . . .

How great a tributary response this is, for all its occasional harshness— a study itself in the ways of the mnemonic imagination.

The next four stanzas work against intimations of immortality, whether found through memories of Eden or through stars in heaven. In stanza iv, the argument "reads a round" in explicitly earthly ways: in the round of the composition of matter, with a buried pun on "compost" (apple and skull are "composed of what comes rotting back to ground"); round shapes in which one reads lessons in mortality (apples, skulls); the rounding of lines, where enjambment brings meaning down to earth ("its acrid juice was sweet, / Untasted"). Stevens, like Byron, combines

---

[13] Ovid, *Met.* I.497–98: "He looks at her hair hanging down her neck in disarray, and says: 'What if it were arrayed?' " (Loeb). "Fictitious doom": *OP* 35.

the Fall according to Genesis and the fall according to Newton with other falls, chiefly sexual, in which the fruit of life falls of its own accord (*Don Juan* vi.lxxvii, x.i–ii). Such a natural fall cannot be sinful, so that the "luscious and impeccable fruit of life" stays impeccable in one sense (unsinning) if not another (neat). Stanza v has a fine implicit comparison of twinkling stars and twinkling fireflies (the strange little lights are mating signals). It is even possible, from a certain perspective, to mistake the light of a firefly for the light of the planet Venus. (This is literally so, not just facetiously, the experiment being of much interest to students of perspective, like Sir Ernst Gombrich, who once got into trouble trying a similar experiment.[14]) "My star, God's glow-worm," said Browning of Keats. But Stevens refuses to move toward any such analogy. Throughout these central stanzas, the tropes come back to earth, this element dominating the elements of air and fire: "rotting back to ground," "mother earth," "basic slate," "the honey of earth."

Through stanzas iv to vi, the language of lessening (Aristotle's topos of depreciation) seems to take over: "merely reads to pass the time," "ticks tediously," "amours shrink." Yet what is being lessened cannot last, and is false if it pretends permanence. Surely the earthly paradise with Eve and untasted fruit, celestial Venus burning for boys, amours that once made even their analysts breathless—surely all these things were once the starry connaissance of the speaker, and he here speaks to himself as much as to the addressee. Though the language may suggest an either-or (either young passion or tedium, etc.), I hear some irony we have not yet read in a book that is "too mad," in the "intensity of love," and in "amours" and "amorists" ("amorists," indeed). Stevens is doing something more than following a topos of depreciation. If I am right that he is moving against a simple either-or argument in stanza iii, then he must also be moving against it here. Our current reading sounds too naive.

With the squash stanza, Stevens begins to move away from pedagogy and toward comic extravagance. He will have nothing to do with Wordsworthian arguments about "maturity" in love and middle age, nor with tropes of the same, that is, all those "ripe fruit" tropes that lead to gentle death: "So may'st thou live, till like ripe Fruit thou drop / Into thy Mother's lap, or be with ease / Gather'd, not harshly pluckt, for death mature" (Milton, *PL* xi.535–38). Not Stevens. His squash, bulging like middle-aged bodies, move with comic rapidity from "golden gourd" to "distended" to "rotting." The question is whether these squash are hu-

---

[14] See " 'The Sky Is the Limit': The Vault of Heaven and Pictorial Vision," in his *The Image and the Eye* (Ithaca: Cornell University Press, Phaidon, 1982), p. 164.

man bodies or human love, and on our answer depends our sense of comedy here.

Stevens also moves unobtrusively from the word "heaven" to "sky," the word "sky" being largely free of doctrinal associations. "Laughing sky" comes to my ear partly as a verbal echo that combats Wordsworth. ("I see / The heavens laugh with you in your jubilee," says the *Immortality Ode*.) Stevens' squashed uncle and lady, undergoing the unavoidable and sometimes funny indignities of the human condition, see no such thing. Instead, "the laughing sky will see the two of us." Yet not laughing with hellish, any more than with heavenly laughter. "Laughing sky" also comes as a faint memory of one standard epithet for the goddess of love, "laughing" Aphrodite. It seems to me that Stevens evokes the mysterious laughter of things (if I may say so)—neither heavenly nor hellish, but earthly, the way things are. After that, his poem is ready for the defiance of an exuberant hymn, and a gesture of reconciliation.

Whatever the sky's laughter may be, it leads to human laughter in the mock-battle of stanza ix ("splashed," "squashes," "washed," then "clashes"). The mock-battle is a replay of the battle of stanza i, as the echoes tell us ("clashed edges" and "loudened by clashes," "spuming thought" and "deadly thought"). Its "quizzing" includes teasing, regarding with an air of mockery, and also looking through a monocle, as in the title—and, incidentally, as in the famous *New Yorker* cover of Eustace Tilley, which had appeared by this date. Stanza x also comes with a memory of the watery tropes of stanza i. Stevens has no intention that "up-pouring" syllables will produce "Memorabilia of the mystic spouts, / Spontaneously watering their gritty soils." Well-composted tropes that come "rotting back to ground," like people washed by "rotting winter rains," make a richer earth for poetry than some "gritty soil"—however hard on tropes and people in the process.

Yet after Stevens' exuberant hymn (stanza ix), his poem gradually loses its sureness of touch. The word "heavenly" illustrates his difficulty. "Heavenly" may imply two things: immortal as against mortal, and nonphysical as against physical. Stevens wants to address both senses of the word, and he has no trouble with arguments about the earthly as that which is mortal. But the earthly as that which is physical is another matter. Stevens tries humor, mockery, hyperbole, play with standard tropes for the body. They go wrong. His gigantic tree may be one of the "lustiest conceits" promised "for your broadening" in stanza ix, but most readers find it too broad, like the frogs of stanza xi. Stevens is summing up his figures, but with a curious awkwardness in his hyperbole. Take the frog and lily pond. The poem's starry language is reflected in its last appearance on a lily pond: "a pool of pink, / Clippered with lilies scudding the bright chromes, / Keen to the point of starlight" (visual "point" punning on conceptual "point"). The poem's earthly and animal language is heard in the frog: "a frog / Boomed from his very belly odious chords." But the language seems to split into starry-erotic language and animal-erotic language. Stevens' frog sounds like a bullfrog, for a bullfrog does indeed "boom" (a pondful sounds like a herd of cattle), and the booming is a mating call; it comes from the throat rather than the belly, or such throat as frogs have. The bullfrog in nature is not at all odious. It is only comparisons that are odious (which may be the point of this word). "If sex were all" (l. 1), then glittering lily surfaces might simply threaten to grow precious, like this language of them (the fear of the female). "If sex were all," then bodily sounds and sights of desire might simply threaten to grow grotesque, like this language of them (the fear of the male). Even "if sex were all," frog and lily pond belong together, frogs commonly sitting on lily pads. But sex is not all, as this whole poem has been arguing. Is Stevens summing up over it before his great closure? Something in his language here remains unclear, perhaps private and hidden, perhaps not fully under control, perhaps as yet unread.

Not so with his beautiful closure, with its sense of change drawing toward conclusion. Change here is not entirely a matter of kind (new bird for old pigeon, new scholar for old rabbi), nor is it entirely a matter of degree (lesser pigeon, lesser rabbi), nor is it altogether sameness in difference (true pigeon, true rabbi) or simply different perspective, though this last comes closest. Stevens retrieves from his earlier stanzas the tropes of flight, color, sky, ground, and scholar. If the blue pigeon is like the sky in its imaginative coloring, and like this monoclear poem in going "around and round and round," the white pigeon is the color of Venus's doves, as it "flutters to the ground, / Grown tired of flight." Stevens moves toward closure in bringing down that bird, but not now in a "rotting back to ground." Imaginative flight, like the circling of young poets and young love, is drawing to a close in one way, but not in another. Stevens delicately suggests in the white color of his last figure that this bird, fluttering to the ground, is the domestic version of Venus's white dove.

What does this poem tell us of Stevens' word-play? Schemes are always easier to read than tropes, and Stevens has provided the pleasure of schemes in abundance, from the near-homonyms in the title through the pairings of "skulls" and "excels," "little kin" and "inklings." The semantic connection always matters. "All-speaking" is not just a clever play on "evoking"; it is as if it compressed a whole sentence by Proust to tell us that braids are all-evocative, that they evoke everything that is at stake here, that they imply a braided (enfolded, intricate) way of re-membering and speaking. That is, Stevens' apparent schemes of word-play seem to become tropes when we pursue them.

Peter Quince at the Clavier is Stevens' version of the story of Susan-nah, the story of how a private place is violated. Here, as in *Le Monocle de Mon Oncle*, there is tension, tension that is obvious in the poem's plot, its rhetoric, and its uncertainty about its own possible comedy. We have taken a long time to hear the odd disjunctions between the opening and closing lyric voices, and between the figures of Peter Quince and the red-eyed elders.[15] Why is it that we have accepted with so little comment the analogy that follows this: "what I feel, / Here, in this room, desiring you, / Thinking of your blue-shadowed silk, / Is music." So far, so good, even if this sounds like no Peter Quince (except as the fruit of desire). It is the next parallel that causes trouble, or ought to, given the tone of the opening lines: "Is music. It is like the strain / Waked in the elders by Susanna. . . ." The simile is so astonishing that it questions itself, and becomes a query or plea: It is like. . . . It is what? Let it not remain like, or why must it be like? Stevens' word "strain" is a fine choice: a musical strain, first of all ("that strain again; it had a dying fall"); the strain of the elders' eyes, and of their desire; most of all, the strain of the simile itself. Why should thinking in desire about a woman awaken thoughts of this story? It is as if a woman, thinking in desire about a man, is reminded of the story of Hosea and his wife, or of Potiphar's wife. And to say this to the addressee, unless the poem is about to turn comic—is this Peter Quince's bumbling?

In the poem's last section, Stevens contains his story of desire, as Peter Quince's drama is contained. Later, he did not contain the better-known biblical story of a woman spied on in her bath, the story of Bathsheba. In a 1924 poem, a man accuses himself, using Nathan's words to David: "You are the man" (*OP* 30). What husband, what Uriah, what shepherd, has this accused man killed? *Peter Quince* simply turns back to song and praise on the viol without resolving the strains of desire. Do we ever encounter a reverse topos, where a female spies on a bathing male? The answer is that we have already encountered it in *Harmonium* in the 1917 echo of Whitman's personified female desire watching the twenty-eight young men bathing. Stevens invents secret erotic desire for Susanna in 1915, invents secret erotic desire for Ste Ursule in 1915 (*CP* 21–22), re-

---

[15] See Mary Nyquist, "Musing on Susanna's Music," in *Lyric Poetry: Beyond New Criticism*, ed. Chaviva Hosek and Patricia Parker (Ithaca: Cornell University Press, 1985), pp. 310–27. Though my conclusion differs, my reading is indebted to this stimulating dis-cussion.

members secret female erotic desire in 1917 (*CP* 6–7), fancies secret erotic desire in the woman in *Gray Room* in 1917, and savagely attacks these inventions and memories in 1924, when beautiful Bathsheba and sinning David and godly Nathan decline into one accusing figure. The play of echo can be bitter.

What interests me especially about these erotic poems, *Le Monocle de Mon Oncle* and *Peter Quince at the Clavier*, is how difficult the arguments are. For Stevens' dialectic is not generally difficult at this time. The ordinary uses of irony suffice for the religious poetry. Not so with the erotic verse. *Sunday Morning* is a straightforward enough 1915 poem, but Peter Quince's "concealed imaginings," also from 1915, are not. In *Le Monocle*, the rhetoric announces its type but conceals the play of dialectic for the most part. Stevens makes us pursue trope and argument both, even as he tells us the kind of pursuit in each stanza. What we see is a play of dialectic—not paradox, but several arguments existing as possibilities, and the reader pausing over them. So also, as we "pursue the origin and course of love," we pause over love's various arguments. Stevens does not leave us in ambiguity. What he attempts to capture, in dialectic as in rhetoric, is the multiple reality of middle-aged love—how it must live with memory, how its disputes and addresses are necessarily complicated, how it may or may not find unexpected newness.

WHEN STEVENS says that mon oncle pursued the origin and course of love when young, he is quite simply autobiographical, as a survey of his reading and early writing shows. But it is Stevens the poet of place who is more familiar, though matters of eros and of place come together in his work. And it is to the Florida poems that I shall turn now.

Stevens seems actually to have begun the plan he outlines in *The Comedian as the Letter C*: a "colony" of poems for various regions of the Americas, using appropriate flora and fauna, and expressing some appropriate sense of the place. So I surmise, from his many regional poems, beginning with the *Primorida* series in 1917. I have already noted how he uses the Midwestern tall tale. Southern and notably Florida poems make up the most considerable group of regional poems. They are generally accessible, so that it is little wonder that early commentary seized on the North-South contrast in Stevens' work as one way of approaching it. Most of the Southern poems stay close to ordinary mimetic uses of language and familiar kinds of trope, and our sense of place remains stable. There is little blocking or displacing or intricate logic. Such play as there is tends to be surface play. There are a number of fluency poems, Stevens experimenting now with early-Tennysonian effects, especially in the Florida group. It is a natural enough way of writing about the seductive effect of a semitropical climate on a Northern body and temperament.

Florida released something in Stevens, much as Italy released something in Browning. "I used to find the place violently affective," he wrote in 1943 (*L* 450). The result was in part a series of fluency poems: *Indian River* (1917), *Fabliau of Florida* (1919), *Hibiscus on the Sleeping Shore* (1921), *The Load of Sugar-Cane* (1921), *Infanta Marina* (1921). Stevens continued to like these poems, choosing the best for his opening group of poems in *Harmonium*, and later recording two. At first, Florida is not troped as Venus nor any scene as female (apart from one painterly scene in *Six Significant Landscapes* ii). It is in 1919 in *Homunculus et la Belle Etoile*, that Venus-cum-Hesperus shines in the sea off Biscayne and evokes a philosophical ideal (the "ultimate Plato") quite different from Plato's celestial Aphrodite: "She might, after all, be a wanton, / Abundantly beautiful, eager, / Fecund." We now know that in 1921 Crispin considered himself "an artful, most affectionate emigrant / From Cytherea and its learned doves" (*Journal of Crispin*, p. 35). We also know that Crispin's poem once referred to Ariosto, Camoens, Virgil, and Petrarch, three of whom invent memorable romance voyages like Crispin's, and all of whom memorably treat Venus, the goddess of smooth voyaging. It seems possible that Stevens emigrated from the Cytherean in the sense of giving up love poetry after about 1919. The erotic poems in *Harmonium* are all written before that date, though they are dispersed through the volume in a way that disguises this (*Cy Est Pourtraicte*, 1915; *Peter Quince*, 1915; *Le Monocle de Mon Oncle*, 1918; *Apostrophe to Vincentine*, 1918; and, more loosely, *The Worms at Heaven's Gate*, 1916; and *Colloquy with a Polish Aunt*, 1919. *Two Figures*, 1923, and *Last Looks at the Lilacs*, 1923, are sexual poems but not erotic, as I use the word). Stevens emigrated from Cythera to Florida without emigrating from the Cytherean at all. He began to trope Florida as Venus, so that what had been an equivocal earth mother in *Primordia* became erotic or exuberant, at least in 1919 with *The Paltry Nude* and *Homunculus* and *Nomad Exquisite*. After that, the troping changes.

In *Homunculus et la Belle Etoile*, Venus is divided between guiding light and abundant mistress. The homunculus is yet another of those c-sound male figures who are personae for Stevens (Peter Quince, Pecksniff, Crispin) and he is closest to mon oncle. For the word "uncle" is etymologically related to the diminutive -unculus, so that we might punningly say that the homunculus is a little uncle of a man; his poem is a postscript to the great 1918 poem. The homunculus sets about rehabilitating the star Venus that mon oncle has undone. Thus the force of Stevens' variation on the famous speech by Theseus in *Midsummer Night's*

Dream, a speech Stevens will echo many times. In *Homunculus*, Venus presides over lovers, lunatics, and poets alike. The evening star shines for drunkards (Stevens' substitute for Shakespeare's lunatics), for lovers (the ladies, anticipating or remembering love), and for poets:

> In the sea, Biscayne, there prinks
> The young emerald, evening star,
> Good light for drunkards, poets, widows,
> And ladies soon to be married.

The poem is mostly arch and charming, like this prinking evening star, which is related to the "princox" evening of *Banal Sojourn*, also a 1919 poem. For this aspect of the poem, the best gloss is Sterne's chapter on the homunculus in *Tristram Shandy* (i.ii), Sterne also being perfectly aware of the relation between "uncle" and "homunculus." But Stevens' poem ends unexpectedly on "the torments of confusion," less like Sterne than like Theseus, who, for all the "cool reason" in the famous speech, wants a play "to ease the anguish of a torturing hour." Stevens forbears from considering what the light of the evening star does for poets, who disappear from or into his poem after stanza i.

In uncomplicated fluency poems, Stevens' muse encounters no problems, but most of the early fluency poems remain only pleasing exercises. The earliest example is *Indian River* (1917), retrieved by Stevens for the 1931 *Harmonium*. The sounds and stresses of the name of Florida's inland waterway are dispersed throughout this hypnotizing little poem, whose "wind jingles the rings," like the poem itself, which is a charm poem. ("Alfred knows how to jingle but Browning does not," said Carlyle,[16] who preferred Tennyson but was hardly known for his good ear.) Stevens is ambivalent here. His "nunnery beaches" play on "none" in a series of negatives, and also substitute for an expected -ery phrase like "flowery beaches." Their springless, pure white is equivocal. *Hibiscus on the Sleeping Shore* (1921) and *Fabliau of Florida* (1919) are paired in *Harmonium* and followed by the Pacific seashore poem, *The Doctor of Geneva*. Both have unthreatening monsters and occasional archaic diction of a Spenserian flavor. Stevens identifies himself with natural processes in these poems, especially in the better of the two, the evocative *Fabliau of Florida*. Both poems are descriptive, impressionistic, and unjudging. (I read nothing pejorative in "droning," and the word "stupid" includes the etymological sense of "sleepy," as in its poem's title. Phosphor means "bringing light," whether of moon or actual phosphorescent

---

[16] Cited in Roma A. King, Jr., *The Bow and the Lyre* (Ann Arbor: University of Michigan Press, 1957), p. 158.

68

sea life, as on a southern shore.) We can hear Stevens avoiding the easy words for noises of water breaking on the shore and choosing unusual colloquial words, a little self-consciously ("blather," which is "voluble talk").

But when Florida's unending wind blows, it can be another matter. Florida as wind is dispiriting rather than inspiring; she does not tranquilize torment, but herself "comes tormenting." Hence Stevens' desire in O Florida, Venereal Soil (1922) that she take herself back to the sky again, to the constellation Virgo or the planet Venus. The poem plays on Venus in numerous ways. "Venereal" is only "of Venus" in an old sense, and the modern sense dominates—what A. Walton Litz calls the "infection of desire."[17] As soil, Florida ought to take an epithet like "virgin," since soil, like Venus, is paradoxically virgin soil and mother earth at once. And what could make a better muse, a better genius loci, than such a paradoxical combination? Here, Stevens' poetic genius ought to have married the genius of place, Florida herself. But this virgin is only a "virgin of boorish births"—a blunter phrase than Eliot's "Lady of situations," who also descends from Pater's Mona Lisa. Stevens' lady is a "donna" who is no madonna. He closes by asking her to present a "bloom," that is, to be more true to her name. There is no sign she will comply.

Floral Decorations for Bananas (1923), though a lesser poem, is somewhat more successful as comedy. Another "(n)uncle" poem, it divides between the precious and the gross, like the lily pond and frog of Le Monocle, yet not quite that patly if we recognize Stevens' descriptive accuracy here. We sometimes miss the referential force of Stevens' lines because we are unaccustomed to think of him as a descriptive poet. I can see why Frank Kermode writes, "Stevens's sense of place is accurate with respect to the imagination only,"[18] yet this is not always true, even if we take Denham or Thomson or Wordsworth or Frost as the norm for "accurate" poetry of place. I shall argue throughout that Stevens is sometimes a poet of simple, accurate, realistic description. For example, the following lines are a precise description of banana leaves and banana flowers just beginning to set fruit. The first time I actually saw this, I experienced what Gombrich calls inverted recognition, "the recognition not of reality in a painting [poem] but of a painting [poem] in reality."[19]

> And deck the bananas in leaves
> Plucked from the Carib trees,

[17] Introspective Voyager, p. 115.
[18] In his Continuities (New York: Random House, 1968), p. 79.
[19] Gombrich, The Image and the Eye, p. 32.

Fibrous and dangling down,
Oozing cantankerous gum
Out of their purple maws,
Darting out of their purple craws
Their musky and tingling tongues.

Floral Decorations for Bananas is something of a riddle poem. What are floral decorations for bananas? Banana leaves and flowers, *tout court*. Stevens' descriptive accuracy does not dissipate the sense of sexual mixed feelings here, but it does complicate this sense. In the end, the poem's earlier division between daintiness and bluntness widens into a division between "pettifogging" and "cantankerous," "cantankerous" being the one nondescriptive word here. In it, Stevens continues the split between preciousness and grossness, as in stanza xi of *Le Monocle*, but without the recovery of that poem. This poem remains comic only if we read it in isolation.

An entirely successful comic poem, *Bantams in Pine-Woods*, is written in the same year, Stevens here eliminating the precious-gross, male-female contrast. Instead, two male antagonists face off, cock versus bantam, as in Landor's epigram on Charles Dickens: "You ask me what I see in Dickens. / A game-cock among bantam chickens." But Stevens' hero is the bantam, pointing his pointed remarks in a fine witty cockfight, which is a fight over cocks in every sense of the word: as male bird, as "cock of the walk" or braggadocio, and as male sexual organ. Why commentators have been so singularly abstemious about the funny phallic subtext here, I do not know, especially when it is barely submerged at all. The one echo is from *Love's Labour's Lost*, and it invites us to listen for this poem's word-play as we listen for that comedy's word-play.[20] (Stevens' general interest in civilizing and humanizing language, without making it precious, would bear comparison with Shakespeare's enterprise in *Love's Labour's Lost*.) Stevens' triple readings are hilarious in their punning play. "Pine" punned as "longing" (a frequent pun in Stevens) thereby suggests a "pine-woulds," which in turn makes the first lines sound like "Chief If-you-can of As-can in caftan of henna hackles, halt!" (The simile of turkey hackles turns up in Sylvia Plath's *Bell Jar*, though in a hostile, ironic mode.) The battles between poets, including poets of the Ashcan school, is only one of Stevens' allegories. His poem has a Shakespearean exuberance, and makes a happy end to bullfrog and banana-tree figures. Students who equate Stevens' sun with phallic power in any simple-minded way should have another look at this poem.

---

[20] Cf. Mario L d'Avanzo, "Emerson and Shakespeare in Stevens' 'Bantams in Pine-Woods,' " *American Literature* 49 (1977), 103–107.

This is one way of getting outside the divisive dialectic of Florida. Another is seen in *Nomad Exquisite*, where the wanderer may be a shade precious ("exquisite") but is certainly seeking out ("ex-quisite," by etymology), in the happiest of Stevens' c-words for his poetic self. Built syntactically on one simile, this poem's strength lies in the language of creation that it unobtrusively borrows from Genesis ("brings forth"), then expands into other biblical diction ("hymn," "behold," "meet for the eye of"). Beauty is in the eye of the beholder, and Florida's beauty is meet for the eye of a young native—though not the poet we expect, but a young alligator. Stevens is wonderfully expansive and fierce.

Stars at Tallapoosa (1922), another Southern poem, is elegiac, perhaps more than Stevens realized. Stevens knows how lines work: imagined lines between stars, lines designating eyesight in old paintings, lines of an eyelid, the line of the night horizon (eye-shaped), sea lines of waves or of wave-leavings, earthlines of plants or of longitude, the trajectory of arrows, lines of poetry, Whitman's lines. He evokes a starry figure here, Orion the hunter with his sheaf of arrows, an appropriate constellation for this studious eye, itself a hunter with arrows. His lines also evoke a figure who is not a constellation, the hunter Eros. For another pattern of lines suggested by the sealines, the earthlines, the arrows flying and falling, and the Whitman echoes is the pattern of lines by which we see and touch the human body—to come back to the poetic habit of reading the earth as a body and vice versa. Whitman had been a productive blocking agent in 1917 and 1919, with *In the Carolinas* and *Plot against the Giant*. But Stevens could not find in 1922 what Whitman found, a generating erotic muse of this earth. If we read mythically, we may see Stevens returning to the heavens, though to Orion and not to Venus. If he wants to be Eros, he will not be the Eros who loved Psyche. He will be a hunting Eros with his sheaf of arrows, an Orion. *Stars at Tallapoosa* is an elegy for Whitman, and for much else. It is also a "starry connaissance" for its writer, and hazardous as poetic and even sentimental escapism. *Le Monocle de Mon Oncle* engaged Stevens' poetic force; this secretive stargazing does not.

After about 1920, something began to happen to Stevens' work, something especially noticeable in the way he revised *From the Journal of Crispin* as *The Comedian as the Letter C* in 1922. Crispin's "affectionate" relation with Venus disappears in *The Comedian*, and the Venus figure in the short poems becomes highly equivocal. A Venus figure appears intermittently throughout Stevens' work. She is one of the very few immortals that he demythologized and then rewrote. It is true that, as Litz notes, the word "Florida" disappears from Stevens' poetry after his ritual farewell to her in 1936.[21] But her ghost is present in the form of "Floréal," "florid," "floral," "flor-abundant," and so on. That most equivocal 1942 lady, Lady Lowzen, is a Florida spirit, as Stevens' word-play tells us pretty directly: "Flora she was once. She was florid" (*CP* 272). And I suspect Florida's ghost lives on in Stevens' poems about bouquets and floral arrangements, some of which have unexpectedly fierce erotic resonance. Venus in her Florida guise, and other guises too, remains a pervasive presence. But, to our loss, Stevens abandoned her specific territory, erotic poetry, together with his remarkable dialectic on "the origin and course / Of love."

[21] "After *Ideas of Order*, the word 'Florida' never appears again in Stevens' verse" (*Introspective Voyager*, p. 201).

*   *   *   *   *

CHAPTER THREE

The Limits of Word-Play:

The Comedian as the Letter C

> I suppose that the way of all mind is from roman-
> ticism to realism, to fatalism and then to indiffer-
> entism, unless the cycle re-commences and the
> thing goes from indifferentism back to romanticism
> all over again. . . . About the time when I, person-
> ally, began to feel round for a new romanticism, I
> might naturally have been expected to start on a
> new cycle. Instead of doing so, I began to feel that I
> was on the edge: that I wanted to get to the center."
> (*L* 352–52, January 12, 1940, about *The Comedian
> as the Letter C*)

WORD-PLAY has no limits, yet in practice it must be limited. Argu-
ment, on the other hand, tries to set its own limits. Word-play tends to
raise a question of limits; argument tends to mask the question of limits.
The Comedian as the Letter C is about limits and possible evasions of
limits. It is about Stevens' younger poetic self, and it first took the form
of a *Bildungsroman*, a form that itself provides a plot about overcoming
limitations. Stevens' revisions changed this form and made the poem
much more difficult, as he tried to evade expected plot lines, troping,
closure, and much else. The poem teaches us, as I think it taught Stevens,
something of the limits of word-play. Chronologically, it is among the
latest poems of *Harmonium*. But Stevens inserted this one long narra-
tive poem of the collection one-quarter way through it. I shall follow his
plotting and consider the poem here.

The Comedian as the Letter C may exasperate the spirit, but for the student of Stevens' word-play it has a grim fascination. For a "radical instability"[1] seems to overtake its language before the end, and most readers agree with Frank Kermode's description of the poem as a "sustained nightmare of unexpected diction."[2] Yet now that we have the earlier version, *From the Journal of Crispin*, such judgments must be tempered. At the least, we must now speak of the poem as an increasing rather than a sustained nightmare, and I shall argue that it is no nightmare at all until the last two sections. *The Journal* also has much "unexpected diction," but it remains intelligible, chiefly, I think, because of its clear plot. We seem able to accommodate a lot of extravagance in language provided we also have some clear plot or decorum. (I am avoiding saying that plot or decorum controls extravagant language, only arguing for some necessary balance.) In *The Journal*, the unexpected diction appears chiefly in the extended episodes along Crispin's journey, those digressions or what rhetoricians call *dilatio*, where Stevens lets both his hero and his language wander. (The romance technique of dilatio was well known to Ariosto and Camoens, both of whom Stevens names.[3]) Such extravagances of language are balanced by the plot pattern of a Bildungsroman, uncomplicated by human or poetic progeny. But when Stevens revised and expanded *The Journal* in the summer of 1922, he parodied a conventional Bildungsroman; he deleted in ways that make the narrative less intelligible; he broke the comic rhythm of expansion alternating with terseness. Above all, he began to close off tropes in a way quite different from his earlier purging of them.

The Journal is altogether more high-spirited than *The Comedian*, and not only in its closure. It is too bad we lost those fourteen laboring mules (p. 36), though the humor is a little heavy-handed (or heavy-footed, to keep the metaphor):

> Crispin arraigns the Mexican sonneteers,
> Because his soul feels the Andean breath.
> Can fourteen laboring mules, like theirs,
> In spite of gorgeous leathers, gurgling bells,
> Convey his being through the land? A more condign
> Contraption must appear.

[1] William C. Carroll, *The Great Feast of Language in "Love's Labour's Lost"* (Princeton: Princeton University Press, 1976), pp. 26–27.

[2] Frank Kermode, *Wallace Stevens* (Edinburgh and London: Oliver and Boyd, 1960), p. 45.

[3] On *dilatio*, see Patricia Parker, *Inescapable Romance: The Poetics of a Mode* (Princeton: Princeton University Press, 1979), passim.

The allegory is obvious: the fourteen mules are the fourteen lines of the Mexican sonneteers, who thereby become muleteers, driving their beasts of burden. ("Mulio celerrimus," fastest of muleteers, says the Virgilian poem that parodies Catullus [*Catalepton* x.2].) "Gurgle" is not quite the *sonante* of the sonnet, and mules are sterile if tough, and also sulky (like those "sulky strophes" that later bear Crispin's song). As mules go, Mrs. Alfred Uruguay's is a "more condign contraption," and in fact all Crispin's vehicles could use a little more condignness. Stevens cheerfully puns on all transport, from referential through metrical feet to a "curricle" that metamorphoses into a "curriculum."[4]

The Comedian does begin with considerable spirit. Like *The Journal*, it opens thus: "Nota: Man is the intelligence of his soil." There is fine polysemous play on both the words "nota" and "soil." "Nota" is first a memorandum, the NB of a narrative notemaker, in this resembling Crispin, who walks about Mexico "making notes" (II), is an "annotator" (II), in *The Journal* "nudging and noting" (IV). As imperative beginning, "Nota" draws attention to the noting process of the poem as well as the thesis that follows: nota as memorandum shifts to nota as nod (Stevens saying, Look how I begin). Nota as epistle is largely lost in *The Comedian*, though at work in *The Journal*, a journal being something of a letter to oneself. The reader who has Latin will also know that *notae* (*litterarum*) means letters or characters in writing, so that the opening *nota* points forward to all the letters of the poem that follows, and especially to the letter which the title has already noted, the letter C. (Note in the notae litterarum this letter and this title, it says.) The most obvious secondary meaning of "nota" is a note in music, here striking an opening note—C, we assume—and alerting us to musical tropes. The standard trope of singing for writing is at work here, as it is in Part II where Crispin hears thunder, "the note / Of Vulcan, that a valet seeks to own."

Similarly with the word "soil," where we easily read an allegorical meaning, and assume a little casually that our allegory is right. Stevens writes an allegory of soil intermittently all through *The Comedian*. "Salad-beds," for example, we read both referentially (those neat European gardens) and allegorically (those neat Old World tropes or poems inappropriate to New World farming or writing). To get away from both old gardens and old poems is clearly desirable, and the first step of a successful Bildungsroman. "Man is the intelligence of his soil" we read

---

[4] A curricle is a light carriage or gig; it is a traveling trope of easy travel as against Crispin's kind. Because of this word-play, I cannot agree with Louis Martz's suggestion that this is an error for "cubicle" (*Journal of Crispin*, p. 33n).

as an Old World view, demolished by the first voyage on the unpastured and unpasturable sea, that is, "reality."

Stevens reverses the proposition to open Part IV of both poems: "Man's soil is his intelligence." We tend to read the sentence approvingly, for all its possible determinism as a general theory and its uselessness as a poetic theory. It may be that the word "soil" still exerts some of its old rhetorical power (as in "native soil," "virgin soil")—the power it exerted in 1917 when Stevens published in *The Soil: A Magazine of Art*. The word is useful as a rallying-cry for a new art but not for much more. Louis Martz has drawn our attention to a 1921 essay by Paul Rosenfeld in the *Dial*, using language like *The Comedian*'s in a plea for new art.[5] Such language is not uncommon, and it is interesting precisely in its inability to be prescriptive and in its reliance on standard tropes. Critics, like artists, often agree that art should "see anew" or "reconceive," but these figures of perception and generation are little help to the artist, who can only reply, Yes indeed, but how?

To one writer in *The Soil*, "soil" implies not only "native" but also "big": "By American Art, I mean the aesthetic product of the human beings living on and producing from the soil of these United States. . . . Something new, something big is happening here. . . . We've dug into the soil and developed the Steam Shovel, we play ball and we box" (1917, cf. *Journal of Crispin*, p. 39). There is a confusion here between bigness as significance and bigness as size (on which, see Longfellow's strictures in *Kavanagh*). *The Journal* implicitly replies to this easy rhetoric of new versus old, fresh versus stale. "Man's soil is his intelligence" can encourage the kind of geographical determinism that Crispin himself flirts with. ("The natives of the rain are rainy men.") From old theories of possible climatic effects on literature, we may move to a deterministic connection between new land and new art, native soil and native writing. In the end, this can only make things harder for the serious artist.

What is "soil"? We may say outer environment, including literary environment. This is all very well, and takes us nicely through Part I of *The Journal* and *The Comedian*. After that, mythos and allegory become a little murky. And even in Part I, Stevens' language is warning us against any simple reading over from "new soil" to a ready "new art," as we shall see. "Soil" in Part II remains outer environment in Crispin's own story, but what is it allegorically? No longer do we have an easy New World troping to attach to the environment. The allegory changes,

[5] Louis Martz, " 'From the Journal of Crispin': An Early Version of 'The Comedian as the Letter C,' " in *Wallace Stevens: A Celebration*, ed. Frank Doggett and Robert Buttel (Princeton: Princeton University Press, 1980), pp. 10–17.

and the basic trope itself—soil as outer world, soil as poetry—becomes problematic, as it should.

A native if poorer soil as against foreign, exotic soil is a common topos, especially for younger poets. Stevens himself was much attracted to its theme, as we saw in the opening poems of *Harmonium*. But it is not at all a topos confined to American writers. Colin Clout sets the pattern in his return to "this barren soyle" (l. 656). Tennyson in *Amphion* inherits land without traveling, and his poem offers in little Stevens' extended metaphor of soil-as-poetic-work.

> My father left a park to me
> But it is wild and barren.
>
> . . .
>
> Better to me the meanest weed
> That blows upon its mountain,
> The vilest herb that runs to seed
> Beside its native fountain.
>
> And I must work through months of toil,
> And years of cultivation,
> Upon my proper patch of soil
> To grow my own plantation.[6]

"Patch," "soil," "plantation": the beginning English poet uses the same tropes as the beginning American poet, though Stevens' wider connotations are different. These include all the earthiness of *Harmonium*, starting with the first poem and including the plowing of soil, a pun on virgin soil, a mother-earth figure, and so on. The play of Stevens' first word, "nota," points to the process of writing. The play of Stevens' word "soil" points to the conditions of writing, both inner and outer, old and new. Both words are key words, and they indicate two dominant complexes of tropes in *The Journal* and *The Comedian*, the tropes of writing and music and other arts, and the tropes of soil, cultivation, food, and eating.

Stevens keeps in play at least seven such groups of tropes, all having to do with the making of poems. Some though not all of these have been observed. I read them as follows: 1) tropes of other arts and crafts, especially of music (along with natural noise) but also of painting and drawing (along with natural visual effects), and printing; 2) tropes of soil and cultivation, together with fruits and vegetables and seeds, as well as acts of eating and tasting and smelling; 3) tropes of the body, notably of hair and clothing, including shoes, with emphasis on barbers, tailors, and

---

[6] For all their "barrenness," these stanzas offer echoes of du Bellay and Wordsworth, and thereby the thought that provincial art does not exclude intimations of immortality.

shoemakers; 4) tropes of water and fluency; 5) tropes of journeying and vehicles; 6) tropes of mixed or patched things; 7) tropes of progeny. Stevens' ingenuity in combining and varying these tropes is formidable. He delights in words that function in two or three contexts, words such as "ground" (actual ground, musical ground, ground in painting). The reader clings to an apparently straightforward story line in order to avoid vertigo.

When the story line does appear straightforward, all the dizzying play works in two ways. First, unless the reader is repelled, it entertains by its wit and exuberance. Second, if we pursue its strategies, it prevents any easy reading of the story. I want to consider some kinds of word-play in *The Journal* and *The Comedian*, reading examples as specifically as possible, for I find most commentaries scant in particular reading as against paraphrase or allegoresis. I want to test just how Crispin's world is "troped to death."[7] For what is most disconcerting in *The Comedian* is the savage closing off of tropes as it proceeds. It is true that we find somewhat disconcerting the gap between overdetermined narrative plot and underdetermined narrative voice. But it is Stevens' concealed attacks on the imaginative power of tropes that give his poem its strangely mixed effect by the end. In fact, the early gap between narrative plot and narrative voice is not disconcerting; it is instructive.

Take the matter of Triton, for example:

> Could Crispin stem verboseness in the sea,
> The old age of a watery realist,
> Triton, dissolved in shifting diaphanes
> Of blue and green? A wordy, watery age
> That whispered to the sun's compassion, made
> A convocation, nightly, of the sea-stars,
> And on the clopping foot-ways of the moon
> Lay grovelling. Triton incomplicate with that
> Which made him Triton, nothing left of him,
> Except in faint, memorial gesturings,
> That were like arms and shoulders in the waves,
> Here, something in the rise and fall of wind
> That seemed hallucinating horn, and here,
> A sunken voice, both of remembering
> And of forgetfulness, in alternate strain.
> Just so an ancient Crispin was dissolved.

---

[7] Harold Bloom, *Wallace Stevens: The Poems of Our Climate* (Ithaca: Cornell University Press, 1977), p. 79.

Just so, indeed. This dissolving is nothing like as simple and straightforward as a first reading might suggest. In this passage, we can hear the history of Triton, from Spenser, who heard "Triton blowing loud his wreathèd horn," through Wordsworth, who longed for an ear that might "hear old Triton blow his wreathèd horn," to Keats. For Keats, Triton is also old and his sound has faded to an echo, itself echoing the word "forlorn," Spenser-like: "shepherds, singers / Whose mellow reeds are touched with sounds forlorn / By the dim echoes of old Triton's horn" (*Endymion* 1.205–206). For Stevens, the sound is so faint as to seem "hallucinating horn" (though not hallucinated). Though almost vanished, "something in the rise and fall of wind" still suggests the old "halloo" of Triton's horn, heard in the first two syllables of "hallucinating." (Stevens remembered this in 1942, when he heard the sea, not the wind, rising and falling, and reduced its sounds to "hoo": "Howls hoo and rises and howls hoo and falls" [*CP* 383].) The "faint, memorial gesturings" memorialize not simply a Triton who is hardly even symbolic for us; they memorialize Spenser and Wordsworth and Keats, to say nothing of Whitman. Stevens here rejects Hazlitt's or Pater's or any later Romantic attempt to revive Triton.[8] The sounds of all these sounds "falsify" the world for Crispin, so Triton is dissolved back into the sea whence he came, as in Ruskin's account of the gods. Crispin rightly purges his world of such ancient gods and their tropes, so that he and his tropes can start anew. So a first reading goes.

It is true that we tend to assume rather casually that a simple cleansing and fresh start can take place. We might ask some questions of Stevens' text above. That voice is "both of remembering / And of forgetfulness." What is remembered and for how long? What interests me here is how the propulsion of the narrative makes us accept the "dissolving" of Triton and all his tropes. No one objects or worries about this process, so readily do we assume like good Coleridgeans that dissolving will issue in re-creation. Nor does anyone protest that Vulcan is not dissolved in Part II, when Crispin wants "the note / Of Vulcan, that a valet seeks to own, / The thing that makes him envious in phrase" (*CP* 33). The process of starting afresh is not simple, as we should know from *Harmonium's* opening poems. Still, it seems very possible at the beginning of both of Crispin's poems. And the diction, if unexpected, is not nightmarish; it is witty, once we have heard its play.

---

[8] See Hazlitt, "On Milton's Lycidas," *Round Table*, August 6, 1815: still "the sea-gods ride upon the sounding waves." Pater's several Tritons escort their mistress Venus, and no fatigue attends their devotion: "one blows softly through his sounding seashell" (ch. 5, *Marius the Epicurean*).

Similarly with other kinds of word-play, for example, the trope of the curling or crisping waves of the sea. When we see Stevens' "silentious porpoises, whose snouts / Dibbled in waves that were mustachios, / Inscrutable hair in an inscrutable world," we are seeing a late comic version of Ovid's or Colin Clout's sea creatures, "with hoary head and dewy dripping beard"—visually comic in transferring the French Crispin's mustachios to the sea,[9] and verbally comic in undercutting "crisp" or "curled" epithets for waves ("inscrutable hair"). "Inscrutable world" is trite, or would be if it did not follow "inscrutable hair," which is to say well-examined and unfigurable hair as against troped hair. "Curling" can mean "troping" as in Herbert's well-known "Curling with metaphors a plain intention," and "crisping" as "curling" takes on the same meaning. Crispin, we surmise, is one who tropes or wants to trope, but here sees only inscrutable hair and hears only silentious porpoises. (The Mock Turtle's question seems entirely apt: "Why, if a fish came to *me*, and told me he was going on a journey, I should say, 'With what porpoise?' ") Stevens plays against our expectations of a curled-or-crisped waves-as-hair phrase—say, one of Tennyson's early crispings of water, for the young Tennyson was much given to the figure ("the babbling runnel crispeth," the "crisped" sea, "the crisp slope waves"). The young Stevens was much given to the same kind of diction, and the irony here is directed as much against Stevens' early Tennysonian self as against Tennyson. But whatever the kind and degree of irony, this sea-cleansing of tropes remains hopeful: such is the propulsion of the narrative.

Similarly with other witty word-play: the sea is "a vocable thing, / But with a speech belched out of hoary darks." That plural, "darks," is unusual, and we want to hear "sparks," especially if we have been reading Milton on belching volcanos. This is a schematic echoing in which Stevens substitutes a like-sounding word for one we expect, here compacting tropes of marine and volcanic voice, which is to say, Triton and Vulcan. The effect is curiously mixed. The comparatively few neologisms can be funny. A "nincompated pedagogue" is a pedagogue with a nincompoop's pate—nincompated and also syncopated (the syllable "poop" is omitted). "Clickering syllables" are syllables that raise the power of clicking by one syllable. They also play on pertinent meanings of the noun "clicker," a foreman shoemaker or a foreman compositor. "What name split up in clickering syllables . . . Was name for this short-shanks?" As a shank is the narrow part of a shoe or else the "body" of a type as against its "shoulder," "face," or "foot," both clicker meanings

---

[9] A. Walton Litz, *Introspective Voyager: The Poetic Development of Wallace Stevens* (New York: Oxford University Press, 1972), p. 122.

are entirely apt. So is the pun on the French printing term *cliquer*, whence our "cliché." Similarly with "minuscule," a term from printing. Crispin as minuscule would have a reduced c, with a short shank.[10]

Stevens' play with archaic words and etymology is generally comprehensible in the early portions of both poems. "Deject" as a transitive verb is archaic but its meaning of "throw down" is not hard to surmise. "He dejected his manner to the turbulence" plays the old Latinate meaning against the dead metaphor of our modern "dejected." This device, like others, throws an odd light on the purported moral of Crispin's story. Should Crispin not be excising an archaic diction? But then, this is the narrator's voice, which, *pace* Crispin, insists on showing with diachronic relish the resources of an older diction. Stevens is establishing a gap between what the argument seems to say and what the rhetoric, just as obviously, seems to imply. (This device we have already seen in *Paltry Nude*.) Similarly with the word "incomplicate," meaning uncomplicated. We need to revive the old Latinate sense in order to keep the word from sounding pretentious in the following line: "Triton incomplicate with that / Which made him Triton." Not simply "unfolded from" (unplicated, so to speak, or, in one sense, explicated) but unfolded from previous enfoldings, from all those *plis* that have come together to make the legend of Triton.

There are very few allusive echoes in either version of the poem; none has been heard. (The Triton lines are not allusive in their echoing, and the line that sounds like Milton is a pastiche, not a verbal echo: "The appointed power unwielded from disdain" [*CP* 37].) In his allusive echoes, Stevens' high-spirited irony begins to sound a little anxious, at least on second reading. The first reading is witty; the second brings a weight of context to bear, and the wit grows heavy. "Behold, I make all things new," says he who sits on the throne in Revelation 21:5. "Crispin beheld and Crispin was made new," says Stevens. What Crispin beheld was the sea, in *The Journal* the pointedly "unregenerate" sea, as if it defied the apocalyptic prophecy that there shall be no more sea. But if we read an easy self-congratulatory irony in this allusive echo from Revelation, a fainter echo five lines later acts as a warning:

> What is this gaudy, gusty panoply?
> Out of what swift destruction did it spring?

Out of St. Peter's swift destruction is the answer, swift destruction being what false prophets and false teachers bring on themselves in 2 Peter 2:1.

---

[10] Such play with the production of a text is also a deconstructionist tactic. "Derrida is also speaking printers' language," Michael Riffaterre remarks of a pun on "bons à tirer," in his "Syllepsis," *Critical Inquiry* 6 (1980), 635.

The first text is followed by: "And he said unto me, write: for these words are true and faithful." The second follows: "For the prophecy came not in old time by the will of man: but holy men of God spake as they were moved by the Holy Ghost." Similarly with the echo from *Richard III* in Stevens' line, "There is a monotonous babbling in our dreams." Shakespeare's line reads: "Let not our babbling dreams affright our souls" (v.iii.308), but the force of Stevens' echo is in the line that follows: "Conscience is but a word that cowards use." To write, to speak, even to babble without prophetic validation is one thing; to write, speak, or babble "but words" is another. Stevens allows a good deal of anxiety even to his first Crispin before rescuing him. For the second Crispin, the echoes are prophetic.

In *The Comedian*, the play begins to take another form. Rather than playing with tropes so as to prevent easy reading or easy writing, Stevens begins to shut off their possibilities. The later tropes turn savage and bitter, as if Stevens were questioning the possibility of any reading. This is not the kind of blocking we found in the opening poems. Nor is it a play of intricate argument, as in the erotic poems. The narrative voice does not say: things are more complicated and demanding than they appear. It says: I dare you to read this extravagant language. And it is to these unhappy tropes that I want to turn now.

In Part VI, we hear "sounds of music coming to accord / Upon his lap, like their inherent sphere." "Lap" is a substitute for the word we logically expect, which is "lip," and the substitution functions as a kind of lapsus linguae—music fallen or lapsed from the lip, whence it should issue, to the lap. At the same time, the echo reshapes earlier echoes, which themselves have to do with voice, for example, the "lapsing . . . clap" of thunder, with a phonetic echo of the word "collapse" faintly sounding. The echoing picks up earlier "clopping footways," then "backward lapses," to culminate in the duenna clapping her hands, which is followed by a memorable silence. A semantic sequence suggests the downward slide of language: "lapsing," "clap" (collapse?), "lapses," "lap." Crispin's lap and knee and leg are active (all that walking, that kneeling) but alas not his lip, mouth, pharynx, or lungs. When he "poured out upon the lips" of his lady, nothing is said about his own making; the verb has no direct object.

Another undoing of tropes is painful. At the end of Part v, Stevens writes several mysterious lines:

> the quotidian
> Like this, saps like the sun, true fortuner.
> For all it takes it gives a humped return
> Exchequering from piebald fiscs unkeyed.

Stevens said of the last line that it was full of c-sounds, and of c-sounds that they were inherently comic. But his remarks are addressed to schemes, not tropes, and even so, his words for the sounds of the last line are "hissing and screeching" and "squeak" (L 294, 352)—a comedy that sets the teeth on edge. And there is little comedy in this conclusion once we have read the tropes. Better some leaven of malice than the terrible bitterness in this sexual-financial-musical-verbal word-play. Stevens is moving against all those familiar figures of unlocking one's heart or one's treasure or one's word-hoard. Giving and taking here is not on the model of an open-and-shut or key-and-lock set of contraries. It is not a question of locked or unlocking but of something unkeyed, whether it be spouses or treasure house or musical instrument or this verse itself—this "piebald language," as Samuel Butler has it.[11]

"Exchequering" may seem an unlikely poetic word until we remember Shakespeare's sex-money word-play: "For she hath no exchequer now but his, / And, proud of many, lives upon his gains" (Sonnet 67).[12] Some faint memory of Milton's beautiful lines, "many a man and many a maid / Dancing in the chequer'd shade" may be at work here, for Milton's "chequer'd" line rivals Stevens' in c-sounds, though any comedy is worlds away. If the echo is persuasive, then we would read "humped" and "piebald" as grim revisions of "dancing" and "chequer'd shade." The sun as a fore-tuner offers no possibility of harmony here. None of Stevens' earlier undoing of tropes is unhappy in the way this is unhappy. Here are narrative marriage and money, but figurative disjunction and loss. When poets expect "their dark figures to open with a logical key," they are practicing traditional obscurity, as Rosemond Tuve observes.[13] That is, they are using enigma or riddle, the "dark allegory" of rhetorical handbooks. Stevens' word-play can be as logical and coded as Joyce's when he practices traditional riddle poetry. But when he throws the key away—not only scrambles the code, as semioticians say, but also throws out the decoder—the effect is highly disconcerting. Something in Stevens here seems determined not to get caught.

Yet it is true that I am attempting a reading using an old key. Ironically, the only key to Stevens' destructive and deconstructive troping seems to be the history of older metaphors of lock and key. The narrator, if not Crispin, seems to be working toward a reengagement with those older metaphors, which have proved unavoidable. I argued for Stevens'

---

[11] Samuel Butler, *Hudibras* I.i (London: Murray, 1869), p. 25.

[12] Cf. Booth on the play on "many-money," *An Essay on Shakespeare's Sonnets* (New Haven and London: Yale University Press, 1969), p. 57n.

[13] Rosemond Tuve, *Elizabethan and Metaphysical Imagery: Renaissance Poetic and Twentieth-Century Critics* (Chicago: University of Chicago Press, 1947), p. 137.

extraordinary subtlety in his opening poems about ways of beginning to write in America. He is hardly likely to simplify the matter in 1921 and 1922 in the Crispin poems. He undercuts all those fables of beginning that assume any fresh start brings lasting freshness—any spring or Psyche or new-Venus tropes, any declaration by any writer that "Behold, I make all things new." As in some of the opening poems, Stevens' own language implicitly questions the easy line of argument that his poem appears to follow. Yet for all the self-conscious rhetoric of *The Comedian*, it lacks the most interesting effects of poems Stevens has already written. So does the similar hyperbole of *Invective against Swans*. William Carroll speaks of the difference between manipulation of language and transformation[14]—a difference depending on the reader's judgment, yet crucial. Stevens' tropes manipulate in Parts v and vi; they do not transform. Nor can we say, as with *Love's Labour's Lost*, that he is mocking the misuse of schemes of wit rather than tropes of language. The mockery is of tropes, all right, and of all the legends of success that seem to be obligatory for American enterprises. The process sounds like self-laceration in *The Comedian* if not in *The Journal*. Richard Ellmann traces in Stevens a continuing vein of self-mockery,[15] and such a vein can turn cruel. That, I think, is what we are hearing in this poem.

Stevens' personal association with Crispin is something of a problem. Crispin's poetic colonizing looks like a program for some of Stevens' poems. Crispin's move into, and then out of, a poetry of local color is like Stevens' own experiments, as Martha Strom has shown.[16] And Crispin's name links him with earlier, self-mocking, comic personae who come with comic c-sounds: Peter Parasol, Peter Quince, Pecksniff. *The Comedian* is a cautionary tale, and such cautionary tales about part of oneself are notoriously hard to read, as witness *Portrait of the Artist as a Young Man* and *Hugh Selwyn Mauberley* and *Sordello*. (*Sordello*, in fact, makes an interesting comparison with *The Comedian*.[17]) Stevens

---

[14] Carroll, *The Great Feast of Language*, p. 61.

[15] Richard Ellmann, "How Wallace Stevens Saw Himself," in *Wallace Stevens*, ed. Doggett and Buttel, pp. 149–70.

[16] See Martha Strom, "Wallace Stevens' Revisions of Crispin's Journal: A Reaction against the 'Local,' " *American Literature* 54 (1982), 258–76.

[17] I can see Alastor the relentless quester as a prototype for Crispin, but *Sordello* (itself deeply indebted to Shelley) makes the better precursor poem. The six-part *Comedian*, like the six-part *Sordello*, is at once an early virtuoso performance and something of a curiosity. Both poems treat writers who undertake journeys, who encounter and disdain lesser poets, who encounter and are shaped by female figures, and who end by doing little despite much will and effort. Crispin never becomes Browning's Maker-See, being no more than a Letter C. Two alternate endings are offered for each poem, though Browning's is high-spirited. As explorations of false starts for the writing self, both poems come too near the bone, but Browning's poem is a step forward to a new style, unlike Stevens'. (For Alastor, see

described Crispin in 1935 in this way: "Life, for him, was . . . picking his way in a haphazard manner through a mass of irrelevancies. Under such circumstances, life would mean nothing to him. . . . In THE IDEA OF ORDER AT KEY WEST life has ceased to be a matter of chance" (L 293). In 1909, he said: "I hate a man that is what he is—the weak victim of circumstances. That involves occasional hatred of myself" (L 129). The struggle we hear in Parts v and vi is partly a struggle between self-hatred and a heroic determination not to hate—or worse, pity—the self. Thus the abhorrence of any tragic reading of Crispin's fate quite as much as any sublime reading. Thus the stubborn adherence to the Party of Hope in American letters, at least briefly in some of the ribald and joyous rhetoric of the four daughters. And thus the heroism that Helen Vendler notes, and not only in the will not to indulge in self-pity. There is also a heroism in the testamentary disposal of Crispin and the benediction on whatever poetry may ensue. The benediction, heard in the unexpected word "benignly" in the last line, may also be Stevens' endeavor to bless his own poetic offspring.

For Crispin was originally "a most affectionate emigrant / From Cytherea" (*Journal of Crispin*, p. 35), who desired to own the note of Vulcan. He ends with four daughters whose musical figuration makes us aware of a play on the figure of harmony itself, whether accord or discord. Stevens calls his volume *Harmonium*. That "homely parlor upright"[18] is differently designed from the European harmonium, appropriately enough. But we should not forget matters of legend. Harmony, allegorized, is Harmonia, who is the offspring of Venus and Mars, marries Cadmus, introducer of an alphabet, and ends as a serpent. Crispin is no Mars, even if his "prismy blonde" has the iridescence of a Venus. As for Vulcan, his muse was presumably Venus, and she was a fecund muse in some ways if not in others. I hear an unresolved play with legend here—the Psyche legend banished, Crispin's connection with Cytherea deleted, a firm ending avoided. Stevens is being evasive.

After the irresolution of *The Comedian*, Stevens did exactly what he said he would do while he was writing the poem: he remained quiet and considered a major change in his work. "The reading of these outmoded and debilitated poems [*Harmonium*!] does make me wish rather desperately to keep on dabbling and to be as obscure as possible until I have perfected an authentic and fluent speech for myself" (L 231, October 28, 1922). That came at last, but I doubt Stevens knew the cost in 1922.

Helen Vendler, *On Extended Wings: Wallace Stevens' Longer Poems* [Cambridge, Mass.: Harvard University Press, 1969], p. 42; Bloom, *Wallace Stevens*, p. 70.)

[18] Hollander, "The Sound of the Music of Music and Sound," in *Wallace Stevens*, ed. Doggett and Buttel, p. 245.

CHAPTER FOUR

* * * * *

The *Ludus* of Allusion:

Poems of Voice and Death

> Voragine may warrant a charge of obscurantism on
> my part or of stupidity on the other fellow's part,
> as the wind blows. Jacques de Voragine or Jacopo da
> Voragino is the immortal begetter of the Legenda
> Aurea, which, as the best known book of the Middle
> Ages, the subject of Caxton's w-k work and
> W. Morris' chef d-o., not to speak of the fact that it
> is obtainable in any book-store and is constantly in
> catalogues, ought to be fairly well-known even to
> book-reviewers. (*L* 216, October 20, 1919)

ALLUSION is always a kind of play, if we go by the built-in *ludus* of its
etymology, and one early meaning (OED2). Paul de Man calls it an "in-
tertextual trope . . . in which a complex play of substitutions and repe-
titions takes place between texts,"[1] and Stevens becomes a master of such
allusive play—"he that of repetition is most master," to borrow a phrase
from *Notes toward a Supreme Fiction* and use "repetition" in de Man's
sense.[2] Only rarely does he use quotation and only sometimes allusion
proper, that is, "part of the portable library shared by the author and his

---

[1] Paul de Man, "The Epistemology of Metaphor," in *On Metaphor*, ed. Sheldon Sacks
(Chicago and London: University of Chicago Press, 1979), p. 13.

[2] This is to be distinguished from "repetitions" in the Renaissance sense that Thomas
Greene elucidates in *The Light in Troy: Imitation and Discovery in Renaissance Poetry*
(New Haven and London: Yale University Press, 1982), p. 49.

ALLUSION

ideal audience"³ or "usages of earlier texts that the reader must recognize in order to read competently."⁴ There is virtually nothing of Eliot's imperative use of quotation and allusion. Yet some of Stevens' work is saturated with another kind of allusiveness, with echo, where the range goes from strongly allusive through clear to possible echo. Of this type, we may say what Daryl Hine says of Theocritus, that his "allusiveness borders on the oriental."⁵

Discussions of allusion or allusiveness may center on various questions. First, the question of property rights, trivial in itself but pertinent if it points us toward a common topos. Thus Tennyson's tart reply to the charge of plagiarism,⁶ and the usefulness of Irvin Ehrenpreis's remark about parallel rather than specific allusion.⁷ It is possible to speak of "allusion" to a formula as well as to a topos, for example, of Dylan Thomas's "allusion" to "Once upon a time" in his line "Once below a time"; but I do not use the word "allusion" in this way.⁸ And I try to make clear when Stevens seems to echo a common topos rather than a specific work.

Second, the question of reader attribution. This includes the matter of multiple echo (a rare case) and private echo. Private echo (not allusion, which by definition must be public) is echo that seems meant for the poet's own ear. This is singularly hard to prove: do we judge by its faintness or obscurity or arbitrariness, or simply by the fact that it remains unheard for some time (a hazardous ground)? It seems more useful to keep separate the question of private satisfaction, and to judge echoes chiefly by how well they function for the reader.

My categories throughout are taken from John Hollander's indispen-

³ Reuben Brower, cited in John Hollander, *The Figure of Echo: A Mode of Allusion in Milton and After* (Berkeley, Los Angeles, London: University of California Press, 1981), p. 64.

⁴ Greene, *Light in Troy*, p. 49. Michael Riffaterre's sense of intertextuality leads him to say that allusion has an "aleatory" relation with the text: "Identification depends on the reader's culture—while the relation of text to presupposition is obligatory since to perceive these we need only linguistic competence." The polarity between aleatory and obligatory for competent reading seems overdetermined. Allusion is not a matter of chance, but of probability, an area in which semiotics sometimes appears weak. See Riffaterre, "Syllepsis," *Critical Inquiry* 6 (1980), 627–28.

⁵ Daryl Hine, Introduction to his translation, *Theocritus: Idylls and Epigrams* (New York: Atheneum, 1982), p. xiii.

⁶ As cited in Christopher Ricks, "Tennyson Inheriting the Earth," in *Studies in Tennyson*, ed. Hallam Tennyson (London: Macmillan, 1981), pp. 66–67.

⁷ Irvin Ehrenpreis, *Literary Meaning and Augustan Value* (Charlottesville: University of Virginia Press, 1974), p. 7. On the problem of plagiarism, see Roger Lonsdale, "Gray and 'Allusion': The Poet as Debtor," in *Studies in the Eighteenth Century*, IV (Canberra: Australian National University Press, 1979), pp. 31–55.

⁸ Cf. Guy Lee, *Allusion, Parody, and Imitation* (Hull: University of Hull, 1971), p. 3.

sable study of allusion, *The Figure of Echo: A Mode of Allusion in Milton and After*. When I use the term "allusive echo," I mean something less than a commonly recognized allusion and something more than a possible or even clear echo. I mean a verbal echo of one specific passage whose presence is highly probable (and consciously so) for demonstrable reasons. (Once recognized by enough readers, such an allusive echo might come to be classified as an allusion. On the other hand, if some competing echo has as good a claim to be present, the allusive echo would cease being allusive and would come to be classified within the range of simple echo.) I use the word "echo" only for a verbal echo, whether intertextual or schematic (like rhyme). Other uses of the word now seem to me evasive or lazy.

The crucial test of significance is partly a matter of limits, for, *pace* the joys of deconstructionist polysemy, not every echo can or should be brought into play. That way lies the impasse of *The Comedian as the Letter C*. Significance is also a matter of context; good allusive effects bring into play a sense of the original context of an echo or allusion. But "bring into play" is a loose term. De Man speaks of allusion as a trope in which a complex play takes place (tropos become topos as *mise en scène* for a drama or game). But Hollander shows that at least two types of trope are at work, metaphor and metalepsis. And Stevens' remarkable patterns of allusiveness in his later poetry suggest a pattern even more complex than metalepsis.

Stevens' early echoing is chiefly what Richard Hurd calls "glancing" or transitory allusion,[9] where we do not take over the full context of the original. In *Sunday Morning*, for example, the echo from Tennyson brings some weight of context that helps build the topos of the earthly paradise, but it functions differently from the Keats-Milton echoing at the end. In poems like *The Emperor of Ice-Cream* or *The Man Whose Pharynx Was Bad*, the echoes evoke full contexts that comment on Stevens' themes and elicit an emotional response far beyond the discourse of the text. If I am right about the echoes in these two poems, they are working in the same way. Each poem includes an echo of one Shakespearean play, just strong enough to be called allusive. Each poem also includes a more diffuse echoing of another Shakespearean play, this time not strong enough to be called allusive and yet still probable. One reason for the probability is the surprising force of the conjunction of the two Shakespearean plays. This is a strategy Stevens will use again, and unmistakably, in later poems.

---

[9] Richard Hurd, "Discourse Concerning Poetical Imitation" (1751) in his *Works*, 8 vols. (London, 1811), 2:109–241, cited in Lonsdale, "Gray and 'Allusion,' " pp. 53–54.

But first a less successful example of allusiveness, Stevens' 1919 poem, *Banal Sojourn*. As description, this poem works well enough; its subject is a heat wave with its oppressive lassitude; thus the yearning for a sky "unfuzzed" of humid air, which seems to invade the sky from that fungoid garden like some fuzzy mildew. But Stevens attempts allegory: he hints at such lassitude as a kind of evil. "Banal" in the title is echoed by "our old bane," though the etymology of the two words is quite different, and our old bane in other contexts is Satan, who is here only in the vegetable form of the "Satan ear." Stevens' repeated "malady" includes the word "mal," and the archaic "Pardie" sets up a "par-dy / mal-à-dy" refrain. Stevens does not use Baudelaire's word *ennui*, but that is the subject of his poem and likely the origin of his mal-banal rhyme. ("Sur l'oreiller du mal c'est Satan Trismégiste . . . Le canevas banal de nos pitieux destins.") Stevens tries to rewrite Marvell's garden, and not only Marvell's but also Milton's. The memory of Satan in at Eve's ear mingles with the origin of the word "earwig," an insect said to creep in at the ear, figuratively a parasite or flatterer. "For who can care at the wigs despoiling the Satan ear?"

Parasites are of the essence here, as Stevens' wild punning itself despoils his own poetic sustenance. Christopher Ricks remarks of allusion that it frequently uses the figure of eating to refer implicitly to its own processes.[10] Here the poet himself suffers the malady of the parasite, the unfruitful feeder or fungus—"mildew," "earwig," "despoiling." I take it that the odd confusion of the sex of the evening star and the beast summer is deliberate, and perhaps part of the general despoiling. (If the star is Venus, as line 8 suggests, is the fat beast male, despite its female fecundity-gone-wrong associations? If the fat beast is female, is line 8 appropriate for a male, even a Hesperus or Lucifer?) Line 8 in isolation is a beautifully Virgilian line (*decurrit*, "came running down," says Virgil of Iris in *Aeneid* v.610) and the sense of despoiling is severe.

As with other *Harmonium* poems, the presence of *Hamlet* is dominant among the echoes here. "Pardie" is used by Hamlet (iii.ii.294); Claudius is called "the bloat king" (iii.iv.182). "Pardie" follows the play within a play, where poison or bane is poured in at the ear. "The bloat king" occurs in Hamlet's scene with Gertrude, where the imagery of plant and animal rankness is associated with corruption in love. "I . . . unpregnant of my cause . . . can say nothing," says Hamlet. So also the persona of this poem, where the "fat beast" is bloated but not pregnant.

I do but jest, poison in jest, Stevens tries to say in this poisonous little

---

[10] In "Tennyson Inheriting the Earth," in *Studies in Tennyson*, ed. Tennyson, pp. 87–88.

poem. But he cannot play the princox. The archaic diction only jars, and far too much is attempted. In the later poem that began here, *The Man Whose Pharynx Was Bad*, Stevens again works with the words "mildew" and "malady," with tropes of throat (but not the ear), with the imagery of summer but also of winter as baneful. He cuts the echoes from *Hamlet*, cuts the connection of eros and conception with writing. He cuts the *mal* theme (bane-Satan-damn-malady). He moves to a regular stanza and approaches the subject more directly through a first-person persona, producing altogether "neater mould." He would try the *Banal Sojourn* effect again only some twenty years later: "I am Solange, euphonious bane, she said. / I am a poison at the winter's end . . ." (*CP* 265).

In *Harmonium*, the prespringtime of "Solange, euphonious bane" is the subject of *Depression before Spring*, which Stevens placed just after *Banal Sojourn*, and it is the better poem. Stevens here works with minimal effects: delicate sexual punning, an obviously displaced simile, variation on a biblical metaphor. (The word "spittle" in "the spittle of cows / Threading the wind" compacts "shuttle"—vacant shuttles weave the wind—and "spindle"—a spindle threads, a shuttle weaves—so that a normal if somewhat archaic word is made to sound like a portmanteau word.) The poem fills with repeated sounds that are said not to be there, "no rou-cou, / No rou-cou-cou." The play between logic and phonetics is a play between absence and presence. In 1945, "This green queen . . . she came, and comes, / And seems to be on the saying of her name" (*CP* 339). In 1918, "no queen comes / In slipper green," for all the saying of her name and much else besides. *Banal Sojourn* and *Depression before Spring* are followed by the entirely nonseasonal *Emperor of Ice-Cream*, the emperor being a man for all seasons; then by the Cuban doctor and Hoon, all three being related.

Most commentaries on *The Emperor of Ice-Cream* allegorize, and some turn didactic and are far removed from Stevens' own phrase about the poem, "essential gaudiness." Rather than speak of coldness and hardness and seeming-versus-being and the expendable, I want to suggest two epigraphs for the poem. One is a claim by Hamlet, which I think Stevens' two concluding lines retort against. Here are his closing couplets:

> Let be be finale of seem.
> The only emperor is the emperor of ice-cream.
>
> Let the lamp affix its beam.
> The only emperor is the emperor of ice-cream.

Here is Hamlet: "Your worm is your only emperor for diet." Hamlet, also coping with a corpse, is reflecting on the variety of dishes set before our last consumer. (So also was Stevens in 1916, when he altered Shakespeare's "hymns at heaven's gate" to the wickedly funny near-homonym, *The Worms at Heaven's Gate*, and made their reconstitutive feast of Badroulbadour, the most beautiful woman in the world.)

My second epigraph is from *The Winter's Tale* and of Perdita:

> Good sooth, she is
> The queen of curds and cream.

This I hear as likely rather than allusive echo. Stevens, I think, compacts the line about Perdita, giving cream a different temperature and ruler, and using it as a rhyme word. Curds come separately, though they are treated like cream, whipped, that is. (Are curds ever whipped?) Hamlet on Yorick is commonly recognized as the model for Stevens' skull stanza in *Le Monocle de Mon Oncle*, but we have here a specific allusive echo crossed with a fainter echo from another play. We have only to recall the climactic recognition scene at the end of *The Winter's Tale* to hear its imagery playing against that of *The Emperor* and to note that it reverses, point by point, the plot and imagery of *Hamlet*.

Commentators usually avert their eyes from "concupiscent curds." Concupiscence we think of as lust of the eye or sexual desire, but there may be a concupiscence of eating and drinking. (The curds themselves are said to be concupiscent: are they desirous of being eaten, or is this just a transferred epithet?) Augustine thought the rein on the throat should be moderately but not excessively tight (an appropriate reminder for the 1921 man whose pharynx was bad) and so did Thoreau, though he did not use this figure. This is not a throat poem though it is a food poem—a poem of "funeral-baked meats," as Helen Vendler most appropriately says.[11] It is a poem of eating and being eaten, and not just *seeming* to be eaten any more than seeming to eat. The tactile things are like Williams's objects in *Tract*: they are ordinary, present, palpable (or at least language makes them seem so). "Seems, madam? nay it is, I know not 'seems.'" "Lord, we know what we are, but know not what we may be. God be at your table!"

As the *Hamlet* echo is dominant, so also the theme of eating and being eaten is dominant. The echo from *The Winter's Tale* points toward a resuscitation, and when we read Stevens' death scene against that resus-

11 Helen Vendler, *Part of Nature, Part of Us* (Cambridge, Mass. and London: Harvard University Press, 1980), p. 100.

citation scene, we can map the consolation he rejects: "warm life, / As now it coldly stands . . . Let be, Let be! . . . If this be magic, let it be an art / Lawful as eating . . . I saw her, / As I thought, dead." If allusive echo sometimes speaks of its own processes, then we may ask if words are eaten by worms (as the *Hamlet* echoes imply) or may be miraculously restored to a mother tongue (as *The Winter's Tale* echo implies). Or, we may say what the man in Kafka's story says to the corpse: "What's the good of the dumb question you are asking?" Stevens adds "cold" to "dumb"; he declines the beautiful regenerative fable of *The Winter's Tale* even as he tries to modify the mordant wit of *Hamlet's* graveyard scene. The poem's intentions are celebratory, if we go by Stevens' phrase, "essential gaudiness." Yet its echoes confirm what Harold Bloom hears in a general way: that the cost of celebration is considerable.[12] We must read "gaudiness" in more than one way, not just gaiety and rejoicing but also a kind of trickery or even deception. As for the common meaning of showiness, sometimes tasteless showiness, this depends on the reader's judgment. Stevens might well say that, as with matters of food and of death, it is all a question of taste.

"I have not had a poem in my head for a month, poor Yorick." Thus Stevens in May of 1920, after *Le Monocle de Mon Oncle* but before *The Emperor of Ice-Cream* (*L* 219, May 16, 1920). The remark confirms one reading of *The Emperor*. But Stevens' concern is also more general: "I've had the blooming horrors, following my gossip about death, at your house. . . . The subject absorbs me, but that is no excuse: there are too many people in the world, vitally involved, to whom it is infinitely more than a thing to think of. One forgets this. I wish with all my heart that it had never occurred, even carelessly" (*L* 206, April 8, 1918). And then, a year later: "I am completely done up by the news of Catharine's death" (*L* 212, May 27, 1919, of his younger sister, dead in France at the age of thirty).

Stevens' witty title, *The Man Whose Pharynx Was Bad*, itself speaks, suggesting numerous tropes of poetic voice, from constricted and sore to open and blowing: larynx, syrinx, windpipe, sore throat, tongue-tied, dried up, at least three meanings of the Latin *fistula*, and so on. One "pent" example is Tennyson's "shut up within himself, / A tongue-tied poet" (*The Golden Years*). One "sore throat" example is Spenser's "Both pype and Muse, shall sore the while abye. / So broke his oaten pype and downe dyd lie," which emphatically effects closure in the January eclogue. *From the Journal of Crispin* includes "shepherds' pipes," which

---

[12] Harold Bloom, *Wallace Stevens: The Poems of Our Climate* (Ithaca: Cornell University Press, 1977), p. 82.

Stevens deleted in *The Comedian*. Like *The Journal*, *The Man Whose Pharynx Was Bad* (1921) is a valedictory poem, but without the rhetorical escape hatch at the end.

If this man cannot speak very well, he can certainly hear, perhaps only too well. His poem is full of echoes of extraordinary force, and I want to approach it through these echoes, at least one of which is strong enough to be called allusive. Stevens starts with a signal that echo may be at work here: "The time of year has grown indifferent."

> The time of year has grown indifferent.
> Mildew of summer and the deepening snow
> Are both alike in the routine I know.
> I am too dumbly in my being pent.
>
> The wind attendant on the solstices
> Blows on the shutters of the metropoles,
> Stirring no poet in his sleep, and tolls
> The grand ideas of the villages.
>
> The malady of the quotidian. . . .
> Perhaps, if winter once could penetrate
> Through all its purples to the final slate,
> Persisting bleakly in an icy haze,
>
> One might in turn become less diffident,
> Out of such mildew plucking neater mould
> And spouting new orations of the cold.
> One might. One might. But time will not relent.

"That time of year thou mayst in me behold." Shakespeare's sonnet would continue to speak to Stevens all his life. Here it is no longer *that* time of year, no longer bare ruined choirs *where* late the sweet birds sang. Shakespeare's unobtrusive deictics make his sonnet a memory-place that still sings. For Stevens, the old, beautiful tropes of voice have themselves grown indifferent. "Indifferent" closes its line and the period, as its locking rhyme word "pent" closes the stanza. The last stanza repeats the effect in the echoing "diffident . . . not relent" rhyme, and it enlarges the effect in the linking of the final rhyme with the terminal word of the first stanza, "indifferent . . . not relent."

"I am too dumbly in my being pent" is uncannily echoing. It sounds as though it should come from a Shakespearean sonnet. It asks for an original of "I am too X X in my Y Y Z," in a regular iambic pentameter line. One possibility, suggested to me by J.R. de J. Jackson, is that I am hearing Milton: "When I consider how my light is spent. . . ." This

93

must be judged as a tentative though very possible echo. Certainly the abba rhyme is similar, certainly there are -ent rhymes, certainly there is a buried "pent" in "spent," certainly Milton rings ironically against Stevens. ("They also serve who only stand and wait.") Nonetheless, the verbal echo is not clear enough to satisfy fully what this dumb, pent line calls for.

The echoes of "pent" work differently. The best-known rebounding echo goes from Milton through Coleridge to Keats, and it has been finely traced by Hollander to its culmination in Stevens. (One wants to murmur "il pent-seroso.") "In 'The Man Whose Pharynx Was Bad' . . . the Miltonic echo voice and the additional returns from Coleridge and Keats both seem not to cancel each other but to induce further reverberation."[13] We should note, too, that Stevens revises the topos of the city in Milton, Coleridge, and Keats; for him, metropole or village, like summer or winter, makes no difference. There is no suggestion that fresh air will help, though freshness is what is lacking when mildew grows. If mildew of summer recalls the Stevens of *Banal Sojourn*, deepening snow recalls the Stevens of *The Snow Man*. The first persona is overcome by outward scene and inward echoing. The second overcomes only by becoming outward scene and making his poetic place bare of echoes. But both of these strategies now come to the same thing.

In his later work, Stevens has an uncanny ability to go back behind a trope, a trope that is in itself a summing up, and to hear a fainter origin for it. This process may be at work here, for the combination of "dumbly" and "pent" recalls to me Spenser's opening lines to the eclogues, where Colin Clout "Led forth his flock, that had bene long ypent," perhaps the origin of Milton's own "long . . . pent." (Colin, the pipe-playing shepherd, leads forth his flock. Satan, the fallen urban voice, wolflike, attacks the pastoral place.) The connection of Spenser's line with voice is clear, and I have already suggested a thematic connection between Stevens' title and Spenser's closing lines. Even more pointed is the connection of sheeplike dumbness. For Stevens, the trope seems to be so indifferent that piper and shepherd and even wolf have declined into a mere sheep, for whom no seasonal mildness will bring Spenserian relief. "Playing a crackled reed, wind-stopped, in bleats," he wrote in 1936 (*OP* 67), in a sad parody of the pastoral tradition— Milton chiefly, but also Spenser and Keats. Here there is not even a bleat. "Voluble of dumb violence," Stevens wrote in 1942 (*CP* 384), recalling a younger poetic self, and also punning on "voluble," for the ephebe tosses and turns on his bed. That adjective "dumb" resounds back against

---

[13] Hollander, *Echo*, pp. 80–81.

"dumbly" here, and also "how cold she is, and dumb," against the two dumbnesses of pent and dead figures in 1921 and 1922. In the night scene of *Pharynx*, nothing stirs, no one tosses and turns. Stevens wrote a version of Coleridge's "hoarse nightingale" in *Banal Sojourn* ("The grackles crack their throats of bone," the first of Stevens' "crackled reeds"), but here he cuts the trope of the poetic bird. It is the man who has the sore throat; pipe gone bad, he is more appropriately sheeplike.

I want now to turn to the third-last line, where Stevens gives us an extraordinary allusive echo: "Out of such mildew plucking neater mould." It is the formula, "Out of X plucking Y," that places the echo. "Tis dangerous to take a cold, to sleep, to drink; but I tell you, my lord fool, out of this nettle, danger, we pluck this flower, safety." This is Hotspur speaking, and at first the context appears unhelpful. But I want to pause over this echo before going on to a series of nonallusive echoes from another Shakespearean play, and considering the two contexts together, as I think Stevens meant us to consider them, once heard. How dangerous it is for Hotspur to sleep, we know from his wife, for he talks in his sleep: "Thy spirit within thee hath been so at war, / And thus hath so bestirr'd thee in thy sleep" (II.iii.56–57). Alas, in Stevens' poem, the wind or *spiritus* blows, "Stirring no poet in his sleep." We know what Hotspur thinks of poetry; nothing sets his teeth on edge as much as "mincing poetry." "I profess not talking," he claims (v.ii.91), at least until the time of his death, when

> I could prophesy,
> But that the earthy and cold hand of death
> Lies on my tongue. No, Percy, thou art dust,
> And food for—
>
>   For worms, brave Percy.
>   (v.iv.83–87)

For the moment, I want to leave these lines from *Henry IV, Part I* (though not without noting their effect on our reading of *The Emperor of Ice-Cream*). To trace another echoing effect in *The Man Whose Pharynx Was Bad*, we need to return to *Banal Sojourn* and its unusual combination of verb and noun in "feel a malady." We commonly say that we have or suffer a malady, and that we feel an ache or pain. But the combination of "feel" and "malady" is Shakespeare's; we may hear it in the heath scene in *King Lear*:

> Thou think'st 'tis much that this contentious storm
> Invades us to the skin: so, 'tis to thee;

> But where the greater malady is fix'd,
> The lesser is scarce felt. . . .

This hardly functions as an echo in *Banal Sojourn*; it is something closer to a source, though the context reinforces the echoes from *Hamlet* that have to do with voice. But to hear the heath scene echoing against *The Man Whose Pharynx Was Bad* is to hear the following sequence:

> Blow, winds . . . spout . . . crack nature's moulds . . . spout, rain!
> . . . I will say nothing . . . close pent-up guilts / Rive your con-
> cealing continents, and cry . . . where the greater malady is fix'd, /
> The lesser is scarce felt . . . seek thine own ease . . . defend you /
> From seasons such as these? . . . mildews the white wheat . . . No
> words, no words, hush. / Child Rowland to the dark tower came. . . .

I have included, besides verbal echoes, four examples of thematically pertinent lines. The last remarks of mad Tom, for example, gave Browning his poem on poetic voice, on speaking out (slug-horn, not windpipe, is his figure), on the struggle against apathy, deceit, phantasmagoria, fear, and knowledge of failure. Seven of Stevens' important words in his sixteen-line poem on the subject of poetic voice appear in what may justly be called Shakespeare's most powerful scene of voice.

I shall now return to the one allusive echo I hear in this poem, "Out of such mildew plucking neater mould." "Out of this nettle, danger, we pluck this flower, safety." But of course, Hotspur didn't; he died instead, plucking bright honor but not safety. Hotspur and Lear: the conjunction has surprising force. Both are impetuous, hot-tempered, courageous, foolish, and loving (to speak of dramatic character mimetically). Both have at once too much and too little voice (to speak of voice in various senses). Both trust too much in the voices of others. Both are betrayed by insufficient wisdom about rhetoric, both their own and others'. And how do these dramatic voices, themselves now images of voice or echoes, re-sound in Stevens' poem? An indifferent reader will hear nothing; the echoes themselves will be pent and dumb. A less diffident reader may hear simple irony. To map the ironies farther leads us, I think, precisely to the impasse of Part VI of *The Comedian as the Letter C*. No danger, no flower (to consider Hotspur). No love or hate, no rage or voice (to consider Lear).[14] Stevens' blocked writing self hears Hotspur chiefly, and

---

[14] According to M. M. Mahood, Hamlet puns more than any other Shakespearean character, and Lear is also given to word-play. Richard III puns more than any other character in his play (apropos of *The Comedian*), and, in the Henry IV plays, most of the puns are spoken by Falstaff, Hal, and Hotspur. "The Henry IV plays are also deeply concerned with the truth and power of words." Stevens has also heard all this. See M. M. Mahood, *Shakespeare's Wordplay* (London: Methuen, 1957, 1968), pp. 166–68, 178.

also Lear on the heath. But he has chosen, or been chosen by, another part in the dramatis personae.

"Out of such mildew plucking neater mould." We ought to be plucking flowers, and, as this poem is about making poetry, we ought to be plucking flowers of speech, as from some Renaissance garden of eloquence, or even from Coleridge's modest roadside flora: "I have plucked therefore these scentless Road flowers from the chaplet."[15] Given the force of this convention, the ear wants to substitute "dew" for "mildew," at least momentarily, before the heavy terminal and referential sense of "mould" takes over. As for "mould," it may be form as well as fungus, and even as fungus it is not always destructive, as mildew is. We may even call our great forerunners "moulds." But Stevens' echo, like his summer, is mildewed. The only mould, as form or fungus, will be his own—"perhaps."

In *The Man with the Blue Guitar*, Stevens returns to the word "mould" in the sense of "form": "The person has a mould . . . / The blue guitar a mould? That shell? / Well, after all, the north wind blows / A horn" (*CP* 174). Stevens here plays with "wind" in the sense of "spirit": this canto is a later version of *Pharynx*. In 1946, he ends the struggle with "mould," laying to rest ghosts that come through a "mould" of tradition, whether through form or through a sense of voice reawakened from the mould of earth. Here are the last two lines of *Two Versions of the Same Poem*: "Perhaps these forms are seeking to escape / Cadaverous undulations. Rest, old mould . . ." It is Hamlet's farewell to his father we are hearing: "Rest, rest, perturbed spirit" (with a memory of "Well said, old mole!" in Stevens' "old mould"). The ghost can rest when his quest is taken up, and so also with the ghosts of poetic fathers. Stevens here uses "mould" in two senses only, as form and as earth, perhaps fertile, partly human. "Rest" also bears two senses, rest as sleep quietly, and rest as stay on. In the meaningful doubleness of Stevens' words, and in their Shakespearean echo, we may hear a most moving closure to a long struggle. And we may hear a way of proceeding. It is not for nothing that this poem ends on an ellipsis and not a full stop.

We may be unaccustomed to think of Stevens as an echoing poet, though Vendler has taught us to listen for Keats's *To Autumn* in his work.[16] There are passages from various authors that echo and reecho

---

[15] Coleridge, *Collected Letters*, ed. Earl Leslie Griggs (Oxford: Clarendon, 1956–1971), 1:141 (no. 75), December 17, 1794.

[16] In her " 'Stevens and Keats' 'To Autumn,' " in *Wallace Stevens: A Celebration*, ed. Frank Doggett and Robert Buttel (Princeton: Princeton University Press, 1980), pp. 171–95.

through Stevens, none esoteric. I shall note them as I proceed. If we listen carefully to Stevens' letters, this will not surprise us. "The fear of the Lord is the beginning of wisdom . . . much like a mote in one's eye . . . a voice cried in the wilderness . . . the proverbial far country." These are biblical echoes, and we might say that they are simply part of the common tongue, or used to be. Other echoes may pass unobserved. "Shine in use," Stevens wrote to Elsie Moll in a time when Tennyson's *Ulysses* was widely known. "I sit at home o' nights," Stevens wrote to her in 1913 (*L* 180)—reading Marlowe, we assume. Or, "agonies and exultations," he exclaims (*L* 48), presumably after reading Wordsworth. Or, in a compliment to Williams, adapted from Samuel Johnson, "to thee do all things tend"(*L* 249).[17] This is a Stevens whose extraordinary ear, especially in his late poetry, can teach and delight our own listening, as we shall see.

We are more apt to think of the words of older writers as things or concepts or figures rather than as voices. But allusion and echo make us hear voices. Whether allusion tropes itself as eating or inheriting or voicing, it engages with the great forerunners, the "old moulds." Insofar as it is not just ornamental, it displaces, slightly or more, if only by making us hear allusion *as* allusion, if only by resetting or replacing the words. To revise radically the way in which we hear the old words: this is to make word-play and word-war meet in one enterprise. It is something that only the greatest writers can do—Milton, Joyce—and it is something that Stevens achieved only in his later years. Here we have been listening to Stevens working out a place for his own voice. He is moving on from *Domination of Black* and *The Plot against the Giant*, but he is also struggling against some silencing force in these poems of 1921 and 1922.

[17] For "shine in use," see Joan Richardson, *Wallace Stevens: A Biography* (New York: Beech Tree Books, 1986), vol. 1, p. 286. For Marlowe, cf. "I walk abroad o' nights," from *The Jew of Malta*. A glance at the printings of the Everyman edition of Marlowe's plays shows how popular they were at the time. For Wordsworth, cf. "Thou hast great allies; thy friends are exultations, agonies, / And love, and man's unconquerable mind" (*To Toussaint l'Ouverture*). For Johnson, cf. "From thee, great God, we spring, to thee we tend, / Path, motive, guide, original, and end" (*Rambler* 7).

CHAPTER FIVE

∗ ∗ ∗ ∗ ∗

Ways of Ending:

Religious and Last Poems

My direct interest is in telling the Archbishop of
Canterbury to go jump off the end of the dock.
(*L* 351, January 12, 1940)

THE STEVENS of *Sunday Morning* is the Stevens with whom most students begin, and rightly so, for it is the first major poem he wrote, and he continued to rewrite it all his life. To open his volume, Stevens chose something in the plain style that Perry Miller associates with New World writing.[1] But in 1915, he actually began differently. His first major poem was an elegiac type of poem, in the Miltonic tradition that Josephine Miles distinguishes as one dominant American style.[2] *Sunday Morning* and Stevens' antipietistic poems are also poems of place, in their way. Or rather, poems against place, if place is conceived in a Christian view of things. I started with a rhetoric of beginning, and I shall close the section on *Harmonium* with a rhetoric of ending, and with Stevens' third subject, questions of belief.

Stevens is a writer "against closure" in the sense of opposing traditional eschatologies. His own use of formal closure is thus of particular interest, as we consider kinds of "againstness." I want to look at Stevens' arguments and rhetoric about "last things," beginning with the religious poetry and then moving to the poems he chose to end *Harmonium*. It is

[1] Perry Miller, *The New England Mind* (Boston: Beacon, 1939, 1961), ch. 12, "The Plain Style," pp. 331–62, chiefly of sermons.

[2] Josephine Miles, *Eras and Modes in English Poetry*, 2d ed. (Berkeley and Los Angeles: University of California Press, 1964), pp. 224–48.

99

his plot of ending I shall consider in the word-play and word-war of the religious poetry and the closing poems. Yet not word-war, really.

As with the erotic poems, Stevens dispersed his religious poems throughout *Harmonium* in a way that disguises their development, or rather their lack of development. For in their arguments, these are less poems of word-war than of skirmishes. They have nothing of the force of Stevens' dialectic when he writes erotic poetry. That must wait until his return to the subject of religion after *The Man with the Blue Guitar*. It is not the presence of homiletics rather than dialectic that causes trouble, trouble that is reflected in critics' divided reactions to the homiletics of *Sunday Morning. Sunday Morning* is a doctrinal poem from the first word onward, engaging Milton and biblical tradition throughout, in ways we have not heard. The trouble is that the explicit homiletics are so boring. The arguments are obvious and stale. But the implicit homiletics: that is another matter. It is in the area of rhetoric that Stevens does battle, not in the area of dialectic.

Of the twenty poems before *The Comedian as the Letter C*, only two touch on a religious subject, *Ploughing on Sunday* and *Cy Est Pourtraicte, Madame Ste Ursule, et Les Unze Mille Vierges*; the two poems are printed on facing pages. The "fanfaronnade" (*L* 338, 1939) of *Ploughing on Sunday* (1919) is antisabbatarian as a matter of course; it defies quiet Sundays and celebrates sunny ones by blowing its own horn, taking all North America as its field, using the old trope of plowing for writing,[3] and fanning great bird tails out to sun and moon. The charming *Pourtraicte* (1915) presents agape surprised by eros. Crispin shows not the slightest interest in religious subjects through his 573 lines, though the first Crispin of 1921 was briefly anticlerical. Halfway through *Harmonium*, we meet two overt attacks on a Christian kind of heaven, *Of Heaven Considered as a Tomb* (1921) and *A High-Toned Old Christian Woman* (1922). Stevens places his great 1915 poem, *Sunday Morning* two-thirds through the volume. Two more antiheaven poems follow later, both from 1921, *Cortege for Rosenbloom* and *The Bird with the Coppery, Keen Claws*. Stevens' earlier antireligious poems have a vitality and scope that the 1921 and 1922 poems do not. I surmise that the religious poems did seem important to him, to judge from his selections for the "representative" 1953 Faber volume.[4] Stevens included all the poems I have mentioned, except *Cortege*, in the thirty-four poems cho-

---

[3] Cf. "Unctuous furrows, / The ploughman portrays in you / The spring about him" (*OP* 9). On the metaphor of plowing for writing, see Ernst Robert Curtius, *European Literature and the Latin Middle Ages*, trans. Willard R. Trask (Princeton: Princeton University Press, Bollingen Series, 1953), pp. 313–14.

[4] See *L* 732 n. 2 (November 12, 1951).

sen from the eighty-five of the second edition of *Harmonium*. These poems can be seen as leading into *Notes toward a Supreme Fiction*, one of the few long poems reprinted completely in Faber's *Selected Poems*.

I shall approach *Sunday Morning* as we approach it in *Harmonium*, beginning with *Cy Est Pourtraicte, Madame Ste Ursule, et Les Unze Mille Vierges*, then touching on *Of Heaven Considered as a Tomb* and *A High-Toned Old Christian Woman*.

But first a few general remarks on Stevens' religious dialectic in *Sunday Morning* and elsewhere. Or rather, his lack of dialectic. Stevens works with a logic of counteraffirmation without arguing through his position or seeing the strength of his adversary. He purges the last bits of nineteenth-century questioning within himself, or rather within his embowered lady. The affirmations and negations are familiar: reversing the topoi of the heavenly paradise to render it a pale shadow of actual earthly paradises; assuming Santayana's position[5] that Christianity is a religion for the Middle East and not for America ("Its [the church's] vitality depended on its association with Palestine, so to speak" [L 140, May 3, 1909]); stressing anthropomorphism as much in the Christian nativity as in the classical gods ("the very hinds discerned it, in a star"). Questions of faith or doctrine do not arise for Stevens; these are dead issues for him. "Unlike so many of the Victorians, Stevens was not worried by his doubts," David Daiches remarks.[6] "Poetry is the supreme fiction, Madam," Stevens says in his witty, antipietistic poem, *A High-Toned Old Christian Woman* (1922). (Things are not quite so simple in 1942 in *Notes toward a Supreme Fiction*.) "I am not in the least religious," said Stevens in 1907 (L 96). And in 1909, a little more precisely, "I am not pious" (L 140). This does not change, nor does his small anticlerical streak, which is there from the beginning:

> I have been pupil under bishops' rods
> And got my learning from the orthodox.
> I mark the virtue of the common-place.
> (*Poems from "Lettres d'un Soldat,"*
> I, "Common Soldier," OP 11)

> Burgher,
> He is, by will, but not his own. He dwells
> A part of wilful dwellings that impose

---

[5] "Transplanted to this country ready made like the Christian religion," George Santayana, "Genteel American Poetry," *New Republic*, May 29, 1915.

[6] David Daiches, *God and the Poets* (Oxford: Clarendon Press, 1984), p. 175.

Alike his morning and his evening prayer.
His town exhales its mother breath for him
And this he breathes, a candid bellows-boy,
According to canon.

(*Journal of Crispin*, pp. 42–43)

We might not guess from these poems that the early letters and journal show a young man who liked to spend time in churches, even during service.[7] Yet Stevens' early religiosity remains diffused, vague, even baffled. His "magnificent agnostic faith" (Geoffrey Hill's phrase)[8] comes later.

Stevens' Sainte Ursule is his second threatened-virgin figure in 1915, along with Susanna. But the saint's martyrdom in defense of her virginity is not a solemn thought here. Stevens is puckish yet tender. He works from a stanza of du Bellay's best-known poem, or best-known in 1873, according to Pater. (Stevens translated what I think of as du Bellay's best-known poem in 1909; both poems appear in the anthology of French verse he read to his future wife.[9]) He closes the poem mischievously and delicately, suggesting that the Lord himself must sublimate sexual feeling from time to time, quite as much as his saints. With the years, Stevens' play becomes increasingly ironic, and the anti-Christian poems of 1921 and 1922 diminish in scope. *Of Heaven Considered as a Tomb* plays on the common trope of the "vault" of heaven, reading it as burial vault for those who go to heaven. Stevens reverses the standard starry-sky topos of, say, the end of Coleridge's *Biographia Literaria*. (Andrew Wilton remarks that "Theorists of the sublime attached much importance to the associational significance of the sky, and usually placed the night sky full of stars at the head of their list of its sublimities. . . . Burke actually preferred darkness to light for sublime power."[10]) Stevens' heaven is at

---

[7] Cf. *L* 170, 176, 181, 219.

[8] Geoffrey Hill, *The Lords of Limit: Essays on Literature and Ideas* (New York: Oxford University Press, 1984), pp. 16–17.

[9] The stanza is as follows: "J'offre ces violettes / Ces lis & ces fleurettes, / Et ces roses icy, / Ces vermeillettes roses / Sont freshement écloses, / Et ces oeilliets aussi." The volume was *The Oxford Book of French Verse*. See *L* 150–51, 156, and: "I keep recalling Du Bellay's sonnet in the Book of Regrets" (*L* 181, September 4, 1913, from his birthplace, Reading).

[10] Andrew Wilton, *Turner and the Sublime* (London: British Museum Publications, 1980), p. 101. Cf. also Gombrich, " 'The Sky Is the Limit,' " in his *The Image and the Eye* (Ithaca: Cornell University Press, Phaidon, 1982), pp. 162–71. Cf. also Leo Spitzer on the "*concierto*, . . . the order, peace, and harmony of the starry night (in the tradition of the *Somnium Scipionis* and of Augustine)" (*Classical and Christian Ideas of World Harmony: Prolegomena to an Interpretation of the Word "Stimmung"* [Baltimore: The Johns Hop-

once burial vault and place of exile. He rhymes and puns on "icy" and "Elysée," a palace for a President of the Immortals presumably. He mixes classical and other diction, including Ottoman ("porte") in this last year of a Turkish Sultan, such syncretism being part of his rather clumsy attack on Christendom. So negative a poem must depend for its force on some gusto or black humor or strength of conviction, but Stevens' poem sounds more and more a clever exercise as we reread it. The same is true of *The Bird with the Coppery, Keen Claws*. *A High-Toned Old Christian Woman* remains wittily belligerent. We can readily work out the contrary musics, architectures, phonetic effects, and doctrines of the rival heavens therein. Stevens' sound effects are wonderfully frivolous in "their clickety-clack in contrast with the more decorous pom-pom-pom that many people expect" (Stevens in 1945, but not of this poem, L 485). He converts the ancient harmony of the spheres into a "jovial hullabaloo among the spheres," with his favorite pun on "Jove." The last sentence, "Wink most when widows wince," is a tongue twister that asks to be read quick as a wink. As in Shakespeare's "when most I wink," as in the biblical use of "wink at," Stevens' "wink" indicates a "studied refusal to recognize evil,"[11] though not quite in the orthodox sense of "evil." Fictive things, like the stars of heaven, may wink and twinkle to all sorts of ends.

Sunday Morning is a poem without word-play in the sense of "points or neat turns of wit."[12] Like some later poems, *Credences of Summer*, for instance, it seems uninterested in obvious puns, riddles, paradoxes, and so on. Such word-play as it has is implicit; etymology and echo are the preferred areas, and rhetoric works to support homiletics, even in the descriptive passages. We can find generic reasons for this style. Louis Martz has connected *Sunday Morning* with a seventeenth-century meditative tradition.[13] We might also note that *Sunday Morning* is like one type of elegy: a meditative poem, whose "meditation typically leads to recognition (*anagnorisis*) of feeling, to revelations and illuminations. Hence its images of light."[14] Alastair Fowler prefers the term, "modu-

---

kins University Press, 1963], p. 112). In English, the two meanings of the word "vault" (burial vault and vault of the sky) both begin in the sixteenth century.

[11] Stephen Booth on Shakespeare's Sonnet 43, in *Shakespeare's Sonnets* (New Haven and London: Yale University Press, 1977), p. 203. Cf. Acts 17:28–31, which reads ironically against the high-toned old Christian woman. Hastings, *Dictionary of the Bible* has an entry under "wink."

[12] Alastair Fowler, *Kinds of Literature: An Introduction to the Theory of Genres and Modes* (Cambridge, Mass.: Harvard University Press, 1982), p. 208.

[13] Louis Martz, *The Poetry of Meditation: A Study in English Religious Literature of the Seventeenth Century* (New Haven and London: Yale University Press, 1954), p. 324.

[14] Fowler, *Kinds of Literature*, p. 207.

lated ode," for this type of elegy, and that is how we should place *Sunday Morning* generically. Stevens' first way of ending the poem, with stanza vii, moves it toward hymn and antielegy. The ending we now have works with a modulated ode like Gray's *Elegy*, hearing its origins in Milton and revising the Miltonic effects.[15] As we know, Stevens placed himself generally in a tradition of elegiac poetry. ("I gave up writing plays because I had much less interest in dramatic poetry than in elegiac poetry" [*L* 729, September 27, 1951].) And how knowledgeable he is about elegy, we may surmise from the following: "What strikes me at first reading [of the *Gita Govinda*] is the refrains. . . . The refrains are like refrains in the Greek elegies" (*L* 380, December 9, 1940).

In *Sunday Morning*, we may hear Stevens combating the homiletics he finds in some etymology, in some allegory and topoi, and in some standard tropes. I shall take three examples: first, the opening word, "complacencies"; second, the difficult fifth stanza on the theme, death is the mother of beauty; third, the justly praised closing stanza.

"Complacencies of the peignoir, and late / Coffee and oranges in a sunny chair": so Stevens begins. "Complacencies": so a 1915 homily against absentees from church might begin. Or rather, with "complacency" in the singular. "Complacencies" in the plural is rare. Stevens' change of number, a device he likes, shifts the word from expected usage. "Complacency" in the singular has fallen, as philologists say, from "true pleasure" to the common meaning of "self-satisfaction." Has Stevens' lady fallen, like this word, into self-satisfaction (to read a Miltonic lesson from etymology)? Or has she a right to complacency in the sense of "true pleasure"? *Complacui*, I am well pleased, is what God says of his beloved Son more than once in the New Testament. (Milton has this text in mind when he has God call his Son "my sole complacence" [*PL* III.276].) Milton's etymology often draws attention to a high, original unity of meaning that fell with the fall of man. His diachronic play with etymology is part of his doctrine of first and last things. So is Stevens' diachronic play with etymology, as he retrieves and asserts true pagan pleasure through this one word.

Matters of etymology also help us to read Stevens' difficult, memorable stanza v:

> She says, "But in contentment I still feel
> The need of some imperishable bliss."
> Death is the mother of beauty; hence from her,

---

[15] But see the recent argument by Peter M. Sacks that Gray's *Elegy* is an elegy for a mute, Miltonic self (*The English Elegy: Studies in the Genre from Spenser to Yeats* [Baltimore and London: The Johns Hopkins University Press, 1985], pp. 133–137).

Alone, shall come fulfilment to our dreams
And our desires. Although she strews the leaves
Of sure obliteration on our paths,
The path sick sorrow took, the many paths
Where triumph rang its brassy phrase, or love
Whispered a little out of tenderness,
She makes the willow shiver in the sun
For maidens who were wont to sit and gaze
Upon the grass, relinquished to their feet.
She causes boys to pile new plums and pears
On disregarded plate. The maidens taste
And stray impassioned in the littering leaves.

Here, the topos of the fallen leaves is not situated in a time of war or apocalyptic fury, as in Homer or Virgil or Milton or Shelley. Rather, Stevens connects thanatos with eros in an extraordinary logical and phonetic and etymological play on "leaves," "obliteration," and "litter." He begins with three allegorical paths, all familiar topoi. "Where triumph rang its brassy phrase," for example, speaks to action, to poetry celebrating action, and to poets' standard claim that their words will outlast monumental brasses. Whatever paths we follow, they lead toward the "leaves of sure obliteration"—leaves as actual fallen leaves, an allegory of death; leaves as that which is left; leaves as leaves of a book; leaves as souls of the dead. We might go on to say that unfallen leaves, on a willow, for instance, "shiver" in apprehension of death. This is what we expect, especially in nineteenth-century literature—a despairing of life if it ends in sure obliteration. As the willow is symbolically the tree of death, and also of unrequited love, its shivering seems right for maidens, sitting on the grass, pursuing no path. They might well be overcome by a death wish, like Eve's. Shivering willows, thus read, are an omen, as in Tennyson's iconography of willows in the erotic, bereaved landscape of *The Lady of Shalott*. ("Willows whiten, aspens quiver, / Little breezes dusk and shiver . . . willow-veiled.") But Stevens says "although." Is this act, after all, a life-giving act?

Stevens encourages us to move on, in our reading of this compact little fable for maidens. We move from the thought that willows shiver in fear of death to the thought that it is we who make the word "shiver" work this way. Whether or not willows have any sense of death, death is part of life for them. And so it is for Stevens, or so he says.[16] Death itself

---

[16] See, for example, *Death of a Soldier* (CP 97). See also Ellmann, "How Wallace Stevens Saw Himself," in *Wallace Stevens: A Celebration*, ed. Frank Doggett and Robert Buttel (Princeton: Princeton University Press, 1980), pp. 149–70.

might well say "Live" rather than "Die," as in Virgil's minor poem: "Death twitches my ear. 'Live,' he says; 'I am coming.' " ("Mors aurem vellens 'vivite' ait, 'venio' " [*Copa* 38].) Oliver Wendell Holmes quoted the line on his ninetieth birthday.

There is a fine schematic play on "leaves," "obliteration," and "littering" that also breaks with our expectations if we listen carefully. We hear a "-litera-littering" echo, as if "litter" were derived from *littera* (letter), whence our word "literature." In fact, "litter" has no proper etymological relation to "littera" nor to "obliteration," though it has an oblique relation.[17] It comes from *lectus* (bed or couch), whose stem is also that of *lector* or "reader." Those tasting maidens, like Persephone or Eve, duly stray down some path in which leaves and litter and *litterae*, and readers too, move toward obliteration. Text and reader, love and action, intricately involved, all move quietly toward death, from whose memory we nonetheless have Eve and Persephone and Virgil and Milton and Tennyson, and Latin echoes too.

Our ample readings of *Sunday Morning* have not recognized how fully Stevens revises biblical and Miltonic tradition, especially in his masterly closing stanza. Stevens' engagement with Milton throughout this poem is quiet. In stanza iii, he responds to Milton's "for then the Earth / Shall all be Paradise" (*PL* xii.463–64) with "And shall the earth / Seem all of paradise . . . ?"[18] In stanza i, he echoes *Il Penseroso*: "I hear the far-off Curfew sound, / Over some wide-water'd shore" (74–75).[19] Stevens himself liked the sound of church bells when he was a young man, and they seem to have sounded no reproach: "It is pleasant to hear bells on Sunday morning. By long usage, we have become accustomed to bells turning this ordinary day into a holy one. The general absence of that familiar ringing here makes the day half a waste" (*L* 117, January 10, 1909). In *Sunday Morning*, that has changed. His lady's dream goes back to origins in Palestine by means of church bells heard as Milton's curfew, and by means of winding thoughts that move like a winding procession to empty out the noisy, active daytime scene:

> The pungent oranges and bright, green wings
> Seem things in some procession of the dead,
> Winding across wide water, without sound.
> The day is like wide water, without sound. . . .

[17] As noted in my Introduction, false etymology can be as useful to a poet as true etymology. See K. K. Ruthven, "The Poet as Etymologist," *Critical Quarterly* 11 (1969), 9–37.

[18] Philip Furia, "Nuances of a Theme by Milton: Wallace Stevens's 'Sunday Morning,' " *American Literature* 46 (1974), 83–87.

[19] John Hollander, *Vision and Resonance: Two Senses of Poetic Form* (New York: Oxford University Press, 1975), p. 159.

Stevens' phrase, "wide water without sound," though referentially soundless, faintly echoes Milton's poem, as if the phrase were itself tolling the knell to parting day—as indeed it is, drawing the stanza from a bright Sunday morning toward darkness, and preparing us for the sun-versus-dark staged debate of the poem. My allusion to Gray is not accidental, for I hear in Stevens a faint, elusive echo of Gray's famous lines. Such a hearing is supported by Stevens' movement toward burial place as well as darkness, and by his "winding" procession (Gray's verb). (Some such subliminal hearing may account for Frank Kermode's description of *Sunday Morning* as Stevens' *Elegy in a Country Churchyard*.[20]) The echo itself seems to wind across wide water—not the wide water that leads to the earthly paradise, but the wide water that separates Milton and Gray from Stevens.

Stevens' quiet revisions of Milton become a little louder in his well-known closing stanza. We have not heard them because of the even louder presence of Keats:

> Deer walk upon our mountains, and the quail
> Whistle about us their spontaneous cries;
> Sweet berries ripen in the wilderness;
> And, in the isolation of the sky,
> At evening, casual flocks of pigeons make
> Ambiguous undulations as they sink,
> Downward to darkness, on extended wings.

Stevens is revising the powerful tradition of the one (not many), causal (not casual) dove (not pigeon, which is the all-too-common member of the dove family)—in short, the one causal dove who is the Holy Spirit, who

> from the first
> Wast present, and with mighty wings outspread
> Dove-like satst brooding on the vast Abyss
> And mad'st it pregnant: What in me is dark
> Illumine, what is low raise and support. . . .
>   (*PL* I.19–23)

This is the bird that closes Hopkins' sonnet, *God's Grandeur*, at sunrise, as it broods over the bent earth with, "ah! bright wings." In Stevens' poem, it is the cockatoo, earthly and domesticated, who has "bright" wings. The pigeons have "extended wings," a fine rethinking of Milton's "mighty wings outspread." Rejecting a contrast of mighty versus puny,

---

[20] Frank Kermode, *Wallace Stevens* (Edinburgh and London: Oliver and Boyd, 1960), p. 41.

pigeons' wings extend as far as pigeons' wings extend, and we may find what comfort we can in that span. Stevens' adjective "ambiguous" reinforces the directional sense of "undulations"—waviness in an up-and-down motion, and not the clear up-down alternatives of Milton. Similarly with isolation rather than divine presence (or "sponsorship"), and sky rather than heaven. Any skeptics about the presence of a Milton-Hopkins bird here, in addition to Keats's, should look at Stevens' late poem, *In the Element of Antagonisms* (*CP* 426).

My sense of Stevens' pigeons is strengthened by the other birds present in this stanza, the quail. The adjective for their cries, "spontaneous," "hearkens back phonemically to our unsponsored state."[21] It has a reason for doing so. Those quail are in an American wilderness, and they revise Keats's domestic scene at the close of *To Autumn*. But Stevens is also revising biblical wilderness, as North American literature does time and again, specifically the wilderness through which the children of Israel journeyed. The quail whistle because of the beauty of the sound and because of Keats's dominant presence. But the presence of quail at all is because of the Book of Exodus: "at even, quails came up and covered the camp" (16:23). "The people asked and he brought quails, And satisfied them with the bread of heaven" (Psalm 105:40). Those are "sponsored" and not "spontaneous" quail, if there ever were any. Lionel Trilling has the most useful note on this matter. "The phrase 'manna from heaven' is a common one, but no one ever says 'quail from heaven,' even though the quail were just as important as the manna in the diet which was divinely provided for the Children of Israel in the wilderness; manna, we might say, was but the divine dessert. Yet because manna was evanescent and is not to be identified with any known edible thing, it has come to serve as a metaphor for miraculous sustenance and spiritual comfort; the quail, being all too grossly actual, have been quite forgotten."[22] No manna falls in *Sunday Morning*, but quail do come in this American wilderness. Stevens echoes the Exodus journey through the wilderness in more than one poem. In *Of Heaven Considered as a Tomb*, we may hear a near-parodic rewriting of the pillar of cloud by day and the pillar of fire by night: "Or does / That burial, pillared up each day as porte . . . / Foretell each night the one abysmal night, / When the host shall no more wander, nor the light / Of the steadfast lanterns creep across the dark?" Stevens wrote this in 1921, but in *Harmonium* it is one of the

---

[21] Helen Vendler, " 'Stevens and Keats' 'To Autumn,' " in *Wallace Stevens*, ed. Doggett and Buttel, p. 174.

[22] Lionel Trilling, Introduction to his *Selected Letters of John Keats* (Garden City, N.Y.: Doubleday, Anchor, 1950), p.12n.

revisionary religious poems that precedes and so prepares the way for *Sunday Morning*.

When Stevens echoes other texts in this poem, he evokes early-morning or evening scenes. The quail come at even. The birds of stanza iv. 13 echo Tennyson's "earliest pipe of half-awakened birds," itself perhaps echoing Milton's "charm of earliest Birds" (*PL* iv.651). And the strongest echoing evokes the final, evening stanza of Keats's *To Autumn*. We might go on to observe what Stevens evidently observed: that Keats, so memorably engaging Milton in the Hyperion poems and in *Ode to a Nightingale*, moves away from such engagement in *To Autumn*. "In all his previous odes," Paul Fry argues, "Keats had tried to reconstruct Milton's sacred fane," but not in *To Autumn*.[23] For Stevens, however, an engagement with Milton is crucial. If the scene in the last stanza is being used partly "as an instance of a thesis, not surrendered to in and for itself," we must remember that "surrendering to in and for itself" is also a thesis.[24] While echoing *To Autumn*, Stevens also chooses to make clear what Keats has kept implicit—Keats's distance from dialectical tensions that the author of *Paradise Lost* would raise in an evening poem of this earth. Even as Stevens accepts Keats's beautiful vision at the end of *To Autumn*, he widens the context to take in what Keats rightly left out. *Sunday Morning* is explicitly a doctrinal poem; we do it wrong to protest homiletics in the final stanza.

Yvor Winters liked what Helen Vendler calls Stevens' "homiletic" diction, for it seemed to him to work at both the "descriptive" and the "philosophical" levels, to use his terms. (He singled out the words "chaos," "solitude," "unsponsored," "free," "inescapable."[25]) Vendler, with a fine pun on "trope," hears in Stevens' closing lines the "coercion of cadence, which forces the innocent landscape to enact a Stevensian entropy."[26] But once we hear Stevens' descriptive as well as his homiletic language as revisionary (Vendler's "homiletic" is more accurate than Winters's "philosophical"), our sense of Stevens' pathos at the end is modified. The naturalistic force of these lines is increased and their possible nostalgia dissipated.

What kind of echo and allusion is this? I hear none of Stevens' echoes as allusive and some as faint. Stevens' strategy is to try to displace heaven, through a change of old troping. I think the logic of his own

---

[23] Paul Fry, *The Poet's Calling in the English Ode* (New Haven and London: Yale University Press, 1981), p. 271.

[24] Helen Vendler, *On Extended Wings: Wallace Stevens' Longer Poems* (Cambridge, Mass.: Harvard University Press, 1969), p. 49.

[25] Yvor Winters, *Forms of Discovery* (n.p.: Alan Swallow, 1967), pp. 272–78.

[26] Vendler, "Stevens and Keats," p. 174.

echoing leads back toward Virgil. Stevens could be wary of "Virgilian landscapes" and endings, as, for example, in 1951 (*NA* 159). But here, I read Stevens as wishing to separate the evening tradition of poetry from Milton's powerful dialectic in *Paradise Lost*, and restore a Virgilian line of inheritance. From Virgil's eclogues and bucolics, through Milton's *Il Penseroso*, through Keats and Tennyson: this is the line of Stevens' poem. And in combating a biblical and Miltonic language of sun and darkness, of evening, of wilderness, Stevens keeps away from simple reversal, from an easy either-or. Hopkins's sunrise is emblematic; it closes his poem on the eternal type of endless fresh beginnings in which all worldly ending is subsumed. A simple reversal would end Stevens' poem on nightfall as a perpetual type of decline and fall in which all worldly beginning is subsumed, a dark and final closure. His final lines read to me like a variation on Virgilian closure, one of those memorable endings on some form of the word *umbra*. The topos is like the wilderness topos that informs Virgil's husbandry in *Georgics* II.429–34—alike at least in birds and berries and, more important, tone. Keats too draws on Virgil's *Georgics*, through Dryden's translation, in *To Autumn*, and we should not underestimate Virgil's importance for Stevens, even this early. John Hollander speaks of how some lines by John Ashbery "conclude his poem with a substitute for the traditional openings-out of landscape, or closings-in of shadows, which the visionary lyric in English derived from Virgil's eclogues and made its own."[27] Stevens' closure seems to me a paradoxical variation on Virgilian alternatives—a movement that is downward to shadow but also outward. And his strategy, like Keats's, is to divide Virgil from Milton. Stevens' cadences are in the Keats-Tennyson line that owes so much to Milton, and Milton's own cadences owe much to Virgil. Stevens, I think, tries to reclaim such a cadence and such an evening ending for a naturalistic sublime poetry.

A comparison of Stevens and Virgil may sound strange in these days of parched classical scholarship. Yet Stevens drew attention to Virgil as a forerunner in several poems, most notably in the epilogue to *Notes toward a Supreme Fiction* with the poet's "Virgilian cadences, up down, / Up down" (*CP* 407, 1942). In 1945, Virgil is a type of major man in *Paisant Chronicle*, with Stevens punning on the word "still," to keep Virgil at once human and enduring and quiet, as he is: "The baroque poet may see him as still a man / As Virgil, abstract." In the clumsy 1936 attack on Milton, *Mystic Garden & Middling Beast*, Virgil is dropped, along with Milton: "The era of the idea of man, the cloak / And speech of Virgil dropped" (*CP* 185). By 1942, Stevens knew better. And in es-

---

[27] *Yale Review* 70 (1981), 177.

says of 1948 and 1951, he quotes from Virgil's *Georgics* (*NA* 116–17; *OP* 239). In two more essays of 1942 and 1951, he mentions Virgil in passing, gently distancing him (*NA* 23, 1942; *NA* 159, 1951).

But Virgil was there from the beginning. In a journal entry of 1899, Stevens outlines a possible scenic sketch that might include "Georgic distances" (*SP* 54). A journal entry for 1906 reads: "Looked up irises in the dictionary & found this line from Tennyson—'In the spring, a livelier iris changes on the burnished dove.' Is it Virgilian, O doctors?" (*SP* 157). (If it is, it appears to be a topos rather than a verbal echo.) In 1916, Stevens attempted without success the poem, *For an Old Woman in a Wig*, an explicit attack on a Virgil-Dante tradition: "It is the skeleton Virgil utters / The fates of men . . . Hell is not desolate Italy."[28] In 1921, Crispin, "if he could, / Would chant assuaging Virgil" (*Journal of Crispin*, p. 34). And to return to 1915, and *Sunday Morning*, stanza v: "boys . . . pile new plums and pears / On disregarded plate. The maidens taste. . . ." Boys who pile fruit for their beloved: this is a topos once well known from Virgil's second eclogue. (Stevens adds pears to Virgil's plums; Dryden added peaches.) One line from *The Comedian as the Letter C* translates, or adapts, line 53 of this eclogue. Virgil writes, "honos erit huic quoque pomo" (this fruit, too, shall have its honor). Stevens writes, "The melon should have apposite ritual" (*CP* 39) and goes on to expand the topos, though here the "ritual," "sacrament," and "celebration" are not for the sake of eros, as in Virgil and *Sunday Morning*.

There is an essay to be written on Stevens and the subject of endings, including matters of formal closure, doctrines of last things, evening, elegy, Virgilian closure, and so on. *Sunday Morning*, which itself had two printed and three proposed endings,[29] is a rich text for this subject. Barbara Herrnstein Smith notes how the last four lines use four strong words of closure yet also keep a sense of "lingering suspension." She also observes how "a principle of closure is readily available . . . when the dialectic process can be represented as internally resolved, when the poet can record his having 'thought it through' to a stable conclusion."[30] The variety of Stevens' three proposed endings is one illustration that he is not interested in such a dialectical process. But the grammar and rhetoric of his ending, like his opening etymology, show a master rhetorical combatant.

[28] *The Palm at the End of the Mind: Selected Poems and a Play by Wallace Stevens*, ed. Holly Stevens (New York: Vintage, 1972), p. 12; hereafter abbreviated in the text as *Palm*.

[29] The other two endings are with stanzas vii and v (*L* 183, June 6 and 23, 1915).

[30] Barbara Herrnstein Smith, *Poetic Closure: A Study of How Poems End* (Chicago and London: University of Chicago Press, 1968), pp. 177, 244–45, 141.

How does Stevens end *Harmonium* itself? His style becomes increasingly hieratic as he approaches the end of his volume, but he does not end in a hieratic style or Virgilian shade. He ends with what appear to be two throw-away poems, slight gestures that may sound almost too slight. Both editions of *Harmonium* close with two early poems, *Tea* (1915) and *To the Roaring Wind* (1917). And Stevens reprinted the seemingly slight *Tea* as the last poem from *Harmonium* in the 1953 Faber selections. As a closing poem, it is the more puzzling of the two, for it seems a little imagist exercise in oriental fashion. Horticulture and word-play take us a little further.

> When the elephant's-ear in the park
> Shrivelled in frost,
> And the leaves on the paths
> Ran like rats,
> Your lamp-light fell
> On shining pillows,
> Of sea-shades and sky-shades,
> Like umbrellas in Java.

"Elephant's-ear" is the popular name for caladium. (Literal readers of the word "elephant's-ear" very naturally find the poem surrealistic.) Caladium is a tender plant, not native to northern temperate zones, grown for its leaves, like tea. The handsome leaves, in the shape of an elephant's ear, come in various colors and are purely ornamental. As far as I know, no one makes infusions of caladium leaves, as we commonly do of tea leaves. Given Stevens' play in 1915 and 1916 with the topos of fallen leaves, I wonder if he is not writing an envoi for his volume using this topos. Not an invocation cum envoi, like *To the Roaring Wind*, but a little fable of leaves. The poem presents a North American variation on the tea ceremony, where each remembered detail of the scene is savored. Outside, tender-leaved plants are dead, leaves run like rats, driven by some wind, perhaps roaring. Within, one may light a lamp, see sea-shades and sky-shades, and, crossing the line, think of them as "like umbrellas in Java." ("Umbrellas" makes the two preceding "shades" pun slightly in a charming effect, an umbrella in Java being presumably a sunshade.) And the poem comes full circle, for the word "caladium" stems from a Malay word and so comes, like Java tea, from the South Pacific. At the end of all the leaves of *Harmonium*, whether tender or hardy, multicolored or green, we come to this little "leaves" poem and the act of drinking tea. We do not have to be tea fanciers, like Stevens, for different teas to evoke different worlds, Java or elsewhere.[31] So also the leaves of a poet, preserved, properly brewed, and ingested, may evoke other worlds and nourish us. Drinking tea is a common domestic habit, and tea is the most common beverage drunk throughout the world, next to water. It is so common a beverage and a habit that we seldom think of the tea plant. But it too can add to the ancient topos of fallen leaves, as well as to the topos of poetry as food and drink. Take my leaves, this little poem says; preserve them, but do not let them grow stale; try them as you prefer.

Invocations usually come at the beginning of a major literary work. Stevens places his at the end—an invocation that is also an envoi, as the little poem, *To the Roaring Wind*, originally was in the 1917 series *Primordia*.

> What syllable are you seeking,
> Vocalissimus,
> In the distances of sleep?
> Speak it.

We take the point of a wind that is to speak rather than sing. And of a wind that seeks not a word but a syllable. Stevens' adjective "vocalissimus" has a most appropriate double meaning of "speaking" and also "causing speech," according to Lewis and Short—superlatively so, as Stevens' favorite form of the adjective tells us. The schematic echo of "seeking," "sleep," "speak," plus the logic of the sentence, make us hear faintly, "What syllable are you speaking?" This is no bare place, with no burst syllable. Stevens seems to call on a spirit or genius loci (why of sleep?), who will speak, and thereby make his book speak, to the reader. Or who will speak one syllable only in all its roaring, one enabling syllable, which it seeks as much as Stevens. This is no "One of Fictive Music," nor like any of the spirits of the opening poems. It sounds more like the note of Vulcan that Crispin longed to own. Why the Latin? Partly for the look and sound and age of it. "I quote . . . in Latin for the sound and sight of it," Stevens wrote in 1909 (*L* 133). Even more, I think, to introduce a question of translation. Not so much translation from a Latin that hardly needs translation, but rather, translation from the wind's sounds to human syllables—all those translations from wind and spirits that we have heard through many books and leaves and harmonies.

To open *Harmonium*, Stevens chose poems that displace the reader slightly, that play a little against customary mimesis or legend or alle-

---

[31] "And coleus comes from Java. Good Heavens, how that helps one to understand coleus—or Java" (*L* 184, July 25, 1915).

gory, that possess various genii loci. In closing the volume, he tries to bring it home. The two grace notes at the end hand his book over to the reader, as an envoi does, and the last poem also invokes the wind as spirit. These two poems do not displace, and their spirits sound beneficent. Here, the interior scene is a shelter against the outside, and the outside has a voice that may be commanded to speak, as Prospero commands the elements. As *Harmonium* draws to a close, Stevens gives his hieratic style more and more room. Apostrophe appears, and invocation. Word-play now supports rather than displaces. Muse figures are allowed, the roaring wind, "the one of fictive music." The volume draws away from ironic poems, from invective, parody. It transfers the language of religion to the realm of art. It transfers the language of religion to the realm of eros. It allows romantic topoi, such as blowing curtains, full scope. The expansiveness of *Nomad Exquisite*, with its appropriation of language from Genesis, comes near the end. Chronologically, Stevens is approaching a dry period, as *The Comedian* forecasts, and as he chose, in part. It was, I think, much drier than he expected; the poems added to the 1931 *Harmonium* make painful reading. And Stevens published nothing between August 1924 and April 1930, a silence only partly explained by poetic choice and by professional and personal activity. He arranged the poems of *Harmonium* to foretell a different story.

II

* * *

Transition

CHAPTER SIX

* * * * *

A Rhetoric of Beginning Again:

Ideas of Order

The law of contrast is crude. (*L* 445, March 29, 1943)

Ideas of Order is a book of ending and beginning again, as we can see from the plots of the opening and closing poems. The opening poems tell us that beginning again is often a matter of returning, and the words "turn" and "return" echo through the volume like a refrain. The trade edition of 1936 opens with *Farewell to Florida*, a voyage from an old love, but not to a new one (the old love is Venus as Florida, the "return" is to a "violent mind"). Next we have *Ghosts as Cocoons*: an address to a much-desired bride still in the cocoon (Stevens is rewriting the muse poem, *To the One of Fictive Music*). Then, *Sailing after Lunch*: luffing in a romantic *bâteau ivre*, which suddenly finds new wind (Stevens is combating some views of the Romantic). Then, *Sad Strains of a Gay Waltz*: no more dancing to the same old tunes, Stevens' own old tunes from *Harmonium* (he gathers up images of the first three poems, echoes from his two volume titles, and characters as well as words from *Harmonium*; that word "strains" is related to the "strain" of *Peter Quince at the Clavier*). Other poems of turning and returning include *The Pleasures of Merely Circulating* on cycles, *Meditation Terrestrial and Celestial* on the "returning sun," and *Anglais Mort à Florence*, an elegy for all aging human beings, with the unforgettable opening line: "A little less returned for him each spring." The last five poems are valedictory, though in no simple way, as I hope to show: *A Postcard from the Volcano*, a remarkable poem about generations, and so naturally about ending and beginning again and returning; *Autumn Refrain*, an evening poem of desolate farewell, where nonetheless something remains; *A Fish-Scale Sunrise*, a minor morning-after-the-party poem; *Gallant Château*, a quest-poem ending without fulfillment but also unexpectedly without grief; and finally, *Delightful Evening*, the most humorous poem, and for good reason.

How haphazard it all sounds, this volume of "order," and indeed it is very mixed in effect, sometimes strained. That is understandable. Stevens' years of silence must have been filled, day after day, with questions of beginning again: how to end some things, return to others, find yet others. A voyage, a bride, spring after a long winter, morning after a long night, the castle after a weary quest—there they are, our common patterns or ideas of order about ending and returning and beginning again. (I read "ideas of order" as any patterning, large or small, aesthetic or social or whatever, that gives order. Stevens' use of the phrase supports this reading.) Stevens sets out these common patterns and examines them as patterns, testing them for his own use. Throughout, he examines them especially for the greatest hazard of beginning again— the easy path of simple reversal.

We have tended to read *Ideas of Order* as either-or: either elegy for a dead poetic self or else rebirth. Certainly, there is much evening imagery; certainly, there is lack of color, even grayness.[1] There are also various ghosts and spirits and angels, as well as one genius. There is also much coldness, though it is usually felicitous, or says it is. All this may be read as elegiac, especially when we observe that the language of rebirth is more often asserted than achieved, and that there is a good deal of waiting. And Stevens is certainly meditating throughout on ways of saying goodbye. As he puts it in *Waving Adieu, Adieu, Adieu*, "One likes to practice the thing." But either-or readings are too simple for many poems in *Ideas of Order*. Nor are either-or readings of Stevens sufficient beyond this volume. Stevens is always wary of simple reversals, and *Ideas of Order* tests them again and again. This chapter will try to show how and why.

How does this Stevens compare with the Stevens we have watched in *Harmonium*? Some of the effects are surprisingly crude and some fall flat. Stevens appears to be deliberately roughening his earlier subtlety and self-consciousness. The elegant diction, the shaded ironies, the implicit plays with language: much of this is gone. At the same time, Stevens blocks the reader less. There is little sense of displacement throughout, for Stevens stays closer to the language of ordinary mimesis and

---

[1] See, for example, Joseph Riddel, *The Clairvoyant Eye: The Poetry and Poetics of Wallace Stevens* (Baton Rouge: Louisiana State University Press, 1965), p. 113.

allegory. Paradoxically, the "I" of this volume, for all that it claims less and mourns more, seems stronger than the "I" of *Harmonium*, more active than acted upon. The triumph of the volume is its title poem, *The Idea of Order at Key West*. If there is an erotic plot in *Ideas of Order* (and I think there is), Stevens moves past *Farewell to Florida* and also *Gallant Château*. *The Idea of Order at Key West* finds "blessed rage for order" while still in a Florida setting, that troubling setting of the Florida poems, that disorderly setting in the opening voyage away from Key West. Stevens is saying farewell to the subject of eros, and finding a way of reshaping its energies. What is the major English poem of a return that is also a renewal? It is Wordsworth's *Lines Composed a Few Miles above Tintern Abbey on Revisiting the Banks of the Wye*. Stevens' *Idea of Order at Key West* speaks to Wordsworth's poem in ways that I shall show.

Stevens explicitly returns to his own work in *Sad Strains of a Gay Waltz*. Music "empty of shadows" in 1935 is empty of ghosts, or almost. It evokes "your blue-shadowed silk" but not as Peter Quince evokes it; here it is as if the lovely shade were the shade of a former feeling. Then, "desiring you" was music; now "the waltz / Is no longer a mode of desire." *Lions in Sweden* also judges Stevens' former self, dismissing the old phrases for the sublime, those phrases found in a literary "savings bank" (a witty trope that would delight the ghost of R. H. Tawney). "I was once / A hunter of those sovereigns of the soul / And savings banks." Stevens' pun on sovereigns as rulers of the soul and sovereigns as coins extends to "sovereign-souvenir." He also puns on the four cardinal virtues, thereby undercutting the solemnity with which we invest such images. (And do not banks commonly decorate themselves with solemn allegorical figures of the cardinal virtues, especially those virtues that help support the banking system?) Stevens' Patientia uses her English meaning to soothe her Latin one (*patere*, to suffer) and so is "forever soothing wounds." These old sublime and new banking images only remind Stevens of Apollinaire's lion; once an image of majesty, "tu ne nais maintenant qu'en cage." Stevens' savings bank, where we store our old sublime words and images, is like his museum in another poem of *Ideas of Order* (CP 153):

Shall I grapple with my destroyers [Reader: Yes, yes.]
In the muscular poses of the museums? [Reader: Laocoon? Well, why not?]
But my destroyers avoid the museums. [Reader: I see.]

There is one important development, or rather desire for development. *Ideas of Order* includes a troubled impulse to speak to and for a society. Stevens is still working this out, and a false path led him to experiment

119

with social satire, here and in *Owl's Clover*. It was a dead end. Stevens does not have a gift for satire (despite many memorable phrases like the "mickey mockers" in *The American Sublime*), and he came to know this. From now on, his desire will be to realize, more than satirize, the ordinary things of earth—air and light, the joy of having a body, the voluptuousness of looking, to quote his one epigraph in this collection (*CP* 136). As for speaking to a society, Stevens found a way to do this through *The Man with the Blue Guitar*. In *Ideas of Order*, he left behind his old heroic, poetic Hoon self who "found all form and order in solitude" (*CP* 121). In *The Man with the Blue Guitar*, he found a true subject, individual and communal at once.

I want to examine some poems with special attention to the ways in which Stevens avoids simple reversals. It is an all-important strategy in argument and rhetoric. Stevens once wrote that "The law of contrast is crude," and few things help more in reading his work than remembering this general principle. Time and again, our stock responses or expectations follow the axis of some "law of contrast." We sometimes do not see that Stevens is playing with the line of axis itself.

We might start with the last poem, the evening note on which Stevens closes his volume. "Good night," says his little poem, *Delightful Evening*, or rather, not a simple good night but "a very felicitous eve"—this to a certain Herr Doktor (any philosopher, particularly one of the German type, said Stevens [*L* 347, January 9, 1940]). Such a Herr Doktor may be part of any reader of Stevens' poetry:

> A very felicitous eve,
> Herr Doktor, and that's enough,
> Though the brow in your palm may grieve
>
> At the vernacular of light
> (Omitting reefs of cloud):
> Empurpled garden grass;
>
> The spruces' outstretched hands;
> The twilight overfull
> Of wormy metaphors.

This little wave of the hand to Stevens' volume and to a head-holding philosopher plays on "light" and "night" throughout. Evening may be a time of fading light, now without angels and nightingales and even grackles, as other poems in this collection tell us. But this evening is not elegiac for Stevens. Herr Doktor presumably reads by the light of reason and seeks enlightenment, so that he should grieve at what happens to an *Abendland*, to evening language, to decline, and so forth. Every evening offers an elegy to such a thinker as surely as "eve" rhymes with "grieve." What is to some the delight of twilight is simply de-light to others. For them, the twilight, alas, is overfull and also de-light-full. (For skeptics about this pun, I should note the even more obvious punning on "light" and "delight" at the end of *Botanist on Alp [No. 2]* [*CP* 135–36].) The "vernacular" is any normal spoken language as distinct from a learned or literary language. Similarly, our experience of light as one of the "unphilosophical realities" (Stevens' phrase) is "vernacular," that is, unlearned. The association of evening and twilight with elegy and grieving is a literary and learned language, so to speak, for all that the association is natural enough. Everything depends on the light in which we see it: whether evening light empurples grass; whether analogy makes spruces have hands; whether the twi-light of metaphor (which is commonly binary, relating A to B) and the metaphors of twilight show things in a troping or turning light.

Is the Herr Doktor grieved because all metaphors are "wormy," being figurative language (wiggly, hidden, turning, and the ruination of good, substantial food and language)? Or because these metaphors are earthly and mortal and may even smell of Satan? Remembering Stevens' earlier poems using worms as transport ("we her chariot") and his echoes of Shakespearean worms, we may hear a break with his own Germanic, philosophical self. There is indeed a buried metaphor in the phrase, "wormy metaphors"—yet less buried than the Herr Doktor's all-prevailing and all-consuming metaphors of light that dominate our thinking. Stevens is undoing many an idea of order about evening—arguments, tropes, genres, iconography, decline, all the westering of things (what he later called "the westwardness of everything" [*CP* 455]). He is mischievously deconstructing our ideas of light and enlightenment as surely as Jacques Derrida deconstructs Kant's kind of "enlightenment."[2] Since this whole volume is a turning from, and a turning toward, and in some ways, a returning, the light and humorous ending is itself very felicitous. It prepares us for Stevens' undoing elsewhere of orthodox thinking and troping on light. And it warns us to be cautious about Stevens' evening and elegiac poems. As with the word-play in the opening poems of *Harmonium*, the word-play in this little poem has far-reaching implications.

Stevens' rabbi in *The Sun This March* is a contrary to his Herr Doktor figure:

[2] See Derrida's remarks on Kant's *Von einem neuerdings erhoben Vornehmen Ton in der Philosophie* in his "D'un ton apocalyptique adopté naguère en philosophie," *Les fins de l'homme: á partir au travail de Jacques Derrida* (Paris: Galilée, 1981), pp. 445–86.

The exceeding brightness of this early sun
Makes me conceive how dark I have become,

And re-illumines things that used to turn
To gold in broadest blue, and be a part

Of a turning spirit in an earlier self.
That, too, returns from out the winter's air,

Like an hallucination come to daze
The corner of the eye. Our element,

Cold is our element and winter's air
Brings voices as of lions coming down.

Oh! Rabbi, rabbi, fend my soul for me
And true savant of this dark nature be.

We hardly need to be told to hear the pun in "turning" and the etymology of "spirit," but it is useful to be reminded of Milton and Shelley. "Dark with excessive brightness" is how Milton describes the light of the Godhead, which "dazzles." The echo sounds faintly through Stevens' opening lines (where Milton's "excessive" is carefully revised to "exceeding") and his later word "daze." "Conceive" is abstract, as in our common way of speaking, but physical and artistic senses of conception also inform the word, especially when we hear the Miltonic echo. (The sun makes things conceive. The poet conceives, and "we are conceived in your conceits," as Stevens says in 1938 [CP 195].) This is a Promethean self speaking, as we may hear in the voice that comes from Shelley, this time in an allusive echo: "Pain is my element," says Shelley's Prometheus (1.477). Stevens liked the echo well enough to open a wartime poem with it: "Force is my lot . . . And cold, my element" (CP 273). If "cold is our element"—and it does seem to be in this volume where Stevens is so suspicious of the tropes and arguments of warmth[3]—then we are leaving our element in March. It is an odd thing to say, unless of course cold is no more our best element than pain is for Prometheus. Perhaps cold is like pain, something to be endured heroically as punishment for defying heaven.

Here we might protest that Stevens attacks conventional analogues of evening and elegy in *Delightful Evening* and yet uses the conventional analogue of spring sun and returning vitality in *The Sun This March*. But we need to take particular care with this argument. Stevens is em-

[3] See Richard Ellmann's comprehensive sense of the place of coldness in Stevens (in *Wallace Stevens: A Celebration* ed. Frank Doggett and Robert Buttel (Princeton: Princeton University Press, 1980), pp. 163–70. My own account is more diachronic.

phatically not just reversing usual patterns any more than he is trying to forbid their use. This would make for obvious irony and little more. He works to make us see that it is we who make these analogues, natural as it may be to project them out on to the turnings and roundings of the actual world. Thus he can rewrite *In the Carolinas* with a far more conventional Aphrodite as earth-mother in *Meditation Celestial and Terrestrial*.

> The wild warblers are warbling in the jungle
> Of life and spring and of the lustrous inundations,
> Flood on flood, of our returning sun.
>
> Day after day, throughout the winter,
> We hardened ourselves to live by bluest reason
> In a world of wind and frost,
>
> And by will, unshaken and florid
> In mornings of angular ice,
> That passed beyond us through the narrow sky.
>
> But what are radiant reason and radiant will
> To warblings early in the hilarious trees
> Of summer, the drunken mother?

Stevens makes semantic meaning coincide with phonetic effect. The flooding l-sounds, as in Horace's Lalage lines, come with associations of song. The enjambment of line 1 causes a kind of migration, where the warblers seem at first to be in the jungle that is their winter home, until we complete our own reading journey and see and hear the figurative jungle of a Northern spring. Stevens' lovely closing lines transfer a standard epithet for Aphrodite, "laughing Aphrodite," to the trees, which are full of warblings, anticipating summer. "Hilarious" sounds more liquid and celebratory than "laughing trees," and, being Latinate, evokes something like a Venus hilaria. "Hilarious trees" and a "drunken mother" can sound like crude comedy. But to know mother earth as trees know her is to drink from her as well as to see her intoxicated with life. This is no aspic-nippled mother, but neither is she solemnly alma and nutritive. This is Venus who laughed and laughs, and was the sometime lover of Bacchus. She is the only Venus Stevens will allow, as he ends the poetic experiment of confining "florid" things to his will, and "radiance" to his will and reason.

Our common ideas of order about cycles are much influenced by Eliot. For Eliot's ironic cycles have helped to make cycles and irony seem synonymous. Not so for Stevens. To "go round and round" may indeed be ironic, as in the *Dance of the Macabre Mice*, or frustrating, as in *Sailing after Lunch*. But going round and round may also be a pleasure, as in some dancing or singing or going around on (and as) this earth. Hence, *The Pleasures of Merely Circulating*. Post-1934 history makes the tone of this W. S. Gilbert play with rounds and revolutions sound inappropriate.[4] Still, we may take the poem's point well enough. As with our dominant metaphors of light, so with our dominant metaphors of rounds. Stevens is not reversing these metaphors but trying to undo them.

In *Sailing after Lunch*, Stevens' old boat "goes round on a crutch." We usually read "goes round" as "goes around," that is, wanders here and there. But Stevens' general sailing metaphor suggests that he is also thinking here of the sailing term "going about," that is, circling so as to return on one's own path (which is what the Romantic must never do). If Stevens just drifts here and there, he needs some wind (inspiration, in the usual pun). If he is retracing his own path, then his sail is luffing, crutchlike, because he is sailing into the eye of the wind (yet another eye for stanza vi). He needs either some wind or a different tack in order to catch the wind. When a "light wind worries the sail," one might be uncertain of the problem. The whole metaphor holds for literary voyages too. At the end, as Stevens' boat rushes along, we are not told exactly what has solved the problem. Stevens crowds his closing metaphors, unable to resist a distracting "pupil-people" word-play. ("Expunge all people" sounds thematically pointless and etymologically threatening, as the "pierce" of *pungere* is too close for comfort to the "pupil" that follows.) But the allegory stays clear enough.

Sailing after Lunch is on the theme of the Romantic. Stevens' literary voyage uses a sailboat, with its easily allegorized sail and rudder and kinds of movement. His sail here is "heavy" and "historical," and his boat turns "vertiginous" by stanza iv—Rimbaud's drunken boat gone dizzy and getting nowhere. It all depends, as he says, on how one defines the Romantic. He himself consistently defines it in two ways, one pejorative and the other not. For the pejorative sense, and the usefulness of watery tropes for it, we might look at Paul Elmer More, whom Stevens was reading in 1906 and again in 1909.[5] More's essay with the telltale title, "The Drift of Romanticism," distinguishes two kinds of romance, historic romance as against the "mystery and wonder of classic art," the so-called principle of difference being the "expansive conceit of the emo-

[4] The reference is to W. S. Gilbert's "For he is an Englishman," from *H.M.S. Pinafore*. Revolutions in the thirties were safer for Swedish babies than for Spanish or German ones.
[5] Paul Elmer More, *Shelburne Essays*, series 8 (Boston: Houghton, 1913, 1967), p. xiii. Stevens quotes from the *Shelburne Essays* in a letter of 1909 (*L* 133).

124

tions which goes with the illusion of beholding the infinite within the stream of nature itself instead of apart from the stream." Stevens' poem might be written against just such a romantic-versus-classic alternative as More offers. A boat is neither within the stream of nature nor apart from the stream. *Sailing after Lunch* refuses such an either-or.

In all three opening poems, there is a tension of turning—a tension of will and desire in saying farewell and saying hail. The second poem, *Ghosts as Cocoons*, is a parable, echoing biblical language from the parable of the bridal feast. ("It is easy to say to those bidden. . . .") It is oddly disjointed in tone, and Stevens sounds close to breaking allegorical decorum, perhaps through both personal and social ambivalence. After all, "those to be born" include a new poetic self. Binding and rebinding is to the point here. "Her mind had bound me round," says the voice of *Farewell to Florida*, and then, "their mind . . . that will bind / Me round." The setting of will against desire makes this speaker sound like Ulysses versus the Sirens, especially when we hear the play on "bind" and remember that Stevens is "bound" for the North, as we say of traveling. Cocoons are also bound round and round. And ghosts as cocoons (not cocoons as ghosts) are not yet butterflies. In fact, Stevens mentions no cocoons in his text, just as he mentions no swans in *Invective against Swans*. We look for cocoons, and find them in the closing invocation to the bridal figure: "Come now, pearled and pasted, bloomy-leafed." "Pearled" bejewels the bride, but "pasted" questions her jewels (are they just paste?)—at least at first. Then we recognize that both words catch the strange, translucent look of a chrysalis just before it emerges as a butterfly, that moment when a seeming leaf that is actually a chrysalis does start to look "bloomy" as it pales, seeming to be "pearled and pasted." Stevens' high-style language and invocation recall the poem he is in fact rewriting, *To the One of Fictive Music*. It is not hard to work out the revision, and to see why *Ghosts as Cocoons* belongs with *Farewell to Florida* and *Sailing after Lunch*. For one thing, turning and re-turning is no easy, automatic matter. As with evening metaphors, so with the story of Psyche (apropos of cocoons and butterflies and a bride). We should not assume easy and automatic rebirth simply on repeating Psyche's story. We should not assume that Psyche's story never happens.

In *Autumn Refrain*, Stevens returns to the subject of birdsong, and to the area of echo and allusion, with a vigor that belies his theme of loss.

> The skreak and skritter of evening gone
> And grackles gone and sorrows of sun,
> Sorrows of sun, too, gone . . . the moon and moon,

125

The yellow moon of words about the nightingale
In measureless measures, not a bird for me
But the name of a bird and the name of a nameless air
I have never—shall never hear. And yet beneath
The stillness of everything gone, and being still,
Being and sitting still, something resides,
Some skreaking and skrittering residuum,
And grates these evasions of the nightingale
Though I have never—shall never hear that bird.
And the stillness is in the key, all of it is,
The stillness is all in the key of that desolate sound.

"The skreak and skritter of evening gone." But this is wrong, surely. The far-off curfew and the whole *Il Penseroso* evening tradition might be gone. Or the curfew tolling the knell of parting day and the great eighteenth-century model might be gone, or the oaten pipe of evening or twittering swallows. It is these evening sounds, and their attendant melancholy and meditation, for which we expect to hear elegies. Stevens begins his refrain well past obvious sorrows, and satires too. His first line is one of the noisiest lines he ever wrote, and all the noisier because we are expected to cut the sound effects abruptly with the last word.

"And grackles gone," too. Like "skreak and skritter," grackles belong only to a parodic or ironic evening tradition. Not only is the oaten pipe of evening gone; Stevens can not even sing like or of his old hoarse-throated birds. What then? Silence? Not quite. We should note that Stevens does not use the word "silence," but the word "stillness," not quite the same thing. The actual fall into silence of birdsong in autumn becomes a figure for the fall into stillness of all the pastoral pipes of evening, poetic grackles and nightingales both.

Stevens is remembering his own pastoral beginnings as well as his ironic or grackle reaction against pastoral. "Now I wish we could rest after so much disquisition and listen to what we have never heard. The wind has fallen. The moon has risen. We are where we have never been, listening to what we have never heard. We are in a dark place listening—contentedly, to—well, nightingales—why not? We are by a jubilant fountain . . . the round moon . . . the air moving, the water falling, and that sweet outpouring of liquid sound—fountains and nightingales—fountains and nightingales . . ." (*L* 149–50, July 20, 1909). In the best commentary we have on *Autumn Refrain*, John Hollander makes a case for Milton's nightingale as much as Keats's, and particularly the nightingale of Milton's first sonnet, where the young Milton wonders whether it is an emblem of love or of poetry.[6] Stevens' letter of 1909 is of both, and it includes not only moon and nightingale but also a refrain of "never . . . never heard," a refrain that he twice breaks in the poem, breaking off memory and breaking the flow of syntax: "I have never— shall never hear."

I want to argue for an even stronger ghostly presence of Milton in this Miltonic sonnet (or rather, variation on the Miltonic sonnet, as the turn comes in the middle of the seventh line, not the middle of the eighth). Stevens, fallen into stillness, cannot still Milton's line from *Lycidas*, "Grate on their scrannel Pipes of wretched straw." He has heard the "scr-grate" combination of St. Peter, chastising false shepherds, and he begins with an "scr-grackle" combination of sounds that makes us hear the word "grate" with peculiar force. There are yet more echoes in this sonnet. I hear that "yellow moon of words" echoing Whitman's "yellow half-moon . . . The yellow half-moon enlarged . . . the yellow and sagging moon" in *Out of the Cradle Endlessly Rocking*. Whitman's mockingbird is the American version of the European nightingale. In his bird poem, the words find a "key," "the key, the word up from the waves," the word being "death." Stevens finds only a musical "key" to his stillness, and a desolate not a triumphant sound in these echoes rebounding from Milton through Keats to Whitman.

Yet "something resides," grating. I do not want to suggest a triumph in this residuum, and certainly there is a sense of belatedness, both personal and vocational. But there is also an engagement with Milton that is anything but desolate. As always, we should keep an eye on Stevens' grammar. Consider the odd omission of a preposition after the verb "grates," an omission that requires us to remedy Stevens' silence and supply a preposition—or rather, three prepositions. For if "some . . . residium" grates *out* these evasions, it sounds out this poem itself, albeit like Milton's false, fallen voices. If it grates *on* these evasions as on ears, then it hurts them, and Stevens once loved both birds and the pastoral mode. If it grates *up* or breaks in pieces these evasions, it attempts to destroy them, for better or for worse. The evasion of univocal meaning here itself depends on silence, the ghostly silence of a defining preposition after "grates." Yet is not Stevens doing all these things at once? A refrain both makes a noise and refrains from making a noise, and (etymologically) breaks. The word "refrain" also "means regularly 'the birds' song' " in more than one language, to follow Leo Spitzer.[7]

[6] In "The Sound of the Music of Music and Sound," in *Wallace Stevens*, ed. Doggett and Buttel, pp. 248–50.

[7] *Classical and Christian Ideas of World Harmony: Prolegomena to an Interpretation*

127

When false shepherds "grate on their scrannel Pipes of wretched straw. The hungry sheep look up, and are not fed, / But swoln with wind. . . ." St. Peter is in *Lycidas* for pastoral reasons, including Christ's final pastoral charge to him, "Feed my lambs," a text that Stevens repeated in his *Adagia*, transferring the vocational charge to the poet.[8] I expect that some fear of false voice as well as silence is at work in *Autumn Refrain*. (Current readings of the poem hear chiefly the fear of silence.) Yet something else is at work. If these are Stevens' own evasions of the nightingale, then the argument moves as I have outlined. But the preposition "of" is ambiguous: the nightingales themselves may be evasive. If so, what Milton's scrannel pipe grates out in *Lycidas* is being defined as Milton's own evasions of the nightingale. Does the nightingale evade? Hollander hears the necessary evasion that all words are by definition. But this does not seem to me Stevens' concern here, as it is in, say, *The Man with the Blue Guitar*. Suppose we rephrase the question, and ask: does Milton's nightingale evade? Of course it does. And what it evades is precisely fall (autumn) or fallen or false voice—that entire "fall refrain" of Milton's. The voice of the nightingale is consistently a figure for his voice, and his mature poetic voice is by definition not false and hardly fallen. This is especially so of the nightingale simile in the Invocation to Light. (I do not mean any antinomian nonsense by this, and I am aware of discussions about the complexity of Milton's poetic voices. The point stands.) Keats heard this, and Stevens has too. In *Autumn Refrain*, I hear him accepting that he himself has an autumn voice but not a fallen or false voice—that is, questioning Milton's dialectic and turning it back on Milton himself. Stevens has listened to the topos of birds in the earthly paradise, as troped by Milton, Keats, and Whitman. He has added his own sonnet to the list, engaging with his great forerunners, learning tactics from them, elegizing what has gone, and finding a way of going on.

Does his meaning lie in the relation of the various readings? I think so. "Evading" and "evasion" are used in two senses by Stevens, one pejorative and the other benign. To evade by running away from nightingales and the words about them is weak. To evade by reversing them into grackles is only a little better. One helpful way of evading them is to remember what they themselves may evade, in the very power of their song. And since all these kinds of evasion are common enough responses,

---

of the Word "Stimmung" (Baltimore: The Johns Hopkins University Press, 1963), p. 180 n. 37, a long and fascinating note on "refrain."

[8] "Feed my lambs (on the bread of living)" (*OP* 178). "(Poet,) feed my lambs" (A. Walton Litz, "Particles of Order: The Unpublished Adagia," in *Wallace Stevens*, ed. Doggett and Buttel, p. 69).

so much the better if there is a way of suggesting all three at once, together with the tension among them.

Stevens implicitly directs us toward Milton's famous line in the poem following *Autumn Refrain, A Fish-Scale Sunrise*, the directing words being, "instruments of straw that you were playing." In 1936, he again returned to St. Peter's pastoral rebuke: "It is not that he was born in another land . . . and lives with us . . . Playing a crackled reed, wind-stopped, in bleats" (*OP* 66–67). In Milton, it is the poor sheep, the congregation, that are "swoln with wind." In Stevens, it is the shepherd—that is, the poet. Not only is his pastoral reed crackled but its windpipe is blocked—either from wind or even worse, by wind. It is no longer a pastoral but merely a sheepish pipe, and with no Keatsean pathos in the word "bleats." Stevens goes on to acknowledge such a St. Peter-Milton-Keats compound pastoral ghost within himself. Such self-knowledge makes possible the "crackled blade" in *Notes toward a Supreme Fiction* (*CP* 393), as well as the late echo of Milton's "grate," now only quietly "gritting," when the earth, poor,

> Touches, as one hand touches another hand,
> Or as a voice that, speaking without form,
> Gritting the ear, whispers humane repose. (*CP* 484)

For a clumsy example of echo and allusion in the thirties, we might listen to Stevens ironically distancing Eliot in the same 1936 poem that includes the crackled reed: "We regret we have no nightingale. / We must have the throstle on the gramophone" (*OP* 66)—Stevens archly (too archly) implying that when Eliot "Paces about the room again, alone, / He smooths his verse with automatic hand / And puts an old thrush on the gramophone." The revision of Eliot's birds in *Notes toward a Supreme Fiction* is much more subtle than this.

Stevens' 1936 poem, *Mystic Garden & Middling Beast*, is also clumsy work. The allusion, "mystic garden," identifies the attack.

> Hymns of the struggle of the idea of god
> And the idea of man, the mystic garden and
> The middling beast, the garden of paradise
> And he that created the garden and peopled it.
>
> (*CP* 185)

"He" is the poet who creates the "he" who peoples the garden, that is, God. Stevens is practicing nothing more hermetic here than a simple reversal of Milton's "not mystic garden" (*PL* ix.439–43): "Spot more delicious than those Gardens feign'd . . . Or that, not Mystic, where the Sapient King / Held dalliance with his fair *Egyptian* Spouse"—which is to say, the garden of the Song of Songs, a biblical and hence real garden for Milton. Stevens also revises Milton's "subtlest beast of all the field" to a "middling beast." Our own remembering ears expect a meddling beast, so that the echo, once heard, may meddle with all Milton's "middles." Stevens' world is emphatically a world of this middle earth.

"Vallombrosa of ears" in *Parts of a World* is obvious allusion and well handled. After that, comes the extraordinary engagement with Milton in the forties and fifties, at once radical revision and loving tribute. The negative side of revision is left behind, and Milton is celebrated, always within strict rhetorical and doctrinal limits. The allusive methods of *Sunday Morning* and *Autumn Refrain* proved most fertile for Stevens, as he absorbed and reworked his poetic inheritance. Where *Autumn Refrain* advances beyond *Sunday Morning* is in the dialectical use of echo. In *Autumn Refrain*, Stevens discovered how to turn an echo back against its author, not just set up a counterclaim. It is a method he would bring to perfection in the poetry of the forties and fifties.

Stevens takes one other step forward in this volume. He writes the extraordinary title poem, *The Idea of Order at Key West*. This is a poem about place and a genius loci—"place" as actual outside place, but "place" also in several senses of topos: as general and specific arguments appropriate to a seashore, especially the Key West seashore; as themes associated with a seashore; and as a place of voice, above all. I began this book with spirits of place and their culmination in two poems of place, *Domination of Black* and *The Snow Man*. I also began with blocking and our slight sense of displacement. This volume also begins with blocking—not a blocking of the reader, but the supposed blocking of the writer, as recorded in the opening poems. But *The Idea of Order at Key West* takes possession of all its places, attacking old ghosts and spirits. Here Stevens moves beyond the genius loci of the opening poems and of the Florida poems, and of the either-or of *Domination of Black* and *The Snow Man*.

Domination of Black started with Stevens' Wordsworthian 1899 poem, "I strode along my beaches like a sea, / The sand before me stretching firm and fair . . . now trembled far / In mystery beneath the evening star" (*SP* 29). In 1916, at the end, night comes striding—a Milton-Wordsworth strider, coming at the speaker and his fire with all the force of night, planets, and death spirits. Once we have heard the resonance of "came striding," we pay attention to the following line in *The Idea of Order at Key West*: "Then we, / As we beheld her striding there alone. . . ." "Alone," among other things, means unhaunted. The listeners ask of the singer's song, "Whose spirit is this?" and well they might if she sings and strides alone. *Ideas of Order* is full of ghosts and angels and spirits, some inimical, but this poem records a triumph over ghosts. Stevens builds on Wordsworth's structure in *Tintern Abbey*: a named place, a first-person narrator with a companion who is introduced late in the poem, the central word "spirit," an insistence on "blessed." But he will have nothing to do with "a motion and a spirit that impels all things." (By this time, he might have read Empson's tart and clear-headed remarks on Wordsworth's "attempt to be uplifting yet non-denominational" in *Tintern Abbey*.[9]) Stevens will not,

> like an agent of the one great Mind
> Create, creator and receiver both,
> Working but in alliance with the works
> Which it beholds.
>
> (*Prelude* ii.257–60)

He avoids the word "creator," going back to the older words, "maker" and "artificer." He avoids all the language of the inspired poet-prophet or bard. The woman does not half-perceive and half-create anything; she is the single artificer of her song. She is what the listeners behold—not a woman made into addressee, listener, younger self, and spirit of place, as Wordsworth made Dorothy. Stevens' woman sings her own song, and she is treated as a fellow craftsman. Geoffrey Hartman speaks of the link between Wordsworth's own "genial spirits" (*Tintern Abbey* 113) and the genius loci, and he notes Wordsworth's various "apostrophes not only to powers of the earth, beings of the hills, and spirits of the springs, but also to 'genii' who form the poet by means of gentle or severer visitations."[10] Stevens refuses to link the poet's genius and the genius loci in this way. His closing apostrophe is to the "blessed rage for order," and his sea does not have a knowable spirit. It is an inverse ghost—not a spirit shorn of body but a body shorn of a knowable spirit. Not a corpse, for it has motion and sound, "like a body wholly body," as far as we can know it. Thus the sea as "ever-hooded," a wonderfully apt compound adjective, more memorable than all *The Comedian*'s oceanic rhetoric. Visually, it works like the famous Hokusai wave, hood-shaped at the point of greatest gathering; conceptually, it reminds us that we cannot truly and finally know outside reality; symbolically, it recalls death's traditional garb, which may hide a skeleton or simply vacancy, mere air.

[9] In *Seven Types of Ambiguity* (London: Penguin, 1930, 1972), p. 183.
[10] Geoffrey H. Hartman, *Wordsworth's Poetry, 1787–1814* (New Haven and London: Yale University Press, 1964, 1971), p. 212.

Yet the sea is present, even if it is not allowed mind or voice, let alone words. And, "It may be that in all her phrases stirred / The grinding water and the gasping wind." In *The Man Whose Pharynx Was Bad*, the wind blows, stirring no poet in his sleep. Now Stevens' wind blows again, but he is on his guard against all those old figures of inspiration, including his roaring wind at the end of *Harmonium*. "It may be" that, somehow, "in" her words (but how, "in"?) there stirred the "gasping wind." That wind gasps in descriptive accuracy, to be sure, but also as if in surprise—surprise that its own mastery of inspiration is being questioned. "Whose spirit is this?" the listeners ask. Not the old spiritus-wind Romantic afflatus. It is enough to make any wind gasp. As with the sea, who can scour her own tropes, so with the wind, which can gasp in astonishment or gasp for breath or gasp in exhaustion, as when giving up the ghost—a very apt thought. Stevens is testing his ghosts and spirits of many a year.

So also with the "grinding water," which moves on from Arnold's grating roar of the sea on pebbles.[11] Arnold's is a late Romantic sea. Stevens' sea is anti-Romantic, withdrawing from even the cadences of Arnold's sea, while still recalling their "gr-" force. He is not specific about the cause of the grinding noise, so that we also hear other appropriate senses of the word—as if the sea could crush and oppress, but equally could grind figurative teeth at losing its power over human imagination. Stevens knows what he is doing, as we realize from *Autumn Refrain* or from these lines from *Harmonium*: "a voice / Rougher than a grinding shale" (*CP* 103). This is standard Arnoldian usage. In 1934, Stevens does something different.

In *Domination of Black*, Stevens contrasted the great lights of the night sky with a small human light, a fire. It became a favorite contrast for him, and he uses it here, this time making the lights on the rigging of fishing boats his human example. This was a conjunction he had marked casually from his New York roof in 1911: "Bye and bye, the stars came out—and down by the docks, the lanterns on the masts flickered" (*L* 171, August 20, 1911). It is important to visualize Stevens' closing scene in *Idea of Order at Key West*; we need to see the lights of the fishing boats against the sky as well as in the sea:

> tell why the glassy lights,
> The lights in the fishing boats at anchor there,
> As the night descended, tilting in the air,

11 It may owe something itself to *Tintern Abbey*: "the still, sad music of humanity, / Nor harsh, nor grating"; *Dover Beach*: "the grating roar . . . the eternal note of sadness . . . of human misery."

Mastered the night and portioned out the sea,
Fixing emblazoned zones and fiery poles,
Arranging, deepening, enchanting night.

Oh! Blessed rage for order, pale Ramon,
The maker's rage to order words of the sea,
Words of the fragrant portals, dimly-starred,
And of ourselves and of our origins,
In ghostlier demarcations, keener sounds.

Such small human lights mark out an order, but we may underestimate this order if we do not listen well to Stevens' words "poles" and "zones." These are terms we use when we "master the night" and "portion out the sea." The polestar and the five zones of earth help us master the night. And the sea, says Rimbaud, is *lassé de poles et de zones*. Zones or lines of longitude are seen on a map of the world, not on actual sea or land, and they are certainly "ghostly demarcations." Yet they are hardly unconnected with reality. Before the lines of longitude were conceived, navigation was far more hazardous. We are now much more masters of the sea, having thought of that idea of order for all that welter. Paradoxically, such demarcations as Mercator's lines become ghostlier as they sink into our minds, accepted as ideas of order, as part of reality. They then also seem to sink into the landscape, much as the old genius loci was conceived as part of the landscape. Flying in a plane, we can think casually that we are passing over some line of longitude, or that we have passed the international date line and lost a day. (That is a very ghostly demarcation, with a genius loci, waiting on a boundary line to give or take a day of our lives.) "Keener sounds" are sharper, in a scale up to keenest where the sound would vanish from ordinary human hearing. So also "acutest" in "She made the sky acutest at its vanishing." An acute angle can become acuter, then acutest when it is 0 degrees and vanishes. (The top angle of a boat's rigging is always an acute angle.) Stevens opens with a human agent singing beyond the genius of the sea. He closes on a sound and a desire for sound that will go beyond and beyond, keener than any genius loci, whose old calling is faintly heard in Stevens' word, for spirits and ghosts also wail or keen.

Stevens deepens and enchants as well as ordering the night. He does so by conceiving of a rage for order, and a rage to order, not just the idea of order. He used the word "blessed" in conjunction with rage earlier, in *Nomad Exquisite*, and with biblical force. So also Hoon, forerunner of the singer here, was given the force of biblical language. But Stevens' sense of place now goes beyond anything in *Harmonium*. Neither romantic rage nor classical order, this rage for order becomes, godlike, a rage to order. "Raging" is a common epithet for the sea, so that Stevens' word orders up the sea's most memorable raging words: the psalmist's "Thou rulest the raging of the sea" (89:19); Shakespeare's unbounded sea that raises the question, "How with this rage shall beauty hold a plea?"; Milton's outrageous sea, outrageous or acting ultra (beyond) even before the Fall. (The "rage" in "outrage" is an English-language bonus that owes nothing to etymology.) The sea itself seems to go beyond any possible controlling or ordering; thus, at least, in Crispin's story. Stevens is aware of this "beyond" pattern for tropes of the sea, and he sets about limiting it from the start: "She sang beyond the genius of the sea."

Such "arranging, deepening, enchanting night" is something different from Stevens' more usual contrast with Blake's or Yeats's "cold star-bane." Here, turning away at the end of the song, away from sea and stars and sky, and the long history of their troping, turning toward town, this pair sees a port. Those are fishing boats, ordinary working boats at anchor, with their own methods of mapping and measuring and calculating their course, like Stevens' two poetic craft at the start of this volume. Stevens' "ghostlier" is more spiritual, to go by its root sense. Along with "keener," it suggests that sight and sound both might be moved further in a quieter, fuller mastery. It suggests a way of going on.

CHAPTER SEVEN

*   *   *   *   *

Concerning the Nature of Things:

The Man with the Blue Guitar

I desire my poem to mean as much, and as deeply,
as a missal. (*L* 790, July 12, 1953)

The Man with the Blue Guitar is pivotal in Stevens' work, at once a
review and a new direction, a refinding of vocation and a preliminary to
the major long poems of the forties. The series has a certain austerity,
and Stevens himself conceded some boring patches, but rightly judged
the poem's overall strength: "THE MAN WITH THE BLUE GUITAR . . . while
it bores me in spots, is a very much better book than IDEAS OF ORDER" (*L*
338, April 27, 1939). Stevens' effects are sometimes abrupt or com-
pacted; there is occasional bitterness and disgust, and the poem ap-
proaches desperation in the middle cantos. It is the record of a struggle.
In terms of subject matter, we are watching Stevens reconsidering the
subject of place, "place" in a very broad sense of the word. The subject
of eros hardly enters the poem. The subject of belief is central, as Ste-
vens' echoes and allusions make clear. He is beginning his move from
the "imagination-reality" axis toward the subject of the supreme fiction.
The importance of Stevens' word-play lies not so much in particular ef-
fects, skilled as these are. It lies in the relation of poetry as "play" to
"things are they are." Or, using Stevens' repeated rhyme, "guitar" and
"things as they are." Stevens comes to desire a necessary balance be-
tween these two sets of terms, and he shows an increasing mistrust of
poetry not thus balanced. One example is pure poetry, and, by implica-
tion, idealized theories of the imagination.

135

Guitar-playing is Stevens' figure for writing poetry—playing on a popular instrument (of ancient origin to be sure), and an instrument he himself played, though not very well, if we are to believe him.[1] He makes his poetic guitar do many things in this series. Not only does it play in the musical sense; it extends the word "play" itself. A. Walton Litz distinguishes three kinds of play in the poem: "The word 'play' [in canto xxxiii] must be taken in all its senses—the senses of the guitar, the senses of an actor's role, and the ultimate sense of poetry as a liberating game with words which renews our feeling for reality."[2] I am going to argue a little with that word "feeling," but first I want to pause over Litz's first two senses of play, guitar-playing and actor's playing. My interest in this chapter is twofold: first, Stevens' renewed and enlarged sense of vocation; second, the concept of *serio ludere* (to choose an old term), the paradoxical seriousness of some play. Such paradoxical seriousness may inform our sense of musical and dramatic playing. It should inform much more, as Stevens' play with balancing and with echo and allusion makes clear.

Stevens represents many different guitar sounds and types of music. Even if we try to confine ourselves to the representation of acoustic sound and to types of music, other matters keep intruding. How do we listen to these musics? How do types of music correspond with genres? How do we read allegories of chord and discord? How do we hear word-play on the word "playing" itself? The poem will not allow us to separate serio and ludere neatly in all this troping of music.

Stevens begins with an audience request for a tune and tries to sing a "serenade." He then turns savagely noisy: "to bang it . . . Jangling the metal of the strings"; then alters the sound, "picks its way . . . This buzzing of the blue guitar." The audience responds in canto v, still desiring music, hymns in fact, "even in the chattering of your guitar." In viii, "impassioned choirs, / Crying among the clouds" inspire only a mere "lazy, leaden twang . . . twang." By canto xv, Stevens' voice is bitter and self-scourging; he refers to a popular, relaxed tune, which we perforce hear sardonically. And in xvi, one can only "chop the sullen psaltery"—a small masterpiece of a line. In xvii, claws and fangs play on the shell of the guitar, or rather, "propound" and "articulate" (two important words in *Notes toward a Supreme Fiction*). The tentative recovery

---

[1] L 95, 110–11, and cf. the title "Sur Ma Guzzla Gracile," *Poetry* 19 (October 1921). In 1953, Stevens wrote: "Are you visiting some new scene? A young man in a new scene, a new man in a young scene, a young man in a young scene—excuse my guitar" (L 767). He is strumming a charm refrain.

[2] A. Walton Litz, *Introspective Voyager: The Poetic Development of Wallace Stevens* (New York: Oxford University Press, 1972), p. 257.

of canto xviii becomes stronger in xix, where a lute is introduced, usually an auspicious instrument. Here a "monstrous lute" must be reduced to a plain "lute," and played, for this is a dragon-slaying canto, a confrontation with Stevens' own mental monsters.

The irrepressible canto xxiii opens the last third of the poem and may even outline its cantos. (I hear a Dantean total of thirty-three cantos altogether, divided into three parts of eleven cantos each.) Canto xxiii proposes a wildly funny set of duets—a few "final solutions," as Stevens says, preparing for this poem's finale, and playing on doctrines of last things, and against falsely solemn teleologies and eschatologies. Even Goethe does not escape, as Stevens sets *Dichtung* playing against *Wahrheit*. Canto xxiv, largely visual, ends simply, "I play. But this is what I think." (It takes just a little longer before thinking and playing are not opposed.) The clown canto, xxv, has a background refrain of "ay-yi-yi," while its "liquid cats / Moved in the grass without a sound." In canto xxvi, "A mountainous music always seemed / To be falling and to be passing away"—a multiple play on words. Canto xxxii, a general favorite, is full of play, though it does not use the word. Canto xxxiii ends the series with "play" in a rich and full sense of the word, to which I shall return.

We might pause over one example of musical play, which raises questions of genre, of the hero, and of the relation of artist and audience. Canto ii defines itself as a serenade:

> I sing a hero's head, large eye
> And bearded bronze, but not a man,
>
> Although I patch him as I can
> And reach through him almost to man.
>
> If to serenade almost to man
> Is to miss, by that, things as they are,
>
> Say that it is the serenade
> Of a man that plays a blue guitar.

If Stevens had said, "I sing a hero," we would hear the formula for epic openings, another variation on, say, "Arms and the man I sing." But he says, "I sing a hero's head . . . but not a man." Is this just simple limitation (as he said) or simple irony? A play against synecdoche? (We read "arms" in "arms and the man" as a synecdoche for war. Stevens tells us not to read "head" as a synecdoche for man, thereby cutting off that head from old familiar ways of reading.) Or is it a literalization of "head," as if we read Virgil's "Arms and the man" and saw arms as limbs, not armor? Stevens' ironic self-limiting leaves uncomfortable questions. Have heroes and leaders become so cheapened that not even a "hero's head" is fit for song in 1937? Virgil became the voice of empire, of a civilization, of a time. Has epic itself so declined that only a serenade is left for the serious writer? The following cantos, iii and iv (the hero and people cantos, or the high and low mimetic cantos), come close to parody. Canto iii catches and lays out man number one, like a trophy or a Pennsylvania bird (as Stevens said) or a Prometheus (as he did not say). The canto has a subtext of "display" versus "play," and Stevens keeps ambiguous the question of who plays and how. The polarity of hero and masses is very ambivalently seen and heard. Is this also the artist displaying himself at whatever cost? Or is the audience playing and thus displaying the artist? Is there a complicity? In any case, the display is murderous. If epic and epic heroes have gone, it is not a serenade that takes their place. This kind of music murders to display.

Stevens' master clown offers an instance of Litz's second sense of "play," the playing of an actor. The master clown whirls the world on his nose, like any master.

> He held the world upon his nose
> And this-a-way he gave a fling.
>
> His robes and symbols, ay-yi-yi—
> And that-a-way he twirled the thing.

An insouciant figure, this clown displays a mastery so complete that it is play, as with Hazlitt's Shakespeare: "He turned the globe round for his amusement" ("On Shakespeare and Milton"). To hold the world on one's nose, like a ball, is a clown's trick. It is a balancing act, just what is desired in another canto: "So it is to sit and to balance things / To and to and to the point of still" (xxix). Not Eliot's still point of the turning world in *Burnt Norton*, just published in 1935, but a balance, and "the balance does not quite rest" (xxix). Still, "the nose is eternal, that-a-way." Too early for Chaplin's balloon scene in *The Great Dictator*, this canto may owe something to Baudelaire's whirling-world, spinning-top figure in some of his remarks on color.[3] Stevens' continual use of the verb "turn" as "trope" makes this figure a master troper, flinging and twirling, with appropriate robes for his magical proceedings. Although he "cannot bring a world quite round" (ii), this turning figure makes *the* world go round.

---

[3] "La nature ressemble à un toton qui, mû par une vitesse accelerée, nous apparaît gris, bien qu'il résume en lui, toutes les couleurs," *Baudelaire: Oeuvres Complètes* (Paris: Editions du Seuil, 1968), p. 231.

There are other actors in the series, and also a mask, which belongs, unexpectedly, to a Franciscan don. Giving a mask to a "clerical figure"[4] is not in the least ironic, for this clerical figure must also perform a mental balancing act. He must balance the world his church makes (as in the "lean Review" and the cathedral) with what he observes elsewhere. He does so through a "fertile glass," part of all the mirroring in the series. And the balancing acts of clown and don become a figure for our own mental balancing acts as we consider the world "both as [we] see it and as it is," to use Stevens' terms (*L* 316, March 17, 1937). Like musical play, the actor's or clown's play seems to belong to the ludic part of *serio ludere*, while our mental reflections are, of course, serious. Stevens will not allow us quite so naive a sense of "play."

We might begin considering Litz's third sense of "play" by thinking about balance. "Play," says Litz, should also be taken in "the ultimate sense of poetry as a liberating game with words which renews our feeling for reality." Stevens' whole poem balances on the repeated rhyme of "guitar" and "things as they are," or the play of "poetry" and of "reality." It balances or is pivotal in other ways too. If we read it with Stevens' earlier and later work in mind, we may see it as a crossing place for him. It is also a poem that tries out or balances arguments—or tries out or balances rhetoric—until it finds the right one or the closest one. The first two-thirds has more imbalance than steadiness, as Stevens shows us settlements that are too easily achieved, then challenges them, and revises them. (For example, canto xxxii rewrites canto vi.) "It is the chord that falsifies," says canto xi, closing the first third, and recalling how much falsifying accord Stevens has fought in cantos i through x. We might then casually suppose that the clash of discord will provide truth. But Stevens moves away from such a falsehood-truth axis. "The discord merely magnifies," he rhymes, quite unexpectedly. And the poem, as if to illustrate, moves toward its nadir in cantos xv and xvi. Overeasy settlement gives way to overeasy succumbing and confusion.

Stevens also rewrites the dark cantos of the middle, as his poem comes to "balance things / To and to and to the point of still." Strength in this poem comes from the tension of contraries, not from the conquering of one contrary by another.

It may be that one or the other of Stevens' two forces, "imagination" and "reality," always tries to take over. So also it may be that one or the other of serio or ludere tries to take over. (Serio has mostly won, as Jacques Derrida keeps pointing out.) This is to "live at war" (xvi), but it

---

[4] "I have no doubt that I intended to use the word don with reference to a clerical figure" (*L* 784, June 25, 1953).

is not how Stevens ends. He ends with a "wrangling of two dreams" rather than a prevailing by one. He begins to probe for a center, and finds, not a still point, but a balance, a "wrangling of two dreams," a wrestling of Jacob with the angel. If the "play" of poetry seems to us like the ludic half of serio ludere, or the circuses half of bread and circuses, we should think again. Stevens will trope poetry as bread at the end, and work to enlarge our sense of circuses, as of play. (There are social implications to all this, though, as Stevens said, they are not his primary concern here.) This is the first caution, then: that we want to beware of cheap and silly notions of the words "play," "ludic," and so on.

So also we want to beware of cheap and silly notions of "things as they are." Stevens emphasizes the phrase by his way of rhyming. The man who rhymed "guitar" and "catarrh" in 1922 is playing on a very differ-ent kind of rhyme. He repeats it eleven times in all, and he also varies it; "things as they are" changes to "things as they were" or "things as I think they are" or "as we are." Only very occasionally does Stevens offer another end-rhyme.

One of Stevens' unnoticed echoes may surprise us if we assume that "things as they are" is an obvious phrase. Or that "things as they are" is an impossible subject. It can sound as vague as the subject "concerning the nature of things," on which we nonetheless have a classic poem that Stevens relates to his own if we listen carefully to canto xxiii:

> . . . as in a refrain
> One keeps playing year by year,
> Concerning the nature of things as they are.

Stevens' other echoes and allusions confirm the desires of his seemingly modest guitar-playing: the Bible, Dante, Milton, Goethe, as well as Lu-cretius. "Things as they are" need not be reductive. Quite the contrary. We all tend to fill in the blank for the phrase "things as they are," and our filler tends to be bleak, and preceded by "but." This common sense of "things as they are" may be found in remarks by Stevens in 1903 and 1905 (L 68, 82). But in The Man with the Blue Guitar, "things as they are" is more question than assertion, the question being: well, how are they then?

Stevens begins by making clear that we cannot finally or exactly know or play "things as they are" because they are unknowable. Or at least we cannot play things "exactly as they are"; an artist can reach "almost to man" but not all the way. "I cannot bring a world quite round," says the guitarist in a fine play on the word "round." To read it as adjective: he cannot bring a world that is a perfect round, but then the earth is a flattened sphere anyway. To read it as adverb: he cannot bring round, or completely realize, a world. Or even, he cannot bring round or reconcile such a world for us, to use Coleridge's word for what the imagination does. (It "reveals itself in the balance or reconciliation of opposite or discordant qualities" [*Biographia Literaria*, ch. 14]. Stevens' balance is not of this sort.) The world remains stubbornly there, and will not be "brought round" by any poet, or by anyone at all. Physicists and art historians can keep our thinking clear in this matter. To quote Einstein and Infeld: "Physical concepts are free creations of the human mind, and are not, however it may seem, uniquely determined by the external world. . . . [Man] will never be able to compare his picture with the real mechanism and he cannot even imagine the possibility or the meaning of such a comparison."[5] A similar point, loosely speaking, is made by E. H. Gombrich in his attack on Ruskin's notion of the "innocent eye," an eye that supposes it actually can see "things as they are."[6] We may hear Stevens' remarks about *The Man with the Blue Guitar* in terms of Gombrich's ideas of order or schemata (the "world about me . . . as I see it") and outside world (the "world about me . . . as it is"). Stevens would then be "mixing and matching," to use Gombrich's terms, or, to use his own terms, dealing with the painter's problem of realization: "[The poem] deal[s] with the relation or balance between imagined things and real things which, as you know, is a constant source of trouble for me. . . . Perhaps it would be better to say that what they really deal with is the painter's problem of realization: I have been trying to see the world about me both as I see it and as it is. This means seeing the world as an imaginative man sees it" (*L* 316, March 17, 1937).

Though it is impossible to know "things as they are," this is what the guitarist's audience wants, indeed demands. Not for them speculative questions on the nature of things. It would be easy to dismiss this as philistine, but Stevens' gloss is without irony: "in [canto] I the poet was required to express people beyond themselves because that is exactly the way they are. Their feelings demonstrate the subtlety of people" (*L* 359, August 8, 1940). To paraphrase Wilde: people desire to see themselves as they really are not. Stevens' point is that people *are* in fact as they

[5] Albert Einstein and Leopold Infeld, *The Evolution of Physics from Early Concepts to Relativity and Quanta* (New York: Simon & Schuster, 1938), p. 31.

[6] E. H. Gombrich, *Art and Illusion: A Study in the Psychology of Pictorial Representation*, 2d ed. (Princeton: Princeton University Press, 1969). On *The Man with the Blue Guitar* and painting, see Rajeev S. Patke, *The Long Poems of Wallace Stevens: An Interpretative Study* (Cambridge: Cambridge University Press, 1985), pp. 69–80. More generally, see Bonnie Costello, "Effects of an Analogy: Wallace Stevens and Painting," in *Wallace Stevens: The Poetics of Modernism*, ed. Albert Gelpi (Cambridge: Cambridge University Press, 1985), pp. 65–85.

really are not; that is, their desire to see themselves expressed "beyond themselves" is part of what they are. If the proposition of canto i is naive, the desire behind it is not. We should not reduce the audience's demand to a desire to see themselves idealized. Rather, I think Stevens means that audience as much as artist reaches toward "reality," toward "things as they are." Despite all that divides artist and audience in canto i, Stevens begins with what unites them.

Two things are exceedingly important in this poem. First, Stevens thinks of "imagination" and "reality" as equally significant. Second, he insists that they best exist for us in tension. (My quotation marks indicate that the unhelpful terms are Stevens' own; each is best defined on a sliding scale, as Northrop Frye most usefully demonstrates.[7]) Years of student essays demonstrate how difficult it is for us to allow equal significance to reality and imagination. We tend toward seeing the imagination as secondary or even trivial, or else exalting it and debasing reality in proportion. Stevens refuses to do so, which means that he will be no party to any idealistic monism, nor to theories of mystical "pure poetry."

The question of pure poetry was running through Stevens' mind at this time, as his letters demonstrate, and a 1936 essay spends some time on Abbé Brémond's once-popular theory of *poésie pure*.[8] Litz parallels Stevens' two different uses of the term "pure poetry" with Croce's in his 1933 *Defense of Poetry*.[9] I want to add one caution. Again and again in the thirties, Stevens qualifies the word "pure." He explicitly or implicitly insists that poetry for him is tied to earth, or, in a better metaphor, wants the earth. As in *The Man with the Blue Guitar*, imagination must be balanced or called by or rooted in or struggle with a reality that has equal validity. Analyzing Stevens' different senses of pure poetry, we may tend to forget this most important condition. Stevens' insistence on balance and not hierarchy is important for any discussion of idealist theories of the imagination.

[7] Northrop Frye, "Wallace Stevens and the Variation Form," in *Literary Theory and Structure: Essays in Honor of William K. Wimsatt*, ed. F. Brady, J. Palmer, and M. Price (New Haven and London: Yale University Press, 1973), pp. 395–414.

[8] *OP* 221–23. Cf. Henri Brémond, *La poésie pure* (Paris: Grasset, 1926), and *Prière et poésie* (Paris: Grasset, 1926).

[9] Litz, "Wallace Stevens' Defense of Poetry: *La poésie pure*, the New Romantic, and the Pressure of Reality," in *Romantic and Modern: Revaluations of Literary Tradition*, ed. George Bornstein (Pittsburgh: University of Pittsburgh Press, 1977), pp. 111–32. See also Milton Bates, *Wallace Stevens: A Mythology of Self*, pp. 127–55. More generally, see D. J. Mossop, *Pure Poetry: Studies in French Poetic Theory and Practice 1746–1945* (Oxford: Clarendon, 1971). Cf. also Margaret Peterson, *Wallace Stevens and the Idealist Tradition* (Ann Arbor: UMI Research Press, 1983).

This, I think, is part of the explanation of what happens to a whole world of "whiteness" in *The Man with the Blue Guitar* and elsewhere. "Whiteness" and cognate words belong to a religious vocabulary sometimes appropriated by the imagination. But idealized imagination as a kind of displaced faith will not survive, severed from reality. At least, that is how I read Stevens' attack on the immaculate, the moon, and the incandescent imagination.

Light first enters *The Man with the Blue Guitar* as underground light in canto v, originally titled "The Place of Poetry: On Earth":

> Do not speak to us of the greatness of poetry,
> Of the torches wisping in the underground,
>
> Of the structure of vaults upon a point of light.
> There are no shadows in our sun. . . .

A wisp is a small twist of straw or hair, or a bit of smoke; as a participle, it sounds like a diminutive whisper, so that Stevens' imperative opening seems to make Dante's flames (the shades of the dead) utter small sibilants. "Torches" are obviously man-made flames, perhaps of wisps, made to light up underground structures—Stevens implying a little clumsily that it is Dante's own imagination that lights up his underworld. Or his heaven, for all that, since heaven is also an imagined vault upon a point of light, the point or *punto* that is God. The word "punto" is important in Dante; Stevens is using allusive echo. His thrice-repeated "There are no shadows" is set against both classical and Dantean shades, and Eliot's "shadows" too. It is also set against any view of the earth as itself a shadow, compared with the true light of heaven. The blue guitar is not to imply a blue heaven; the guitar is colorless for the first time.

Canto vii has an odd-sounding argument. We call the moon "immaculate": yes, fine, despite its spots. But "good . . . the merciful good"? This sounds like language appropriate for Mary as the Virgo Immaculata. Stevens' gloss also uses biblical language, the familiar language of the Twenty-third Psalm: "I so often speak to the moon, calling it mercy and goodness." Insofar as the moon is a symbol of the human imagination, Stevens could stand in moonlight and use devotional language. Or so we say. But we might note how often the word "immaculate" is equivocal in Stevens. One example is combative. "The sheep-like falling-in of distances" (*OP* 62) was first written as "The immaculate falling-in of distances"—the change emphasizing how obediently those distances fall into line (into the line of the horizon, into the poetic line, into the usual line of thought about horizons and poetry). In *The Man with the Blue Guitar*, we need to listen with special care to Stevens' turn against the apparently straightforward word "immaculate" (vii) when he comes to canto xiii:

> The pale intrusions into blue
> Are corrupting pallors . . . ay di me,
>
> Blue buds or pitchy blooms. Be content—
> Expansions, diffusions—content to be
>
> The unspotted imbecile revery,
> The heraldic center of the world
>
> Of blue, blue sleek with a hundred chins,
> The amorist Adjective aflame. . . .

"Unspotted" is the Germanic equivalent of "immaculate," and words like "immaculate," "pale," and "white," can themselves be coercing, even "corrupting." And "corrupting" in the strong biblical sense of the word, where corruption is a synonym of decay and death. (We lay up treasures in heaven where no moths corrupt, or we are sown in corruption and raised incorruptible.) Stevens' exercise is much like Melville's remarkable exercise in the chapter entitled "The Whiteness of the Whale" in *Moby-Dick*. "Corrupting pallors" tells us what words like "immaculate," "white," "pale," "pallor," and "candid" may become and do, as they intrude into blue. They may become pale blue, that is, strongly imagined as heavenly reality, or, for all that, the contrary, hellish ("pitchy") reality. Stevens' puzzling double gloss on this canto in fact makes perfect sense. His first comment was: "the amorist Adjective means blue (the amorist Adjective) as a word metamorphised into blue as a reality" (*L* 783, June 18, 1953). A few days later, he rightly corrected any notion that this "reality" was real for him; the canto "has to do with pure imagination," he wrote (*L* 785, June 29, 1953). Canto xiii "is a poem that deals with the intensity of the imagination unmodified by contacts with reality, *if such a thing is possible*. Intensity becomes something incandescent. . . . The poem has to do with pure imagination" (my italics). Stevens is past the easy satire of his antireligious poetry in *Harmonium*. He is also past the easy appropriation of religious vocabulary. There is a kind of fattening on such words. They can fatten one past a double chin to "a hundred chins," and never make a muscle. Stevens is now too rigorous with himself for that.

"Immaculate," that is, "unspotted," is now associated with "imbecile," a synonym for the more usual moon adjective, "lunatic." (Stevens makes the same substitution in 1945: "As one of the secretaries of the moon, / The queen of ignorance, you have deplored / How she presides over imbeciles" [CP 333].) *Amoureuse flamme* is so conventional a French phrase that it seems to echo behind Stevens' attack on the adjective. (Why is he so wary of adjectives? The muted discussion goes on in 1949 [CP 475]. Are they too easily added and so unearned?)

Canto xv reacts against the various lights of xii and xiv—"incandescent," "chandelier," "candle"—and the reaction is extreme.

> Is this picture of Picasso's, this "hoard
> Of destructions," a picture of ourselves,
>
> Now, an image of our society?
> Do I sit, deformed, a naked egg,
>
> Catching at Good-bye, harvest moon,
> Without seeing the harvest or the moon?
>
> Things as they are have been destroyed.
> Have I? Am I a man that is dead
>
> At a table on which the food is cold?
> Is my thought a memory, not alive?
>
> Is the spot on the floor, there, wine or blood
> And whichever it may be, is it mine?

This is an ekphrastic canto, recreating and interpreting a Picasso painting with the Picasso properties of food on a table and a bottle of wine. Picasso's phrase, which Stevens could have read in *Cahiers d'Art* for 1935, is *somme de destructions*.[10] Stevens' translation as "hoard" adds the sense of something saved and treasured, possibly a word-hoard. (He punned on his own translation in 1951 by varying it to "horde" [NA 161], a fine personifying of Picasso's notion.) The light is presumably moonlight; there is a spot on the floor that cannot be interpreted. This is a different phase of the moon from canto vii's immaculate, good, merciful moon.

Stevens' sinister closure is a study in the poetics of the question. One answer is: yes, the wine or blood is mine, and I am a dead man, with the immaculate moon now only a spot on the floor, and not white but red, not light but spilled wine or blood. Stevens plays with memory here, including the memory of the immaculate good as the incarnate, sacrificed Christ, though the fleeting memory of transubstantiation or communion is "not alive" for Stevens. The table here is purely earthly, as is the last supper—perhaps just the latest supper in a still life painting, but perhaps the final supper in a painting of *nature morte*. To catch at the moon is

---

[10] See Litz, *Introspective Voyager*, p. 238; Judith Rinde Sheridan, "The Picasso Connection: Wallace Stevens' 'Man with the Blue Guitar,'" *Arizona Quarterly* 35 (1979), 77–89.

foolish fantasy that does not see the moon any more than the catch or refrain, "Shine on, harvest moon." (Surely not "Good-bye, harvest moon?") We usually read the last question as rhetorical, with an implied yes or as-good-as-yes to the deadly question. But there are other answers. One is literal, in Picasso's terms: no, it is a spot of red paint. Which is to say that allegories of destruction are read into paintings as much as allegories of progression. That might lead to the either-or impasse of *The Comedian*. But the man who worked through the evening and light troping of *Ideas of Order* is not going to return to such an impasse. What happens in the end to light, we shall see in the final canto.

When Stevens says that canto xiii "has to do with pure imagination," he does not say *what* it has to do. Surely it is skeptical or at least wary of "pure" imagination, as it is at least wary of a whole family of white and pure words. In Stevens' remarks on Abbé Brémond's theory of pure poetry, he carefully distances his own sense of pure poetry from such mysticism. We may hear an example of such distancing at the end: "The poet . . . must be possessed, along with everything else, by the earth and by men in their earthy implications. . . . We know Sweeney as he is and, for the most part, prefer him that way and without too much effulgence and, no doubt, always shall" (*OP* 229, 1936). Who are "we"? Not Eliot, we say at first, not the Eliot who thought apelike Sweeney's heavy beard looked like "maculate giraffe." Eliot would like a Sweeney shining with effulgence, with Miltonic, celestial effulgence, an immaculate Sweeney. Or would he? Eliot the poet surely prefers Sweeney as he is—earthy, a useful *homme moyen sensuel*. If Sweeney were not there, Eliot would have to invent him.

The same insistence on the "earthy," and a submerged quarrel with Abbé Brémond's *poésie pure*, help explain Stevens' play on the word "animal" in canto xvii.

> The person has a mould. But not
> Its animal. The angelic ones
>
> Speak of the soul, the mind. It is
> An animal. The blue guitar—
>
> On that its claws propound, its fangs
> Articulate its desert days.

We are used to thinking of etymology when we hear words like "anima" and "animate." But "animal"? Yet the word "animal" has the same etymology. Stevens is using it in its older and etymologically purer sense of "a living being." Some unpublished notes to Renato Poggioli make this clear. " 'IT is an animal'—the soul. The body has a shape. The soul

146

does not. The soul is the animal of the body."[11] We tend to read the above lines using the modern sense of "animal," and so read "animal" as roughly synonymous with the body. In restoring the old sense, Stevens questions the whole history that has lowered this word, philologically speaking. He also conducts an undercover war with Abbé Brémond (my nomination for an "angelic one"). Brémond took over Claudel's "Animus" and "Anima," or "l'esprit et l'âme."[12] Stevens translates these as "the soul, the mind," in line 3, and decides to retranslate the soul as an "animal"—not a word for the mystical Abbé, who sticks entirely to Animus and Anima. Like Milton, Stevens can make the diachronic meaning of words do battle.

Theories of pure poetry in the old sense do not hold much interest for us nowadays, though there are discussions about whether a diction purified of rhetorical divisions is possible.[13] If these discussions are the last remnants of idealist theories of pure poetry, we might listen to Stevens' wariness about all purities separated from reality.

At the end, Stevens returns to people's hunger for what is real. "A poem like a missal found / In the mud": so begins canto xxiv, which Stevens paraphrased as: "I desire my poem to mean as much, and as deeply, as a missal" (L 790, July 12, 1953). Stevens' clerical figure, whether poet or reader, is hungry, like a hawk, and hawks can find food in the mud.

> A poem like a missal found
> In the mud, a missal for that young man,
>
> That scholar hungriest for that book,
> The very book, or, less, a page
>
> Or, at the least, a phrase, that phrase,
> A hawk of life, that latined phrase:
>
> To know; a missal for brooding-sight.
> To meet that hawk's eye and to flinch
>
> Not at the eye but at the joy of it.
> I play. But this is what I think.

[11] Note to Renato Poggiolo, Houghton Library, Harvard University. Quoted by permission of Holly Stevens and the Houghton Library.

[12] Brémond, Prière et poésie, ch. 12, "Animus et Anima."

[13] Cf. Geoffrey H. Hartman, "Purification and Danger," in his Criticism in the Wilderness: The Study of Literature Today (New Haven and London: Yale University Press, 1980), pp. 115–57. He omits "mystical currents" (p. 149n 12), which is a pity.

Part of Stevens' play here is with a "latined phrase," just as he says: *accipiter* (hawk) and *accipere* (to perceive or comprehend, i.e., to know). A hawk of life, as he commented, is "one of those phrases that grips in its talons some aspect of life that it took a hawk's eye to see. To call a phrase a hawk of life is itself an example" (*L* 783–84, June 25, 1953). Latin puns are running through Stevens' mind, for an "aspect" is a looking-at, from Latin *adspicere*. The hungry scholar is seized by something equally hungry. Rather than finding words, the scholar is found by them, though only when ardently wishing them (unlike a mouse or other hawk food). The process of seeing and knowing and hunting is finely caught by Stevens, whose hunt will be understood only by those who are hungry. In canto iii, the great hero-bird is pinned down for specimen and admonition; so also we say that we "pin down" words or thoughts. In xxiv, the poet or reader is more like those who hunger and thirst after righteousness in Isaiah. ("Ho, every one that thirsteth," begins the beautiful passage.) "Brooding-sight" faintly evokes Wordsworth's "brooding mind," itself revising Milton's bird of the Holy Ghost, which, "dove-like satst brooding on the vast Abyss." Stevens' bird here is no dove, and its "brooding-sight" is not nidification but hunting. He is revising the Christian iconography of the hawk, so memorably used by Hopkins.

It is this sense of a hunger for what is real that makes Stevens' "play" utterly serious, and not with any inflated "high seriousness." His echoes and allusions bear witness to this. And that is why I would quarrel with Litz's word, "feeling,"—feeling is a word that concedes so much. Biblical literature and Virgil and Lucretius and Dante and Goethe do not speak to people because they renew a "feeling" for reality. Even as we pay tribute to Stevens' genius for play, we can slide back into the old divisions that he is attacking.

In the last third of the poem, no moon or night appears. The penultimate canto conquers the dominance of dark, and more than conquers, with its play in space and darkness, its "jocular procreations." The final canto conquers the dominance of light, and more than conquers, too:

> That generation's dream, aviled
> In the mud, in Monday's dirty light,
>
> That's it, the only dream they knew,
> Time in its final block, not time
>
> To come, a wrangling of two dreams.
> Here is the bread of time to come,

> Here is its actual stone. The bread
> Will be our bread, the stone will be
>
> Our bed and we shall sleep by night.
> We shall forget by day, except
>
> The moments when we choose to play
> The imagined pine, the imagined jay.

Monday is the day after Sunday. It is the not-always-welcome start of the working week; etymologically, it is the day of the moon. To sleep by night is a tranquility, fitting for the closure of this poem. To see an old dream "aviled / In the mud, in Monday's dirty light"—this is also surely a tranquility. By now, we should know better than to read this as simple repudiation of all the old dreams, whether of the Bible or of Lucretius or of Dante or of Goethe. Stevens places mud and moon in one line, connecting them by alliteration and by logic. I read an allegory here, saying that the immaculate, merciful good of the moon, or its unspotted, imbecile reverie, or its spot on the floor—all may be made part of an ordinary working Monday. And an ordinary Monday is not just anti-Sunday. It is part of Stevens' balance or dialectic, as he returns to questions of religion, this time in earnest.

"Is the function of the poet here mere sound? . . . All this . . . has no more meaning than tomorrow's bread." Thus Stevens in 1923 (*CP* 144). Tomorrow's bread, or the lack of it, may have a lot of meaning, and did in the thirties. Litz hears how Stevens echoes Christ's first temptation in canto xxxiii,[14] a temptation whose allegory of bread and stone always speaks to human hunger. (Brecht uses it in *Der Steinfischer*.) He hears Stevens thereby rebuking the palliatives of the thirties, the facile saviors with fake miracles and illusions. Poetry cannot alter the "stone" of reality—or rather of actuality. (Stevens says "actual stone," not "real stone.")

There is one more important echo, marked by enjambment. "The stone will be"—what, after the various stones of this poem? Our stone, to keep the parallel? Turned into men, as in the Deucalion myth? Metamorphosed into bread, as in Satan's temptation? No, it will be "our bed." We may read this as a rather uncomfortable acknowledgment of actual nature as a place of rest. Not the alma mater of Lucretius, nor the aspic mater of "you lovers that are bitter at heart" (xvi), but, quite simply, "actual stone," that part of the earth that does not produce bread. That hardly sounds like a comfortable bed, despite the comfort of "bedrock" in the implicit pun. Yet a stone was once a bed, and the place of a famous

---

[14] Litz, *Introspective Voyager*, pp. 236–37.

dream, also part of "that generation's dream." It was Jacob's pillow when he dreamt of a ladder between earth and heaven, with angels ascending and descending and God at the top (Genesis 28:10–22). And he "took the stone that he had put for his pillows, and set it up for a pillar," and he called the place Bethel, in memory of the dream: "And Jacob vowed a vow, saying, If God will be with me, and will keep me in this way that I go, and will give me bread to eat, and raiment to put on, so that I come again to my father's house in peace; then shall the Lord be my God: and this stone, which I have set for a pillar, shall be God's house: and of all that thou shalt give me I will surely give the tenth unto thee." Stevens' bread and bed and stone and dream (or dreams) are different. His language even suggests that Jacob might better have wrestled, or wrangled, with the angels on the ladder as he did in his other wondrous dream— wrestled until he was blessed and renamed. I have quoted all of Jacob's vow so that we may hear the language of covenant, including its firm cadences, and so recognize it in Stevens' last canto. I do not know of a stronger closure in Stevens' work to this date, and I cannot but hear it as a vow made with himself. It is a vow of calling, of vocation, of faithfulness. And that last word is not too strong: "This was / Who watched him, always, for unfaithful thought" (CP 483). Stevens would keep his vow of 1937 for the remaining eighteen years of his life.

When he ends with the verb "play," we should hear it in the context of this language of covenant. We hear all the rich senses of musical play, of the actor's or clown's play, of punning, and so on. There is one use of "play" that I have not mentioned and at first it sounds slight. It is the schematic echoing in canto vi of "place," "placed," "play," "space," and this in a canto first entitled, "The Place of Poetry: On Earth." In canto xxxii, "jocular procreations" are the ways we reimagine space and so find a place for ourselves in it. Of this canto, Stevens said: "The point of the poem is, not that this can be done, but that, if done, it is the key to poetry, to the closed garden, if I may become rhapsodic about it, of the fountain of youth and life and renewal" (L 364, August 10, 1940). From the beginning of this book, I have been exploring connections between word-play and our sense of place. Here Stevens works with a sense of place different from place in the opening poems of Harmonium or the Florida poems. It is a sense of place that defines itself against the sense of place in the biblical writers or Lucretius or Dante or Goethe. It is not an individual and solitary sense, as in Domination of Black and The Snow Man, or like Hoon's. Stevens now wishes to make a communal sense of place, as did the great writers just mentioned. His opening cantos address that subject. At the end he can make that covenant with himself because, in one way, his poetic self has come home. He has found his subject.

"The moments when we choose to play": Litz quotes R. P. Blackmur on the play of poetry: "Poetry is a game we play with reality; and it is the game and the play—the game by history and training, the play by instinct and need—which make it possible to catch hold of reality at all."[15] But Blackmur is not prepared to allow Stevens full status in this game and play. In the same essay, he diminishes Stevens to a dandy, and this in 1952 after *The Man with the Blue Guitar* and *Notes toward a Supreme Fiction*. Blackmur's "play" and "game" of poetry simply reinscribe old divisions under a guise of aesthetic criticism. For him, Stevens' play is not serious, nor would it be serious for the old Platonic and neo-Platonic and Christian practitioners of serio ludere.[16] They would not hear how Stevens takes the old language and reality of temptation and miracle, vision and covenant, and replays it on a blue guitar for things as they are.

[15] Blackmur, "Lord Tennyson's Scissors: 1912–50," in his *Form and Value in Modern Poetry* (New York: Doubleday, Anchor, 1957), pp. 369–88.

[16] For the old sense of serio ludere, see for example Edgar Wind, *Pagan Mysteries in the Renaissance*, 2d ed. (New York: Norton, 1968), pp. 222, 236–38.

* * * * *

CHAPTER EIGHT

Against Synecdoche:

Parts of a World

> I began to feel that I was on the edge: that I wanted
> to get to the center: that I was isolated, and that I
> wanted to share the common life. . . . Instead of
> seeking therefore for a "relentless contact" [like
> Crispin, *CP* 34], I have been interested in what
> might be described as an attempt to achieve the nor-
> mal, the central. (*L* 352, January 12, 1940)

STEVENS enjoyed himself more in this volume than in *Ideas of Order*
or *The Man with the Blue Guitar*, and he was disappointed when readers
showed no corresponding enjoyment (*L* 429–30, 433, 501). We can hear
him indulging his old sense of fun from time to time, for example, in the
casual, nudging asides on his own processes ("Shucks," "Pftt"). Or in a
courtly bow to the reader after an unforgettable line and point: "The
squirming facts exceed the squamous mind, / If one may say so." Or in
the play with things that fall: stones fall, night falls, moonlight falls, we
drop off to sleep. (This begins to sound like the old Spike Jones record
where "night falls" and a great clunk sounds out—an aural pun.) Or we
may hear him at play in *Metamorphosis*, a poem Stevens liked, where
he disintegrates our names for the fall months into the unpleasant par-
ticulars of those actual months: "Oto-otu-bre" sounds out "Oh, brrr."
After the restraint of *The Man with the Blue Guitar*, Stevens seems more
at ease here, an ease that allows much experimentation, not always suc-
cessful. Yet the volume does sustain his sense of achievement: "by far

the best thing that I have done," he wrote to Alfred Knopf (L 501, May 17, 1945).

A synecdoche in the usual sense is always a part, but not every part is a synecdoche. Despite our assumptions about the title, *Parts of a World* is largely written against synecdoche, that "most seductive of metaphors," to quote Paul de Man.[1] De Man is skeptical about synecdoche because it so easily implies a wholeness or completion, a rounded and finished unity. His own enterprise, like all deconstructionist enterprises, continually questions such unity. Stevens is entirely aware of the seductiveness of sliding from parts to whole.

Parts of a World is a book of "parts" in many ways. We may map the relations of parts to wholes and parts to other parts all through the volume. Consider, for example, subject matter: of metaphysics, as in one unified truth or Logos, and the parts thereof, or not thereof. Or the subject of war and the army; this is very much a war volume, as A. Walton Litz notes,[2] and the relation of parts and whole is vital in time of war. Or the subject of aesthetics, as this is also a painterly volume, with frequent mention of painting or drawing or names of painters or problems of light and space. (The word "light" appears in twenty of the sixty-three poems; effects of light in fifty-one poems. Our sense of light and space can be partial or a whole world or something other.) Or the subject of exile, which is also a matter of being a part or apart (*A Dish of Peaches in Russia*, the several echoes of the psalm of exile).

We might also consider the word "parts" itself. The concordance to Stevens' poetry shows that this word and like-sounding equivalents rise in frequency with this volume and all succeeding ones, especially *The Rock*. We may think of this collection as musing on what and how things are held in common. Common, ordinary, domestic things figure in *Parts of a World*, though they do not always figure in an ordinary way. Sometimes they are dwarfed and sometimes they are enlarged: there are several giant figures and several tiny ones. Throughout, Stevens is wary of themes that commonly give a sense of unity or wholeness, whether war and nation, whether old ideas of light and space, whether home or heaven or the quest for either. (This means he is wary of part of his earlier self, but we know this already from *Ideas of Order*.) He is equally wary of rhetorical patterns that commonly give a sense of unity or wholeness: synecdoche, metaphor, symbol, closure. This is a volume of "parts" in numerous senses, but all senses agree on this: that they should question

[1] Paul de Man, *Allegories of Reading: Figural Language in Rousseau, Nietzsche, Rilke, and Proust* (New Haven and London: Yale University Press, 1979), p. 11.

[2] A. Walton Litz, *Introspective Voyager: The Poetic Development of Wallace Stevens* (New York: Oxford University Press, 1972), pp. 264–66.

the relation of parts to whole. This remains true for all the pertinent semantic meanings of the word "parts" in *Parts of a World*. Whether parts are particulars (the dominant sense in this volume) or dramatic roles or musical parts or regions or parts of speech or the divisions of oration or parts of the body or factions or duty—whatever meaning of "part" dominates, there is always a question of the whole.

I hope it is not necessary by now to say that Stevens' questioning does not result in some simple reversal where we turn from wholeness and unity to fragmentation and chaos. Rather, he examines how parts seem to lead on to wholes—seem, because we are accustomed to certain ideas of order. Since there must always be some order at work, Stevens' particulars test orders, reshape orders, keep them flexible, keep them visible as orders. We may read Stevens' volume usefully in E. H. Gombrich's terms, for if *Ideas of Order* looks at orders or schemata, then *Parts of a World* looks at the contrary—at the language of particulars that must be matched with the schemata. This is a matter of degree, of course, for ideas of order still occupy Stevens' mind in this volume, as witness the two theses of *Connoisseur of Chaos*. But the stress is on particulars. The squirming facts exceed the squamous schemata.

A catalogue of vivid effects would pall pretty quickly, and Stevens' sensuous particulars do not pall. He keeps them simple, often short, and sometimes achieves a remarkable sense of presence. "Clear water in a brilliant bowl, / Pink and white carnations." "The pears are not viols, / Nudes or bottles. / They resemble nothing else." "It was . . . not so much / That they were oak-leaves, as the way they looked." "There was the cat slopping its milk all day, / Fat cat, red tongue, green mind, white milk." "It is April as I write. The wind / Is blowing after days of constant rain." "The chandeliers, their morning glazes spread / In opal blobs along the walls and floor." "To think of a dove with an eye of grenadine." "The dogwoods, the white ones and the pink ones, / Bloomed in sheets, as they bloom." "The dog had to walk. He had to be taken. / The girl had to hold back and lean back to hold him." "It is she that he wants, to look at directly, / Someone before him to see and to know." This is a side of Stevens that we tend to underestimate, and it is worth noting in a volume where Stevens sometimes indulges in "Gothic excess."[3] In the dog-walking lines, we can hear Stevens clearly imitating action as the line itself walks, holds back, walks. There is a kind of holding back in all these particulars, a holding back of too much vividness, too much inge-

---

[3] The phrase is Helen Vendler's, of *Oak Leaves Are Hands*, in *On Extended Wings: Wallace Stevens' Longer Poems* (Cambridge, Mass.: Harvard University Press, 1969), p. 152.

nuity, too much "apposite ritual," as Crispin called it. Stevens uses gestures of pointing instead (you visualize pears, oak leaves, and so on). The desire for presence comes in passionate language, as do the effects of presence, even the presence of seemingly small things.

I have been speaking generally about parts and wholes and worlds, thereby giving my own sense of such wholeness as this volume has. It is time to turn to particulars. I want to pause over Stevens' play with echo and allusion in this collection before turning to the question of associative language as a type of word-play.

Stevens is very combative in his use of allusion and echo in *Parts of a World*. He often raises the volume of his sound to include allusive echo and allusion proper, thus drawing attention to his own processes. He allows some crude effects. It is as if he had grown impatient because his chosen area of combat had not been heard. Is this not what the allusion to Milton's leaves of Vallombrosa is telling us? "Queer, in this Vallombrosa of ears, / That they never hear the past" (CP 225). Not "ears of Vallombrosa," which our own remembering ears expect. That would suggest Milton's fallen "leaves of Vallombrosa," drying into little, cupped, earlike shapes—listening leaves, a figure for reader response. But Stevens' ears do not respond; they stand in place of Vallombrosa, a place of the shades that is also a Valley of the Shadow of Death, where Milton's own leaves fall on deaf ears. Queer that we may hear only the present schematic echo of the triple rhyme, "queer, ears, hear," and not the allusive echo of Milton.

Stevens is on clear and familiar ground in the poem, *On the Road Home*, which is one of a series alluding to a well-known text from John's Gospel. "I am the way, the truth, and the life," says Jesus, who is the Word, the Logos. ("I wish I could tell you how much I enjoyed getting your letter. It was like going to the Evangelical Church in Reading and hearing old Dr. Kuendig preach in German on the text 'Ich bin der Weg, die Wahrheit, und das Leben.' "[4]) Here, Stevens' words, "way," "truth," and "life" are not informed by the Word, the way, the truth, the life. "Words are not forms of a single word," even a single lower-case word. "In the sum of the parts, there are only the parts." *On the Road Home* makes us hear "parts" as anti-Johannine in other lines than the ones quoted above: "You said, / 'There are many truths, / But they are not parts of a truth.' " The quarrel extends to *The Latest Freed Man*, for Stevens knows that the well-known text is preceded by another well-known text, usually detached from context: "Ye shall know the truth

[4] Joan Richardson, *Wallace Stevens: A Biography* (New York: Beech Tree Books, 1986), vol. 1, p. 525.

and the truth shall make ye free." (Stevens himself quotes it detached from context in 1943 [*NA* 51].) Thus when "the latest freed man" rises at six and sits on the edge of his bed, he muses on how he has "just escaped from the truth." But what kind of "freeing" is this? How is Stevens' combat anti-Johannine?

If we do not ask this question, the poem sounds a little bald, as if Stevens were returning to the word-play in, say, *Of Heaven Considered as a Tomb*. This is "how he was free . . . how his freedom came":

> To be without a description of to be,
> For a moment on rising, at the edge of the bed, to be,
> To have the ant of the self changed to an ox
> With its organic boomings, to be changed
> From a doctor into an ox, before standing up,
> To know that the change and that the ox-like struggle
> Come from the strength that is the strength of the sun,
> Whether it comes directly or from the sun.
> It was how he was free. It was how his freedom came.
> It was being without description, being an ox.

Five poems earlier, Stevens calls the sun "bull fire," which is nearly a ball of fire and nearly an American idiom, Mark Twain style. ("It was bully," Huck says frequently.) It recalls the classical oxen of the sun, which the repeated "ox," in *The Latest Freed Man*, recalls even more clearly. "Organic boomings" call out Bous, bous, if it "booms" its own name—the call to Stephen Dedalus by his classmates. Stevens is summing up over a history of the "doctrine of this landscape." ("Doctrine" is what makes the "doctor" of the lines above, presumably a modern version of the angelic doctor whose symbol is an ox, Thomas Aquinas, who turns up in *Les Plus Belles Pages*, also in *Parts of a World*.) Stevens' freed man ends with "himself / At the centre of reality, seeing it," and "everything bulging and blazing and big in itself"—himself now a sun, insofar as human language allows. If *The Latest Freed Man* suggests itself as a simple example of being "free" from doctrine, we should look again. Modern art, we hear ad nauseam, "frees" us from older conventions of art. It does, and it does not, as Stevens' play in this poem tells us. This is also true of freedom from religious orthodoxy.

Stevens uses allusion proper in *A Dish of Peaches in Russia*, his moving poem of exile. "With my whole body I taste these peaches, / I touch them and I smell them . . . I absorb them as the Angevine / Absorbs Anjou." "My village," he says later in the poem, speaking as an exiled Russian through the words of du Bellay, native of Anjou. ("Quand revoiray-je, helas! de mon petit village . . . la doulceur Angevine.") "Who speaks? But it must be that I, / That animal, that Russian, that exile, for whom / The bells of the chapel pullulate sounds at / Heart." As in *The Man with the Blue Guitar*, Stevens is playing on the etymological paradox of animal-anima, a play against dualisms of body-soul, physical-metaphysical, outside-inside, past-present. "Pullulate" ("sprout" or "bud") is what peach buds do. Russian bells, heard in exile, only ululate, for they are not heard at dawn or dusk, as the enjambment leads us to think. They are heard "at heart." "The exile at the bottom of his heart": this is one of the most moving phrases in Stevens' letters.[5] *On the Road Home* is glad to be rid of old ways and homes, but Stevens also knows the price of exile.

Stevens sometimes repeats echoes and allusions in this volume, so that, having heard one, we hear others. It is true that *Examination of the Hero in a Time of War* starts with an echo of Stevens' *The Sun This March*, but the echo of both poems is from Shelley's heroic, suffering Prometheus. Hence also the scene of snow and rock, and the phrase, "hangs heavily." This is an epic voice we hear, or at least a memory or parody of epic voice.[6] The stanza closes with a barrage of echo, for Stevens is examining past warrior-heroes: Prometheus, Othello ("bright arms"), Aeneas ("fate / In its cavern," "sybils"), David, soldier and psalmist ("wings subtler than any mercy," "psalter"; cf. Ps. 57:1–3). He goes on to another hero and to outright quotation from a book much on his mind at this time, the Book of Daniel. We have heard the idiom of Stevens' Dutch ancestors in the line, "The Got whome we serve is able to deliver / Us," but we have not heard the text they are quoting. It is a repeated formula in Daniel, a favorite wartime text, naturally enough (Dan. 3:17, 6:17, 6:20, and cf. 6:27). Stevens makes a rather crude parody of it. The other text from Daniel that enters his work is from Belshazzar's feast. It informs a new version of a scene that haunted him, the scene of someone alone in a moonlit room trying to read something from, or by, the moonlight. The question is whether such a person is another Belshazzar, trying to read a fateful writing on the wall. ("The moonlight in the cell, words on the wall. / To-night, night's undeciphered murmuring" [CP 260–61].)

One use of echo is especially interesting because it does not work at all. In *Country Words*, Stevens attempts word-play on "country," "canton," "singing" (*cantare*), "cunning," in a poem of sexual and verbal

---

[5] "I feel the constancy of a man who in the exile at the bottom of his heart cries If I forget thee, Jerusalem—and then works for years at a task of this sort with all the cunning of his love" (L 681, June 2, 1950).

[6] I am arguing against a sense of a lyric strain here; cf. Vendler, *On Extended Wings*, p. 155.

exile. He takes two well-known passages from the Old Testament, one from Daniel (the writing on the wall) and the other from the great psalm of exile, Psalm 137. Belshazzar provides argument: the speaker wants no writing on the wall, no hidden text requiring a prophet to disclose its meaning. He wants simple pages that Belshazzar himself can read. The psalm of exile provides echoes, so that we hear its words filtered through this poem: "If I forget thee, O Jerusalem, let my right hand forget its cunning . . . We hanged our harps Upon the willows . . . they required of us a song . . . How can we sing the Lord's song in a strange land?" Stevens writes: "Cunning-coo, O, cuckoo cock, / In a canton of Belshazzar . . . Underneath a willow there / I stood and sang and filled the air." The "country" of Stevens' title is any country from which one is exiled, including a sexual country. Stevens' usual wit and tact have failed him here. He might have done something with the land of Switzerland, as "canton" and "cuckoo cock" suggest. But the words of the psalm of exile say no to Stevens. There are some words that refuse to be played upon as Stevens plays on these, and the words of this psalm are such words. Some historical or literary or other sense in us protests, remembering how these words have been echoed and reechoed through the centuries. Sexual "cunning-country" refuses to be punned with the psalmist's "cunning" and his country. Stevens leaves the words of exile behind after stanza i, as he does the singsong, ticktock rhythm of his parodic song. But the harm has been done, and the poem falls apart. It makes a cautionary tale for matters of word-play and allusion.

The psalm of exile sounds out differently at the end of Stevens' intricate eight-part *Extracts from Addresses to the Academy of Fine Ideas*. Stevens said the poem grew out of the "lightness with which ideas are asserted, held, abandoned, etc." in "the world today" (*L* 380, November 18, 1940). In the last section, he prints the following lines in a separate paragraph, thus:

> How can
> We chant if we live in evil and afterward
> Lie harshly buried there?

"How shall we sing the Lord's song in a strange land?" Stevens rewords the exile's cry, in a question from someone doubly exiled, and he offers no answer. He takes words from one of the great cries of faithfulness to set against a world where ideas are lightly asserted, held, abandoned. He takes words from one of the great cries of faithfulness to set against that faith, for he finds no home in that Lord's land. Only in "the heart's residuum" can the "brooder" seek "music for a single line, / Equal to memory." Two years later, as we shall see, he again remembered the sense of true place in the Old Testament, and again found no home there.

One other echo should be mentioned, for it is from someone whose best-known lines Stevens continually echoes. In stanza x of *Examination of the Hero*, Stevens writes, "And if the phenomenon, magnified, is / Further magnified, sua voluntate" (CP 277). This is a poem about war and peace, written twelve years after Eliot quoted Dante's line, "Our peace in His will" in *Ash Wednesday* ("E'n la sua volontade è nostra pace" [*Para.* III.85]). Stevens goes back from Dante's Italian to Latin, and substitutes a human will for magnifying. Once heard, this echo awakens earlier echoes in *Parts of a World*, for example: "He is the transparence of the place in which / He is and in his poems we find peace" (CP 251). Here as elsewhere in this volume, Stevens makes very clear where he stands apart from echo and allusion, and where he has made it a part of himself. His work with echo and allusion is more embattled here than anywhere else in his work. Hence perhaps its occasional lapses.

Parts of a World opens with three poems that are object lessons against synecdoche. *Parochial Theme* is a title that speaks to our sense of "parts." Not our usual easy phrase, "universal theme," nothing so grand. Perhaps "parochial" in the neutral sense of a parish; perhaps "parochial" in the pejorative sense of narrow and provincial. Stevens' text offers no clear solution of this ambiguity, leaving us to piece poem and title together, or not. The parts of this poem are violently disjoined. Perhaps this is the point in the world of 1938.

Harmonium closed by calling to the wind. *Parts of a World* opens with the wind, and what it means to say simply, "The wind blows," we may surmise from *The Man Whose Pharynx Was Bad* and the poems of absent wind from the early thirties. In a traditional scene of inspiration, there are only two characters, the wind and one's writing self. Stevens breaks with this inside-outside pattern. He suggests various voices in the wind. He introduces the figure of the glassblower, who will continue to appear in his work, but he does not identify the blower exclusively with wind or with poet. Some combining of inner and outer forces is at work, with Stevens wisely refusing to define it too schematically. (It would vary from blower to blower in any case; this blower sings a mi-me pun in falsetto.) Voices in the wind may be contemporary voices quite as much as voices from the past. Stevens is reminded of Whitman, hearing himself heard by others. "Barbarous chanting" is his tribute to the "barbaric yawp" of Whitman's searching and hunting close to *Song of Myself*.

Stevens called the poem "an experiment at stylizing life": "consequently the references to health are to be thought of in connection with the stylizing of life. . . . The poem may be summed up by saying that there is no such thing as life; what there is is a style of life from time to time" (*L* 434–35, January 12, 1943). A style of life: 1) Hunting, torturing, executing; 2) hunting, health, hallooing, chanting, holy. Stevens begins with one word, "hunting," and expands its various associations: hunting for an animal, hunting for a word, hunting for wholeness. ("Hale" or "whole," which is cognate with "health," is the only wholeness admitted here. "I shall be good health for you nevertheless," says Whitman of the barbaric yawp.) One hunts for what one pines for; thus the "pine-lands," in Stevens' usual pun, and thus also, I think, the "ponies." Stevens made himself a "secretive hunter" in 1922, and then abjured hunting for some things in 1934 (*CP* 71–72, 124–25). The thirties had hunters and hunted too, some desperate, and the thirties also hunted after various "salvations," both civil and religious. The poem's disparate parts come together at the end without unifying, in an outrageous pun on "glamorous hanging," a pun usually omitted when we quote the closing lines. Whether a picture-hanging or an execution, "life . . . is more than any scene: / Of the guillotine or of any glamorous hanging. / Piece the world together, boys, but not with your hands." The poem is a small lesson on parts and wholes, quests and endings.

We usually manage to domesticate such statements as Stevens' second title, *Poetry Is a Destructive Force*. But Stevens is bald enough about this anti-Coleridgean sentiment: "It can kill a man." When we read that poetry can kill a man, we may think of self-destructiveness and a few odd cases. But Stevens' wide sense of the word "poetry" includes anything one "has at heart," including convictions. Such things can cause death quite readily, now as in 1938. Stevens begins with ambiguity, taking us back again to the paradoxes of *The Snow Man*: "That's what misery is, / Nothing to have at heart." The grammar offers two meanings, and they come to much the same thing. The alternatives of having versus nothing run through this volume; "having" has a strong sense of possession, whole and utter. "Being nothing otherwise, / Having nothing otherwise" (*CP* 194). "There was not an idea / This side of Moscow. There were anti-ideas / And counter-ideas. There was nothing one had" (*CP* 229). This is another sense of parts and whole, where poetry is all or nothing. We note also Stevens' passionate language of conviction, even as he plays against some patterns of wholeness.

Stevens has begun with two very different rhetorics of part and whole. They indirectly challenge the reader. Piece me together, piece your world together, says the first poem, but not with your hands any more than the old biblical house was a house made with hands. Stevens' colloquial "piece together" plays against our usual, decorous "compose" or "unify" (as does "patch together" in the epilogue to *Notes toward a*

Supreme Fiction). The second poem asks indirectly what we have at heart, and both poems may be read as introductions to the third and powerful poem, *Poems of Our Climate*. This poem has no overt violence, no play with outrageous puns or paradox. Stevens stills life here, and he brings it home. This is "our" climate, whoever "we" may be. We are in a room, or looking at a painting, or seeing a room as in a painting. This poem is much more a poem of reminiscence than we have recognized:

I love this snowy light. (*SP* 9)

Every Spring I have a month or two of semi-blackness. . . . Perhaps, it is simply a revulsion against old things. . . . One has a desire for the air full of spice and odors, and for days like junk [junks?] of changing colors, and for warmth and ease. . . . I'd like to wear a carnation every morning. . . . You must always have pink cheeks and golden hair. . . . Old people are tremendous frauds. The point is to be young—and to be a little in love, or very much—and to desire carnations and "creations"—and to be glad when Spring comes. (*L* 97–98, March 2, 1907)

Stevens could have developed his poem as he developed his letter—extolling springtime, with its natural flowers grown in the ground, in contrast with these out-of-season carnations, which are not "of our climate." He could have developed the poem like *Stars at Tallapoosa*, whose "delight" and "simplicity" and "bright-edged" and "cold" he now revises. But the analogy of the mind's sky-lines and the heart's lines of desire is too easy. There are other lines now. Another poem, the painful and crude 1932 *Good Man, Bad Woman*, also informs *Poems of Our Climate*, as we may hear by its phrase "blossoms snow-bred pink and white." It is a poem bitterly divided between a hard heart and a susceptible heart, "brass" heart and "bared" heart. *The Poems of Our Climate* is past such antinomies, past such corroding. It knows and tastes and places its "bitterness," without being a bitter poem. Quite the contrary.

> Clear water in a brilliant bowl,
> Pink and white carnations. The light
> In the room more like a snowy air,
> Reflecting snow. A newly-fallen snow
> At the end of winter when afternoons return.
> Pink and white carnations—one desires
> So much more than that. The day itself
> Is simplified: a bowl of white,
> Cold, a cold porcelain, low and round,
> With nothing more than the carnations there.

I used the word "taste" of Stevens' word "bitterness," but this is a word and sense that we do not have until Part III, the third poem of our climate. Carnations have a spicy fragrance, but nothing of that scent enters Part I in the way it enters Stevens' 1907 letter with almost Miltonic force. Beauty here is distanced and unsensuous—nothing like the sensuous peaches that are tasted, smelled, eaten, possessed. So also with the unobtrusive echo of Keats's "cold pastoral," as "a bowl . . . Cold" becomes "cold porcelain." Keats's "cold pastoral" is a frozen world of desire, on that Grecian urn, and again Stevens might have gone on to develop Keats's paradoxical dialectic. Instead, Stevens shifts the dialectic. In Keats, the possibility of fulfillment lies in his still world of art. In Stevens, a scene of still life says no to desire, no to thoughts of fulfillment. Stevens' lines are utterly of limitation, not of frustration.

This is true of the pictorial lines of the poem, as well as its poetic lines. The clearness and brilliance and simplifying of things are very subtly made limiting, even slightly claustrophobic. We do not notice this at first, for Stevens starts by enticing us. But there are oddnesses. For one thing, the bowl is glass in lines 1 and 2. It is the day that is a "bowl of white, / Cold," in the ancient figure of the vaulted sky as a bowl. But not a bowl of wine, to tip and drink, as in classical poetry. And not a vault of heaven to parody. Stevens is far from parody here, in this quiet analogy. We see an overcast sky, low clouds, an inverted bowl, ourselves as incarnate pink-and-white humans (this is *our* climate), contained within that bowl of the sky. This slight oddness makes clearer Stevens' play with light. Just for a moment, at the end of line 2, we expect him to go on and talk about the light of "clear water in a brilliant bowl," as he does in *The Glass of Water*. But no, it is the light in the room that he defines so precisely, as if in a painting: the peculiar light of reflected snow. We have three enclosures, sky, room, bowl, all simplified. Part I comes to center on simplifying—or rather being simplified. There are only two verbs in ten lines, the first being delayed past three full stops, the second in the passive voice. Both are unexpected. Who or what simplifies?

Then we cross the divide to Part II and find ourselves in another world, a hypothetical purgatory, as Stevens begins to work with the word "simplicity":

> Say even that this complete simplicity
> Stripped one of all one's torments, concealed
> The evilly compounded, vital I
> And made it fresh in a world of white,
> A world of clear water, brilliant-edged,
> Still one would want more, one would need more,
> More than a world of white and snowy scents.

"Evilly" makes Stevens' "world of white" take on the connotations of biblical whites (white-robed elders, washing that makes one whiter than snow). Then the picture narrows again to the water of line 1, as if to wash away larger associations of evil. But the action of returning to this object suggests diminution; the water and its brilliancy will not function as symbols that imply a whole. Stevens is quietly, insistently, working against such reading. If this bowl evokes some larger whole, as bowls often do—if ever the golden bowl be broken—that larger whole may just be oppressive. And Stevens' phrase, "never-resting mind," plays against all the stillness of Part I. To my ear, it also plays against St. Augustine, and the Dante-Eliot line of thought. "Our hearts are restless until they find their rest in thee." This is said to be Augustine's most quoted line, and I hear Stevens' word "never-resting" declining an Augustinian repose, his mind refusing the comforts of the heart. What is chiefly astonishing in this 1938 poem is its range of association. The scene begins as both an ordinary American indoor scene and a painting. And slowly, the snow-cold-white associations begin to make a context. It is a whole way of looking at things that Stevens is disputing.

We may hear word-play in the more usual sense in the juxtaposition of "bitterness, delight," and not only because we have read *Delightful Evening*.

III

There would still remain the never-resting mind,
So that one would want to escape, come back
To what had been so long composed.
The imperfect is our paradise.
Note that, in this bitterness, delight,
Since the imperfect is so hot in us,
Lies in flawed words and stubborn sounds.

We expect to hear the opposite of bitterness if there is to be a contrast—something like "bitterness, sweetness" or "bitterness, honey." We expect this especially because desire in this poem includes, without any focusing, erotic desire, and "bitter-sweet" is a standard erotic formulation. (It begins with Sappho, and Catullus is the acknowledged Latin master of it.[7]) Why do we not have sweetness? For all that, why do we not have sweetness and light, since we began by looking at light? Then we begin to hear why Stevens says "delight." "Bitterness and dark" is the logical opposite of sweetness and light. Stevens' position is de-light to some but unhyphenated delight to him, as he makes his own claim for

---

[7] Sappho, Frag. 40; Catullus, LXVIII.18, "dulcem . . . amaritiem." My edition of Catullus also quotes Goethe's *Egmont*: "freudvoll und leidvoll . . . die Seele die liebt" (III.2).

light. It is not just a way of looking at things that Stevens combats but also a way of hearing things—the way they lie both visually and aurally. That last punning paradoxical verb, "lies," has a stubborn sound of its own that tells us delight "lies" in sounds, and so it does. A sound of "lie" is inherent in the word "delight," but it is equally inherent in the opposing party's "light." Those remain stubborn sounds in English.

I want to mention one other play on words, a play that will inform Stevens' poetry from now on. This is the play of *cum-* words. Depending on what letters follow it, Latin *cum-* takes the form com-, cor-, col-, co-, or con- in English. Stevens' play extends to the Germanic near-homonym, "come." The full sequence in *Poems of Our Climate* runs: "complete," "concealed," "compounded," "come back," "composed." Part I uses no such words. Part II begins with a unifying *cum* ("complete"), then undermines it as "concealing." That Stevens is consciously playing with a schematic and semantic echo is clear by Part III, with its terminal near-rhyme, "come back . . . composed." The never-resting mind desires to come back, not to the *cum-* of "complete simplicity," but to an undefined "what had been so long composed"—the imperfect in any case (grammatically the past perfect, as we may say of verbs and paradises both). It is "composed" in the etymological sense of "pieced together" but not in the sense of "tranquil." The still life of *Poems of Our Climate* is a painterly composition whose composedness Stevens will not allow to entice him into some kinds of composition. Leo Spitzer has analyzed the "well-known Ciceronian con- pattern" as it is expanded in an "Augustinian world harmony." "*Cum-* is to him [Augustine], grammatically speaking, perfect."[8] Not so for Stevens. "The imperfect is our paradise."

This is one kind of word-play which I have not discussed—the play within an associative field, where the rhetorical force of words is informed by dialectical assumptions. Stevens plays very finely in the difficult area of association—the area that Eliot hears as part of the "music" of poetry,[9] the area that I think Stevens means by the "sound of words" (as in his essay, "The Noble Rider and the Sound of Words"), the area which tests the translator and for which no dictionary is adequate. "It doesn't sound right," we say, very simply, of a translation that is "off."

Stevens' group of "common" words, including all the *cum-* words I have mentioned, makes an excellent example of the play of association. We may read such words as a word-complex, using a method of the great

[8] Leo Spitzer, *Classical and Christian Ideas of World Harmony: Prolegomena to an Interpretation of the Word "Stimmung"* (Baltimore: The Johns Hopkins University Press, 1963), p. 33.

[9] T. S. Eliot, "the greater or less wealth of association" of words, from "The Music of Poetry," in *Selected Prose*, ed. John Hayward (London: Penguin, 1953), p. 60.

philologists, such as Leo Spitzer. Or we may read them as a word-complex using a method of the deconstructionists. We know from the great philologists how such word-play can illuminate the history of thought. We know from the deconstructionists how such word-play can subvert the history of thought. Stevens, I think, follows neither of these courses. For all his pleasure and skill in subverting what he believes to be false, he will move toward a supreme fiction, retrieving from the past what he can, and imagining the possibility of a new mythological form (*CP* 466). This will come in the forties, for example, in *Notes toward a Supreme Fiction* and *An Ordinary Evening in New Haven*. I think *Poems of Our Climate* shows Stevens turning from an imagination-reality axis and reaching toward a supreme fiction. I want to pause over Stevens' use of the word "common," for it is essential for his 1949 poem, *An Ordinary Evening in New Haven*, and it begins to be important in this volume.

Stevens is an exacting and fastidious writer, so that his genuine passion for what he calls the "common" is sometimes hard to understand. Not, of course, the common as that which is stale and trite. "Common," like "ordinary," "plain," and "vulgar," may be understood in either a neutral or a pejorative sense. Ruskin preaches a small sermon on the matter. "A daisy is common, and a baby, not uncommon. Neither is vulgar."[10] Stevens' early uses of the words "ordinary" and "common" are all synonymous with "banal," as in the conventional contrast between "commonplace" and "revelation" in 1908: "Thus the landscapes, largely impressionistic in a half-decided way, are only transcripts of common-place Nature—lovely in itself, but, as Art, common-place. There is no revelation. There are no remarkable styles. It might happen anywhere" (*SP* 189). Similarly, in 1918, there is an attack on the tyranny of the "common-place" for the "common soldier" (*OP* 11): "I mark the virtue of the common-place. / I take all things as stated." In other poetry written from 1918 through 1923, we can hear Stevens working out reactions to a stale commonplace: in *Anecdote of the Abnormal* (*OP* 24), *Banal Sojourn, The Ordinary Women, The Man Whose Pharynx Was Bad*. He ends *The Comedian* with the figure of "illuminating" the commonplace, but when it is illuminated by words like "fancy" and "apparition," we are hearing a fear of Mauberley-like triviality, and not any sense of transforming.

Stevens will continue to use such words as "common" in their pejorative sense, for example, in a letter of 1951 (*L* 735). But after *The Comedian*, he returned to grapple with "plain" and "common" things in

[10] John Ruskin, *Works*, ed. E. T. Cook and A. Wedderburn (New York: Longmans Green, 1903–1912), vol. 27, *Notes and Correspondence*, p. 470.

his poetry. In 1942, after the opening poems of *Parts of a World*, Stevens chose as the fourth poem *Prelude to Objects*. The conclusion starts this way:

> Poet, patting more nonsense foamed
> From the sea, conceive for the courts
> Of these academies, the diviner health
> Disclosed in common forms.

In these gay, punning lines, Stevens combines an erotic and sculptural diction to evoke a figure he refuses to name except by the evasive, good-humored word "nonsense." As mythical figure, she is Aphrodite, rising from the foam of the sea, most pattable and capable of bringing to birth a poet's conception. As matter or material cause, something foamed from the sea does need a little patting into shape in order to disclose "the diviner health . . . in common forms" of poetry. As formal cause, non-material or non-sense, the figuration is abstract. And as mere nonsense, the conception is gaily defensive. Like other poems in *Parts of a World*, this is a poem of healing and uses the vocabulary of health.[11] Paradoxically, the common Aphrodite is said here to be diviner and healthier than the ideal Aphrodite, that distant star of *O Florida, Venereal Soil*. Stevens has turned his back on the Platonic contrast of the Aphrodite Pandemos and the Uranian Aphrodite in order to invoke a common Aphrodite. So also, in 1933, he copied the following extract into his commonplace book: "Good common flesh, blood, and mind are beside us here and now, yet we hardly recognize that mistress's real, useful and excellent companionship, hardly consider her presence, thinking to find a matchless beauty in every other neighbourhood than our own. It is seldom that the normal is sought with excited zeal, yet it is the normal that is good, and it is the normal that fortunately can most easily be gained."[12] Stevens will have nothing to do with old patterns of synecdoche, of parts and whole, of *cum-* and common. Nor is his idiom "common," in various senses of the word. That should not keep us from taking seriously his desire for something communal. His echoes and allusions in *The Man with the Blue Guitar*, his four great poets of 1942, Virgil, Dante, Shakespeare, Milton (*NA* 23), his echoing in *Examination of the Hero in a Time of War*—these are of words and makers of words that have made a sense of com-

---

[11] The vocabulary of health ("hale," "health," "inhale," "ease," "disease") is important in Stevens. It might usefully be compared with Goethe's, for all that Eliot supposed Goethe's notions of health to be outdated (*Selected Essays*, pp. 420–21). Cf. also "Poetry is a health" (*OP* 173) and *NA* 17.

[12] Commonplace Book, I, 3, WAS 70–73, Huntington Library. Quoted by permission of Holly Stevens and the Huntington Library.

munity. And Stevens closes his volume with this last poem, and its musing on a false and a true "common." If I am right about this sense of the communal in Stevens, then he parts company with the deconstructionists here, for all his wariness about the rhetoric of synecdoche. His word-play and word-war desire a new sense of the whole. He is ready to write *Notes toward a Supreme Fiction.*

III

* * *

Transport to Summer

CHAPTER NINE

* * * * *

Transport and

the Metaphor Poems

The title, TRANSPORT TO SUMMER, is in itself a gift, and I thank you for giving my Swedish cart the savor of poetry. This use of words—strange but also natural—makes me realize why I used to think I would like to be a writer. (Marianne Moore) [1]

Transport: (1) The action of carrying or conveying a thing or person from one place to another; conveyance.
(2) Transference of a word to a different meaning; metaphor. (Obs. rare)
(3) The state of being "carried out of oneself" . . . vehement emotion (now usu. of a pleasurable kind). (OED)

THE TITLE, *Transport to Summer*, plays in all its words. We should annotate, and we may allegorize or go even further. The annotation is from Stevens himself, who said flatly that by the word "summer" he meant "reality" (L 719, June 19, 1951). "Transport to Summer," then, offers to convey us to where and what and how this summer-reality is. What usually transports us to summer is the turning earth itself, and the

[1] Marianne Moore, Letter to Wallace Stevens, March 16, 1947, WAS 52, Huntington Library. Quoted by permission of the Huntington Library and of Clive E. Driver, Literary Executor of the estate of Marianne C. Moore. The reference is to *The Prejudice against the Past* (CP 368–69) and to Moore's *A Carriage from Sweden*.

Stevens who wants to write a poetry of earth, and who has punned so long on turning as troping, must have smiled at this little allegory. It makes his own volume into a turning poetic world. We may figuratively ride on metaphor too (only in modern Greece do we literally ride on a bus called *metaphora*).[2] Thus read, "transport" is metaphor that takes us to summer-reality. Stevens' unobtrusive preposition, "to," is also important, as his prepositions so often are. It reminds us that there are different ways of getting from A to B, from transport to summer: a journey, a scale, a speaking. On the vehicle of metaphor to summer-reality: this is a journey. From the point of metaphor to summer-reality: this is a scale or spectrum, from imagination to reality. From speaking metaphor to summer-reality: this is a soliloquy where transport speaks. (Or is it a dramatic monologue, where summer-reality is a responsive, influential auditor? The difference is important.) Transport as ecstasy moves in similar ways.

We may be transported back in time to a remembered summer-reality, which is what happens in the first part of *Certain Phenomena of Sound* (*CP* 286), and in this letter: "Being in his [a friend's] old-fashioned house in which he has made no changes transports me in time as Mrs. Church's movements transport me in space. The difference is that once I lived in just such a time" (*L* 827–28, April 19, 1954). We may be transported out in space to places we have never seen, as in the above letter or in *Description without Place*. We may be transported while in actual summer, which is strongly evoked in this volume. Stevens begins with three high-summer poems, and his descriptive language of summer is forceful throughout.

I want to look at the opening poem before pursuing some of Stevens' word-play and word-war with one kind of transport, transport as metaphor. Stevens began playing with the figure of metaphor early in his work. He literalizes metaphor, provides it with various stories, considers its different kinds, delights in it, rejects it. Metaphor leads a complicated life. Some of the metaphor poems in *Transport to Summer*, as well as two earlier poems, suggest possible areas of discussion for those cognizant of metaphor's habits.

Transport to Summer begins with an odd-sounding poem that is nonetheless affirmation for Stevens, and closer to traditional invocation than any opening poem so far. The first stanza has the motion and metaphor of transport on a summer night:

> Look round, brown moon, brown bird, as you rise to fly,
> Look round at the head and zither
> On the ground.

---

[2] See Derrida's play on this in his "*Retrait* of Metaphor," *Enclitic* 2 (1978), 4–33.

This moon of 1942 is not white, not the 1915 Blanche of an early version of this poem, *Blanche McCarthy* (*OP* 10). It is brown: descriptively a darkish rising moon, and by association something other than the unearthly white or immaculate or unspotted round moon that so haunted Stevens' imagination. Earthy in its color, this moon visits earth, and becomes an agent of song for him once more. It is his old moon-watcher who speaks this poem, we assume. By a pun on "round," the moon is told to make itself appear round and to look around (as if it had a hidden side, which it does). In *The Man with the Blue Guitar*, Stevens' punning on "round" is negative. Here the rounds work differently, whether round shapes (moon, head, rose), roundish trajectories (of the moon), rounded stanzas (by a three-syllable last line that sounds like refrain), or rounding cycles of time (marked by a returning moon, night after night). Every "rise" will become a "rose," and may rot, as from white to brown, as from fresh flower into "rotted rose" in Stevens' "rise-rose" pun that also recalls *The Man with the Blue Guitar* and its "rotted names." It is important for Stevens that the moon can be brown, and it is important that we are the ones who give to it a sense of perfection in its roundness and its whiteness. This might issue in complete rejection of moony worlds, but Stevens is past that now.

Stevens' head on the ground, though apparently decapitated, has life of a kind:

> In your light, the head is speaking. It reads the book.
> It becomes the scholar again, seeking celestial
> Rendezvous,
>
> Picking thin music on the rustiest string,
> Squeezing the reddest fragrance from the stump
> Of summer.

Wary of prophetic voice in *The Comedian*, calling out to the rabbi-scholar in *The Sun This March*, hating a bloody moonlit scene in *The Man with the Blue Guitar*—Stevens is healed of this now, and can reanimate prophetic voice and scholar and moon and even blood, without fear. If this were classical literature, we would say that a shade of the dead (perhaps Orpheus?) was being blooded, and so could take form and speak. What seems at first a grotesque, self-conscious figure makes sense. Stevens' reimagined moon is once more a muse and also a genius of place, inspired not by afflatus but by ancient blood-sacrifice legends. If there is any echo of Joel's apocalypse, where the moon is turned into blood, such terrors of the moon are transformed by Stevens.

And what of the title? We speak of the "body" of a text, and of its title as a "head." The "head" of this poem is: "God Is Good. It Is a Beautiful

Night." Title is detached from text, as the head in the poem is detached from its body. But both heads speak, in a way. We may not recognize Stevens' opening poem as an invocation, but that is what it is. The moon is invoked, a bird presented, the scholar returned, the head blooded, prophecy faintly echoed, the night acknowledged as beautiful, and God allowed without irony. Stevens is ready to begin his best volume.

His title, *God Is Good. It Is a Beautiful Night*, quietly introduces questions of metaphor, at least metaphor according to Stevens, for not everyone would agree that the first sentence of his first title is metaphor. Stevens begins with a hidden and important dispute, how to read the sentence "God is good." Is this metaphor or not? Orthodoxy says no. He himself said yes: "In metaphor . . . the resemblance may be . . . between two imagined things as when we say that God is good" (*NA* 72, 1947). The dispute continues when we ask how we are to relate the two sentences of the title. Stevens simply juxtaposes them. His titles have played with such juxtaposing metaphors already, using single words, *The Candle a Saint, The Bagatelles the Madrigals*. Sentences are something else. Is the night beautiful because God is good? Orthodoxy says yes. Or vice versa? And does this make God a kind of metaphor for a beautiful night? Stevens leaves these questions unanswered, but they bear on metaphor as analogy.

The sense of "transport" as metaphor is implicit in the first two poems of *Transport to Summer*, then emerges explicitly in the third poem, the powerful and difficult *The Motive for Metaphor*. I shall go back to two earlier poems before approaching the metaphor poems of *Transport to Summer*. But first I need to pause over the figure of metaphor itself.

We are still some way from any comprehensive grasp of Stevens' notions of metaphor. Such comprehension would have to take account of essays and notebooks and poems, including a few poems in which metaphor is not mentioned by name. I do not think Stevens' notions can be readily assimilated to any one current theory of metaphor. Rather, he seems to challenge theories in his own compact, elusive way. His language of metaphor sometimes sounds like a gloss on recent philosophical writing about metaphor, so close are some of the terms and plots. Metaphor is easily the most prominent figure of thought mentioned by Stevens; as in Aristotle, an "eye for resemblance" is the sine qua non for the poet. (As not in Aristotle, resemblances themselves have an eye that may "catch" the poet's: "the eye of a vagabond in metaphor / That catches our own" [*CP* 397].) I have no sense that metaphor swallows all other figures in Stevens (a current complaint about critical writing on metaphor).[3] I have no sense that he identifies it essentially with logo-

---

[3] For example, Gérard Genette, *Figures of Literary Discourse*, trans. and selected from *Figures* I, II, III (1966, 1969, 1972) by Alan Sheridan (New York: Columbia University

centrism. This last is a current argument I do not altogether understand. I suppose it is because metaphor is thought to be essentially analogy, and analogy is thought to be spiritualizing, as in a Thomistic doctrine of analogy. Or else because metaphor is thought to be centered on anagogic metaphor, to use Northrop Frye's term.[4] Stevens is exceedingly wary of anything approaching anagogic metaphor, at least until late in his life.

As for analogy, in his 1948 essay, "Effects of Analogy," it is widened into a general principle of resemblance, governed not by God, but by something Stevens calls a "discipline of rightness" (*NA* 115). I read this as a quiet replacing of the divine in a Thomistic doctrine of analogy. In a Thomistic view, the principle of analogy of being allows us to say that God is good, it being "the principle that since God is the cause of good in each genus, he can be called by the name of the perfection of these goods."[5] When Stevens starts *Transport to Summer* by saying God is good, he means something else. And we might note how he connects Aquinas and moonlight in 1941 in *Les Plus Belles Pages*—not by Thomistic analogy but by something he loosely calls "interaction, inter-relation." "This is an idea of some consequence," Stevens commented, "not a casual improvisation." *Les Plus Belles Pages* is best read as a discussion, in little, of doctrines of analogy. This would make sense of Stevens' comments on this short and seemingly slight poem. "Nothing exists by itself. / The moonlight seemed to . . . The moonlight and Aquinas seemed to." As for Thomistic theology, "the idea that [this] is involved is dismissed in the last line," Stevens drily noted. Poetically, he said, "Theology after breakfast sticks to the eye" (*CP* 244–45, *OP* 293–94).

Stevens suggests in a 1947 essay that "metamorphosis" would be a better word than "metaphor" (*NA* 72), and his play with the figure of metaphor is especially suggestive about "interaction, inter-relation." He is sensitive to the metamorphosis of A into B in the A and B of metaphor. We might recall I. A. Richards's words for crossing the space between the A and B of metaphor ("a borrowing between and intercourse of thoughts, a transaction between contexts").[6] Or Frye's interrelations of

Press, 1982), pp. 113–21. Genette speaks of the process of "centrocentrism" (p. 114). See also Wayne Booth, in *A Rhetoric of Irony* (Chicago and London: University of Chicago Press, 1974); or in *On Metaphor*, ed. Sheldon Sacks (Chicago and London: University of Chicago Press, 1979), pp. 47–49. Cf. also Jonathan Culler, *The Pursuit of Signs: Semiotics, Literature, Deconstruction* (Ithaca: Cornell University Press, 1981), p. 188.

[4] See below for Frye's five types of metaphor in the *Anatomy of Criticism* (Princeton: Princeton University Press, 1957).

[5] Monroe Beardsley, "Metaphor," *Encyclopedia of Philosophy*, ed. Paul Edwards (New York: Macmillan, 1967), p. 288.

[6] I. A. Richards, *The Philosophy of Rhetoric* (New York: Oxford University Press, 1967), p. 94.

A and B in his five categories of metaphor. (Of these, archetypal metaphor and anagogic metaphor are especially useful—the first because it is usually omitted, and the second because it distinguishes radical metaphor.[7]) Or Christine Brooke-Rose's sense of the movements of metaphor in grammatical constructions.[8] Or Ricoeur's predicative sense of metaphor in his theory of statement-metaphor as against word-metaphor.[9] Or more recent work on the movements and behavior of metaphor.[10]

I want to consider five poems: *Metaphors of a Magnifico* (1918) and *Thinking of a Relation between the Images of Metaphor* (1945) as treating questions of archetypal metaphor, *Oak Leaves Are Hands* (1942) as a poem of demonic metaphor, *The Motive for Metaphor* (1943) as a play between grammar and metaphor, and a poem of the making of metaphor, and *Man Carrying Thing* (1946) as a problem of metaphor and identity.

Stevens plays with rhetorical figures from the beginning, and with metaphor starting with *Metaphors of a Magnifico*, the thirteenth poem of *Harmonium*. The poem is variously read as a problem in psychological identity (Helen Vendler) and a problem of totality (Helen Regueiro).[11] I read it as a problem of archetypal as against other types of metaphor, and

[7] Frye maps metaphors as follows: 1) metaphor as simple juxtaposition (A; B); 2) metaphor as simile (a descriptive definition: A is [like] B); 3) metaphor as an analogy of proportion, that is, four terms of which two have a common factor (a formal definition: A is as B); 4) metaphor as the concrete universal, the individual identified with its class (an archetypal definition); 5) metaphor as total identity (an anagogic or radical definition: A *is* B). See the *Anatomy of Criticism*, pp. 123–25. Charles Altieri extends Frye's anagogy (I think too far) in his "Wallace Stevens' Metaphors of Metaphor: Poetry as Theory," *American Poetry* 1 (1983), 85.

[8] In her *Grammar of Metaphor* (London: Secker & Warburg, 1958).

[9] In *La métaphore vive* (1975), trans. R. Czerny, *The Rule of Metaphor* (Toronto: University of Toronto Press, 1977). Ricoeur works, as he says, from a distinction made by the French linguist, Emile Benveniste, between a semantics, where the sentence carries the minimum complete meaning, and a semiotics, where the word is treated as a sign in the lexical code (*Rule of Metaphor*, pp. 4, 176, 179). Such a distinction may also be found in W. B. Stanford's *Greek Metaphor: Studies in Theory and Practice* (Oxford: Blackwell, 1936): "Aristotle, like nearly all his successors until the nineteenth century of the Christian era, neglected the true principle of language, that *the phrase or sentence, not the word, is the unit of speech.* For metaphor this is a more vital truth than for any other form of words" (p. 9). Stanford refers to a 1922 article by A. H. Gardiner in the *British Journal of Psychology*. This distinction between discourse and sign, which is fundamental in reading metaphor according to Stanford and Ricoeur, is a distinction that a substitution theory of metaphor ignores.

[10] See especially the collection edited by Sheldon Sacks, *On Metaphor*. See also David S. Miall, ed., *Metaphor: Problems and Perspectives* (Sussex: Harvester, 1982).

[11] Helen Vendler, *Wallace Stevens: Words Chosen Out of Desire* (Knoxville: University of Tennessee Press, 1984), pp. 22–23. Helen Regueiro, *The Limits of Imagination: Wordsworth, Yeats, Stevens* (Ithaca and London: Cornell University Press, 1976), pp. 180–82.

so a problem of both identity and totality. (Archetypal metaphor seems to me a distinct kind rather than Rugiero's "variation," and I do not read the first sentence as any metaphor at all.) With a title like *Metaphors of a Magnifico*, we expect a series of metaphors, perhaps magnificent, certainly magnified. But the point about the magnifico's metaphors seems to be that he has none. Or more precisely, that he cannot reach any, for he keeps trying to get his men across a bridge, like some officer in charge of transport. (This is a wartime poem, and the scene is European.) Clump, clump, go the boots of twenty men on to the bridge of metaphor, but never across, or at least never past archetypal metaphor, which seems to get nowhere:

> Twenty men crossing a bridge,
> Into a village,
> Are twenty men crossing twenty bridges,
> Into twenty villages,
> Or one man
> Crossing a single bridge into a village.
>
> This is old song
> That will not declare itself . . .
>
> Twenty men crossing a bridge,
> Into a village,
> Are
> Twenty men crossing a bridge
> Into a village.
>
> That will not declare itself
> Yet is certain as meaning . . .
>
> The boots of the men clump
> On the boards of the bridge.
> The first white wall of the village
> Rises through fruit-trees.
> Of what was it I was thinking?
> So the meaning escapes.
>
> The first white wall of the village . . .
> The fruit-trees. . . .

The poem centers its five symmetrical stanzas on the one-word line that is the bridge of all metaphor, the verb "to be." But "are" only carries A back to A, and no meta-, no "beyond," comes. Then two verbless lines give an elliptical, trailing closure. The magnifico's problem seems to be archetypal metaphor. His twenty men either remain discrete particulars or a lifeless whole, unlike the sensuous intruding countryside. The trouble is that archetypal metaphor goes dead and seems inimical to the language of sensuous particulars. Stevens is drawn to particulars, yet something in him also wants archetypal metaphor, as we realize from his hero and major-man figures. In 1918 archetypal metaphor is only ironic, here and with the common soldier in *Poems from "Lettres d'un Soldat"* (*OP* 10–16). By 1942, Stevens has learned how to approach a sense of the communal, as in *Examination of the Hero in a Time of War*. In the magnifico, I hear Stevens testing his own "magnifying" poetic self against his sensuous, particular, poetic self. In *Sunday Morning*, m-sounds say "mmm" to "magnificent" Jove and his mythy mind. "Mmm" may express pleasure or express skepticism—a fine double sense for *Sunday Morning* and for the "magnifico" among Stevens' own selves. By 1945, archetypal metaphor and the metaphors of sensuous particulars can work together, as in *Thinking of a Relation between the Images of Metaphor*. Thinking of a relation between the A and B of metaphor is just what we have been doing. Perhaps it is better to think of fishing in a stream between A and B than of crossing a bridge between A and B.

> The wood-doves are singing along the Perkiomen.
> The bass lie deep, still afraid of the Indians.
>
> In the one ear of the fisherman, who is all
> One ear, the wood-doves are singing a single song.
>
> The bass keep looking ahead, upstream, in one
> Direction, shrinking from the spit and splash
>
> Of waterish spears. The fisherman is all
> One eye, in which the dove resembles the dove.
>
> There is one dove, one bass, one fisherman.
> Yet coo becomes rou-coo, rou-coo. How close
>
> To the unstated theme each variation comes . . .
> In that one ear it might strike perfectly:
>
> State the disclosure. In that one eye the dove
> Might spring to sight and yet remain a dove.
>
> The fisherman might be the single man
> In whose breast, the dove, alighting, would grow still.

Here, as elsewhere in Stevens, the poet searches for the perfect metaphor, again and again, fishing, looking, listening, spearing, fixing. Here, as elsewhere in Stevens, there is a play on "still." To "grow still" makes a double closure, as the dove grows quiet and also keeps on growing, which is how the A and B of poetic metaphor should work. Poetic metaphor sits quietly on the page, finally, and also goes on growing in our heads.

The 1942 poem, *Oak Leaves Are Hands,* allows no such images of metaphor. Lady Lowzen, the strange spirit of this poem, is one of several weaving ladies in Stevens' poetry. "She held her hand before him in the air, / For him to see, wove round her glittering hair." This is from another hand poem, which Stevens placed just before *Oak Leaves Are Hands,* a poem with the pointed title, *The Hand as a Being.* Both poems center on mysterious ladies, associated with trees, who do odd things with their hands, notably weaving with glittering effect in seven triplets. In *Notes toward a Supreme Fiction,* also from 1942, "The spouse, the bride / Is never naked. A fictive covering / Weaves always glistening from the heart and mind" (CP 396). My guess is that *The Hand as a Being* is a rejected canto for *Notes toward a Supreme Fiction*: the stanzaic and metrical form is the same, and, as in the final "fat girl" canto of *Notes,* this "first canto of the final canticle" is beneath a tree, with a "nameless dame" who is known by the end. She is related also to Nanzia Nunzio, who comes echoing the Canticles, and finds out about weaving and glistening. I shall approach Lady Lowzen partly through legend and partly through word-play, especially the play of metaphor.

The metaphors of *Oak Leaves Are Hands* are not logical, except for the analogy in the title. (The leaves of one oak family do look like hands.) And they are singularly hard to read. Stevens gives us one clue in his fine portmanteau word, "metamorphorid." All metaphor is a kind of metamorphosis, which is to say, change of meaning. This is all very well, but sinister or horrid metamorphosis? We are not accustomed to think of metaphor in this way. Stevens' full phrase is "evasive and metamorphorid," and clearly his lady is evasive in the pejorative and not the benign sense of the word. (He uses it both ways.) In *The Hand as a Being,* the speaker seizes the "naked, nameless dame." (The verb is Miltonic; Stevens, who was sensitive to such things, may have noticed how Adam "seizes" Eve's hand both before and after the Fall.) In the final canto of *Notes,* the speaker holds the fat girl. Evasion versus seizing, flirtation versus consummation, we may say, and of reading as of ladies in the very different pleasures of these texts. The elusive figuration of *Oak Leaves* tantalizes; the naked, nameless dame and the fat girl are auspicious muses, and grant consummation, which is to say, naming, for the poet. They are related to Eve, and their classical type would be Calypso, also one of Milton's types for Eve. But Lady Lowzen is related on the sinister side. She is closer to Lilith than to Eve, and her classical ancestress is Circe, also a powerful weaver and singer.

Singing is an old trope for the making of poetry, and so is weaving, as recent criticism on the "texture" of a text has reminded us. Poems, though now written, are conventionally sung or chanted, and may exercise some enchantment. *The Hand as a Being* opens with *cantare* words, "In the first canto of the final canticle," a line repeated three times in all. "Canto," "canticle," "composed" (also thrice repeated), "wove": we move on to *Oak Leaves Are Hands* with tropes of singing and weaving in our ears, and phrases from the Canticles. What we hear, after the promise of the title's metaphor, is a parody of one of the great singing and weaving poems in the English language, Coleridge's *Kubla Khan*.[12] Everything goes slightly off: expected ancestral halls become "ancestral hells." An expected bachelor of fine arts becomes a "bachelor of feen masquerie," going one better than Byron's Don Juan, who was "a bachelor—of arts, / And parts, and hearts" (C.xi). The usual female spinner and weaver would be a "spinster," not a bachelor, but Flora has taken a course in "feen masquerie." ("Feen" plays on archaic and Scottish "fine" and perhaps on German fairies or *Feen*;[13] "masquerie" is a neologism from "masque-mask-maquillage," as if metamorphosing the word "mask" into its various possibilities.[14]) This is metaphor as practiced by a witch—hence metamorphorid in Stevens' memorable word. Stevens hears the "-or" of metaphor and morphosis and horrid, as of the name Flora, and, less comfortably, Mac Mort.

What if metaphor "carries beyond" or transports in this queer horrid way toward a world of death? Why should the transformations of metaphor, its crossings over the bridge of "to be," its metamorphoses, be assumed to be benign? Perhaps they are malign. This is metaphor as metamorphosis, horrid variety, best understood in relation to Frye's theory of metaphor. For *Oak Leaves Are Hands* is, I think, about the disabling muse, for which we have no clear figure. Similarly, we may follow Frye in conceiving of anagogic metaphor as well as other, less radical kinds. But Frye's map moves upward. There is no demonic metaphor, which would be a contradiction in terms for Frye. Or, more precisely, demonic metaphor is the shadow side of anagogic metaphor, just as evil is lack of goodness in orthodox Christian theology. Stevens is more Manichean. Suppose we want a figure not only for the disabling muse

---

[12] Vendler notes the parody in *On Extended Wings: Wallace Stevens' Longer Poems* (Cambridge, Mass.: Harvard University Press, 1969), p. 151.

[13] Cf. Marie Borroff, cited in ibid., p. 152.

[14] See below, on the "mic-mac of mocking birds" in *An Ordinary Evening in New Haven*, and see the "mask-mimic" play in *Sombre Figuration* (*OP* 67).

but also for demonic metaphor: it would transport all right, but transport down or back. Such a muse would be powerful and sinister among singers and weavers and text-makers. Yet of course, once you can invent her and write about her in this funny way, you are on the road to recovery. That is to say, *Oak Leaves Are Hands* is a charm poem, perhaps quite personal. This lady, after all, is Florida in another guise, as Stevens tells us: "Flora she was once. She was florid. . . ." She is the sinister aspect of Stevens' one-time muse, and Stevens is working his way out of her web, out of her ancestral hells-cum-halls. Circe works "transformational magic," as Angus Fletcher says,[15] and you need to be Ulysses and have moly in order to get out of her metaphors. In Circe's garden, oak leaves *are* hands.

Bardic writing helps in reading this poem: Collins and Gray and Blake. Collins's *Ode on the Poetical Character*, with all its weaving and its magic notes and its enchanting Spenser-Milton heritage, is very useful. We might note the standard trope of a tree's "brow": "strange shades o'erbrow" the Poet's Eden. Stevens also uses the trope: "merely by putting hand to brow," a wonderful thinking, writing, sylvan figure. We might also note that Milton's "ev'ning ear . . . its [Heaven's] native strains could hear" by "that oak," the oak of *Il Penseroso*. We should also add the Gray-Blake line.[16] Here is Blake's comment on Gray's poem, *The Bard*: "Weaving the winding sheet of Edward's race by means of sounds of spiritual music and its accompanying expressions of articulate speech is a bold and daring and most masterly conception." Then we should turn this whole Collins-Gray-Blake bardic pattern upside down. Lady Lowzen, being a tree-spirit, "merely by putting hand to brow," can function like a bard, enlivening past and future. Rather than inspiring a Miltonic evening ear, she goes odd, and her pensiveness is far from pastoral. Stevens has highly mixed feelings about the "feen masquerie" of any bard within him. We have seen this in his mixed reactions to his own gift for euphony and charm poetry, and to his early love of birdsong. And we shall see, in the birdsong canto of *Notes*, how he tends to extremes when he exorcises such charm. Gray's oak trees sigh revenge on the king who has murdered bards. Stevens takes his own revenge on the bard within himself. Prophetic or bardic metaphors that get out of hand deserve their bewitching, demonic counterpart.

Metaphors of a Magnifico is a forerunner of *The Motive for Metaphor*, as Vendler argues, and also, I think, of the fourth poem of *Trans-*

---

[15] Angus Fletcher, *The Prophetic Moment: An Essay on Spenser* (Chicago: University of Chicago Press, 1971), p. 79.

[16] Cf. Vendler, *On Extended Wings*, p. 327.

port to Summer, Gigantomachia. In 1943, Stevens divided the problem of the magnifico by treating two different kinds of metaphor in the third and fourth poems of *Transport to Summer. Gigantomachia* centers on archetypal metaphor, and again uses soldier figures. It too is a wartime poem, and questions of archetypal metaphor are apt to be important in wartime. But *Gigantomachia* is a rather weak poem, for all the bluster of its title. It is *The Motive for Metaphor* that we think of as Stevens' chief poem on the subject of metaphor. It is an inviting puzzle, though its word-play is so intricate that I am not sure we shall ever untangle it—which means that metaphor's motive, like all deep motives, stays partly hidden. The play begins with the title itself, in the schematic echo that raises further echoes (what's a meta for?). Etymological play connects motive and metaphor, reminding us that "motion . . . is always the essence of metaphor."[17] We are not surprised to find motion in this poem, then, though the tropes and grammar of motion may surprise us. The first half has ordinary grammatical sentences and describes disabled figures. The second half has no verb at all, but astonishing cumulative vigor in its appositive phrases, and a most puzzling syntax:

> You like it under the trees in autumn,
> Because everything is half dead.
> The wind moves like a cripple among the leaves
> And repeats words without meaning.
>
> In the same way, you were happy in spring,
> With the half colors of quarter-things,
> The slightly brighter sky, the melting clouds,
> The single bird, the obscure moon—
>
> The obscure moon lighting an obscure world
> Of things that would never be quite expressed,
> Where you yourself were never quite yourself
> And did not want nor have to be,
>
> Desiring the exhilarations of changes:
> The motive for metaphor, shrinking from
> The weight of primary noon,
> The A B C of being,
>
> The ruddy temper, the hammer
> Of red and blue, the hard sound—
> Steel against intimation—the sharp flash,
> The vital, arrogant, fatal, dominant X.

---

[17] Christine Brooke-Rose, in a classic formulation, in her *Grammar of Metaphor* (London: Secker & Warburg, 1958), p. 258.

"You like it": who is "you" in this core sentence? The primary reading is of "you" as reader. But a secondary reading of the title suggests something more. It suggests that "the motive for metaphor" is not just our human motive but also metaphor's own motive. Stevens sometimes personifies figures of speech and thought, as I have noted, and he personifies metaphor more often than we have realized. So read, "you" becomes the personified figure of metaphor itself. I find this reading helpful because Stevens does seem to be working with a land of metaphor, a *pays de la métaphore*. ("It is only *au pays de la métaphore qu'on est poète*," says Stevens, with Mallarmé [*OP* 179].) Or rather with two *pays de la métaphore*: a natural, changing world of metamorphosis, and a place of art, of fixing, of againstness, a forge.

Suppose we conceive of a land of metaphor, a true place for this trope: not the standard country of standard taxonomies, where tenors of metaphor are too often solid concepts, while vehicles of metaphor are light contraptions; but a world where metaphors live, metaphors past and present, potential and actual, written and read. Such a land would include unmade metaphors, moving to or from completeness, or just moving about, content not to be themselves. Such a land would also include the place where metaphors are made—not a landscape as in the first part but a forge or crossing-place as in the second. Not nature but art. Not safe simile ("you like it") but dangerous metaphor. In short, Stevens has attempted a poem like Yeats's *Byzantium*, with a similar ambivalence about fixing things in art, a similar figure for doing so (a smithy),[18] with a weaker, less tormented world of flux. Our motive for metaphor is motion or change, new art, which we go on desiring. Our motive for metaphor is to achieve and fix powerful metaphor, which we go on desiring. What does metaphor itself desire? To wander sometimes as mere potential? To be made? To be read? To prevail and become a sovereign metaphor (anagogic?), which is to say, a "reality"? To prevail over logic and grammar?

Such a reading helps account for the senses of an artistic plot, and a plot of primal forces, throughout the poem. It also helps account for the sense of the Vulcan figure in both halves of the poem, first as cripple, then as archetypal artificer with his great forge. For there is a play through the poem on impotence and potency. This is the contrast we hear between the grammar and tropes of the first part, and of the second

---

[18] Patricia Parker, in a fine charting of Stevens' ambiguous syntax, compares Browning's use of the goldsmith and his "ABC of being" in Book I of *The Ring and the Book* (I.1358–60) in "The Motive for Metaphor," *Wallace Stevens Journal* 7 (1983), 76–88. On this poem, see also David Walker, *The Transparent Lyric: Reading and Meaning in the Poetry of Stevens and Williams* (Princeton: Princeton University Press, 1984), pp. 77–80.

part. The stresses of the last line come like hammer blows, and we hear the sound of something like Vulcan's forge or his famous pinnings-down. Something animate seems to shrink here, as if a horse were being shod. (We recall the fish that "shrinks" from the fisherman's spear.) Or as if Vulcan were hammering the fetters of Prometheus or the net to catch Venus and Mars. Once caught, once pinned down, Prometheus can no longer storm heaven and steal fire, nor Venus take more lovers. These primal forces will have been stilled, and transport stopped. Art does that when it catches things in metaphors, and yet it does not. Poetic metaphors get made, finally, and printed on a page. Poetic metaphors also go on generating endless meanings. If I am right that the figure of Vulcan has a vocational force for Stevens, as well as a personal force, this would support Vendler's psychological reading of the poem.[19] Yet I would argue against too exclusive a psychological reading, which downplays questions of metaphor that greatly interested Stevens.

Some current tropes for metaphor explore erotic and biological language. "Steel against intimation," says Stevens. Ted Cohen commends to us the "topic of linguistic intimation" in his "Metaphor and the Cultivation of Intimacy." He ends by warning that metaphor's intimacy "is not . . . an invariably friendly thing" and may even be "lethal."[20] His plot sounds curiously like Stevens' plot in *The Motive for Metaphor*. But Iris Murdoch comes closer: "Any artist both dreads and longs for the approach of necessity, the moment at which form irrevocably crystallizes."[21]

I began by observing the odd behavior of grammar and trope in this poem. Can we extend the plot? Suppose we think of *The Motive for Metaphor* as posing the following question, a natural enough question when we look at the tension between its grammar and its metaphors. What is the relation between grammar and rhetoric? Sometimes it is a dull affair. Perhaps we should think of grammar and rhetoric as like artist and material, or like two primal forces that desire yet resist each other like some lovers. Perhaps we might say of them: 1) each will try to dominate the other; 2) each will desire and resist domination; 3) neither can finally dominate; 4) this will go on.

One metaphor poem in *Transport to Summer* comes disguised as a riddle poem, so well disguised that it has thus far resisted identification. The first line and a half of *Man Carrying Thing* are often quoted, but the rest of the poem hardly ever. As the rest is said to be an illustration of

---

[19] Vendler, *Wallace Stevens: Words Chosen Out of Desire*, pp. 23–26.
[20] Ted Cohen, in *On Metaphor*, ed. Sacks, pp. 6, 9, 10–11.
[21] "The Sublime and the Beautiful Revisited," *Yale Review* 49 (1959–60), 271.

the famous saying, this seems fair enough, for "The poem must resist the intelligence / Almost successfully."

> The poem must resist the intelligence
> Almost successfully. Illustration:
>
> A brune figure in winter evening resists
> Identity. The thing he carries resists
>
> The most necessitous sense. Accept them, then,
> As secondary (parts not quite perceived
>
> Of the obvious whole, uncertain particles
> Of the certain solid, the primary free from doubt,
>
> Things floating like the first hundred flakes of snow
> Out of a storm we must endure all night,
>
> Out of a storm of secondary things),
> A horror of thoughts that suddenly are real.
>
> We must endure our thoughts all night, until
> The bright obvious stands motionless in cold.

Certainly the words "brune figure" seem to resist identification. (I shall come later to identity.) "Brune" is an obsolete English adjective for "brown," so that this is an obsolete or dead metaphor, to read symbolically. But perhaps "brune" is French, and the figure is alive, to read bilingually. (*Figure* in French is feminine and so would take the form *brune*.) But "brune" is also a noun in French, and it means "dusk" or "twilight"—say, a "winter evening," as the poem says. In that case, a "brune figure" is a twilight figure or metaphor. (The pun is also at work in Eliot's meeting at dusk with the figure of Brunetto in *Little Gidding*.) The light wanes; a storm comes. We cannot identify figures specifically or generally, as Stevens plays back and forth between figure as man and man as figure.

For what is "Man Carrying Thing"? If man is transporting thing, this is, quite simply, the figure of metaphor. (I. A. Richards would call it "Vehicle Carrying Tenor.") If man is carrying thing so both may face a problem of identity, this is the figure of a man as a philosophical or psychological type. (Identity: the sameness of a *person* or *thing* at all times or in all circumstances. OED 2.)

Descriptively, the figure is a man as obscure as the thing he carries. Stevens' imperative mood tells us to accept man and thing as secondary, and the poem moves through his customary appositions toward something obvious, white, primary, so that we come to expect the last line:

"The bright obvious stands motionless in cold." (The terms in the parenthesis sound like terms from a problem of identity, and they include the part-whole opposites that Stevens knows so well.) The intelligence can presumably perceive something, since that something is bright, obvious, and motionless. But things are not quite right. For one thing, we must "endure" the storm until the bright obvious stands. And what is that "horror of thoughts that suddenly are real" (the hardest line in the poem)?

In the secondary reading, the figure is a figure of thought, that is, metaphor. To read this way, taking the parenthesis as a true or elidable parenthesis, is to read the man and thing as a simile in which thought is horrible, and to be endured, until something different from thought stands. Christopher Ricks has taught us ways of reading parentheses and their disjunctions.[22] And Frank Doggett notes how the poem "carries" the parenthesis, like man carrying thing.[23] How oddly this parenthesis works, for it reverses the logic of the sentence to make one extreme instead of another. There is a question of clarity here, and of turning inside out, as there often is with metaphor. ("Some things are, however, expressed with greater clearness and precision by means of metaphor than by means of the precise terms themselves," says Demetrius [*On Style* II.82, Loeb].)

How useful is it to connect problems of identity and metaphor? Frye uses personal identity as the best example of anagogic metaphor.[24] Stevens finds the relation of metaphor and identity problematic. In *The Motive for Metaphor*, he says, "you yourself were never quite yourself / And did not want nor have to be." Is this a metaphor? Is it a desirable state, and in what ways? Vendler reads this poem as a problem in identity. What does it mean when a figure "resists" identity? Should metaphor, or should we, resist identity? If identity is being identical, like newspapers coming off the press (Stevens' 1947 example [*NA* 72–73]), yes indeed, though the point is hardly worth making. If identity is logical identity, where A = A (or twenty men crossing a bridge are twenty men crossing a bridge), yes indeed, though again the point is hardly worth making. If identity is philosophical or psychological identity, the question becomes more interesting. Perhaps we should reverse things and ask if identity is a problem of metaphor.

[22] Christopher Ricks, "Geoffrey Hill and 'the tongue's atrocities,' " *Times Literary Supplement*, June 30, 1978.

[23] Frank Doggett, *Stevens' Poetry of Thought* (Baltimore: The Johns Hopkins University Press, 1966), p. 130. Doggett suggests that the word "secondary" is used in a Lockean sense.

[24] Frye, *Anatomy of Criticism*, pp. 124–25.

In any case, Stevens' clear bright closure is most equivocal. If transport and change stop, there is an end to the problem of metaphor and identity, but also an end to man and metaphor (taking this as motionless man and motionless metaphor). If transport and change have been swirling among possibilities and suddenly grow clear, this is achieved metaphor and identity. As with *The Motive for Metaphor*, the plot is double and turns inside out and outside in. As with *The Motive for Metaphor*, the end is still and yet moving.

One interesting aspect of metaphor in Stevens is the "againstness" that seems part of its function. Wayne Booth thinks of metaphor as "additive" or a "synthesis."[25] But Stevens' metaphor ends in an X not a +. I read this as a sign of the action of having crossed and also of crossing, something achieved and fixed and finished, and also something that goes on. Such a reading is both synchronic (this is how metaphor works) and diachronic (this is how metaphors have worked). Diachronically, it makes a way of proceeding, as we leave dead or crossed metaphors, and keep moving or crossing ones. This may also speak to Karsten Harries's sense of metaphor as sometimes "collusion" and sometimes "collision."[26] Perhaps it is both.

To follow Stevens' play with some figures of metaphor is only a beginning. I touched on Herr Doktor's notions of metaphor in *Delightful Evening*, and on metaphor as juxtaposition and metaphor as analogy before coming to the five poems above. I have not touched on metaphor (or trope) as deviation, a continuing and far from simple idea in Stevens. Nor on Stevens' rewriting of Keats and Hopkins in

> Adam of beau regard, from fat Elysia,
> Whose mind malformed this morning metaphor,
>
> While all the leaves leaked gold. His mind made morning,
> As he slept. He woke in a metaphor: this was
> A metamorphosis of paradise. . . . (CP 331)

Nor on Stevens' one-line series of metaphors for a pineapple (*NA* 83). Nor on *Metaphor as Degeneration*, a late poem. Nor on Stevens' play with that strange, most common verb "to be." Nor on much more. Our own chief danger in reading Stevens' word-play and word-war with metaphor is neatness of identification, to come back to one epigraph for this book.

We might end the metaphor poems of *Transport to Summer* with the

---

[25] Wayne Booth, *A Rhetoric of Irony* (Chicago and London: University of Chicago Press, 1974), p. 177.

[26] Karsten Harries, "Metaphor and Transcendence," in *On Metaphor*, ed. Sacks, p. 71n.

poem just after *Man Carrying Thing*, called *Pieces* (1946). There is no problem of identity here, though for identification we need to know what Christmas tinsel looks like in February. Though the subject is similar to that of *Man Carrying Thing*, the terms and tonality have shifted. This poem sings.

> Tinsel in February, tinsel in August.
> There are things in a man besides his reason.
> Come home, wind, he kept crying and crying.

And Stevens repeats the last line, like a refrain. Its force is in that word, "home" (most of us would say, "Come back, wind"). The poem speaks to matters of summer, voice, part and whole, simile and metaphor. In this, it is like the last canto of *Notes toward a Supreme Fiction*, written four years earlier, but chosen to close *Transport to Summer*. It is this last crossing between artist and material, between lover and fat girl, that is Stevens' most felicitous in the entire volume.

* * * * *

War and the Normal Sublime:

Esthétique du Mal

> The fundamental difficulty in any art is the problem of the normal. (*OP* 169)

> For myself, the inaccessible jewel is the normal. . . . (*L* 521, 1946)

> Is evil normal or abnormal? (*NA* 154, 1948)

WHAT KIND of word-play is the title *Esthétique du Mal*? Weakly provocative might be one answer—a mixing of aesthetics and ethics, a calling-up of Baudelaire. The word "esthétique" suggests a question of translation, and not just French to English. Greek is also pertinent in the etymological sense of the word, and Stevens said he had this sense in mind. "I was thinking of aesthetics as the equivalent of aperçus, which seems to have been the original meaning" (*L* 469, 1944; cf. OED, "aesthetics," 1a, and the headnote, especially on Kant). John Crowe Ransom may have suggested one starting point, by his inability to translate from one sphere to another. "The time scarcely comes when there is enough of dedicated public service to fight evil in the world, and improve the lot of the citizens; when is there a time for art?"[1] Stevens will not separate the spheres of ethics and aesthetics in this way. He would later protest when people spoke "as if the discipline of the arts was in no sense a moral discipline" (*NA* 175, 1951). "The question of the existence of spheres [of

---

[1] John Crowe Ransom, "Artists, Soldiers, Positivists," *Kenyon Review* 6 (1944), 276–81.

value] and the question of what is appropriate to them are not settled"
(*NA* 148, 1948). And in 1943, he copied into his commonplace book a
sentence by Flaubert: "L'esthétique est une justice supérieure."[2]

Mal sounds detached, as though Stevens were evading the associations
of words like "pain" and "evil." Yet the French word gives him what no
English word does, a test we must always apply to foreign words in his
text, as R. P. Blackmur knew.[3] It gives him one term for both necessary
(or natural) and unnecessary evils, that is, for evils apparently unavoid-
able, and those deliberately done and suffered. (The question then be-
comes what evils are truly unavoidable, and whether they should be
called evils. Death is unavoidable, but Stevens will work against calling
death an evil. The human will is more controversial—the principle of
evil, said one reader of Balzac, and Stevens recorded the remark.[4]) One
dictionary definition of "mal" reads: "evil, wrong, harm, hurt, ache,
malady, difficulty, trouble," so that "mal" also includes smaller afflic-
tions as well as larger. *Avoir le mal du pays* is to be homesick, to have
nostalgia, our Greek-rooted word that Stevens uses so memorably in
canto x. The word "mal" is untranslatable in some ways, thus providing
in little an allegory about pain. For the experience of pain cannot be
translated directly, only indirectly. All words, not just some, are "cut off
from pain," to quote the soldier's words that inspired this poem. It is a
question of what words sound appropriate and when.

As for Baudelaire, he too had written an antiinfernal collection ninety
years before, but antiinfernal in a very different sense from Stevens'.
Baudelaire transfers hell to earth, and centers his poetry on the abnor-
mal. He knows what hell is, says Eliot, who likes him for that, and con-
trasts *Fleurs du Mal* favorably with the contemporaneous *Leaves of
Grass*.[5] Stevens' great desire is to write a poetry of earth, but one of the
difficulties of this enterprise is the force of a poetry of hell. Tropes of
evil, pain, and suffering take on peculiar force from their association with
hell or the demonic. Eliot assumed that humanism and liberalism did not
take seriously the fact of human evil, evil so monstrous that it seems as
if only a divine, transcendent force beyond the merely human can com-
bat it. Stevens' response is different:

---

[2] Commonplace Book, II, 4, WAS 70–73, Huntington Library. Quoted by permission of
Holly Stevens and the Huntington Library.

[3] R. P. Blackmur, "Examples of Wallace Stevens," in his *Form and Value in Modern
Poetry* (New York: Doubleday, 1957), pp. 183–212.

[4] The remark, by William Troy, appeared in the *Kenyon Review* 2 (1940), 334, according
to Stevens' Commonplace Book, II, 2, WAS 70–73.

[5] Eliot, "Baudelaire," in his *Selected Essays*, 3d ed. (London: Faber & Faber, 1951), p.
420, and "Whitman and Tennyson," *Nation & Athenaeum* 40 (1926), 426.

Is evil normal or abnormal? And how do the exquisite divinations of the poets and for that matter even the "aureoles of the saints" help? . . . But when we speak of perceiving the normal we have in mind the instinctive integrations which are the reason for living. Of what value is anything to the solitary and those that live in misery and terror, except the imagination? . . . the chief problems of any artist, as of any man, are the problems of the normal and . . . he needs, in order to solve them, everything that the imagination has to give. (*NA*, 154–56, 1948)

One possible way of responding to evil is through the force of the normal rather than the force of the divine, and this is Stevens' response. His notion of the normal is very different from that in Eliot's 1930 essay on Baudelaire, which would make any sane person detest the normal. Stevens had an uphill battle if he wished to establish the normal as something powerful and desirable. As he says, "To be able to see the portal of literature, that is to say: the portal of the imagination, as a scene of normal love and normal beauty is, of itself, a feat of great imagination" (*NA* 155, 1948). "Portal" is a high Romantic term, and we expect to hear of extraordinary and elevated love and beauty there, that is, we expect to hear of the sublime. Stevens' strategy is to place normal things there. "For myself, the inaccessible jewel is the normal and all of life, in poetry, is the difficult pursuit of just that" (*L* 521, 1946). "The fundamental difficulty in any art is the problem of the normal" (*OP* 169). In *Esthétique du Mal*, Stevens implicitly rebukes Eliot's Baudelaire for killing off God and retaining the devil. (So also, we kill off idealized readings of texts and cheerfully retain all the tropes and shudders of the *abyme*.) He sets about undoing the dialectic of evil versus good, *mal* versus *bon*, where the good is understood in transcendent, notably Christian, terms. What he works toward is a dialectic of evil versus the normal, of evil versus the good understood as normal, everyday, earthly good. It is all-important to understand this strategy of Stevens.

Given this strategy, it is a stroke of genius to begin with a natural example of mal, the erupting volcano Vesuvius. I shall pause over that volcano and canto i, in order to add one fact, some associative readings, and a suggestion about topos. The fact is that there was an eruption of Vesuvius in 1944: "In World War II, after the Allies had gained control of the area in 1944, Vesuvius erupted again. This eruption was preceded by several days of seismic activity. Then at 4:30 on the afternoon of March 18, molten lava welled up through fissures in the floor of the crater. It poured over the rim and flowed down the side of the volcano. At 5:30 pm on the 20th the explosive phase began. The ruins of Pompeii were reburied under nearly a foot of ash."[6] Some two months after this eruption, Stevens read the spring issue of the *Kenyon Review* and began *Esthétique du Mal*; six weeks later, the poem was complete. "What particularly interested me," he wrote to Ransom, "was the letter from one of your correspondents about the relation between poetry and what he called pain. Whatever he might mean, it might be interesting to try to do an esthetique du mal. It is the kind of idea that it is difficult to shake off" (*L* 468, June 17, 1944). Here is part of the letter Stevens read:

> What *are* we after in poetry? Or, more exactly, what are we attempting to rout? The commandos of contemporary literature are having little to do with Eliot and even poets of charming distemper like Wallace Stevens (for whom we all developed considerable passion). ["Prone to distemper he abates in taste," said Stevens of Crispin, and the line is turned against him here.] Not necessarily a poetry of time and place, either. The question of poetry as in life (and in the Army) is one of survival, simply. . . . Men like Karl Shapiro (his "Anxiety"), John Berryman, Delmore Schwartz transcend the aesthetic of poetry—thank God! I find the poetry in *Kenyon Review* lamentable in many ways because it is cut off from pain. It is intellectual and it is fine, but it never reveals muscle and nerve.

When Stevens wrote the poem, then, Naples had just passed into Allied hands and Vesuvius had just repeated the geological phenomenon known to ancients and moderns alike. The place and time seem made to order for a war poem about an aesthetics of pain, as desired by Ransom's correspondent. More than one observer of Vesuvius in eruption compared the sight and sound to the guns of war. Quite apart from war, volcanoes are places of terror, where warlike language sounds appropriate. They are conceived as mouths of hell, again an appropriate wartime metaphor. "Here is the famed gate of the nether king," says Aeneas to the Sibyl of Cumae in her cave (*Aeneid* VI.106–107, Loeb). "Hemmed in between Elysium and Tartarus"; "in a Paradise . . . the neighbouring jaws of hell"; "this peak of hell, thus rearing itself in the midst of a Paradise." Thus Goethe on Naples and Vesuvius in his *Italian Journey*. Volcanic fire and also ethereal fire are regarded with wonder by humans, says Longinus. The contrast of nether and ethereal fires accounts for Stevens' unusual word "ether," so long associated with things heavenly in a classical and Christian scheme of things. "The volcano trembled in an-

---

[6] *Encyclopedia Americana* (Cambridge, Mass.: Harvard University Press, 1981), "Vesuvius." See also Richard Wilbur, *Responses: Prose Pieces 1953–1976* (New York and London: Harcourt, Brace, Jovanovich, 1976), pp. 16–17.

other ether, / As the body trembles at the end of life." The two fires, destructive and heavenly, had been used by Eliot two years before in *Little Gidding*, in a paradoxical Christian use. Stevens distances both from human experience. Nor will he have anything to do with an apocalyptic view that "the fire and the rose are one" (*Little Gidding* v)—a very possible reason for separating the fire and the rose so sharply in this canto.

Vesuvius is, then, not only a volcano in the general theater of war in 1944, whose sight and sound are like the great, terrible guns of war. It is not only a volcano near Naples, providing actual contrast of earth as a fruitful paradise and earth as hellish. It is not only associated by ancients and moderns with the mouth of hell. It is also commonly one of the objects that elicits feelings of the sublime in classical and modern writing on the sublime (in Longinus, Burke, Kant, etc.). And by these last two associations, it is connected with the gods (sublime feelings connecting us with the gods, and infernal regions showing the wrath of the gods or of God, whether in the old war against the Titans or Dante's hellfire or Freud's associations of Yahweh with volcanoes).[7] It is, finally, a figure of poetic voice.

Over this last category, I need to pause. I spoke of volcanoes as mouths of hell, concentrating on hell rather than mouths. A crater is naturally enough troped as a mouth. (The Sicilians call them mixing bowls but we call them mouths or throats, says Lucretius [vi.701–702].) This mouth speaks differently from the mouth and flowing of a river in fluency poems. For one thing, a "volcano" is etymologically from Vulcan, presumably since it sounds like his great forges at work. Here, then, is another "note of Vulcan" that Crispin might long to own. (Stevens made the Vulcan-volcano connection clear in lines that he cut from *The Comedian as the Letter C:* "Virgins on Volcan del Fuego wear / That Volcan in their bosoms as they wear / Its nibs upon their fingers" [*Journal of Crispin*, p. 42]—a very different kind of volcano.) For another thing, "Every new writer, as Emerson wrote, is only a new crater of an old volcano,"[8] and writers as various as Byron and Browning have used the figure for their own poetic voice. For another thing, Stevens used a volcano-as-voice figure twice in 1936 in quite contrary ways. He amused himself with the notion of cheap and easy "volcanic" outbursts in the figure of the "volcano Apostrophe," which he glossed as follows: "A man who spouts apostrophes is a volcano and in particular the volcano

[7] Sigmund Freud, *Moses and Montheism* II, vol. 23 of *The Standard Edition of the Complete Psychological Works of Sigmund Freud*, trans. James Strachey (London: Hogarth, 1973–1974), p. 45 n. 2 This work was published in English and in German in 1939.

[8] Emerson, cited by Richard Howard, in his *Preferences* (New York: Viking, 1974), p. 6.

Apostrophe" (*L* 372, 1940; cf. *OP* 63). But *A Postcard from the Volcano* is something else: not the tourist's postcard from the safe slopes but a voice from within the volcano addressed to future generations. Something like Yeats's late, ghostly voices, this is Stevens' own dead voice, as he imagines it speaking after he has gone—that is, as it now speaks to us.

If the volcano is a place of voice, we might go on and ask if it is also an image of topos. I argued that the hearth-fire in *Domination of Black* was an image of a topos, and I think the volcano is a powerful, late image of topos in Stevens—this time not a common place in the sense of a hearth-fire, but instead a common place for mighty spirits, whether of the underworld or Vulcan's forge or vanquished Titans or earlier poets or one's own poetic spirit. We would not go seeking kinds of argument here, as in Aristotle's storehouse or Quintilian's hunting ground. If we come here, we are likely to hear prophecy not argument, and to need a priestess and a golden bough quite as much as Aeneas did in order to reemerge alive. This is postclassical topos as a place of voice with a vengeance.[9]

It is disconcerting, then, to find Stevens firmly turning his back on all this potential weight of tradition and moving over to argument and away from prophecy. What we expect to happen here does not happen. The "sounds" of the words, "potent for so long, [have] become merely the emblem of a mythology," to quote Stevens' 1942 essay on the sublime (*NA* 4). (He calls it nobility.) Given this subject, surely Stevens' first two cantos, like his title, run the risk of sounding merely moderate or even "mean," to use Longinus's contraries to the sublime. Certainly our common reading objects to the man in canto i because he is so cool toward that erupting volcano. Like some readers of the once-famous lines of Lucretius about enjoying disaster from afar, we dislike the gap between pain and theorizing about pain. Something in us objects to the sentence, "His book / Made sure of the most correct catastrophe." We are following Burke or Kant in our objection; according to them, the man in this canto has lost the sublime, for all that he reads about it. He ought to be using rhapsodic language and thinking of his Maker, that is, moving from contemplation of the natural sublime to expression in the rhetorical sublime and conviction of the transcendental sublime. Instead, he

---

[9] Cf. Harold Bloom's remarks on the image of the empty pyramid in Hegel, Derrida, Shelley, and Melville, in the course of an argument against sublime-as-sublimation literary reading and for sublime-as-repression reading. A volcano, erupting or extinct or between, is an even better image, being almost too uncomfortably connected with the sublime. Cf. *Agon: Towards a Theory of Revisionism* (New York and Oxford: Oxford University Press, 1982), pp. 242–43.

experiences the natural sublime without any corresponding sublimity of feeling or conviction or language.

"Pleasant" Naples and the paroxysms of Vesuvius: the contrast is extreme. "Pleasant" is pointedly not a sublime term. Nor is the picturesque a sublime category. Stevens' clause, "the sultriest fulgurations, flickering, / Cast corners in the glass," is a fine, precise observation of the odd effect of brilliant light reflected just for a moment in a squared piece of glass. It also glances at theories of the picturesque. Does this man read about the sublime and see only the picturesque? Stevens implies more than one sense of reflection in his mirrored sublime. Is the sublime limited or cornered into its own "little brother,"[10] the picturesque? Stevens raises the question without providing the standard answer of yes. Schiller says that "the relative grandeur [of the natural sublime] outside him [the observer] is the mirror in which he perceives the absolute grandeur within himself."[11] Stevens' cunning use of mirrors throughout his work suggests that the glass here, like some iconographic detail in a painting, is meant to remind us of several things: of actual flashing light, of the sublime versus the picturesque, and of the mirroring function in theories of the sublime.

Similarly, "It was almost time for lunch" is first a descriptive statement but also obliquely introduces canons of taste, again a nonsublime category. (I am arguing for a submerged pun on the word "taste," not for the notion that aesthetic taste originated with the taste of the tongue, as, for example, in Dugald Stewart.[12])

This student of aesthetics may well be related to American aesthetes in Europe,[13] for whom loss of the old sublime was a problem. He is certainly related to those famous visitors to Naples who saw Vesuvius in eruption and wrote "letters home" about it: Berkeley, who also said that Vesuvius "groaned"; Winckelmann, for whom the sound was most like an artillery bombardment; Goethe, who is for Stevens the most obvious forerunner; and many another. (Once we start looking, they seem legion, as can happen with Stevens' types.[14]) But this man is hardly a

[10] The phrase is Angus Fletcher's, in *Allegory: The Theory of a Symbolic Mode* (Ithaca and London: Cornell University Press, 1964), p. 244.

[11] Friedrich von Schiller, *Naive and Sentimental Poetry and On the Sublime*, trans. Julius A. Elias (New York: Ungar, 1966), p. 203.

[12] Dugald Stewart, *Collected Works*, vol. 5, *Philosophical Essays*, ed. Sir William Hamilton (Edinburgh: Thomas Constable, 1855), "On the Sublime," pp. 275–329.

[13] Harold Bloom, *Wallace Stevens: The Poems of Our Climate* (Ithaca: Cornell University Press, 1977), p. 229.

[14] They include James Fenimore Cooper, Athanasius Kircher (who said, "O altitudo, O the greatness of God," on seeing Vesuvius in eruption), Samuel Rogers (who said, "Volcani Domus . . . like the explosion of great Ordnance"), John Ruskin, and many others.

Goethe, contrasting Eden and hell, or even a Tischbein, who at least had some strong feelings, if not sublime ones, about the phenomenon. He may be a composite, something of a self-parody whose purpose is to make us question our own way of thinking about the sublime. Stevens gives us little information, and so tries to maneuver us away from dramatic readings based on character, and toward an examination of terms and arguments. We do not know whether this man is young or old or what he thinks or even that he thinks derivatively.

The proposition of canto i is that "Pain is human." Stevens sets aside the matter of animal pain, which can be connected with human pain, evil, and war, in the Pauline view that the "whole creation groaneth and travailleth," as in Lowell's *Quaker Graveyard in Nantucket*. He is careful to confine the language of pain to Vesuvius, emphasizing that we project pain on to natural phenomena that do not experience the pain felt by creatures with a central nervous system. The notion that the world apart from us feels no pain "is a part of the sublime / From which we shrink."

But why? If we cannot have a sublimely magnificent and good natural world, we seem to prefer a sublimely terrible one to one just "there" and innocent of human feelings. Melville observes that we may add to the natural world "whatever is sweet, and honorable, and sublime." The actual natural world may have the "colorless all-color of atheism from which we shrink." (Both sentences are taken from his famous chapter on the whiteness of the whale, and Stevens may be echoing the second one.) Stevens' point is that we add pain quite as much as sweetness, honor, and the sublime. The significance of this point becomes clearer when we extend the argument to the word "evil." That too we project on to the nonhuman world. Stevens makes this very clear in a letter to Delmore Schwartz: "You are fascinated by evil. I cannot see that this fascination has anything on the fascination by good. A bird singing in the sun is the same thing as a dog barking in the dark" (L 693, October 9, 1950).

I have spent some time on canto i, and I shall now move forward more rapidly, concentrating on some of Stevens' word-play and word-war, for this is both full-dress play and war. At the end, I shall comment briefly on how the poem speaks to theories of the sublime.

But first I need to map the arguments, if only roughly. Stevens' fifteen cantos all center on a proposition, usually explicit. The first three form an introduction on the subject of pain, after which he shifts the subject from pain to evil, then to the imperfect. (We should distinguish these categories.) The propositions of the first three cantos are: 1) pain is human; 2) pain is not to be blamed on nature ("It is pain that is indifferent to the sky."); 3) nor is it to be blamed on the demonic. Cantos iv and v are on the subjects of radical evil and radical love. ("The genius of misfortune / Is not a sentimentalist." "So great a unity, that it is bliss, / Ties us to those we love.") Canto vi treats the subject of perfection and imperfection, playing with celestial orbits. Canto vii breaks the sequence for an elegy on the war dead. Its difficult proposition is: "His wound is good because life was." Cantos viii and ix consider a world without the sublime. Three cantos follow on the subject of the innocence of living, working against most "nostalgias." Cantos xiii and xiv treat of necessity. (Ananke, "the unalterable necessity / Of being this unalterable animal." Leninist necessity or the political sublime.) Canto xv closes on the proposition that "The greatest poverty is not to live / In a physical world."

Canto ii is a rather puzzling fable of the beautiful as against the sublime, with Stevens' old figure of the moon-watcher. If it is a dark night of the soul, Stevens' astringent view of such nights would help explain the tone: "Most of the dark nights of the soul consist of self-pity."[15] Canto iii like canto ii comes to a sense of this earth as sufficient for "salvation," but only after a journey through Dante's world:

> His firm stanzas hang like hives in hell
> Or what hell was, since now both heaven and hell
> Are one, and here, O terra infidel.

"Firm" stanzas? Stevens is playing with the phrase *terra firma*, earth now being no such thing but rather a terra infidel, at least from a Dantean view. Dante's hell was in its way a terra firma and his earth not at all firm ground, considered metaphysically. But Dante's terra firma, whether earth or hell, depended on his *stanza firma*. "Hang" echoes back against the double "hanging" of canto ii (scent hangs, hives hang), as this stanza catches up the heavy alliterative h-play five lines earlier. Kinds of hanging or depending are of the essence here. The last clause, "as if we were sure to find our way," plays against the famous opening lines of Dante's *Inferno*, where, in the middle of life's way, he has lost his way. Stevens' argument is familiar enough: that a pitying god (a Jewish or Christian God, primarily) induces self-pity. This is an argument from experience, and it is a possible but not necessary argument, for all Nietzsche's polemic. Stevens' desire and his courage are moving, if not logically connected with belief or unbelief. His meditation on pity addresses itself also to the connection between the sublime and the pathetic.

For the first time in the series, Stevens plays with echo and allusion, echoing three of his "four great poets" or forerunners in "The Noble

---

[15] *L* 863, whence also: "Nietzsche was one of the inventors of the dark nights of the soul" (December 28, 1954).

Rider and the Sound of Words," Dante, Shakespeare, and Milton (*NA* 27; Virgil is the fourth). "The fault lies with an over-human god . . . a too, too human god, self-pity's kin / And uncourageous genesis." Whose fault? Stevens does not say precisely, but we need to retain the word, for it is important in the following canto in a "fault / Falls . . . false" sequence that recalls Milton. So does "woe" here. "Too, too human" recalls something else to my ear. "O that this too, too solid flesh would melt": this, rather than Nietzsche's *Human, All Too Human*, is the echo that tells. (Stevens read volume one of Nietzsche in March 1944, and thought little of it, though he liked the sound of the German [*L* 462].) It is not that Stevens supposes Hamlet to be self-pitying; this would be a simple and boring Nietzschean point. Stevens is making a parallel of Hamlet and his father with Christ and God the Father, a parallel already exploited by Joyce. "Who by sympathy has made himself a man" is *in nuce* the doctrine of the Incarnation. Stevens' echo whispers a wish that such too, too solid doctrinal flesh would also melt. (This doctrinal war does not apply to the earthly Jesus, as witness the language of *The Good Man Has No Shape*.)

Once we hear this echo, the unusual word "kin" in "self-pity's kin" also takes on Shakespearean resonance. Addressed by Claudius as "son," Hamlet interrupts, "A little more than kin, and less than kind," the word "kind" meaning "natural," among other things. It is precisely what is natural or properly "in kind" for human beings as offspring of earth that concerns Stevens here. This is a canto about parenthood. Like Hamlet, Stevens distances himself from the claimed kinship of a usurper, a too, too human god. In stanza ii, Stevens rejects the supernatural, calling it "over-human" ("over" as excess, not superiority). Here excess takes the form, "too, too human." For a psychological reading of this canto, Neil Hertz's remark on excess is most apt: "It [is] possible to think of excess in terms of Freud's discussions of excessive identification, of that supererogatory strength of investment that turns the superego into a harsher taskmaster than the father on whom it is modeled."[16] Stevens' attack is familiar, the technique sometimes rather too close to Joyce's, without Joyce's panache. Stevens is always hard on himself when he suspects the least self-pity, and his rigor may adversely affect the poetry here. After the ellipsis, as he reclaims health and honey from a Christian iconographic tradition, Stevens takes on his own voice in a strongly assertive mood.

---

[16] Neil Hertz, "The Notion of Blockage in the Literature of the Sublime," in *Psychoanalysis and the Question of the Text*, ed. Geoffrey Hartman (Baltimore: The Johns Hopkins University Press, 1978), pp. 74–75.

Canto iv begins: "Livre de Toutes Sortes de Fleurs d'Après Nature. / All sorts of flowers. That's the sentimentalist." That's the philanderer too, as it happens, in Stevens' two unexpected allegories of the seriousness of evil, properly so called. We hardly expect the passionate, single-minded, intense quests of artist or lover to be analogues for the passionate, single-minded, intense quests of an evil genius. But these are the analogues Stevens chooses. "The genius of misfortune is not a sentimentalist": thus the proposition of this canto. When we hear that a Spaniard of the rose, who adores one flower (one woman), is not a sentimentalist; when we hear that "toutes sortes de fleurs" defines the sentimentalist, then we can see the sense of Stevens' various examples, and the connection with writing. Tennyson may make this even clearer: "And well his words became him—was he not / A full-cell'd honeycomb of eloquence / Stored from all flowers?" Not Stevens' poet. We have just finished a canto in which honey and golden combs play back against stanza-hives, storing their sustenance and sweetness, like Dante's *stile dolce*. Here, a book, in the once popular form of a "flora," culls its material from every flower. As a "flora," it is dead (see Robert Browning's first letter to Elizabeth Barrett); as a flora from "every" flower, it is sentimental. Ruskin said that a "flower-loving mind" should be distinguished from "minds of the highest order," that is, minds capable of the sublime and not confined to mere earthly flowers.[17] Stevens refuses this analogue. The test of seriousness is not heaven as against earth. It is single-mindedness as against anthologizing: "anthology" is etymologically "toutes sortes de fleurs."

Stevens is claiming for his work what Eliot and others would deny him: that he does have a sufficiently serious view of evil. His main point is clear, even if the characters of B. and the Spaniard are not. Evil, properly so called, is not philandering, short term, dispersed casually in miscellaneous affairs, venial. Just as canto i asserted that pain is human, so canto iv asserts that evil is human. The notion of an evil genius hovers in these lines but cleansed of any Gothic associations. Stevens does not address the question of the origin of evil, beyond its origin in the self; the question of how widespread it is; or the question whether the genius of misfortune may possess all minds (always or sometimes) or some only. He only observes that there may be, as he puts it later, an "imagination of evil" (*NA* 154). Though an imagination of evil may be abnormal, such a thing appears to exist. Given Stevens' powerful sense of how the imagination works in human affairs, the thought can be chilling.

[17] Ruskin, *Modern Painters*, pt. vi, ch. x. par. 7.

Here he does not pursue the theme of radical evil any further, and the word returns only with cantos xiii and xv.

If we watch Stevens' use of the word "evil" throughout his work, an interesting pattern emerges. Until the late thirties, there are only minor or heavily ironic uses. In 1936, Stevens uses the word in an important compact argument about the death of evil. He works against an argument like Dostoevsky's at the end of *Crime and Punishment*: that without God, "anything is permitted." He will not accept a "fear that, from the death / Of evil, evil springs" (*OP* 69). In the war poems, Stevens is at first concerned to balance evil with good, and equally not to imply a Christian metaphysic of evil. These are poems of 1940 through 1942, the most substantial being the difficult and witty eight-part *Extracts from Addresses to the Academy of Fine Ideas*. (This modulates from the fierce ironies against "evil death" in ii to a revision of evil through a revision of the psalm of exile in viii.) The concerns of the earlier war poems are present in *Esthétique du Mal*, but also the desire to acknowledge fully the seriousness of evil. After this, there are only two minor uses in Stevens' poetry (*CP* 423, 528). In Stevens' 1948 essay, "Imagination as Value," the subject returns.

"Softly let all true sympathizers come." *Piano*: that is how to hear canto v, a canto whose "in-bars" and "ex-bars" and opening adverb, together with its echoes, suggest music. Stevens' hushed language admits no rhetorical flourishes. It is a bare language, simple to the edge of sentimentality, yet worlds away when we hear what he is doing. His "true sympathizers" are those he can honestly admit, past the bars and limits of his sublime. (Sympathy, not pity, we should note.) This is an *odi profanum* or "stay back" canto, where hell and heaven are equally "barred." It is a hymn of simple beauty to human love. As in iii, Stevens works with echo and allusion, using them to keep out Dante and Eliot but to embrace Milton and (I think) Tennyson for those times in their work when a profound sense of human love seems stronger than religious doctrine. One extraordinary metaleptic echo turns against a Dante-Eliot tradition; this is the echoing of "obscurer selvages." Another, more dispersed echoing is gentler in effect, as its subject is gentler; it is of Milton's beautiful hymn to wedded love in *Paradise Lost* iv.750–75. This is Stevens' chief pattern for his own hymning, and it is a full-hearted tribute to Milton. Stevens implicitly shears off Milton's doctrines of heaven and hell (and so, to some, un-Miltonizes him), but his aim is not to undercut him. His aim is to welcome Milton in the fullest way possible.

Within Stevens' "phrases / Compounded of dear relation," the words "dear relation" signal his own dear relation to the human Milton. For

Milton's hymn to wedded love says: "By [wedded love] . . . Relations dear, and all the Charities / Of Father, Son and Brother first were known." Stevens adapts the lines:

> So great a unity, that it is bliss,
> Ties us to those we love. For this familiar,
> This brother even in the father's eye,
> This brother half-spoken in the mother's throat . . . we forego
> Lament, willingly forfeit the ai-ai
>
> Of parades in the obscurer selvages.
> Be near me, come closer, touch my hand, phrases
> Compounded of dear relation.

Stevens' lines resemble Milton's: the tone is similarly intense, the diction similarly straightforward, the polemic similarly mingled with praise. This passage in Milton is framed by "bars" ("corporeal bar," 585, and "bars of Hell," 795) and it is generally informed by a sense of proper bars—to Eden, to marital rites, to knowledge. Milton ends: "O yet happiest if ye seek / No happier state, and know to know no more." Stevens quietly revises Milton's bars and Milton's closure and Milton's sublime: "Before we were wholly human and knew ourselves"—"wholly" with a w, pun intended, as we realize from *Mystic Garden & Middling Beast*. Stevens has marked how Milton's hymn addresses itself to all wedded love, explicitly "Present, or past," with no distinction of pre- and post-lapsarian, no dwelling on the Fall. It is the beautiful middle space of Milton's human love that Stevens evokes. Stevens' ex-bars and in-bars are shelters for his place of human love, not only against the demonic but also against the divine. So also "Be near me" quietly revises Tennyson's *In Memoriam* (L), and perhaps Bach's lovely song of that name ("Bist du bei mir").

The proposition of this canto reverses canto iv's proposition. If evil is of the self and is evil and not minor folly, so also love is of the self and is love and not sentimentality. A distinction between the places of evil and love is made by Stevens' unobtrusive use of the deictics, "that" and "this." "That" as adjective occurs three times in canto iv, never in canto v. "This" or "these" occurs eight times in canto v, never in canto iv. As canto v is much concerned with in-ness and ex-ness, in-bar and ex-bar, such a use of "this" and "that" suggests that love belongs to the "this-ness" of life or the normal, and evil to the "thatness" or the abnormal.

For the sake of such human love, "we forego / Lament, willingly forfeit the ai-ai / Of parades in the obscurer selvages." The word-play in these lines is some of the most remarkable in all Stevens' poetry. The first reading of "ai-ai" is as a Greek word, an exclamation of pain. But Stevens' ai-ai takes place in the Dante-Eliot "obscurer selvages," so that we are invited to hear a wailing there. ("Where is there an end of it, the soundless wailing?" asks Eliot in *Dry Salvages*. Stevens' voice replies: in human love.) An Italian ai-ai is a first-person suffix, so that an English ear, following Stevens' line of argument, hears a pun on "I-I," and thereby the question whether Eliot rewrites Dante's ai-ai's as self-pitying I-I's. Stevens' own later lament, "ay-mi" (xiii), is said to be one of "politest helplessness,"something very different from "parades," an angry word directed against Eliot.

As for "the obscurer selvages," this is a canto on the subject of edges and limits. But for a long time, the words made no specific poetic sense to me. One day, I was looking at Dante's opening lines to the *Inferno*, and considering how his wood echoes the sound of *selva* in lines 2 and 5: "selva oscura . . . selva selvaggia." Suddenly the adjectives detached themselves and combined in a memory of Stevens: "oscura selvaggia," "obscurer selvages." The wit and intelligence and precision of such Joycean word-play came as a delight and a revelation. For of course, Dante's *selva oscura* or "dark wood" is not in the middle of life's way for Stevens, neither as doctrinal allegory nor as personal allegory nor as a place for poetry. As allegory, it remains on the edge of things, peripheral to Stevens' earthly vision. *Selva* does not lead toward *salvatio* or salvation, as it does in Dante and in Eliot's *Dry Salvages*. Thus "selvages," punning brilliantly against a complex of "selva" words. *The Dry Salvages*, written three years earlier, is even more on the edge of things than Dante: thus the "obscurer selvages."[18] The phrase "obscurer selvages" touches on questions of etymology, both true and false; on literary echo and allusion; on the long history of a well-known trope; and on a topos, which Dante's "obscure wood" has become. Stevens is speaking back against one line of succession, a Dante-Eliot line—acknowledging it, foregoing it, trying to divert its force.

To forego so great a quest as a Dantean pilgrimage is no light matter for Stevens. We should not so misread his word-play. It is a forfeiting, as he says, and perhaps an impoverishment. Yet it is possible to be "exquisite in poverty," that is, to seek out, in the etymological meaning of the word. "Within what we permit, in-bar / Exquisite in poverty" accommodates a seeking or quest or pilgrimage of a kind. If limited, it is also of consummate excellence. The minutiae of such a quest "mean more / Than clouds, benevolences, distant heads." Clouds are thereby "ex-barred," as if visually in Derrida's kind of erasure. Or as if recalling,

[18] See my "Senses of Eliot's Salvages," *Essays in Criticism* 34 (1984), 309–18.

only to disbar, Coleridge's clouds of "bars" in the *Dejection Ode* and even Keats's "barred" clouds in *To Autumn*. The imagery of light, the function of clouds, the wonderful phrase, "nebulous brilliancies," the possible play of Coleridge's disbarring clouds coming through Keats,[19] the Joycean words "in-bar" and "ex-bar," the Miltonic bars of Eden—all this is part of the entire imagery of light that appears through the whole series. It begins with the light of volcanic fire and the mention of ether, and it ends with gleaming fields of harvest. Stevens is rewriting the language of sublime light. And all his bars speak to theories of the sublime, with its bars and limits, including the *limen* of the OED's sub + limen, basis of a much-disputed etymology.[20]

By contrast, the charming and difficult fable of big bird and the yellow grassman in canto vi turns from exclusion to another pattern of seeking and a different sun. The terms shift to imperfection versus perfection and away from human agents. Our readings tend to allegorize the fable, and helpful as some of these are, we still lack a reading of the particulars of Stevens' language. Among several at work are the language of desire, with the sun as a masculine force, chasing through the heavens; the language of quest, with the earth re-turning and the sun re-searching; the language of eating and fruit growing; and the language of astronomy, which seems to dominate, with its shapes, circuits, revolvings, orbits, lapses, corrections, and something askew. (It sounds as if a great clock is being playfully described, one in which the sun appears as a yellow orb on the face; the lunar cycle is also calculated, with the minute hand "pecking" its way around the dial.)

If we watch the cumulative language of the center from v through viii, we see the following sequence: "central senses" and "selvages" (v), "concentre" (vii), "eccentric" (viii). In vi, there is much awareness of shapes and symmetry, and we recall that "perfection" includes the perfection of geometrical form, the perfect circle or sphere. I would hazard the guess that Stevens is moving against the old and powerful symbolism of the perfect circle, so beautifully developed by Dante at the end of the *Paradiso*. Against this, he offers the movement of actual celestial orbits, of lapses in the astronomical sense. Is the big bird with a bony appetite a humorous figure for a night-shadow-death matrix of imagery as against a sun-light-life matrix? Stevens likes this kind of play, and he may be using it to alter the relation between the two. Certainly there is no "still point of the turning world." The sun may even bring to perfection and

---

[19] Paul Fry makes the connection in *The Poet's Calling in the English Ode* (New Haven and London: Yale University Press, 1981), p. 163.

[20] Cf. Jan Cohn and Thomas H. Miles, "The Sublime: In Alchemy, Aesthetics and Psychoanalysis," *Modern Philology* 74 (1976–1977), 289–304.

then fail different systems of belief, as in Keats's Hyperion poems. The sun as "yellow grassman" is like the haymaker in an early letter. "However, the haymaker is out . . . (haymaker is Woods-ese for sun)" (*SP* 119). Stevens prefers grass to hay, partly because of its connection with "gross." And the adjective "yellow" applies both to the sun (as in Dickinson's "yellow man") and also to what the sun does to grass. It also stays well away from "golden" (on which, see canto v).

Stevens is rewriting *The Poems of Our Climate*, with its perfect-imperfect dialectic. He will not allow the imagery of the "consummate" (from *consummare*) to escape the logic of "consume" (from *consumere*)—a pun implicit in canto i. "Consummate" means "utmost" so that a volcano puns to "consume / In fire the utmost [consummate] earth." This is an echo from the Song of Moses, to which Stevens adds that word "utmost" and thereby the implicit pun: "a fire . . . shall consume the earth" (Deut. 32:22). To be consumed in consummation is a familiar mystical or sexual paradox. Stevens' evasions of such consummation are handled with wonderful humor.

"How red the rose that is the soldier's wound": this old figure, familiar enough when used of the blood of the martyrs, can be offensive to modern ears. Eliot, deliberately using even more violent old language in *East Coker*, at least prepares the reader. Yet to a historian of war, like Paul Fussell, Stevens' elegy in canto vii makes sense.[21] It works with a series of "concentric circles," not Dantean but of shadows. Stevens returns from lapses to symmetry, though a symmetry of dark and shadow and death. The poetry itself is smooth and calmed. Its stillness is like Owen's in his sonnet, "Anthem for Doomed Youth," and the closure on a grieving female figure is also like Owen's. Stevens' soldier lies in memory beneath a woman's forehead and even seems to receive her touch: "A woman smoothes her forehead with her hand / And the soldier of time lies calm beneath that stroke." Stevens wishes to hymn, not death, but all life even including death. The mode is one that Whitman made his own, and Stevens' greatest difficulty is not with the unfamiliar opening image but to match Whitman's own great hymns. I do not think he does, but his elegy remains moving. Our differing reactions to it demonstrate problems of genre and of association.

Cantos viii and ix consider, not the death of God, but the death of Satan. Stevens is at home here, and his opening is almost whimsical: "The death of Satan was a tragedy / For the imagination. A capital / Negation destroyed him in his tenement. . . ." Derrida remarks on how

[21] Paul Fussell, *The Great War and Modern Memory* (London, Oxford, New York: Oxford University Press, 1975), p. 244.

"Mallarmé prescribes a suspension of the title, which—like the head, or capital, or the oracle—carries its head high, speaks in too high a voice."[22] Stevens prescribes, not a suspension, but a decapitation and a decapitalization in this capital punishment. (The "satanic" in "satanic mimicry" has already been printed in lower case.) Satan is seen as puzzled, because he is denied rather than being fought with "filial revenge" (the warrior Christ is one reading, Stevens here rewriting the battle in heaven as a revenge tragedy). This is for Satan an "eccentric" or off-center death. Better to be at the center of Dante's *Inferno*, upside down in ice, than not to be at all. Stevens wrote in 1951 that "To speak of the origin and end of gods is not a light matter. It is to speak of the origin and end of eras of human belief" (*OP* 205). We must suppose that Stevens is not speaking of the end of Satan as a light matter, or else that Satan is not a god.

If the death of Satan is puzzling for him, it is a tragedy for us—that is, for our imagination. Stevens dissociates evil from a figure of Satan, and considers our emptied world in something of Eliot's perspective in the essay on Baudelaire. "Phosphored" in canto ix evokes the morning star, that is, the planet Venus in her morning appearance as Lucifer. The word also describes the moon's peculiar light, light of lunatics and lovers and poets, all subject to the "folly of the moon." "Nothing is left but comic ugliness / Or a lustred nothingness" when Satan dies and that bright and morning star falls. Stevens' old moon-haunting is at work in these phrases. I do not think he can reuse the word "lustre" without remembering his bitter 1932 use (*OP* 34–35). Stevens had his own erotic moon gods and moon demons; they once threatened his entire world, and their vanquishing must have left it bare. The argument here is kept very general: to each, his own demons. Stevens simply offers a comic version of a stripped-down world. The mode is reminiscent of *The Comedian as the Letter C* but well in control. Still, the mode helps account for the bursting forth at the end of a language of desire and grief that sounds almost incongruous. Whatever gods and demons we lose, there is loss, at least at first. As this is a war poem, we should note how Stevens also addresses himself to the psychology of war, for there may be a peculiar emptiness when battle ceases for once and for all.

Canto x has given us the memorable plural use of "nostalgia": "He had studied the nostalgias." This type of pain is the *algos* for a return home, a *nostos*, which we may read in Jungian terms, though we should also remember the mystical Abbé Brémond, with his anima and animus and lack of animal. Thus "His anima like its animal" and thus the

[22] "The Double Session," in his *Dissemination*, trans. Barbara Johnson (Chicago and London: University of Chicago Press, 1972, 1981), p. 177.

woman "with a vague moustache"—the Jungian anima having recessive male characteristics, and Brémond's anima being in need of an animal. For Stevens, in fact, the anima *is* an animal, as we know. This is not the "mauve / *Maman*," a female type easy to read, whether we think of Renoir or the mauve decade or (my preference) Proust's Mme Swann in a mauve scene at the end of *A l'ombre des jeunes filles en fleurs* (i.i). Whatever the resonance, it is sentimental rather than romantic. Stevens thinks of the true romantic as "dyed through and through with the most authentic purple" (*OP* 256, 1934), and mauve is presumably the diluted or sentimental romantic. The mauve maman contrasts with the fierce mother, whether Whitman's or Jung's.

We know that Stevens studied the nostalgias. He noted in his commonplace book a remark by André Rousseaux: "La nostalgie de l'éternel est au fond de toutes les oeuvres des philosophes, des romanciers et des poètes."[23] But he says it is reality that his imagination quests for, and *l'éternel* is not reality for him. "The imagination with its typical nostalgia for reality" is his phrase (*L* 364, August 10, 1940). We may think of nostalgia in the widest sense: "Philosophy is really homesickness" (Novalis) or "All the poems of the poet who has entered into his poethood, are poems of homecoming" (Heidegger).[24] Homecoming is a return to some kind of mother figure here. Stevens insists that it be an earthly mother—not the mother of mal, Eve, or the redemptive mother, Mary, or Goethe's redemptive mothers at the end of *Faust*. In arguing for "innocence of event" (Helen Vendler's phrase)[25] or a Whitman-like acceptance "that he might suffer or that / He might die," Stevens asserts that life is innocent. Life has no intent to injure, and no redemptive mother is needed. It is very like him to turn on his final stance and examine that, too: "It was the last nostalgia: that he/ Should understand"—a comment on Stevens' own meditation but also on psychological understanding, itself no more immune from patterns of homesickness than philosophy or poetry. A passion to understand may be Jung's or Freud's form of homesickness.

Canto xi, by contrast, is a poem of violent protest against popular nostalgia or a debased sublime, with some of Stevens' most angry wordplay. The proposition governing its two mirrored sections is: "A man of

---

[23] Commonplace Book, ii, 10 WAS 70–73. Huntington Library. Quoted by permission of Holly Stevens and the Huntington Library.

[24] Novalis and Heidegger are cited in Thomas McFarland, "The Place beyond the Heavens: True Being, Transcendence, and the Symbolic Indication of Wholeness," *Boundary 2* 7 (1979), 287.

[25] *On Extended Wings: Wallace Stevens' Longer Poems* (Cambridge, Mass.: Harvard University Press, 1969), p. 217.

bitter appetite despises / A well-made scene." The two sections are divided by the often-quoted couplet: "Natives of poverty, children of malheur, / The gaiety of language is our seigneur." But not much else gets quoted from this puzzling canto. Stevens' protest against "well-made scenes" of war is offered in violently dislocated language. His wild punning and black humor may have something to do with the blockage that is part of the sublime—a feeling of helplessness before the flood of pretty, saccharine phrases about death. He selects four well-made scenes in which death is sweetened, then re-presents them as something he despises, in a mood of "bitter appetite."

Here are the two separated versions of the first scene, brought together: "At dawn, / The paratroopers fall and as they fall / They mow the lawn . . . [he despises] A well-made scene in which paratroopers / Select adieux." We have been able to do something with "mow the lawn": the grim reaper, all flesh is grass, Marvell's mowing poems, and later versions of this topos, like Frost's. But even so, Stevens sounds awkward and arbitrary, and what is the relation of the first and second scenes? Surely, this: it is an old joke to pun on *coup de grâce* and "couper le grass," that is, "mow the lawn."[26] To give or receive a coup de grâce certainly means coming to a final adieu. Stevens is adding to this old topos a wicked pun. The *grâce*-grass association plays back against the sun as yellow grassman and the gross-grass play there. If the sun is associated at all with grace, it is a purely earthly grace, issuing in grass—which flesh is as, flesh that is mowed down in war, not in pretty scenes.

The second topos is the ship going down, an example chosen by Lucretius for our experience of danger: "A vessel sinks in waves / Of people . . . [he despises] / A ship that rolls on a confected ocean, / The weather pink, the wind in motion. . . ." "Waves of people" is a phantasmagoria, with a pun of people waving farewell. Waves of the ocean, waves of people waving, and the old trope of sea waves as arms—all are at work here. Stevens extends the punning to sound waves in the phrase "bell-billows," making the bell in the village steeple toll as the vessel sinks. "Confected" judges wartime rhetoric.

Stevens' third topos is the tolling of a bell in a steeple: "as big bell-billows from its bell / Bell-bellow in the village steeple . . . people, for whom the steeple, / Long since, rang out farewell, farewell, farewell . . . [he despises] / A steeple that tip-tops the classic sun's / Arrangements." "The bells are the bellowing of bulls," Stevens wrote, rather more clumsily, in *The Man with the Blue Guitar*. It is all too easy for a writer to have bells tolling, whether the writer is Longfellow in a standard school

[26] My former student, Linda Munk, heard this word-play.

poem or Eliot in *Four Quartets*. So also with the final topos of violets:
"Violets, / Great tufts, spring up from buried houses / Of poor, dishonest
people . . . [he despises] the violets' exhumo." The grave as a "buried
house" is a standard topos, as is the springing of flowers from it. "And
from his ashes may be made, / The violet of his native land," Tennyson
wrote in *In Memoriam* (xviii), in a figure as old as Persius [Sat. 1.39–40].
Pater's use is memorable.

We might well ask how far these "well-made scenes" play against
Eliot's *Dry Salvages*, with its vessels, tolling bell, and especially its kind
of farewell ("Not fare well, / But fare forward"). Stevens had reason to
be sensitive to Eliot's use of Arjuna on the field of battle, especially if he
thought Eliot was remembering *Lettres d'un soldat*. He too had read the
book during World War I, and he wrote a series of poems from it, using
the introductory passage on Arjuna as epigraph (*OP* 110–16). But he did
not read Eliot's metaphysical lesson from Arjuna. No more will he read
cycles of falling and rising as Eliot does, whether cycles of death falling
from the air (paratroopers or Eliot's bombers), death by the rising and
falling of water, death marked by bell and tip-top steeple, or death in the
buried houses of the grave from which flowers spring. This kind of sub-
merged quarrel works with topoi rather than verbal echo.

Canto xii refuses a purely stoic world, which is free from pain because
one lives essentially without other people, and "accepts whatever is as
true." It is a world of self-sufficiency. The place of Stevens' argument is
not clear to me, though we might relate it to Kantian and Hegelian the-
ories of the sublime, to follow Iris Murdoch. Perhaps such theories are
too exclusively concerned with isolated individuals.[27] Together with the
hymn to human love in canto v, this shows a Stevens we sometimes
forget.

Canto xiii is more readily placed in our post-Freudian age:

> It may be that one life is a punishment
> For another, as the son's life for the father's.
> But that concerns the secondary characters.
> It is a fragmentary tragedy
> Within the universal whole. The son
> And the father alike and equally are spent,
> Each one, by the necessity of being
> Himself, the unalterable necessity
> Of being this unalterable animal.

Stevens' "politest helplessness" carries a high sense of civilization in the
face of necessity. The diction suggests a plot ("assassin," "disclosed"),

---

[27] Cf. "The Sublime and the Beautiful Revisited," *Yale Review* 49 (1959–60), 255.

with the scene of recognition as self-recognition. What one recognizes, I think, is one's own coming death ("the assassin . . . One feels its action moving in the blood"). "The force that destroys us is disclosed"—not necessarily a physical force, of course. The plot of father and son makes our life sound like a type of revenge tragedy, whether the son is Oedipus or is Christ. (Stevens chooses diction and syntax that work for both stories.) There is little sense of the sublime as sublimation here, except in the sense of civilization which I mentioned. And the sense of a Freudian plot is clear. I think, in fact, that Stevens' source for the word "helplessness" is in the standard English translation by James Strachey of Freud's *Future of an Illusion*, from which Stevens quotes in 1942 (*NA* 14–15). There, the son-father relation widens by analogy into the relation between the individual and nature. In the face of nature, the individual eventually feels helpless, as helpless as he once felt before the father. Stevens' own plot in this canto parallels Freud's plot, as he shifts from the father-son story to the larger story of an individual confronting what will destroy him. Freud repeats the key word "helplessness" seven times. Some of his phrasing sounds like Stevens': "man's helplessness remains and along with it his longing for his father, and the gods. . . . You transform everything that was once the father complex into terms of helplessness." Stevens departs from Freud with the term,"destiny unperplexed." For Freud writes: "As regards the apportioning of destinies, an unpleasant suspicion persists that the perplexity and helplessness of the human race could not be remedied." Stevens quietly disagrees. His sense of destiny is unperplexed for all that it is helpless.

The canto on Leninist necessity is usually thought to be a blemish in this series, an odd anomaly. Odd it may be, but this is because we so seldom consider the matter of a political sublime. Explorations that connect Burke the political philosopher and Burke the theorist of the sublime are rare. And who has considered a Marxist idea of the sublime? Here, Stevens starts with Yeats's sense of what happens to "hearts with one purpose alone" (*Easter 1916*) or what Stevens calls "the lunatic of one idea." His lake pointedly revises the grand sublime ocean, a standard property of the natural sublime. Auden's sense of lakes in his *Bucolics* is much the same: "Sly Foreign Ministers should always meet beside one." Stevens plays off our associations with the words "logic" and "lunatic," and ends with paradox.[28]

He chooses to close his series with images of fertile, food-bearing land, a standard contrast with destructive volcanic fire in the literature of the sublime and elsewhere. The "green corn" of August indicates that he

[28] See D. L. Macdonald, "Wallace Stevens and Victor Serge," *Dalhousie Review*, forthcoming.

has moved home to North America. (The "corn" of Europe is our wheat, and it is yellow in August. Green corn in August is North American.) He comes to a place of plenitude, a summer place in this volume of summer. And it is defiantly a place of cultivation—defiant because "lack of cultivation . . . was essential to the sublime," to quote Schiller.[29] It is defiantly physical too—against all metaphysicals, especially sublime ones. "We must of necessity go beyond the physical order, and seek the principle of conduct in quite another world," to quote Schiller again.[30] Stevens disagrees. His last canto is generically a hymn (a "chorale," a "thesis," a "psalm" using the biblical word, "scrivened" and recalling the psalmist's sentence, "My tongue is the pen of a scrivener" [Psalm 44:2]). Canto xv is, in its own way, also a transport to summer.

Esthétique du Mal deserves the close attention of theorists of the sublime. Stevens begins historically, with a sense of the old sublime, natural and transcendental both, as it speaks in images of voice. Battles with the transcendental sublime, old style, run all through the poem. There are submerged debates with Dante, Milton, Eliot, and other representatives of a transcendental sublime through the first six cantos. Stevens marks out his own middle space in canto v, excluding both the up and down of the old sublime. After the elegy for the war dead, the death-of-Satan cantos face the dilemma put by Thomas Weiskel: "to find either a mode of sublimation which does not attenuate what the sublime pretends to be or a mode of desublimation that is not merely natural."[31] The attack on a debased sublime in canto xi is not hard to read, once we hear the wild punning and the topoi. I should like a theorist of the sublime to enlighten me about Stevens' meditation on the psychological sublime. And does the canto on solitude speak to theories of the psychological sublime? What is there to be said about a political sublime?

I began by connecting Stevens' word-play and word-war in *Esthétique du Mal* with actual war. That is where I shall end, though the connection I want to make is different. It is best put by a question: what have theories of the sublime to do with war? They certainly have to do with psychic war, to consider the psychological sublime. They certainly have to do with metaphysical and ideological war, to consider the transcendental and political sublime. But what of actual war? The question can be a little uncomfortable, for all that we admire acts and seasons of courage in war. Let me go back to Longinus and to one point where Stevens'

---

[29] Cited in Andrew Wilton, *Turner and the Sublime* (London: British Museum Publications, 1980), p. 30.

[30] Cited in Angus Fletcher, *Allegory*, p. 251.

[31] Thomas Weiskel, *The Romantic Sublime: Studies in the Structure and Psychology of Transcendence* (Baltimore: The Johns Hopkins University Press, 1976), p. xi.

theory of the sublime differs from his. This is a passage from which I. A. Richards quoted in his *Coleridge on Imagination*; Stevens made a note of the quotation in his copy:[32]

> She [Nature] therefore from the first breathed into our hearts an unconquerable passion for whatever is great and more divine than ourselves. Thus within the scope of human enterprise there lie such powers of contemplation and thought that even the whole universe cannot satisfy them, but our ideas often pass beyond the limits that enring us. . . . So it is by some natural instinct that we admire, surely not the small streams, clear and useful as they are, but the Nile, the Danube, the Rhine, and far above all, the sea. The little fire we kindle for ourselves keeps clear and steady, yet we do not therefore regard it with more amazement than the fires of Heaven, which are often darkened, or think it more wonderful than the craters of Etna in eruption, hurling up rocks and whole hills from their depths and sometimes shooting forth rivers of that pure Titanic fire. . . . Other qualities prove their possessors men, sublimity lifts them near the mighty mind of God . . . in literature, as I said before, we look for something greater than human (xxxv–vi).

Against Longinus, we hear Stevens repeatedly holding the small candle of the human imagination. (Not that he underestimates the force of cosmic fires or sentimentalizes small ones, as we know from *Domination of Black* and *Auroras of Autumn*.) Longinus prefers huge and strange phenomena to smaller everyday ones. Such preference for large effects need not extend to human acts, but it often does. Longinus prefers the *Iliad* to the *Odyssey*. A note in the Loeb edition says, apparently without irony, that this is because the *Iliad* describes real fighting, the serious business of life. If Longinus seems safely remote, we might consider the following connection of war and the sublime:

> War itself, provided it is conducted with order and a sacred respect for the rights of civilians, has something sublime about it, and gives nations that carry it on in such a manner a stamp of mind only the more sublime the more numerous the dangers to which they are exposed, and which they are able to meet with fortitude. On the other hand, a prolonged peace favours the predominance of a mere commercial spirit, and with it a debasing self-interest, cowardice, and effeminacy, and tends to degrade the character of a nation.

---

[32] *Coleridge on Imagination*, p. 24. Stevens, inside back cover: "Longinus, p. 24." His marked copy of the book is at the Huntington Library. Noted by permission of Holly Stevens and the Huntington Library.

This is Immanuel Kant, in a seldom-quoted passage from the *Critique of Judgement* (II.i.263, trans. Meredith). Granted that this is eighteenth-century war, where civilians, duly protected by "sacred respect" (indeed yes), safely watch from the sidelines, forgetting the ironies of Lucretius. Granted that Yeats said similar things. In 1944, as today, the alternatives sound false. Angus Fletcher notes how we stress the subjectivity and experience of the sublime, isolating the psychological interest of writers on the sublime, and ignoring the philosophical or religious basis that is for some the sine qua non of the sublime.[33] We ignore other things too. Stevens did not.[34]

For his sense of the sublime, we should turn to his 1942 essay, "The Noble Rider and the Sound of Words," substituting the words "sublime" and "sublimity" for the words "noble" and "nobility." Stevens begins with the old sublime, an example of Plato's "dear gorgeous nonsense" (Coleridge's phrase). He ends with a present and living sublime. It is not subjective, as with Kant, with no object sufficient for it. It is defined only in relation, like the old transcendental sublime. And like all theories of the sublime, it has to do with violence. We sometimes isolate the one sentence which is a favorite quotation, and read it as if any inner violence would do, but we should remember the context.

> Nobility is a force and not the manifestations of which it is com-
> posed. . . . It is a violence from within that protects us from a vio-
> lence without. It is the imagination pressing back against the pres-

---

[33] Fletcher, *Allegory*, pp. 243–44.

[34] Stevens' response to the war may be seen in part from his letters: "Somehow or other, with so much of Hitler and Mussolini so drastically on one's nerves, constantly, it is hard to get around to Buddha" (*L* 337, April 12, 1939). "When the war broke out I was in Virginia . . . . As the news of the development of the war comes in, I feel a horror of it: a horror of the fact that such a thing could occur" (*L* 342, September 20, 1939). "I hope . . . that you are free from the effects of the more or less universal disaster" (*L* 353, January 18, 1940). "I make no reference in this letter to the war. It goes without saying that our minds are full of it" (*L* 356, May 24, 1940). "When we were facing the great evil that is being enacted today . . ." (*L* 373, August 30, 1940). "The hope that the coming year will bring an end to the great disaster in which we are all involved" (*L* 381, December 9, 1940). My sense of Stevens' response to the war is closer to Charles Berger's in his *Forms of Farewell: The Late Poetry of Wallace Stevens* (Madison: University of Wisconsin Press, 1985) than to Marjorie Perloff's in her "Revolving in Crystal: The Supreme Fiction and the Impasse of Modernist Lyric," in *Wallace Stevens: The Poetics of Modernism*, ed. Albert Gelpi (Cambridge: Cambridge University Press, 1985), pp. 41–64.

The most telling criticism of some of Stevens' writing about war is made by James Merrill: " 'How gladly with proper words,' said Wallace Stevens, / 'The soldier dies.' Or kills" (*Late Settings* [New York: Atheneum, 1985], p. 26; see the epilogue to *Notes toward a Supreme Fiction*).

sure of reality. It seems, in the last analysis, to have something to do with our self-preservation; and that, no doubt, is why the expression of it, the sound of its words, helps us to live our lives.

It takes some time to see the strength of Stevens' title and the scope of his answer to the soldier of 1944. I hope that soldier also saw it.

CHAPTER ELEVEN

* * * * *

Notes toward

a Supreme Fiction

My own way out toward the future involves a con-
fidence in the spiritual role of the poet. (*L* 340, June
1, 1939)

I need badly to find one man in history to admire. I
am in near peril of turning Christian and rolling in
the mud in the agony of human mortification.[1]

The *Fiktion* of [Nietzsche's] Aphorism 34 is the
commonplace idea that the world exists only in the
mind. So considered it is an unreal thing, in which
logic does not have a place. Since an *Urheber* is a
projection of logic, it is easy to dispose of him by
disposing of logic. . . . This is quite a different fic-
tion from that of NOTES, even though it is present
in the NOTES. We are confronted by a choice of
ideas: the idea of God and the idea of man. The pur-
pose of the NOTES is to suggest the possibility of a
third idea: the idea of a fictive being, or state, or
thing as the object of belief by way of making up for
that element in humanism which is its chief defect.[2]

---

[1] Henry Adams, copied by Stevens in his Commonplace Book, II, 1, WAS 70–73. Quoted
by permission of Holly Stevens and the Huntington Library.
[2] Letter to Henry Church, WAS 3512, Huntington Library. Quoted by permission of
Holly Stevens and the Huntington Library.

It Must Be Abstract

Stevens arranged the poems of *Transport to Summer* in approximate chronological order, except for the greatest, *Notes toward a Supreme Fiction*. This poem, first printed privately in 1942, closes *Transport to Summer*, a collection written between 1942 and 1947.

What is Stevens doing in this poem? To put it oversimply, *Notes toward a Supreme Fiction* is a poem that rewrites "supreme" writing, that is, our sacred scriptures; or points toward ways of rewriting them. It has its own kind of Genesis at the beginning, and its own kind of Revelation at the end. Stevens foregoes the usual genres of beginning and end for such writing, choosing the unexpected genre of the lecture to open and close his series. (Or is it unexpected? As Paul Ricoeur says of Genesis, "Ce prologue apparaîtra d'abord comme un récit didactique destiné à donner une instruction."[3]) At the beginning, we are inside the lecture; at the end, we are outside. We begin by identifying ourselves with the much-lectured ephebe taking instruction. We end with the poet and his beloved "fat girl," walking down a street in Paris after a lecture at the Sorbonne (a mark of Stevens' Francophilia and a tribute to the dedicatee, his friend Henry Church). The notes of the title are from the lecture. There are three, all in the optative mood, each heading a section of ten cantos: It Must Be Abstract, It Must Change, It Must Give Pleasure.

Stevens begins with an ephebe—in ancient Athens a beginning citizen and a beginning soldier. Thus the citizen in the last canto, someone who says, "Civil, madam, I am," with a full sense of the associations of "civil." Thus the soldier in the epilogue. Stevens' ephebe is also a beginning poet, though we do not know this until canto v. If the poet is one who writes our sacred scriptures, or our most noble words, then he or she *is* an essential citizen, an essential soldier. I take the word "noble" from Stevens' 1942 essay, "The Noble Rider and the Sound of Words," for this essay, and the 1943 essay, "The Figure of the Youth as Virile Poet," are important if oblique glosses on *Notes toward a Supreme Fiction*. Here, too, Stevens is fascinated by the question of authority: why could we once yield ourselves to supreme or noble words and now cannot? What words can take their place? Stevens' ephebe is not just any developing poet (to read synchronically), not just Stevens' earlier self (to read retrospectively), not just ourselves as readers. He is also specifically the virile poet, that future poet who will some day write what we now

---

[3] Paul Ricoeur, in *Exégèse et hermeneutique* ed. Roland Barthes (Paris: Editions du Seuil, 1971), p. 71.

lack, some work that will mean what sacred scriptures and noble works once meant. This poem is also addressed to him or her.[4]

But whom does the prefatory verse address? As it stands, it is a riddle poem. What possible "you" fits its conditions?

> And for what, except for you, do I feel love?
> Do I press the extremest book of the wisest man
> Close to me, hidden in me day and night?
> In the uncertain light of single, certain truth,
> Equal in living changingness to the light
> In which I meet you, in which we sit at rest,
> For a moment in the central of our being,
> The vivid transparence that you bring is peace.

If Simone Weil or some equally rigorous Christian addressed these lines to the Supreme Being, they would make sense. (We would read the preposition "except for" as both excluding and including: only for God do I feel love and, only by means of God do I feel love at all.) Stevens says "And for what," not "And for whom," and my tentative answer to the riddle of "you" is the supreme fiction itself. Every word of Stevens' title revises orthodox religious language, and so does this prefatory verse, and so would this answer. The second and third lines distance him from religions of a sacred book, chiefly Judaism and Christianity. ("Thy word have I hid in my heart," says the psalmist.) And the language of certitude, revelation, and finality is introduced only to be undone by antonymous modifiers.

"Begin, ephebe" opens the text proper, which begins, and dramatizes beginnings, and studies strategies of beginning a poem about supreme things. Tone and the imperative mood call attention to voice and stance and the act of starting, as "In the beginning" and "In the middle of life's way" do not. And as Stevens' own fables of beginning at the start of *Harmonium* do not. This is patently, self-consciously, an initiating voice. But it will have nothing to do with a high, sublime style, with a *fiat lux*. It is brusque, even imperious. It seems to come out of nowhere (this is as close as Stevens will come to creation *ex nihilo*). It suggests indirectly that we should map the voices in *Notes*, and also the voices in *Paradise Lost* or *Four Quartets* or Dante or even the Bible. It speaks with slightly exaggerated authority, and makes us reflect on the authority with which other supreme stories begin. (And how effective Stevens'

---

[4] "The centuries have a way of being male," Stevens wrote in "The Figure of the Youth as Virile Poet" (*NA* 52). Thus, I assume, the word "virile"; yet the "masculine nature" of the new poet "that must be master of our lives" is enlarged at the end of this essay (*NA* 66–67).

216

strategy is, for we are certainly obedient to the instruction here, perceiving as we are told to perceive.) The prefatory verse is full of the preposition "in," which also opens some of our best-known sacred texts. The first canto offers only the somewhat odd phrase, "in the idea of." It obliquely suggests that we pay attention to kinds of in-ness, and what they enclose, particularly if they enclose us.

Great religious texts commonly begin with origins, but there is no orthodox firstness in this canto, no first light, first humans, first disobedience. It is a canto of returning, of becoming ignorant again, of washing clean. Or rather, it is a canto of both origins and returning, as Stevens plays between beginning and continuing. His argument stresses beginning, his rhetoric stresses continuing, notably in the echoing of begin-be. Though it is not as striking as Beckett's wonderful pun on *commencez* and *Comment c'est*, it makes a similar point. We may map a series of continuities, the being or "comment c'est" of things—rounded time and space, rounded shapes (sky, sun, eyes), sources and flourishings and declining. We may also map a series of discontinuities, the beginning or "commencez" of things: the sharp "Begin," the hortatory negatives, washing clean, "Phoebus is dead." Yet this is not an either-or process. This is a canto of roots: human roots (mentor-ephebe), vegetable roots (autumn harvest), word roots (per-ceiving and in-con-ceivable, sup-pose and com-pose). And roots are themselves both a beginning and a continuing. We may establish new roots as well as go back to old. (Thomas Greene uses a metaphor of roots apropos of a Renaissance sense of imitation.[5]) As with roots, so with this canto. Its strength lies in the tension between what is kept and what is discarded. (Such a tension also marks any engaged act of reading. Northrop Frye puts this in terms of father-son stories.[6]) As we ourselves read Stevens' title and first canto, we also keep and discard, perhaps in the spirit of Stevens, perhaps not.

How many texts about supreme things start with a mentor and a student? Dante begins with Virgil, Milton begins with the teaching Heav'nly Muse. And the Book of Genesis itself? As Milton says, the Heav'nly Muse taught Moses as well as John Milton, and Moses is the putative author of Genesis. "Begin, ephebe" is also how God might address Moses, before the Book of Genesis starts. Or how Moses might hear God addressing him, to follow Stevens' logic. Or how a supreme

[5] Thomas Greene, *The Light in Troy: Imitation and Discovery in Renaissance Poetry* (New Haven and London: Yale University Press, 1982), p. 19.

[6] Frye: "Perhaps a text does not exist at all except as somebody's recreation of it. In all recreation there is a son/father relationship which has a double aspect: an Oedipus relation where the son kills the father and a Christian relation where the son identifies with the father" (*New Literary History* 12 [1981], 225).

fiction might start addressing the beginning poet or reader or poem. My reading is something more than playful analogy. Stevens will later use Moses' story of the burning bush, and God's naming therein, "I am that I am."

Stevens once thought of giving the first canto of *Notes* a title: "At first I attempted to follow a scheme, and the first poem bore the caption RE-FACIMENTO. Jean Wahl picked that up right off. The first step toward a supreme fiction would be to get rid of all existing fictions" (*L* 431, December 8, 1942). "Refacimento" means a "new-modelling or recasting of a literary work" (OED), here of "existing [supreme] fictions." Johnson uses the term of Dryden in his *Lives of the Poets*: "His last work was his *Fables*, in which he gave us the first example of a mode of writing which the Italians call *refacimento*, a renovation of ancient writers, by modernizing their language." Refacimento is the first step in a process that Stevens will later call "decreation," a term he borrowed from Simone Weil. ("Décréation: faire passer du créé dans l'incréé. Destruction: faire passer du créé dans le néant. Ersatz coupable de la décréation.") In 1951, Stevens translated both definitions, though not the last phrase, and added: "Modern reality is a reality of decreation, in which our revelations are not the revelations of belief, but the precious portents of our own powers. . . . Poets and painters alike today make that assumption and this is what gives them the validity and serious dignity that become them as among those that seek wisdom, seek understanding [cf. Proverbs 4:7]. I am elevating this a little, because I am trying to generalize" (*NA* 175). Stevens adapts Weil's religious term to secular use; decreation is seeing the created world transformed to a world that is uncreated by any god. The gods have been "dispelled in mid-air and dissolve like clouds" (*OP* 206, 1951).

Or: "Let purple Phoebus lie in autumn harvest, / Let Phoebus slumber and die in autumn umber." Phoebus ("the shining one") is to be reclaimed by earth, to darken into umber. Yet living things that die rot slowly back into compost and become soil that gives new life to plants. "But do not use the rotted names," Stevens wrote in 1937, and he puns on "rotted rose" in the first poem of this volume. Neither poem develops Whitman's trope of the compost pile (*This Compost*), though a 1949 poem does:

> . . . as of an exhumation returned to earth,
> The rich earth, of its own self made rich,
> Fertile of its own leaves and days and wars,
> Of its brown wheat rapturous in the wind. . . .
>
> (*CP* 491)

(And how gently Stevens reawakens the shades of Hesiod and Ceres and Proserpine, who all speak to his composting fable.) Stevens' painterly word "umber" in *Notes* I.i puns on classical *umbrae* (shades of the dead), and umbra (the shadow of the sun), as well as the brown umber of harvest. The name of Phoebus dies into the uncreated, but part of it reemerges in the word "ephebe." Something like the law of the conservation of matter is at work here, a law of the conservation of language, so to speak. If I read Stevens rightly, he is making use of the analogue between plants and words beloved of poets and linguistic philosophers alike. But he is seeing an entire process, plant to rot to compost to soil to new plant. This too is part of Stevens' opening fable of decreation. It may usefully be compared with Derrida's remarks on dissemination,[7] and it speaks to and through older writers. So does Geoffrey Hill's decreation— to and through Stevens, Eliot, Tennyson, and more: "That decreation to which all must move" (*Lachrimae* 5).

One point should be made about the matter of naming. Stevens writes, "The sun / Must bear no name, gold flourisher." We variously account for Stevens' or the mentor's defiance of his own injunction. (A first principle of disobedience, poetic as against mythic or religious naming, and so on.) Stevens' mentor has dramatized his doctrine, being a good teacher, but he is subtler than he appears, also being a good teacher. We read: "The sun must bear *no* name." We should also read, "The sun *must* bear no name"; that is, there is no name that the sun is required to bear, neither Phoebus Apollo nor Christ. The point of this becomes clearer at the end of Part I.

Cantos i through v form a unit, as much through their hortatory tone and strategies of decreation as through theme and addressee. The addressee appears in line 1 and is left at the end of canto v, "voluble of dumb violence," reappearing only in canto x for some last advice. The word "idea," also in line 1, moves in canto ii into the theme of the "first idea," which continues in iii, iv, and v, vanishes in vi, reappears in vii and viii, and shifts in x to the "idea of man." After that, no form of the word "idea" appears again in the poem. We may read cantos i through v as on the subject of a true dwelling place, that poetic home Stevens desired from the beginning. We may read them as on the subject of the first idea. (My one caution about the first idea is that it is still an idea, and that it must fit all six propositions about the first idea in Part I.[8]) As

---

[7] Cf. Derrida on insemination and dissemination, in his *Dissemination*, trans. Barbara Johnson (Chicago and London: Chicago University Press, 1972, 1981), p. 304.

[8] We should not equate the first idea with Valéry's icy *réel*. (Valéry uses the word *idée* only in passing.) I wonder if the first idea is not the first germinal idea of any supreme fiction. The giant who thinks the first idea would then be one of those poets with "huge

with all the cantos, we should remember matters of genre. Stevens chooses not to call attention to genre, as he does in each stanza of *Le Monocle* and each canto of *Esthétique du Mal*. We ourselves must map the variety of type—riddle, parable, hymn. We ourselves must map the place of each canto—the place of its argument among arguments about supreme things, the topoi if any, the kind of memory-place. For Stevens contrives to build the cantos as appropriate structures for their dialectic and rhetoric, just like the old memory-places. At least, this is true of the cantos we have read well.

I shall touch on canto ii as a canto of places (apartments and the celestial, and how we get and stay there); I shall argue that Stevens says "Yes: but" to the "I am" of Coleridge and the "I am" of Descartes in cantos iii and iv. I shall pause over the difficult and lovely canto vi, and finally argue for one sense of "abstract" for Stevens' "major man."

Canto ii is a canto of dwelling places. It opens on apparent oxymoron, "celestial ennui": "It is the celestial ennui of apartments / That sends us back to the first idea." This oxymoron is apparent, however, only to readers of Baudelaire, especially Baudelaire seen through Eliot. Anatole France was of a different persuasion: "Même le sublime ennuie."[9] And Stevens, as we know, expected to be bored in heaven. The ephebe is a little slow to grasp the point: "May there be an ennui of the first idea?" To which his instructor replies in genial mock-ferocity: "What else, prodigious scholar, should there be?" So much for an obligatory *frisson* of horror over the word "ennui."

As for the word "apartments," we want to be on the lookout for words using the prefix a- or ab-, this section being a gloss on the note, "It Must Be Abstract." Abstraction is "drawing out from," and Stevens here enjoys his old play on the opposites "apart" and "a part."[10] The pun is even older than I have indicated. Here is the postcard he and Elsie sent to her parents just after their marriage. Stevens begins it: "Our house is under the mark. Our floor is next to the top. Therefore, we face the chapel, which is only across the street. Chimes every evening. *We are not a part of the chapel*—but apart from it. Hence, the word apartment. Hope this is clear." To which his bride added: "Wallace is crazy. Don't mind him" (SP 246). "Apartment" as a metaphorical dwelling place is unusual now,

---

imagination" (*NA* 23, 1942). As in *Notes* I.i, Stevens hopes he has "washed the imagination clean," so that the new poet and his community can recognize the poet's function.

[9] Anatole France, cited in Samuel H. Monk, *The Sublime: A Study of Critical Theories in Eighteenth-Century England* (New York: MLA, 1935), p. 9.

[10] Patke infers that "the ephebe-hermit dwells in an apartness of regression and defeat"; he notes "the pun on a-partment" but assumes "Stevens's phobia of modern housing" from *NA* 18, *SP* 242, 246 (*The Long Poems of Wallace Stevens: An Interpretative Study* [Cambridge: Cambridge University Press, 1985], p. 146).

though Edward Young thought it appropriate to consign God to one. ("Vast concave! ample dome! wast thou design'd / A meet apartment for the Deity?" [*Night Thoughts* ix.782–83].) This was before the days of high-rise apartment buildings, but after the King James Bible, where "in my Father's house there are many mansions." The apartment in *Notes* i.ii is part of the troping of dwelling places all through the series. It is also related to iii.i: "To sing jubilas . . . And so, *as part*, to exult with its great throat." In 1943, Stevens wrote of how "the philosopher dwells in his reason and the priest dwells in his belief." The poet also "dwells apart in his imagination" (*NA* 66). Hermit and philosopher figure in this canto, but who lives in apartments? Those who are part of a structure of belief or reason or imagination, and so live apart from the world? "The sacred" etymologically means "set apart," and to abstract is "to draw off or apart" (OED 2). I expect Stevens is using the word "apartment" in this sense, with the implicit observation that so-called belief, reason, imagination rarely set anyone apart these days. Most spiritual dwelling places are more like modern apartment houses than hermits' cells or cathedrals or the original groves of academe.

Canto ii is not only a canto of dwelling places; it is also about how we get there. Sometimes we get there by appointment. The "philosopher / Appoints man's place in music," says canto ii, faintly echoing a text that gave Stevens two of his well-known lines. "I will appoint a place for my people Israel, and will plant them, that they may dwell in a place of their own, and move no more" (2 Sam. 7:10). Stevens makes the appointer human, and anticipates his later echoing in canto iv: "we live in a place / That is not our own." Stevens' gloss on this canto in his letters is a close, flat paraphrase, except for the start: "If 'I am a stranger in the land,' it follows that the whole race is a stranger" (*L* 444, March 29, 1943). His mind is running on biblical dwelling places, for he is recalling an Old Testament formula: "I have been a stranger in a strange land" (Moses, in Exodus 2:22). The displacement in Stevens' letter is from a biblical sense of place, which once determined our sense of actual place, and still does for some. It did for Stevens' mother, who, dying tranquilly, said she would like a room in the bright sky (*L* 173, July 1, 1912). In canto ii, he is summing up over the memories of biblical dwelling places. And there are more to come.

What is such a strange canto as canto iii doing in a poem about a supreme fiction, or rather what is its second part doing? Its reversal is extreme. Word-play with whiteness—"immaculate," "candid"—runs through the first twelve lines, recalling many another white and shining world in Stevens' poetry. We are right to hear these lines telling us what poetry can do, but we tend to read naively. We shear off or domesticate the second part, which also tells us what poetry can do. "Poetry is a

destructive force. . . . It can kill a man," Stevens wrote in 1938. I think
the canto is precisely *about* reversals, reversals of white, immaculate te-
leologies. It is not that such refreshing does not happen. It is that such
refreshing may be too easy, and so easily reversed, as Stevens knew.
Here, he shows us an undoing of his first world, and with it all such
immaculate, idealized first worlds or homes—childhood or erotic or re-
ligious paradises—and perforce an idealized theory of poetry. Or at least
an idealized Coleridgean theory of poetry, for Coleridge is the chief an-
cestral voice echoing through this canto.

> The poem refreshes life so that we share,
> For a moment, the first idea . . . It satisfies
> Belief in an immaculate beginning
>
> And sends us, winged by an unconscious will,
> To an immaculate end. . . .
>
> We say: At night an Arabian in my room,
> With his damned hoobla-hoobla-hoobla-how,
> Inscribes a primitive astronomy. . . .
>
> And still the grossest iridescence of ocean
> Howls hoo and rises and howls hoo and falls.
> Life's nonsense pierces us with strange relation.

I shall only touch on the close reading of this canto I have already made,[11]
which hears a riddle based on *Kubla Khan* echoing back against the echo-
ing of "candid" in the first part. (Hoobla-how, Kubla Khan.) The strat-
egies of undoing dominate the first five cantos of *Notes*, and *Kubla Khan*,
with its magical transformations of biblical and Miltonic paradises, and
its yearning poet, serves Stevens' purposes wonderfully well. And Ste-
vens' work invites us to read in this way. Twice he parodies Coleridge's
great poem, once in 1942 in *Oak Leaves Are Hands*, once in 1923 in a
"mythy goober khan" (*CP* 142). In 1942 and 1943, Coleridge appears in
Stevens' essays, once as "one of the great figures" (*NA* 41, 3). And in
one of the final climactic cantos of *Notes*, Stevens echoes part of Cole-
ridge's definition of the primary imagination (III.viii), altering Cole-
ridge's own echo of the "I am."

Canto iii will not tell us how to read reversals. We may be undone by
them, as by a riddle, if we stay inside them. We may escape from them,
as from a riddle, by observing that "we say" these things ourselves,

---

[11] In "Riddles, Charms and Fictions in Wallace Stevens," *Centre and Labyrinth: Essays
in Honour of Northrop Frye*, ed. Eleanor Cook et al. (Toronto: University of Toronto Press,
1983), pp. 227–44.

though this is to put in jeopardy the power of words over us. Stevens' last line comments on the whole preceding canto—on its strange relation (story), its strange relation of first and second parts, its strange relation to seeming nonsense language. It offers a way out of the usual inside-outside readings of reversals, including the reversals of supreme or sacred fictions.

From Coleridge to his mental foe, Descartes: this is the movement from canto iii to canto iv, which opens: "The first idea was not our own. Adam / In Eden was the father of Descartes. . . ." Adam is the father of mankind, and so perforce of Descartes, but Adam himself as a Cartesian in Eden is another matter. Dryden, rewriting Milton, was happy to make Adam a Cartesian: "What am I? or from whence? For that I am I know, because I think . . ." (*The State of Innocence*, iii.i). For Coleridge, Descartes is the great schismatic, one of the dividers of the world, so that a Cartesian Adam in Eden is unthinkable. But Stevens' sentence in effect collapses the whole high Romantic struggle epitomized in the figures of Coleridge and Descartes. We may suppose for a moment that he is simply turning away from Coleridgean idealism and moving toward a kind of Cartesianism, for he goes on:

> Adam
> In Eden was the father of Descartes
> And Eve made air the mirror of herself,
>
> Of her sons and of her daughters. They found themselves
> In heaven as in a glass; a second earth. . . .

In *Paradise Lost*, Milton made water a mirror of Eve, rewriting Ovid's story of Narcissus. Here the Miltonic-Ovidian mirroring water undergoes a metamorphosis into air, and this mirroring air is made to echo St. Paul's famous mirror, that speculum or glass through which we see darkly (1 Cor. 13:12). If canto iii is about and uses enigma or riddle, this canto is about and uses mirrors. In Milton, Eve supposes she sees another creature; tempted toward self-absorption, she is recalled by Adam, taught what a reflection is, and turned toward him; the incident adumbrates the temptation and the Fall. In Stevens, Eve and all her progeny make the air into a mirror, projecting their own reflection into another being, that is, God. This is to make a mirror of "mere air," as Stevens has it in *Botanist on Alp (No. 2)*. If Adam-qua-Descartes were to come along, he might equally tell Eve, and us, that such projections are only ourselves writ large in the air or "in heaven." Stevens returns more than once to St. Paul's famous text, always to combat it. Converting St. Paul's mirror into Eve's mirroring water—this is clever, though the anthropomorphic doctrine is a little heavy-handed. And as argument, it seems to leave Descartes fully in charge—Coleridge's Descartes, of course, not the sufficiently orthodox seventeenth-century one.

Here we need to return to the opening sentence of the canto: "The first idea was not our own." We need also to give full weight to the turn in the argument marked by the word "but." For after the Eden scene, the canto proceeds thus:

> But the first idea was not to shape the clouds
> In imitation. The clouds preceded us.
>
> There was a muddy centre before we breathed.
> There was a myth before the myth began,
> Venerable and articulate and complete.
>
> From this the poem springs: that we live in a place
> That is not our own and, much more, not ourselves
> And hard it is in spite of blazoned days.

"First idea . . . in Eden . . . second earth . . . imitation . . . preceded us . . . before we breathed . . . before the myth . . . we are the mimics . . . we add." A question of priority is very much at issue here, whether the priority is chronological or ontological. Stevens insists on the priority of clouds and of a "muddy centre," thus veering away from numerous tropes of clouds as accommodating the unbearable full light of God or obscuring true revelation. Clouds, in these traditional tropes, are always waiting to be swept away; light or revelation or the sun is the "pedagogue." The "sweeping meanings we add" at the end of this canto recalls all those heavenly stringed instruments that a poet sweeps, and also the sweeping of clouds from the air, together with the "sweeping meaning" that we add to such troping. To make clouds into pedagogues rather than obscuring, accommodating, adumbrating, veiling, enfolded phenomena is to revise a long-standing hierarchy. As for the "muddy centre before we breathed," this restores a center to that mud into which God breathed and made man.

But Stevens is puzzling when he calls the anterior myth "venerable and articulate and complete," especially in that word "articulate." This seems an odd or even quite wrong word, for human speech alone is articulate. Or is it? In canto v, Stevens will move on to animal noises, which we assume are fully "articulate" for them, for all the OED may say. I think Stevens is refusing priority to the creation of humans, refusing to see this creation as unique, and thereby also refusing priority to Descartes' *cogito*. Other parts of the world have being, even if they do not have human reason or speech. To allow a "muddy centre before we breathed" and an earlier myth is to undo Eden and Descartes in one blow. What Stevens does here is to attack *both* a Coleridgean and a Cartesian view of origins and being. Against Coleridge, he allows Descartes into Eden and puts him to work against St. Paul. Against Descartes, he allows priority to things that can never say *cogito, ergo sum*, and he attacks our assumption that human language is the first and only way of articulation. Stevens hardly undervalues human language; he loves it too much. To say that clouds and mud and so on preceded us has little point until we see how things look in our dominant Cartesian mirror, which is dominated by a human self quite as much as Eve's "mere air." Canto iv is as much an attack on the Cartesian "I am" as canto iii was on the Coleridgean "I am," Stevens wishing to destroy neither, only to prevent them from becoming supreme.

Thus, I think, the reason for canto v, where the argument seems much thinned after the intricacies of iii and iv. Stevens develops tropes of voice, the voices of three kingly animals, lion, elephant, and bear. (For the elephant as king of the beasts, see E.M.W. Tillyard's *Elizabethan World Picture*, and for the bear, see Amerindian legends.) These kingly animals do not live in a place that is their own, either. The desert is enraging for the lion, whose stanza is triply reddened but who is not allegorized into red Wrath. In Stevens' favorite pun on "voluble," the ephebe is said to be "dumb, / Yet voluble of dumb violence." (The line in the *Collected Poems* omits "of," which the 1942 printing by the Cummington Press includes.) The ephebe's violence is directed as yet against himself, and not against the first idea, for the roofs still "cow" him. Despite the latent bovine sense in "cowed" (this being an animal canto), I hear little irony in calling the ephebe "heroic." He is right to look across the roofs,[12] for if they belong to structures of belief or supreme fictions, then they are the true challenge. It is their words the ephebe must confront, and that is what he or someone does in canto vi, where we hear a new voice.

Cantos vi and vii function as a transition from the opening five cantos to the climactic major-man cantos. Yet in a sense canto vi is the true beginning of Stevens' poem:

> Not to be realized because not to
> Be seen, not to be loved nor hated because
> Not to be realized. Weather by Franz Hals,
>
> Brushed up by brushy winds in brushy clouds,
> Wetted by blue, colder for white. Not to
> Be spoken to, without a roof, without

[12] Cf. "the distant company of strange yet friendly windows burning over the roofs" (*L* 67–68).

First fruits, without the virginal of birds,
The dark-blown ceinture loosened, not relinquished.
Gay is, gay was, the gay forsythia

And yellow, yellow thins the Northern blue.
Without a name and nothing to be desired,
If only imagined but imagined well.

My house has changed a little in the sun.
The fragrance of the magnolias comes close,
False flick, false form, but falseness close to kin.

It must be visible or invisible,
Invisible or visible or both:
A seeing and unseeing in the eye.

The weather and the giant of the weather,
Say the weather, the mere weather, the mere air:
An abstraction blooded, as a man by thought.

Nothing sings in cantos i through v as some of these lines sing. What seems most remarkable is the toughness of the argument and the fluidity of the lyric lines, themselves "loosened." Both Frank Kermode and Harold Bloom find this the hardest canto of Part I,[13] and I shall pause over it.

The referent of the opening sentence, like the mysterious addressee of the prefatory verse, is unspecified. And surely the argument, taken baldly, is untrue. God is unseen; whether or not we are religious, we can hardly say that God has not been loved. And "weather by Franz Hals"? Like the Sherlock Holmes story whose point is that the dog does not bark, surely the point of the second sentence is the *lack* of weather in Franz Hals's paintings. (Only Bloom seems to have noticed this oddity though he accounts for it differently. Most commentators demonstrate the power of suggestion by writing of Hals as if he were Constable.[14]) Stevens uses language that is both painterly and descriptive of actuality ("colder for white"). Yellow does "thin" the Northern blue. (More blue should be added in contrast to yellow "in order to achieve that equivalence to daylight," said Henry Richter to the ghosts of Dutch seventeenth-century masters, of which Hals was one.[15]) Some things Hals and

[13] Harold Bloom, *Wallace Stevens: The Poems of Our Climate* (Ithaca: Cornell University Press, 1977), p. 188; Kermode, " 'Notes toward a Supreme Fiction': A Commentary," *Annali dell'Istituto Universitario Orientale: Sezione Germanica* (Naples, 1961), p. 181.

[14] Bloom, *Wallace Stevens*, p. 187.

[15] As cited in Gombrich, *Art and Illusion: A Study in the Psychology of Pictorial Representation* (Princeton: Princeton University Press, 1969), p. 322.

others did not see and hence did not realize in the French sense of *réaliser* (*L* 828). I read Stevens' emerging spring weather as a synecdoche for all weather, and weather as a metonymy for this earth, and in the substitutions of these tropes I find no loss of love for actual spring weather. "The image of New England in early spring is an image not yet exploited," Stevens wrote in 1954 (*L* 827).

Stevens' lovely weather and earth are released from old allegories and symbolism in lines 5 through 8, which we may approach through the allusive echo of "first fruits." Literal first fruits are commonly a harvest sacrifice to the gods or to God. Figurative "first fruits of the Spirit" might be Milton's "Sighs / And Prayers" (Rom. 8:23, *PL* xi.23–24). The "first fruits of them that slept" is the resurrected Christ in the reverse-harvest metaphor of 1 Corinthians 15:20, 23, which we are likely to know from Handel's *Messiah*. Given this echo, "the virginal of birds" takes on wonderful punning force in a musical-procreative-Virgin-birth word-play. To be "without a roof" similarly plays on the release from old structures of belief (the roofs of canto v, the roof of old John Zeller) and the memory of the Son of Man who has no place to lay his head. In this context, "not to / Be spoken to" is also a release rather than a loss. Without Stevens' eighth line, all this might seem too easily antiallegorical. But "the dark-blown ceinture loosened, not relinquished" is one of Stevens' loveliest and most suggestive lines. It is an exquisite image of earth and sky as Venus, Stevens playing over all those tropes of wintry earth as bound, and all our memories of statues of Venus loosening her garments. "Ceinture" just suggests the girdle of Venus without itself being bound by that equivalent, and the language of Christendom is itself loosened by this shift from "virginal" to loosened ceinture. Yet not relinquished. Stevens "relinquishes" nothing in this extraordinary summing-up of a history of troping and painting. He has, of course, moved back toward earth in this line, and not only through evocations of Venus. "Dark-blown ceinture loosened" approaches descriptive language for early spring phenomena—clouds and streams, say—yet the compound adjective is too unusual and general to fit the particulars of one referent.

The difficult last lines I can read only so far, on the assumption that "it" is the supreme fiction. Stevens' seeming paradoxes about the visible and/or the invisible allow for an embodied supreme fiction without requiring any incarnation. As for abstraction, "thought" is an abstract noun and "blooded" a concrete one. If we can flesh out a thought, we can "blood" one too, figuratively speaking. And blood does fill thought processes in the sense of brain cells. But how is a man blooded by thought? Surely our or Stevens' analogical reasoning is wrong here—that is, unless we read "blooded" as if Faulkner had written it. "To blood" is to give a hound its first taste of the blood of the game it is to hunt (OED 3) or to make a man eager for combat (OED 4). "Put on the whole armor of God," St. Paul wrote. "For we wrestle not against flesh and blood but against principalities, against powers." "Soldier, there is a war between the mind / And sky," Stevens will end. "Blooded, as a man by thought."

Stevens chooses to end Part I with three climactic cantos on what he calls "major man." His greatest challenge is to present such a figure and still avoid the dominant "major man" patterns we have inherited, notably that of Christ. Canto viii opens:

> Can we compose a castle-fortress-home,
> Even with the help of Viollet-le-Duc,
> And set the MacCullough there as major man?

Not very likely, to follow the rhetoric of the question, and we note that structures do vanish from Part I after this, though every canto until now has included one that is more or less allegorical. In the final canto, the clown figure is spied "beyond the town." The imagery and allegory of dwelling places cannot go much beyond Stevens' all-encompassing compound noun, "castle-fortress-home." As so often in Stevens, the word is first of all a precise description, here of some of the buildings Viollet-le-Duc did restore. (An old French château was at once a castle and a fortress and a home.) Allegorically, it recalls Stevens' longtime desire for a poetic home, at once a majestic dwelling place for some ruler in an inner life, and a true inner home. As for the fortress, we might recall Luther. "Ein fester Burg ist unser Gott": "A mighty fortress is our God," says Luther's famous hymn, which Stevens inherited from his ancestors, used in another poem, and punned on in his letters. "One's own fortitude of spirit is the only 'fester Burg' " (L 403, February 18, 1942). "Spreading out fortress walls like fortress wings," he wrote later in *The Old Lutheran Bells at Home* (CP 461).

Stevens prefers "violet space" rather than Viollet's places, and he sets the MacCullough tentatively there—"the pensive giant prone in violet space." MacCullough is one of the sons of *Notes*, and spoken of with a definite article, as of the head of the clan.[16] The argument is not hard to follow once we understand that Stevens wants the major man to be embodied, but only as a possibility and never as a necessity. The embodiment, if it happens, will be as random as the name, and perhaps short lived. It is the abstraction that is necessary, not the incarnation. We can hear this implied in canto i, if we listen with care to Stevens' play on the

---

[16] John Hollander has remarked that he once heard a MacCullough referred to as "the MacCullough" or head of the clan, in Pennsylvania.

words "inconceivable" and "sun." If we listen also to the logic of his incomplete syllogism: "The death of one god is the death of all. Phoebus is dead." Stevens does not add the third sentence, "Therefore all gods are dead," and especially the successor to Phoebus Apollo, that is, Christ. (The succession is explicit at the beginning of Dante's *Paradiso*.) I hear a pun on "son" in Stevens' phrase "inconceivable idea of the sun." He made this argument explicit in another 1942 poem about the hero, playing an abstract "conception" against a physical one: "It is a part of his conception, / That he be not conceived, being real" (*CP* 279).

In the old tradition, the created world was made by the Son, who would later be conceived within it. A world that is the "inconceivable idea of the sun" will not accommodate either conceivable idea of the Son. For Stevens, such a conception is not possible, and his fiction must be abstract. A compendium, yes (this is one sense of "abstract"); possible of being made flesh, yes; but with no necessary historical incarnation. "The pensive giant . . . May be the MacCullough" (I.viii). "He is and may be but oh! he is, he is, / This foundling of the infected past" (I.ix). Major man, even when he takes over Christmas imagery, as in I.ix, always "may be," and only may be. It is not that Stevens is proposing a discarnate major man when he uses the word "abstraction." He is de-creating the doctrine of the Incarnation, so to speak. ("The NOTES start out with the idea that it [a supreme fiction] would not take any form: that it would be abstract" [*L* 430, December 8, 1940].) Theologically, Stevens is moving back to neo-Platonic allegorical interpretation, rather than Augustinian figural (not figurative) interpretation. He would make a fine neo-Platonist but never an Augustinian, and orthodoxy followed the path of Augustine.

My sense of Stevens' word "abstract" is consistent with I. A. Richards's use in his *Coleridge on Imagination*, which Stevens read and annotated. Richards conceives of an " 'all-inclusive myth' that would provide the kind of nature 'that the religions in the past have attempted to provide for man.' "[17] Stevens starts "It Must Be Abstract" with a play on "be," and a doctrine of being is at the center of Christian "supreme fictions." We recall how it informs Thomist analogy. We might note also how the verb "to be" functions in the name of God, I am that I am, and in the statement of Incarnation, Jesus is God. (We sometimes assume in discussions of metaphor that "the doctrine of Incarnation is in essence a theory of metaphor."[18] That depends on your doctrine. A good deal of

[17] I am indebted for this point to B. J. Leggett, "Why It Must Be Abstract: Stevens, Coleridge and I. A. Richards," *Studies in Romanticism* 22 (1983), 489–515.

[18] Charles Altieri, "Wallace Stevens' Metaphors of Metaphor," *American Poetry* 1 (1983), 45.

patristic anguish went into arguments about whether it was or it was not at the time of the Council of Nicaea.) It does not do to underestimate Stevens' awareness of all this, as we may see from his extraordinary de-creation of the language of orthodoxy in these lines from canto viii:

> Logos and logic, crystal hypothesis,
> Incipit and a form to speak the word
> And every latent double in the word. . . .

Stevens restores logic to logos, which may be a short step, or a leap, depending on our sense of both. If we go from logos to logic as from Coleridge to Descartes, then it is a leap. The Johannine Word, though it encompasses all logic, is beyond logic, being paradoxical and a-logical; it would not take kindly to a logic on equal footing. Hypotheses are conventionally cloudy, and wait for clear thesis or revelation. Stevens keeps his major man both a hypothesis and crystal clear. (Thus also, I think, "cloudless the morning" of I.x, and thus also the full play over the word "crystal" in Stevens' last canto.) "Incipit" *is* a form, or at least a formula, "to speak the word," just like Stevens' opening "Begin." "Every latent double in the word" revives Augustine's formula, "In Vetro, Novus latet; in Novo, Vetus patet" (In the Old Testament, the New lies latent; in the New Testament, the Old stands patent). Stevens' line evokes this principle of typological or figural interpretation, but shies away from saying what is patent. He is unobtrusively insistent about lying in this canto: the giant is prone, doubles are latent in the word, MacCullough lay lounging by the sea. The memory of Whitman's "loafing" is insufficient explanation, and I cannot read fully. But there is some play with proneness, latency, and lying that I think we should connect with the mysterious hiddenness of major man in canto ix. Cantos ix and x are both revelatory in their way, yet canto ix also includes injunctions against naming and making images, as if Stevens were undoing the major man of the New Testament according to some laws of the Old. The revelation of major man in his particulars should remain private, though in his abstraction, major man is part of—rather, *is*—the commonal.

"Beau linguist" sums up over this stanza, as "linguist" takes a full range of meaning: interpreter, master of languages, translator. Though there is no patency, no opening of the word, no radical metaphor, but only the simile of "as if," still there is ease at the end of canto viii, in the lovely flowing lines, like the waves of the sea, with water and words flowing back and forth, and no sense of barrier between. Stevens' lines play back over all his watery and fluent poems:

As if the waves at last were never broken,
As if the language suddenly, with ease,
Said things it had laboriously spoken.

Cantos viii and x seem to me fully realized, canto ix less so. Stevens distances his major man from both apotheosis and reason, both logos and logic, so to speak:

The romantic intoning, the declaimed clairvoyance
Are parts of apotheosis, appropriate
And of its nature, the idioms thereof.

Reason sounds and looks differently: "reason's click-clack, its applied / Enflashings." (We may recall Bernard Shaw as he appeared in Yeats's dream—a sewing-machine that clicked and shone, and smiled incessantly.) After this double distancing, Stevens must bring major man to life, and he chooses a revised annunciation and nativity language. There are fine lines and phrases, such as "My dame, sing for this person accurate songs." And we can hear the play throughout with a- prefixes, a play calling on the note, "It Must Be Abstract." Yet I cannot hear Stevens meeting the demands he makes of himself in this canto.

Canto x is another matter. "God is the only president of the day, and Webster is his orator." Thus Thoreau in the Islamic formulation that is, or used to be, commonplace rhetoric. And thus also Stevens: "The major abstraction is the idea of man / And major man is its exponent." The formulation, smiling a little at its form, is ironic at very little expense to itself, as Stevens prepares to close Part I of *Notes*. His movement of comic through high sublime is congenial to him, and the canto is at ease. Its most important movement is away from major man as an "exception" and back toward a concept of "part of." For if Stevens' supreme fiction is to be heir to older supreme beings, it must function as more than a "fortuitous, personal" fiction. Though Stevens' significant "moments" come randomly, his fiction in the abstract must be able to speak to a community. He knew this at the time of *The Man with the Blue Guitar*, and it is important in 1949 in *An Ordinary Evening in New Haven*. It is also clear in this poem: "In being more than an exception, part, / Though an heroic part, of the commonal." Then comes the leap: "The major abstraction is the commonal, / The inanimate difficult visage." "Abstract" as compendium merges with "abstract" as "inconceivable" or "invisible or visible or both," as Stevens plays among the senses of "abstract" in the preceding nine cantos. He offers a figure, who is separate yet only one, and with much yet to read.

And the ephebe is recalled, to be sent on his way, to make, to "confect" (a more artful form of "compose" and a play against "infected" in I.ix). Negatives return: "not to console / Nor sanctify, but plainly to propound." The word "console" moves with biblical force down through Wordsworth: "from the blank abyss / To look with bodily eyes, and be consoled" (*Prelude* VI.470–71). Wordsworth is himself echoing and revising Milton, and Stevens will echo and revise both more loudly at the end of his series. Here he chiefly registers his dislike of the premise that makes consolation necessary. "To propound" is to put forward for consideration or debate (not quite what we expect of a supreme fiction or major man). But it is also to represent by figure or description (an obsolete meaning), to conceive or imagine to oneself (also obsolete), and to put before the proper authority for the purpose of having legality established (a legal meaning—in the context, as if one were to come before Constantine, propounding Christianity). Propounding is also, rarely, a name for the rhetorical figure of prolepsis ("the Greekes call him *Prolepsis*, we the Propounder, or the Explaner which ye will," says Puttenham [*The Arte of English Poesie*, III.xii.179]). The old religious word for "prolepsis" would, I suppose, be "prophecy." Such a refacimento of visionary prophecy is a fitting end to Part I.

IT MUST CHANGE

"Change and decay in all around I see: / O thou, who changest not, abide with me." Thus the well-known hymn. Something subject to change cannot be the true God, says Augustine (*City of God* VII.27). It seems too obvious for Stevens' note to say that his supreme fiction must change. Of course it must change, we want to say. What has Part I been arguing if not that? We may best consider this matter by asking what Stevens' subjects are in Part II. This is not a section about God or gods or major man. Its subjects are the forms and tropes in which our dominant "supreme fictions" linger on: an old seraph, cycles of nature, bourgeois tributes to an old warhorse and an old monument, the earthly paradise, birdsong as earnest of a heaven, moony eros, tropes of naked truth and final revelation. (Some of these we recognize as Stevens' own personal "vestigial states of mind.") The only way that the title of Part II makes sense to me is when "must" is emphasized: It *Must* Change. Stevens is testing some continuing tropes of a supreme fiction. That is why he will end with the translation and transformation cantos, and a Theater of Trope. Part I begins with ideas and ends on the verb "propound"; it is a propounding section, with doctrinal matters to the fore. Part II begins with sensation and desire, and ends on the verbs "propose" and "write," with reflections on "metaphor" in a Theater of Trope. In Part I, dialectic is to the fore, in Part II, rhetoric. Both are matters of being, as we may hear from the intricate play on "be" in I.i and II.i (begin, ephebe, Phoebus, to be, the bee to be, etc.). But Part II proceeds not so much by argument, though there are certainly arguments at work—questions of repetition, randomness, constancy, and so forth. It proceeds by testing tropes. Stevens knows full well that "metaphors are harder to get rid of than arguments."[19]

His choice of angels as part of a supreme fiction also looks a little obvious, and mischievous too. Angels were once believed in much more widely than they are today. Attempts to explain this change are likely to take place just where Stevens wants them to—on the ground of human imagination. Time has altered angels; Stevens amusingly enacts this in canto i by having the seraph himself grow old, the Chronos implicit in his "chronologies" moving through the canto relentlessly to arrive at its standard pun on Cronos or Saturn. Stevens does not argue overtly about where and how angels exist. He simply puts his seraph outside, and then inside, a text, making him wander easily off the page and back on to it. In thus decreating an easy inside-outside way of reading, Stevens imitates very well the ambiguous way in which we usually read angels.

> The old seraph, parcel-gilded, among violets
> Inhaled the appointed odor, while the doves
> Rose up like phantoms from chronologies.
>
> The Italian girls wore jonquils in their hair
> And these the seraph saw, had seen long since,
> In the bandeaux of the mothers, would see again.

Doctrines of angelic being are hardly central in theological debate. Is Stevens being the village atheist with the standard test cases that attack something inessential and ignore important matters? The answer might be yes, if Stevens had left off angelology with canto i. But he likes angels, and they keep reappearing through the rest of his series: in Nanzia Nunzio, in the apostrophized capital-A Angel of III.vii, in the comparative angel of III.ix where "I can do all that angels can," and in the leaping angel of III.viii, as remarkable a modern angel as Rilke's. This old seraph is only Stevens' first angel, if his most tired.

"Parcel-gilded" is a wicked word: itself old, like the seraph, it means "partly gilded." A seraph ought to be golden, surely, even more golden than spring's "golden fury" (II.ii). (Jonson makes the contrast: "changing his parcell guilt to massie gold" [*Alchemist* III.iii].) Through this

[19] Paul de Man, *Allegories of Reading: Figural Language in Rousseau, Nietzsche, Rilke, and Proust* (New Haven and London: Yale University Press, 1979), p. 4.

adjective, the old seraph also enters the "part of" debate of *Notes*, though he ought to be wholly whatever he is, just as he ought to be golden. Was he always "parcel-gilded" or has he worn down to this? Gold or gilded, he does seem to live on the illuminated page of an old chronology, inhaling the appointed odor, whether of incense or of sanctity, surrounded by violets and doves. Yet the enjambment of lines 1 and 2 suggests that he has momentarily strayed into the natural world and there inhales the odor of violets. Doves "like phantoms" are doves like ghosts, with the word "phantom" evoking the Holy Ghost yet also making its iconographic doves spectral rather than symbolic.

The argument of cantos i and ii is not hard to follow, though we tend to underestimate its reach and miss its engagement with Eliot. Both these matters are illuminated by word-play. "The distaste we feel for this withered scene," that is, the withered scene of a repeating springtime: Eliot has so dominated this subject that we all too easily assume the natural recurrence of seasons calls for the ironic or elegiac mode. We should know better after *Ideas of Order*. Is not stanza ii in the same mode as *The Waste Land*, Part I? Well, no, but this is not clear until the end of canto ii, where Stevens openly attacks Eliot's assumptions about memory, sleep, spring, death, and returning:

> Why, then, when in golden fury

> Spring vanishes the scraps of winter, why
> Should there be a question of returning or
> Of death in memory's dream? Is spring a sleep?

But Stevens' quarrel with Eliot is apparent enough before this. Eliot's nostalgia for the prophetic voice of Isaiah's seraph is clear in his pained parody of this seraph in *The Waste Land*, Part II, the "sylvan scene" of the "withered stumps of time." When Stevens speaks of "the distaste we feel for this withered scene," he refers to actual springtime gone dead, and also to all spring scenes made dead by a "waste land" point of view.

It is true that the profusion of imagery can be bewildering in this canto, as Helen Vendler says,[20] at least until we recognize that it is focused on a traditional Christian iconography of annunciation, as seen in Italian art. (Those "Italian girls" are the models for countless Madonnas.[21]) Such iconography makes much use of natural springtime rebirth, always seen as sustained by the supernatural. For a few stanzas, it looks

---

[20] Helen Vendler, *On Extended Wings: Wallace Stevens' Longer Poems* (Cambridge, Mass.: Harvard University Press, 1969), pp. 193–94.

[21] "We find the poetry of mankind in . . . the madonnas of all Europe" (*NA* 159, 1951, and cf. *NA* 73).

as if Stevens' old seraph will watch girls and flowers, birds and bees, much like an orthodox seraph. Then we realize that he has not been purely seraphic all this while. Mixing memory and desire, he can become a "satyr in Saturn"according to—not Isaiah or any scripture, but—"according to his thoughts." The seraphim are distinguished by their ecstatic fervor of devotion ("seraph" is thought to derive from the Hebrew word, "to burn"). They are angels of love, spiritual love, that is. Stevens' seraph belongs "in a universe of inconstancy," like all of us, and so, "The seraph / Is satyr in Saturn, according to his thoughts." The line has caused some problems, though it need not. "Saturn troubles nativities," says the *Greek Anthology* (ii.183), and it certainly troubles the archetypal Christian annunciatory imagery here. Other beginnings, other annunciations and nativities than the Christian one, are evoked: Saturn's golden age, with what Milton calls its "pleasing license"; hence a Satyrnalia (Vendler hears this pun, where, to my ear, the old seraph and his long experience of Italian girls threaten to become distasteful); a saturnine or sour satyr (as in the *vers saturnien* of the French symbolists); and a seraph-become-satyr by a troubling conjunction of stars "in Saturn." In all this word-play, the seraph never speaks. Isaiah's great seraph touches the prophet's lips with a coal, and he prophesies. This seraph inhales but does not inspire; sees girls but no longer annunciates; transforms himself, but not "as a man by thought," only as an old seraph "according to his thoughts," and they get no farther than goatishness (unless we think "in Saturn's reign, / Such mixture was not held a stain"). The canto dwindles altogether: the appointed odor to "an erotic perfume"; the doves to clattering pigeons. The bees also start to repeat, and Stevens breaks off in a refrainlike recollection of the first "bees" line. Cantos i and ii form a pair. "I don't particularly like the first one or two parts," Stevens remarked when considering what to read from "It Must Change."[22] And canto i does finally take on some of the bluntness and distaste that it describes. "Thus spake the seraph, and forthwith," we cheerfully sing at Christmas, but Stevens cannot find any refreshment in this old form of a "supreme fiction."

Stevens calls attention in canto ii to his least subtle trope, what Vendler calls the fable of the bees. The trope that by repetition becomes the chief trope of repetition—it would seem impossible to rescue such a figure, but Stevens does, beginning with an obvious pun and obvious play with enjambment:

[22] Stevens: "There are three or four parts of it ["It Must Change"] that I like very much. I don't particularly like the first one or two parts" (Letter to Robert G. Tucker, February 24, 1954, WAS 2431, Huntington Library, quoted by permission of Holly Stevens and the Huntington Library).

The President ordains the bee to be
Immortal. The President ordains. But does
The body lift its heavy wing, take up,

Again, an inexhaustible being, rise
Over the loftiest antagonist
To drone the green phrases of its juvenal?

The bee is hardly a literal test case for a doctrine of immortality (though one remembers the wasp and the courteously inquisitive Hindu in *A Passage to India*). But Stevens is not proceeding by direct doctrinal engagement with matters that are not provable. He is interested in the assumptions of rhetoric, especially the assumption that there should be a "question of returning" in spring. (As so often, "of" is ambiguous.) Vendler's is the best commentary on the fable of the bees in cantos i and ii. I would add only the observation of how the bees move through different contexts: reference (bees out there), punning (bee-be), image of human life, exemplum in doctrinal argument, traditional image of the successful imitator, metonymy for voice (with the obsolete meaning of "booming" revived), and metaleptic comment on its own figuration by means of echo. Stevens' third stanza is addressed both to a doctrine of immortality and a history of trope:

Why should the bee recapture a lost blague,
Find a deep echo in a horn and buzz
The bottomless trophy, new hornsman after old?

"To drone the green phrases of its juvenal" refers, among other things, to the juvenal of troping, say the time of Gray, whose beetle "wheels his droning flight" (*Elegy Written in a Country Churchyard*). Or the time of Collins, "where the beetle winds / His small but sullen horn" (*Ode to Evening*). Why should Stevens' bee "find a deep echo in a horn . . . new hornsman after old?" Not this chase for him. Or why should it rise "over the loftiest antagonist," the Miltonic phrase marking the antagonist as either Satan or the lofty Milton himself, over whose phrases Stevens' own phrases must rise if he works in a Miltonic mode. The old mode will not of itself "rise up" for him; it must be "taken up." Whatever is inexhaustible, it is not this mode of being.

After such elaborations, we are ready for the plain allegory of canto iii. Its point seems overobvious, unless it is an argument against the genetic fallacy. The General Du Puy and the Place Du Puy, in which his statue rests immobile, pun on the general "sinceness" of things. "Puy," meaning eminence, is now obsolete except in place names like Place Du Puy. "Depuis" means "since," and the word suits Stevens' purposes bet-

ter than, say, "passé," because "depuis" talks about what is past but re-
quires a verb in the present tense. Stevens has found an allegorical pun
in a grammatical construction. He chooses for this canto a stiffness of
syntax and diction and imagery, right down to the geraniums, and its
plainness is unappealing, unlike that of the catalogue poem, canto iv.

Canto iv begins as abstraction and ends as hymn. It begins with the
"origin of change" and ends with an address to a spirit contrary to Eliot's
and Baudelaire's "hypocrite lecteur, mon semblable, mon frère": "Fol-
low after, O my companion, my fellow, myself, / Sister and solace,
brother and delight." This is Whitman's kind of address and apostrophe,
and as in Whitman it includes the reader. Stevens' own voice sounds
more distinctly early in the poem with the play on "copulars" and the
memorable next line: "Winter and spring, cold copulars, embrace / And
forth the particulars of rapture come." The hymn moves into Stevens'
own earthly paradise in canto v—his Southern lands, and his poem *Sun-
day Morning* with its island and wide (here "sky-wide") water and or-
anges and pungent fruit. Stevens' island is inhabited by a planter, and
thereby we may hear once more the force of Milton's Eden for him. That
planter is surely a human version of Milton's "sovran Planter," who was
God (*PL* iv.691). Stevens' echoes are softly rebounding, as so often, over
the history of a topos. For it is Goethe's earthly paradise that is most
recalled here, the earthly paradise of his famous song, "Kennst du das
Land wo die Zitronen blühn?" In Goethe, we may find blooming citron
trees, golden oranges, blue sky, myrtle, a great house, and the refrain,
"Dahin! Dahin!" Stevens' orange trees bloom, his oranges are painterly
"blotches," his island is blue, his myrtle is sea-myrtle, his house is un-
specified. He has no refrain, though we may hear là-bas, là-bas, as a quiet
echo of Mignon's impassioned Dahin! Dahin! This quiet recollection
speaks of Stevens' love for Goethe.[23]

Stevens turns sharply from this topos of the earthly paradise to a very
different canto, an attack on his own enemy within, birdsong.

> Bethou me, said sparrow, to the crackled blade,
> And you, and you, bethou me as you blow,
> When in my coppice you behold me be.

What is that crackled blade, imperiously called by sparrow, who demands
more elevated address than it is prepared to give. We recall Stevens' line,
"Playing a crackled reed, wind-stopped, in bleats" (OP 67), with

[23] "For a long time Goethe was to me what Sainte Beuve was to you. The other day, for
instance, I happened to be saying something with respect to one of my grandfathers when
I noticed that he was born in 1809. I thought automatically Goethe was still alive" (L 457,
October 11, 1943).

its harsh revision of Milton and Keats in an attack on Stevens' own early pastoral self. "Crackled" in 1942 as in 1936 takes a full range of meaning: making crackling noises; trilling or quavering (used contemptuously, says the OED, of this obsolete sense); breaking off in small pieces (thus related to refrain); and the transitive nonce-use of cracking jokes in a small way (OED 4). Stevens' 1942 reed plays the cracked tune of a debased or lost pastoral, breaking the pastoral instrument, reducing the song to crackles, recalling contemptuous treatments of song, and joking on the whole procedure—all in one word. As for a crackled blade of grass, it is normally impossible to use this except to produce a piercing whistle. Logically, the sparrow should be a song sparrow, and Stevens' journal supports this, as noted below. But the speeded-up repetition and rhythm of line 2 turn the song into something else. (Stevens suggested the nasal note of a catbird [L 435, January 12, 1943].) If we juxtapose our memories of a song sparrow's song and our memories of a grass-blade whistle, we may begin to read Stevens' stanza. The incongruity is funny—unless you yourself happen to be a blade.

How is one to answer this bird, this age-old trope for poetic voice which has taken to ordering the poetic voice around, especially when that bird has been reading Shelley? For this is an intimidating creature, just as the Arabian fable in I.iii can be intimidating. Stevens uses a similar defensive strategy here: he suggests another reading of the same words, this time through punning on two words three times over, and devising a syntax to suit all three sets of puns. We come first to the reading outlined above, as the most obvious and the one anticipated by Stevens' earlier writing. But to what extent it retains any priority is very much in question. To quote John Hollander: "as is so often the case with Stevens' ambiguous constructions, it is the relation between two or more possible meanings that itself not only enters their array, but seems to dominate them."[24]

For Stevens' syntax is so devised that this blade may blow *in* the wind quite as readily as itself blow wind. This brings the figure closer to an actual blade of grass and also closer to Whitman, as if it evoked classical or Miltonic reeds or pipes or straw at a distance only, and preferred the modern image of voice as closer to actuality. This is a more cheerful state of affairs for a writer, since a blade, crackled or other, has as much natural vitality as a bird. Even if it is blown in the wind, rather than blowing wind, it may retort by bearing seed, etc. (We recall the tropes of voice as seed in *The Comedian*.) If the first reading is intimidating, the second is

---

[24] John Hollander, *The Figure of Echo: A Mode of Allusion in Milton and After* (Berkeley, Los Angeles, London: University of California Press, 1981), p. 92.

not quite so bad. So also the first reading of the Arabian fable in i.iii is intimidating, and the second not quite so bad.

But there is yet a third reading for "blade" and "blow." The coppice of this sparrow is etymologically a "blow" or "cuff"; it is cognate with French *couper*, being a small wood grown for purposes of cutting. Stevens' word "blow" also means "cut down by a blow," and so "blade" retrospectively takes on the meaning of "axe-blade." Stevens is triply punning. The old pastoral reed is being intricately mocked, even as the crackled blade of grass is blowing in the wind, and the old glade of the singing bird is being destroyed. Triple punning is rare, as W. B. Stanford notes,[25] and to pun triply on a complete clause is very rare. Stevens' word-play captures something of his mixed feelings about birdsong and bethouing—the sense of intimacy, with all the poetic and spiritual implications. (One addresses as "tu" either intimates or servants or God, and the muse may function in all these ways.) Stevens' old nostalgia about pastoral is here, with a recognition of how intimidating it can be. So is his sense of being Whitman's heir and part of an American scene. And so also is his sense that, even as he remembers all this, he is surreptitiously chopping down the habitat of that imperious bird by himself insisting that the supreme fiction must change. Little does sparrow know what awaits its hubris.

Stevens' exuberant punning abates only slightly in the second tercet:

> Ah, ké! the bloody wren, the felon jay,
> Ké-ké, the jug-throated robin pouring out,
> Bethou, bethou, bethou me in my glade.

"The jug-throated robin pouring out" combines nightingale and robin, for the nightingale by convention says "jug, jug," and song by convention "pours out," as we remember from *Le Monocle*. Thus a jug-throated bird pouring out. But why combine nightingale and robin? Because we live in North America is one answer; like Thoreau, we may substitute our own well-known songbird for the non-American nightingale. A little ornithology and a glance back at earlier Stevens suggest that another answer is Eliot. For Eliot's two memorable birds in *The Waste Land* are the wretched nightingale singing jug, jug, and the redemptive hermit thrush singing its famous water-dropping song. The robin is our most domesticated member of the thrush family; it is to the thrush (hermit, wood, etc.) as the pigeon is to the dove. Stevens' bird overgoes Eliot's considerably. It does not merely say "Drip drop drip

---

[25] Stanford, *Ambiguity in Greek Literature: Studies in Theory and Practice* (Oxford: Blackwell, 1939), p. 71.

drop drop drop drop"; it pours. After this poem, we have no need of any more "bethous," whether Shelley's or Eliot's. (I am thinking of Eliot's vocative "O thou," as in "O swallow swallow"—which reads very strangely after Stevens' watery attacks.) This is a much more skilled attack than in 1936.

Scr- and cr- and k-sounds are usually assigned to the enemies of song—to those who grate on their scrannel pipes of wretched straw, or to the cracked tune that Chronos sings. Here birdsong takes over the k-sound, rendered as ké-ké in a phonetic approximation of the songs of jays and wrens. (Stevens is most likely hearing marsh wrens, for the songs of house or winter wrens are sweet.) At first, I read all these sounds as one, only coming to hear a contrast under Stevens' own tutelage: "Bethou is intended to be heard; it and ké-ké, which is inimical, are opposing sounds. Bethou is the spirit's own seduction" (L 438, January 28, 1943). Stevens does not make the argument or syntax indicate this contrast but he did say that *Notes* should be read slowly. I assume he expected the attentive reader to hear the contrast, just as Tennyson expected the attentive reader to hear the rooks in *Maud*, and was much irritated with the conventional little girl who opted for nightingales. If the "bethous" are the spirit's own seductions, "ké-ké" sounds like the spirit's mockery, something altogether more risory and raucous. The two stanzas with Stevens' comment, as well as Tennyson on his rooks, make a most interesting test case for questions of referential language.[26]

It might seem curious that Stevens should choose birdsong, well troped or not, for such an attack. We have to take fully into account the insidiousness of a bird who utters imperatives, and whose sense of being is so strong. In this, the bird is like the ephebe's instructor, and its canto also opens and closes with "be-." At the same time, we have to take fully into account our own memories of birdsong and the long history of birdsong in literature. Stevens' remark that the sparrow represents the spirit's own seduction is helpful, and so is his journal entry of July 26, 1899. ("One finds immense satisfaction in studying the lyrics of song-sparrows, catbirds, wrens and the like" [L 30].) For the journal demonstrates first that Stevens studied birdsong, and second that he once loved it. He came to think of it as the spirit's own seduction for two reasons, I think. One is that it was associated with erotic seductiveness, and the second (and this is the cogent reason here) is that it is so often heard as earnest

---

[26] Stevens: "Such poems [as *Notes toward a Supreme Fiction*] have to be read slowly" (letter to Robert G. Tucker, February 24, 1954, WAS 2431, Huntington Library, quoted by permission of Holly Stevens and the Huntington Library). Tennyson's remark is quoted in *Studies in Tennyson*, ed. Hallam Tennyson (London: Macmillan, 1981), p. 176.

of a heaven. Even Hardy's coppice-bird so works on him that he "could think" of some blessed hope. Hardy demonstrates how persistently bird-song may be heard as vestige of a heaven, or at least some hope out there. Stevens is out to undo all such "vestigial states of mind." And so he insists on the natural thievery and belligerence and general bloodiness of birds. So also he attacks poets like Eliot, who locate birdsong in a paradise.[27] Stevens' sentence, "It is / A sound like any other," makes sense only when read against such a persistent and stubborn history of bird-song. Canto vii turns against such a "seducing hymn," rewriting *To the One of Fictive Music* but Stevens does not quite recover himself. In canto viii, he does so fully.

Nanzia Nunzio announces her own annunciation in canto viii, in a conflation of the seraph and the Italian girls of canto i in one female figure. As the Queen of Sheba comes to Solomon, so Nanzia Nunzio comes to Ozymandias. Among female ancestresses for Nanzia, the Queen of Sheba is much to the point, also bearing gold and gems though a little differently; also a traveler, and a "confronting" traveller, again a little differently. "The queen of rich Arabia came . . . to prove Solomon with dark sentences," as Coverdale translates 2 Chronicles 9:1. "And king Solomon gave to the queen of Sheba all her desire, whatsoever she asked" (Authorized Version, ibid., 9:12). Those "dark sentences" are more pointedly *aenigmata* in the Vulgate, a word that emphasizes Solomon as the wise leader who solves riddles and unveils mysteries, Milton's sapient king. "I am the spouse," says Nanzia Nunzio. "As I am, I am / The spouse . . . I am the spouse, divested of bright gold, / The spouse beyond emerald and amethyst . . . I am the contemplated spouse." She speaks, not in the plain style of one intent on stripping off ornament, but in the language of the Song of Songs, the only place in the Authorized Version of the Bible where the word "spouse" appears. Nanzia Nunzio evokes not only this powerful and beautiful text but also its fulfillment in the Apocalypse (or sudden unveiling), where the marriage of the Canticles is transformed into the marriage of the Spirit and the Bride. Ozymandias demonstrates his wisdom by answering her in kind, that is, by extending "spouse" into the more usual biblical allegorical "bride." He replies that "the spouse, the bride / Is never naked." As it happens, Ozymandias is perfectly orthodox, for the biblical bride is not naked. Her troping as the spouse, the bride, that is, as type and antitype

---

[27] Eliot is a possible candidate for the "bloodless episcopus" here. Eliot would be a new Bishop (Episcopus) of Hippo (the old one is St. Augustine), rather than his own engaging flesh-and-blood hippo-potamus. ("Flesh and blood is weak and frail," and so on.) Stevens' antagonism threatens to get out of hand.

in Canticles and Revelation, is among the most beautiful in biblical literature. Nanzia comes dressed in a version of the bride as New Jerusalem; her gold and amethyst and emerald may all be found in St. John's vision, as Emily Dickinson knew. Nanzia Nunzio is more erotic, shedding her jeweled ornaments slowly, New Jerusalem metamorphosing back into spouse, and spouse behaving like the Aphrodite of the Homeric hymns.

Nanzia has more than biblical ancestresses. The great classical veilers and unveilers are also part of her heritage: Calypso and Isis and the Aphrodite just mentioned. Yet these are figures whose mystery remains, if their clothing does not. And some remain mostly clothed, like the Isis who lies behind Keats's Moneta, and who also utters a portentous "I am": "I am all that has been, that shall be, and none among mortals has hitherto taken off my veil." (Female figures of authority like Moneta and Beatrice tend to uncover their faces only.) "The . . . ceinture loosened, not relinquished," said Stevens earlier of his Aphrodite spring weather. But Nanzia is a desert lady, on the sand and with a burning body, a vestal "long prepared," and with no hesitation about relinquishing ceintures. Her language is of high ceremoniousness, and we readily read it as both erotic and allegorical (as we are trained to read the Song of Songs). We also find a slight humor in her solemn ardor, especially where the language moves to include the phallic.

She is the first utterer of an "I am" in *Notes*, and she not only utters "I am"; she utters the first variation on Jehovah's "I am that I am." For a moment, the enjambment makes her sound like a rival to Jehovah, but she wants a predicate, and, when the line turns, the verb "to be" turns out to be a copula. Nanzia defines herself as a spouse and so needs that "inflexible / Order."

The mystic marriage of Spirit and Bride in Revelation ushers in the end of mystery or veiling. The trope of clothing or veils as symbol of mystery, and asking to be removed, is so common that we pause before clothing that seems meant to stay on. "The garment stands for a mystery," says Augustine of Noah's nakedness (*City of God* xvi.2), and Noah's garment was clearly one mystery that should have stayed that way. So is Nanzia's, and our students easily read her as the exemplum Ozymandias makes her out to be:

> Then Ozymandias said the spouse, the bride
> Is never naked. A fictive covering
> Weaves always glistening from the heart and mind.

Yet Stevens cuts off the story of this memorable encounter without conclusion, except for the lesson. And his inconclusive closure makes us return to ponder Ozymandias, or it should. Perhaps we should ask if an order is ever so inflexible that it cannot weave a fiction; weaving, like all texts, requires some bending of ourselves. Commentators seem singularly incurious about Ozymandias. (Feminists might be interested in how we take him as a figure of authority, for all Stevens' signs of reservation and Shelley's parable, and how readily we take the delectable Nanzia to be a shade dimwitted.) One wants to ask Ozymandias: Can't you clothe her? If he had the right words, he could (she assumes) "speak to me that, which spoken, will array me . . . Clothe me." Is Ozymandias refining her metaphors before acceding to her request? Are his words already a kind of clothing? Is he saying: I won't array you because you're arrayed already (and by whose heart and mind?)—for "Solomon in all his glory was not arrayed as one of these"? Or is he saying: get dressed, I can't array you. Or: start weaving. At the least, if we smile a little at Nanzia's solemnity, we ought also to smile at the solemnity of Ozymandias. Nanzia, so ardently attracted by the prospect of an inflexible order, has met one so inflexible it appears not to desire to bend to her in any way, and this despite the note "It Must Change." She succeeds no more than Flaubert's Queen of Sheba did with St. Anthony. "On s'étonne qu'il ne soit ni plus séduit, ni plus ébloui," says Valéry.

In I.iii, "the poem sends us"—at least, as long as we say, like Samuel, here am I; send me. But where does the poem itself go or stay or live? Canto ix insists that the poem is always between, not at or in. Wherever we locate it or however we define it, the poem is moving. As with objects seen by modern physicists, the poem is not an inert mass but a field of force. Stevens avoids telling us whether this poem is being written or being read; he chooses language that is valid for both processes. We have hardly begun to read this intriguing canto, but how clumsy and sophomoric it makes many a discussion of poetry sound:

> The poem goes from the poet's gibberish to
> The gibberish of the vulgate and back again.
> Does it move to and fro or is it of both
>
> At once? Is it a luminous flittering
> Or the concentration of a cloudy day?
> Is there a poem that never reaches words
>
> And one that chaffers the time away?
> Is the poem both peculiar and general?
> There's a meditation there, in which there seems
>
> To be an evasion, a thing not apprehended or
> Not apprehended well. Does the poet
> Evade us, as in a senseless element?

Evade, this hot, dependent orator,
The spokesman at our bluntest barriers,
Exponent by a form of speech, the speaker

Of a speech only a little of the tongue?
It is the gibberish of the vulgate that he seeks.
He tries by a peculiar speech to speak

The peculiar potency of the general,
To compound the imagination's Latin with
The lingua franca et jocundissima.

Critics of Stevens' poetry are fond of the word "hovering" for the way his poetry refuses to settle in one place. If we say that poem or meaning "hovers," then we can also say that poem or meaning has "the concentration of a cloudy day." Or that a poem like some hawk may hover over a field of meaning. More often, we are assuming that the poem hovers above two or three meanings. Perhaps, then, it would be more accurate to say that it "flitters to and fro." Even when we say that Stevens centers his poetry in a space between two areas or when we say meaning lies between tropes in his poetry—even this sense of betweenness may be insufficient for what Stevens is doing. It is not so much that he *locates* his poetry in a space, a betweenness. Rather, he plays with that space itself, seeking a figure for it. He considers our various senses of betweenness—flittering back and forth between categories, or else hovering over the gap.

Does this mean then that Stevens is forever shifting, evading, escaping, flittering—that is, playing irresponsibly with one notion of meaning after another? Again, I find this an inaccurate way of reading Stevens. If I had to name the subject of canto II.ix in one word, I should say "translation" in a wide sense of the word. Translation is always a crossing, more or less conscious, from one meaning to another. In II.ix, Stevens foregrounds the act of crossing over that mental space that translation must always cross, offering various figures for it. He draws our attention to translation at the beginning and end of the canto: "the vulgate," "the imagination's Latin," and "the lingua franca et jocundissima." How simple it sounds, and a simple reading is possible and not wrong, only inadequate. "Vulgate" means of the vulgar or common tongue. A lower-case vulgate is not the Vulgate, yet cannot but evoke Jerome's Vulgate, especially when that great church father appears two cantos later. Is the vulgate related to the Vulgate as a god is to God? Is it our true "sacred text," written or thought, a text of what we actually hold precious and supreme, if we hold anything precious and supreme? Jerome's Vulgate is no longer

244

a common tongue. Is Stevens'? In any case, the poem goes from one "gibberish" to another, the poet's to the vulgate's. "Gibberish" also takes a full range of meaning, even granted that the term has some irony. (If my work is gibberish, Stevens implies, consider carefully the communal text. Is it not another kind of gibberish?)

The Vulgate was a translation into Latin, this once being a common European tongue for educated men. The lingua franca, literally the Frankish tongue, is mixed jargon used for communication between people of different languages. The poet, Stevens concludes, tries "To compound the imagination's Latin with / The lingua franca et jocundissima." As with "two things of opposite natures [that] seem to depend / On one another" (II.iv), so here. The imagination's Latin is in English, and "the lingua franca et jocundissima" is in Latin. (Jocundus is late Latin, from the classical *jucundus* or "pleasing," compounded with *jocus* or "jesting"—a fine example of a compounding.) Stevens' "jocundissima" qualifies any common lingua franca, offers a compounding of two Latin words, reminds us of the diachronic history of words (classical to late Latin, then to English), and suggests that Stevens is doing what he describes, making a most pleasing jest, altogether jocund. There is no difficulty in communicating this jesting and jocund closure, even to a reader with no Latin. The poet, like the reader, begins with two kinds of gibberish, that is, sounds that need translation into some, into any, language. By the end, poet and reader are beyond gibberish, and a most pleasing translation has been prescribed and achieved.

From translation to transformation: that is the movement from canto ix to x, which opens:

> A bench was his catalepsy, Theatre
> Of Trope. He sat in the park. The water of
> The lake was full of artificial things,
>
> Like a page of music, like an upper air,
> Like a momentary color, in which swans
> Were seraphs, were saints, were changing essences.
>
> The west wind was the music, the motion, the force
> To which the swans curveted, a will to change,
> A will to make iris frettings on the blank.

"Catalepsy" is a Latinate term for a disease in which trances occur, or else for apprehension by the mind. A poet's state of mind might be called cataleptic by those who think it is pathological or by those who think it is essentially philosophical—or by a poet smiling a little at both. For Stevens, the poet's trance or apprehension is more accurately a Theater of Trope, and he begins to sum up over the nine one-act plays we have seen in cantos i through ix. That is why the seraph reappears, now refreshed; that is why "these beginnings" echoes "this beginning" (ii); that is why the west wind blows (vi). Stevens transforms a park bench, making it a spectator's seat in the capital Theater of Trope that is both outside and inside his own head. And not just a spectator's seat but also a playwright's and director's. The score and script of his series of tropes appear before him in a canto that moves like canto ix. Or rather, moves in and through and about a particular park, probably his favorite Elizabeth Park, Hartford. Stevens keeps it ordinary: bench, park, lake, swans, west wind. Shelley's ode of transformation stays above or below the habitable surfaces of the earth and sea. As Paul Fry says, "The only region that the 'Ode to the West Wind' cannot inhabit . . . is the region of the familiar."[28] Stevens' wind is of this earth. St. Paul's great text of transformation moves us away from this earth: "For now we see as through a glass darkly, but then face to face." In i.iv, Eve "made air the mirror of herself, / Of her sons and of her daughters. They found themselves / In heaven as in a glass." Here, there is no heaven, though there is an "upper air," punning on musical air. Here we have "rubbings of a glass in which we peer." Stevens is cleaning St. Paul's glass. Do we peer into it or do we peer about inside it? For St. Paul, the glass is a figure of separation from God. But Stevens has transformed our sense of how reflections on a lake may work. His Theater of Trope is full of tropes. If the Chaplin figure of i.x is also a vagabond, then he too is here, "in metaphor": "The eye of a vagabond in metaphor / That catches our own."

Stevens' revisions are funnier in Part ii than in Part i. He works from staleness at the beginning to triple freshness in canto x. His tropes take on lives of their own, and act out their usual arguments, together with a few variations when they get bored. Stevens has a little trouble at the stale end of his range, in cantos i through iii, but most of the other cantos are remarkable. The play of rhetoric with and through dialectic is dazzling.

It Must Give Pleasure

How can pleasure be required from a supreme, a highest fiction? Do not supreme things have to do with belief? Denis Donoghue sees the problem very clearly: "Stevens's true idiom is an idiom of pleasure: it bewilders

---

[28] *The Poet's Calling in the English Ode* (New Haven and London: Yale University Press, 1981), p. 206.

me to find him resorting to an idiom of belief."[29] I want to enlist the unlikely aid of the Westminster Catechism, even if the common reader now knows no more of it than Topsy. The first and best-known question reads: what is the chief end of man? And the perhaps surprising answer is: to glorify God and enjoy him forever. (I realize that it is another matter to *require* enjoyment or pleasure, but then it is another matter to require abstraction or change or anything at all of a supreme something.) The divines who put together the Westminster Catechism had in mind the eternal enjoying of God in heaven, but they did not confine glorifying or enjoying to the hereafter. Stevens opens Part III with a powerful example of glorifying God in which he himself takes no pleasure.

Stevens' word "pleasure" is pretty clearly belligerent. The Christian word would be "joy." The Catechism's "enjoy" is a little startling to modern ears, this word having fallen into secular use. In canto ii, we hear of "desire"; in iv, of "love"; in v, of a "sensible ecstasy" and of "a fugue / Of praise"; in vii, of being "satisfied," of "an hour / Filled with expressible bliss," of being "happy," of "majesty" as mirror of the self. Not until canto ix do we come back to joy, this time in the form of "enjoy": it is that powerfully emerged first person who lays claim to enjoyment. And not just enjoyment, for this is also the first mention of pleasure in the section, "It Must Give Pleasure." Pleasure is now associated with joy, for joy is not, as in canto i, a "facile exercise."

> I can
> Do all that angels can. I enjoy like them,
> Like men besides, like men in light secluded,
>
> Enjoying angels. . . .
> And we enjoy like men. . . .
> So that we look at it with pleasure. . . .

I surmise that Stevens had in mind precisely such readers as Denis Donoghue when he chose to open Part III with a pointed use of the word "joy," which he knows perfectly well has different associations than the word "pleasure." (And the associations of "pleasure," he had pondered at least as early as 1915: "*Complacencies* of the peignoir. . . .") Thus also the point of closing his poem with a repeated "enjoy" that is synonymous with pleasure, a pleasure finally allowed and finely extended in the word "Pleased" in canto x. Here is the opening of Part III:

[29] Denis Donoghue, "Two Notes on Wallace Stevens," *Wallace Stevens Journal* 4 (1980), 43. Cf. also his *Ferocious Alphabets* (Boston and Toronto: Little, Brown, 1981), p. 210.

To sing jubilas at exact, accustomed times,
To be crested and wear the mane of a multitude
And so, as part, to exult with its great throat,

To speak of joy and to sing of it, borne on
The shoulders of joyous men, to feel the heart
That is the common, the bravest fundament,

This is a facile exercise. Jerome
Begat the tubas and the fire-wind strings,
The golden fingers picking dark-blue air. . . .

"Make a joyful noise unto the Lord": this is the English version of the best-known plural jubilas of the Vulgate, Jubilate Deo. Stevens' sense of the word "joy" includes also his sense of jubilas and jubilate. But it includes much more. We may approach it by asking why Jerome begets the tubas.

Stevens' answer in his letters is carefully and courteously straightforward and also carefully limited: "Jerome is St. Jerome who 'begat the tubas' by translating the Bible. I suppose this would have been clearer if I had spoken of harps" (L 435, January 12, 1943). If we ask, why tubas and not simply harps, we may find a poetic answer. It is not simply that Jerome begat sundry *tubae* as well as the "jubilas" of line 1, when he translated the Bible into Latin. For all that, he begat the association of "exult" and "jubilas" through his several pairings of forms of *exultare* and *jubilare*, and the assonanatal association of *tuba-jubilate*, to say nothing of Jubal and Tubalcain. Joyce exploited the associations three years before Stevens in his "jubalent tubalence" and "tubular jurbulence." Beyond this, Stevens' delight in Latin leads us to the Lewis and Short Latin dictionary he owned, and to the word *juba*. Two of its meanings are "the flowing hair on the neck of an animal, the mane" and "crest," precisely the tropes of Stevens' second line in a happy mingling of echo and metaphor, the metaphor being, "A multitude is a lion." Stevens' huge Christian lion—not so much the Church triumphant as the Church rampant—is related to the lion of I.v and to the lion that iconography commonly notes beside St. Jerome. "Tubas" awakens "jubas," and much more besides.

"This is a facile exercise" dismisses exultation, and takes us aback. Stevens turns immediately to the human agent, the begetter of great words, though not in derision. He is well past the mode of *A High-Toned Old Christian Woman*, and the language is of seeking and finding: "To find of sound . . . To find of light." ("To find, / Not to impose," he will say in III.vii.) To find of sound and light an ancestor "for companies of voices moving there." Stevens is searching his own poetic and ancestral voices, and "moving" takes as a secondary meaning, "affecting." He offers an exemplum, then reads it, first in a "facile" way (we accept that singing "as part" of it), then in a searching way (we seek something more from those companies of voices), then a way of "difficultest rigor." This last is hard to read—a catching from a moment, as "when the moon hangs on the wall / Of heaven-haven." Stevens returns once more to his moonlit room, with the firmament now like a shelter and a promise. The phrase "heaven-haven" is Hopkins' phrase, and, given Stevens' mistrust of the word "heaven," and his first seven lines here, it may be startling. Stevens has found himself responding to that moon and that sky in a way something like Hopkins: how to explain this? Or as he puts it, how "to catch from that / Irrational moment its unreasoning." Not for a moment does he think that moon and sky are "things transformed." "Yet we are shaken by them as if they were." The echoing here is very faint and very fine, and we may not hear it at all till we are once more rereading Milton's *Lycidas*, hearing its echoing too. "Yet once more I shake not the earth only, but also heaven" (Heb. 12:26–27). "Yet once more, O ye laurels . . . I . . . shatter." Yet once more, Stevens quietly adds, we, and not the earth or heaven, are shaken—shaken as if earth and heaven were transformed.[30] "We reason about them with a later reason," Stevens ends, very simply, reasoning about his own responses and about Hopkins's and Milton's and even St. Paul's. Part II ends with a "transformation." Part III begins with things that are "not transformed," as Stevens yet once more refuses Christian "companies of voices" or "an innumerable company of angels" (Heb. 12:22).

The pleasures that a supreme fiction may give: this is a dangerous topic. Exalt them too far, and they become banal, no different from a "celestial ennui." Debase them too far, and they become ludicrous. The great challenge is Wordsworth (not Keats, for Keats came to matters of supreme fictions only at the end of his short life). Stevens began this subject in 1915 in *Sunday Morning*, with earthly pleasures easily substituted for supposed heavenly pleasures. He knows by 1942 that things are not that easy. One pleasure that *Sunday Morning* omits, except by indirection, is erotic pleasure. Stevens knew by 1918, the time of *Le Monocle de Mon Oncle*, that heavenly and supreme matters are not always neatly separate from erotic matters. And a great poetry of earth, even if it is noting its way toward a supreme fiction, must consider eros. This, I think, is why we hear echoes from the great love poem of biblical literature, the Canticles or Song of Songs. And more than echoes: we

[30] Cf. John Hollander, *Echo*, p. 128.

hear how we have read these words. But that is in Part II, "It Must Change." In Part III, we have the blue woman (ii), the marriage in Catawba (iv), and the exquisite final fat-girl canto (x).

Stevens moves at once to this earth after the final shaking of canto i. His lovely seasonal language in canto ii is of natural and erotic seasons both. He insists on two things: first, that some metaphors of these things not be used, and, second, that these things be seen in memory only. I see the logic of the first point, but not of the second, unless it is personal. "That frothy clouds / Should foam, be foamy waves, should move like them," is an innocent enough trope, one would think. But the blue woman will have none of it. "The blue woman . . . Did not desire . . . that the sexual blossoms should repose / Without their fierce addictions . . . the frothy blooms / Waste without puberty." "Frothy": clouds, sexual blooms, early spring blossoms, Venus of the sea foam. Stevens thought the blue woman was the April weather of the time of writing, a weather he is reading very fully. I hear a full assent to air, light, the joy of having a body, the voluptuousness of looking, to quote Stevens' 1934 epigraph (CP 136). I hear also Stevens' old attack on escapist fantasies. And I hear a move against any allegorical exaltation, as in our usual reading of the Canticles. Stevens is once more rewriting his "one of fictive music" (CP 87–88). She was "of the clearest bloom, . . . and of diviner love the day / And flame and summer and sweet fire." In 1942, she is a woman for all seasons, and the bloom is specific. "No thread / Of cloudy silver sprinkles in your gown" in 1922, but in 1942 Stevens will distinguish silvers and find a use for clouds. In 1922, "that music is intensest which . . . vaunts the clearest bloom . . . sees and names, / As in your name, an image that is sure . . . O bough and bush and scented vine." This is an attempted language of the Canticles. In 1942, Stevens clearly and firmly keeps himself from such language, making his muse herself see and name, name a specific, earthly bough and bush, the dogwood.

> The blue woman looked and from her window named
>
> The corals of the dogwood, cold and clear,
> Cold, coldly delineating, being real,
> Clear and, except for the eye, without intrusion.

The dogwood has white and pink blossoms, as we know from Stevens' dog-and-dogwood poem, *Forces, the Will & the Weather*, if not from nature. But it is wrong to read Stevens' "corals" as primarily metaphoric. Coral is the color of the stems of the dogwood shrub; nursery catalogues advertise this color as especially appealing in the winter. Stevens is simply being accurate—"clear and, except for the eye, without intrusion."[31] What seemed appropriate "clear blooms" in 1922 were not: they were sexual blooms idealized into "one of fictive music." A supreme fiction is clearer and more rigorous. A supreme fiction must give right bodily pleasure—of eros, of weather, of all senses and seasons.

Canto iii is a red and angry canto after the blue woman one. It stands out oddly in Part III, which mostly eschews fierce attacks. Stevens' composite Jehovah figure has turned into that graven image which the second commandment forbids, but a shattered graven image, like the remains of Shelley's Ozymandias. (The frown in line 8 marks the inheritance.) Stevens "lasting bush" plays quickly against the dogwood bush, before its own color of "unending red" evokes another bush, the burning bush— symbol of the church of this "dried-up Presbyterian" (L 792), the place of God's "I am that I am," the place where Moses must cover his face and *not* see God. I do not know if Stevens misremembered the Old Testament account, or deliberately plays against it here. Nothing burns, no voice speaks, and Stevens includes all gods in this rather overdone attack. So also, he includes both Orpheus and Christ in the phrase "dead shepherd" (and Orpheus is a standard figure for Christ). I take it that bidding the sheep to carouse is a shepherd's invitation in Stevensian form. "Feed my sheep," said Christ to Peter, and Stevens made that bidding into the poet's task. To carouse is to engage in a drinking bout. We began with grapes in III.ii, we go on to marriage wine in III.iv, to Meursault in III.v, to wine at a table in a wood in III.ix, and to meats and wines and sacramental bread in the epilogue. Carousing is not the way most of us think of mass or communion, at least not since the first century A.D. But the word is not altogether hostile. Remembering *A High-Toned Old Christian Woman*, we might even say it is a tribute of sorts.

Having refused to consummate the union of Nanzia and Ozymandias, Stevens now offers his own tale of an appropriate "mystic marriage." He begins with the concluding line of III.i: "We reason of these things with later reason," and canto iv is a reasoning of sorts about heaven and earth. Not that heaven and earth are themselves transformed, but that Stevens allows the old metaphor of the marriage of earth and heaven a full expression. Adelaide Morris rightly says that the "marriage place," Catawba, fuses the names of the captain and Bawda.[32] Catawba was there first, of course. It is the actual name of a river and region in North Car-

---

[31] Milton Bates argues for late-summer coral berries, but coral stems fit the time of the canto. See his *Wallace Stevens: A Mythology of Self* (Berkeley and London: University of California Press, 1985), p. 226.

[32] In her *Wallace Stevens: Imagination and Faith* (Princeton: Princeton University Press, 1974), pp. 185–86.

olina. The sounds of the actual place name expand into the male-sun and female-earth characters of the captain and Bawda. ("Bawda" is not coarse if one hears its old meanings as well as its current ones. "Thus, our bawdiness . . . indulged at last, / Is equally converted into palms" [CP 59].)

Why Catawba? The name is said to mean "divided" and Stevens divides it wonderfully, to be sure. But I think it appealed for another reason than its acoustic sounds and their possibilities. Catawba is known for its wine, in whose praise Longfellow wrote a bouncy poem, maligning overseas wines: "Drugged is their juice / For foreign use, / When shipped o'er the reeling Atlantic." By contrast, this native wine is "pure as a spring," from "such a grape / As grows by the Beautiful River" (Catawba Wine). The waters of Catawba eventually become wine through the "mystic marriage" (Stevens' phrase) of sun and earth, so that when we hear of the "sipping of the marriage wine," we think of Catawba wine. Then we hear the following injunctions:

> Each must the other take not for his high,
> His puissant front nor for her subtle sound,
>
> The shoo-shoo-shoo of secret cymbals round.
> Each must the other take as sign, short sign
> To stop the whirlwind, balk the elements.

Stevens' "shoo-shoo-shoo of secret cymbals round" is like his "hoobla-hoobla-hoobla-how," though the play is friendly and not derisory. It imitates the sound of round cymbals around us, cymbals that are brushed and not clanged, as in a familiar jazz sound. And it puns with cheerful obviousness on secret symbols around us, especially the great central symbols of roundness. "Shoo-shoo-shoo," it says, "Be off." We must read no doctrine of symbolism from this mystic marriage, and symbolism often takes marriage as a figure for its own way of thinking. When we hear of such symbols round us, we should hear cymbals, and a secular dance sound.

Stevens allows signs, if not symbols, though not eternal signs, only "short signs." John Hollander has written very finely on these signs, and how "rhyming for the later Stevens does the imagination's work." He has heard the Spenserian lines within Stevens' lines.[33] There is also a mischievous play with Milton's language at the end of Book VI of *Paradise Lost*. This is, appropriately, the end of the war in heaven. Christ goes forth, armed with God's bow and thunder, which sounds right to us, partly because of Blake. He girds on God's "Sword upon thy puissant

---

[33] *Vision and Resonance: Two Senses of Poetic Form* (New York: Oxford University Press, 1975), pp. 132–33.

Thigh" (VI. 713–14). A puissant thigh can be dispersed into "his high, / His puissant," though this reading may sound at first a little forced. But not when we hear the "whirl-wind sound" of "the Chariot of Paternal Deity," whose wheels "shake Heav'n's basis" (VI.749–50, 712). As with the phrase, "ever-hill Catawba," which compacts the long troping of the "everlasting hills" in the Old Testament, so here with "the whirlwind." This mystic marriage may echo the marriage service ("Each must the other take," "I take thee for . . ."). But it is in no way sacrament or symbol, though it is a pleasure and a sign.

Marriage, service, wine, water. I have been moving toward the biblical prototype for this mystic marriage, the marriage at Cana, for I think Stevens is offering Catawba as an American Cana. Cana is the place of Christ's first miracle, the changing of water into wine at a marriage feast, to the delight of the worried bridegroom. It was for centuries a favorite biblical scene,[34] and it is often quoted at marriage ceremonies. Catawba wine, from Catawba water and earth and the sun, is a wholly natural miracle. Stevens is moving against the center of Christian symbolism, against its ceremonies, figures, acts.

We sense this from the beginning of the canto, as Stevens picks up earlier arguments, and moves on. It is true that "we live in a place / That is not our own and, much more, not ourselves." But when we see clearly—and this is how the ephebe is told to see the sun—we can make "a place dependent on ourselves."

> We reason of these things with later reason
> And we make of what we see, what we see clearly
> And have seen, a place dependent on ourselves.

This is a powerful move forward, and Stevens is putting a good deal of weight on that word "dependent," itself a powerful Virgilian and Miltonic word.[35] We remember that "two things of opposite natures seem to depend / On one another" (II.iv). Dependencies can be mutual, can have a fruitful tension for Stevens. By the end of canto iv, we realize that he is once again returning to St. Paul's text about seeing clearly, and rewriting it. "For now we see as through a glass darkly, But then face to face." We begin this canto seeing clearly, and not in a glass darkly. We end with "love's characters come face to face," characters as dramatis personae and characters as in an alphabet. Stevens ends with rhyme, an

---

[34] Cf. Emile Mâle, *The Gothic Image: Religious Art in France of the Thirteenth Century* (New York: Harper, 1913, 1958), pp. 176–81.

[35] Cf. Owen Barfield on Latin *pendere* and English "hang," in his *Poetic Diction: A Study in Meaning*, 3d ed. (Middletown, Conn.: Wesleyan University Press, 1928, 1973), pp. 127–28.

unusual closure, and the rhyme is on "place" and "face." He has not forgotten, I think, Eliot's repeated rhymes on "place" and "face" and "grace." Nor has he forgotten that St. Paul's text is the culmination of his great chapter on the love of God. He does not attempt a similar ex- altation here, and there is a sense of holding back, of limitation, of slight stiffness. Stevens' tone is not that of someone participating in a marriage feast or writing spousal verse. He sounds a little like the worried bride- groom.

Not so in the remaining cantos, beginning with the three Canon As- pirin cantos, which open with a French wine and an Indian recipe: "We drank Meursault, ate lobster Bombay with mango / Chutney." This is a canto that I cannot read very far, for it is a riddle poem, and no one as yet has solved the riddle of the Canon's sister. This mysterious canto is a trap for the unwary, inviting allegoresis but so far resisting our intel- ligence quite successfully. I shall add only two glosses to our present knowledge, one on the Canon's fugue and one on his name. Both depend on word-play.

> The Canon Aspirin, having said these things,
> Reflected, humming an outline of a fugue
> Of praise, a conjugation done by choirs.

"Canon" is the standard general term for "fugal" imitation. Browning makes a useful comment: "A 'canon' in music, is a piece wherein the subject is repeated—in various keys—and being strictly obeyed in repe- tition, becomes the 'Canon'—the imperative *law*—to what follows."[36] The Canon Aspirin thinks the same way he hums, that is, in a *fuga per canonem*—orderly, in a harmony that is "amassing" and "complicate." (Did Stevens remember his fine use of "incomplicate" in *The Comedian as the Letter C*?) In short, Stevens will now allow all that he can to the heritage that he loved in a way, and also fought—the biblical heritage of Milton, Coleridge, Wordsworth, Browning, and others. Attacks like Ste- vens' attack on the old seraph, and many of his earlier attacks, are simply insufficient against this tradition. Stevens must give it its due if his own rejection is to be persuasive.

For the name, Canon Aspirin, we might note a 1943 remark by Ste- vens: "just as Bergson refers to the simpler representations of aspiration occurring in the lives of the saints, so we may refer to the simpler rep- resentations of an aspiration *(not the same, yet not wholly unlike)* oc- curring in the lives of those who have just written their first essential

---

[36] Cited in Lilian Whiting, *The Brownings: Their Life and Art* (Boston: Little, Brown, 1911), p. 260.

poems" (*NA* 49–50, my italics). In 1909, Stevens copied into his journal two unidentified lines, which come from Browning's *Rabbi ben Ezra*: "What I aspired to be, / And was not, comforts me" (*SP* 220). Shortly afterward, he also copied the following unidentified quotation: "le tourment de l'homme de pensée est d'aspirer au Beau, sans avoir jamais une conscience fixe et certain du Beau" (*SP* 221). Stevens' journal and early letters demonstrate how attractive the sentiment of aspiration was for him. And in 1909 he called himself "a willing courtier and aspirant" (*L* 134). The Canon's surname is connected with his title by the fact that a candidate is an aspirant (OED, candidate, 2a). (As Faulkner notes, a French military candidate in aviation is what "the French so beautifully call an aspiring aviator."[37]) Stevens begins by loving aspiration and hating the canonical, as in the attack in *From the Journal of Crispin*. But a choirboy's sense of the canonical is hardly a threat to the great biblical texts or to Milton. Stevens must face the strength of what he decreates.

Canto vi allows Canon Aspirin's mental world a great deal:

> Thereon the learning of the man conceived
> Once more night's pale illuminations, gold
>
> Beneath, far underneath, the surface of
> His eye and audible in the mountain of
> His ear, the very material of his mind.

The enjambment is very fine, turning inside out our sense of up and down, above and beneath. The ancient trope of the vault of heaven is imagined, with the eyeball becoming a reverse sphere, like a mirroring globe, where illuminations are either reflected or buried. "Audible" stops any easy apposition, yet Stevens manages to build a modern version of the old microcosm and macrocosm.

Stevens knows the attraction of an "utmost," a *telos*, and we want to watch the various movements, wings, and so on, throughout the series. Here, he cunningly makes the word "point" the terminal word in the line, as if he were conceding some utmost mental point, and remembering Dante's extraordinary play with "punto." Then he goes on. He will use this tactic with the word "point" again.

> Forth then with huge pathetic force
> Straight to the utmost crown of night he flew.
> The nothingness was a nakedness, a point
>
> Beyond which thought could not progress as thought.

[37] Faulkner, *Soldier's Pay* (New York: Liveright, 1926), p. 7.

The lines make the Canon's limits very clear, as does his action of "imposing orders." Stevens desires something other in canto vii, which abjures every fiction but one, "the fiction of an absolute," and moves to apostrophe, though unusual apostrophe. A capitalized Angel is told to be silent and listen, Stevens now reversing the usual hierarchies of angel and human, speaking and listening.

> To be stripped of every fiction except one,
>
> The fiction of an absolute—Angel,
> Be silent in your luminous cloud and hear
> The luminous melody of proper sound.

We should listen here for the enjambment, notable in every line quoted, and listen also to the repeated "luminous." It tells us that Stevens' "luminous cloud" is not an accidental echo. This is what Stevens is hearing:

> Ah! from the soul itself must issue forth
> A light, a glory, a fair luminous cloud
> Enveloping the earth—
> And from the soul itself must there be sent
> A sweet and potent voice, of its own birth. . . .
> This light, this glory, this fair luminous mist . . .
> Joy is the sweet voice, Joy the luminous cloud—
> We in ourselves rejoice!
>
> (Coleridge, *Dejection Ode*)

And Stevens prepares to rewrite the Coleridgean canto i.iii in the light of these lines, read in the spirit of Stevens rather than the spirit of Coleridge. Here is what follows:

> What am I to believe? If the angel in his cloud,
> Serenely gazing on the violet abyss,
> Plucks on his strings to pluck abysmal glory,
>
> Leaps downward through evening's revelations, and
> On his spredden wings, needs nothing but deep space,
> Forgets the gold centre, the golden destiny,
>
> Grows warm in the motionless motion of his flight,
> Am I that imagine this angel less satisfied?
> Are the wings his, the lapis-haunted air?
>
> Is it he or is it I that experience this?
> Is it I then that keep saying there is an hour
> Filled with expressible bliss, in which I have

No need, am happy, forget need's golden hand,
Am satisfied without solacing majesty,
And if there is an hour there is a day,

There is a month, a year, there is a time
In which majesty is a mirror of the self:
I have not but I am and as I am, I am.

These external regions, what do we fill them with
Except reflections, the escapades of death,
Cinderella fulfilling herself beneath the roof?

What are we to ask of these lines? As so often with Stevens' mature poetry, the general sense is not hard to read. It is the particulars that may puzzle us. We should note the kind of question and answer here. Stevens does not say, "What do I believe?" And he does not answer with doctrine or with its reverse, with some symbolism or a "flippant communication" (*CP* 418). The question is not rhetorical, neither a sonorous, solemn rhetorical question nor an ironic rhetorical question. The answer is oblique and fictive, yet nonetheless something of a parable, which is one way of answering questions. (Who is my neighbor? A certain man went down from Jerusalem to Jericho. What am I to believe? A certain angel leapt downward.)

We may hear this canto gathering up earlier cantos, especially I.iii, and we may map the language of direction, the language of angels, the language of belief and satisfaction. Here the assertive statement that the poem "satisfies / Belief" (I.iii) becomes interrogative: "What am I to believe?" Satisfaction is implied but limited: "Am I that imagine this angel less satisfied?" "Is it I then that . . . am satisifed." All the sentences are interrogative, though one modulates through its clauses into a sufficiently assertive mood to drop the question mark. This canto does not send us, "winged by an unconscious will" (I.iii). The "I" both sees as a spectator and experiences as angel, and sees his experience, of a movement downward "on his spredden wings," a movement protracted and without landing, a suspension. The time of fulfillment is not in terms of undefined beginning and end, but is specifically limited. Ex- words here (expressible, external) are limited in comparison with the outward movement—the ex-ness, so to speak—of such words in I.iii (exhilaration, excitation). We might suppose that a movement from first-person plural to first-person singular, from assertive to interrogative mood, from winging our way from immaculate beginnings to immaculate ends to seeing and being a falling angel, from extended to modified adjectives, from excited participation in power to a multiple stance where power is examined—that all these limitations would make for a lesser canto. But this is not what happens. Stevens' first world is represented here in strength. It lives, not in spite of its careful limiting, but because of it. Stevens' "I am" claims no more than he can sustain: "I have not but I am and as I am, I am."

An angel who leaps downward automatically evokes the figure of Milton's Satan, and yet Satan is a curiously dead figure for this canto. Is Stevens merely joining the revisionists, with a serene Satan rather than a Promethean one? We have recognized the influence of Wordsworth's angel from the end of *The Prelude*,[38] but we have not heard the verbal echoes from Milton himself. It is that word "serene" that helps, once we hear Milton's and Stevens' play with the word. Milton's "serene" occurs in his Invocation to Light, a passage echoed repeatedly in Stevens' work:

> Thee I revisit now with bolder wing . . .
> Taught by the heav'nly Muse to venture down
> The dark descent, and up to reascend,
> Though hard and rare: thee I revisit safe
> . . . but thou
> Revisit'st not these eyes . . .
> So thick a drop serene hath quencht thir Orbs. . . .

"Drop serene," as editions of Milton note, translates the *gutta serena*, the Latin medical term for "all blindness in which the eye retains a normal appearance."[39] Standard editions do not note, though Wordsworth does, that Milton goes on to an English pun on the word:

> But cloud instead, and ever-during dark
> Surrounds me, from the *cheerful* ways of men
> Cut off, and for the Book of knowledge fair
> Presented with a Universal blanc . . .
> > (my italics).

"Serenus" is translated as "serene," "cheerful," and so on. Here is Wordsworth, remembering Milton's word-play, and drawing strength therefrom in his *Elegiac Stanzas [on] Peele Castle*: "I speak with mind serene . . . farewell the heart that lives alone . . . for 'tis surely blind. / But welcome fortitude and patient cheer / And frequent sights of what is to be borne."

What, then, if that serenely gazing angel is Milton himself, Milton

---

[38] Bloom, *Wallace Stevens*, pp. 213–14.
[39] Hughes, *Milton*, note to *PL* iii.25, p. 258.

who created and so includes Satan? In *Prelude* xiv, Wordsworth holds Milton at arm's length in a discursive mode. Stevens enacts what Wordsworth describes. He projects Milton in an intuitive or angelic mode. His angel gazes "serenely" in its Latinate as well as its English sense. Milton's gaze is tranquil but it is also blind, and for Stevens not just physically blind. And it is Milton in the act of creation who leaps downward here—downward because he is projecting himself into his own created world, in a "drop serene," so to speak. Downward because he begins by hovering above his created world, brooding like the Holy Ghost. Downward because he may be identified with Mulciber,[40] who also fell from heaven, who is also Stevens' patron god, whose leisurely fall has cadences very like the slow fall of Stevens' angel:

> thrown by angry *Jove*
> Sheer o'er the Crystal Battlements: from Morn
> To Noon he fell, from Noon to dewy Eve,
> A Summer's day; and with the setting Sun
> Dropt from the Zenith like a falling Star. . . .
> (I.741–45)

There is this difference: Mulciber or Vulcan lands, just as Satan does. Stevens' angel does not land. We may say, and rightly, that Stevens is playing against the phrase, "leap to conclusions." For this is not how we read great imaginative literature; it prevents us from leaping to conclusions. To follow Coleridge, we agree to suspension—that "willing suspension of disbelief *for the moment* which constitutes poetic *faith*" (*Biographia Literaria*, ch. 14, my italics). That is one answer to Stevens' opening question, "What am I to believe?"

I have spoken of the angel as Milton the creator, and then of the process of reading great imaginative literature. Stevens, I think, chooses language that works for both writing and reading, as he does elsewhere. His angel begins the leap "on spredden wings," a seventeenth-century phrase, though not Milton's. (It is in Henry More and perhaps elsewhere.) As the lines proceed, the diction changes and we move on from Milton's language to Wordsworth's in a familiar line of succession. Stevens' superb ear has heard how Wordsworth himself makes use of Milton. He starts with archaic diction, then slowly makes us hear Milton, then Milton *through* Wordsworth. Stevens lets the words tell their own

---

[40] On Mulciber as a figure for Milton himself, see John D. Guillory, *Poetic Authority: Spenser, Milton and Literary History* (New York: Columbia University Press, 1983), pp. 144–45.

history if we care to listen. So wonderfully evoked is this line of succession that we do not read as we read most literary histories. We respond, just as if we were reading powerful imaginative literature, for this is precisely the question we ask of Milton's and Wordsworth's greatest lines: "Is it he or is it I that experience this?" The "he" is at once the creator (Milton, Wordsworth) and the creation (Satan, Mulciber, Milton). We are both inside and outside this text, reading both synchronically and diachronically. Yet it is also and especially Stevens who is speaking. He too becomes the angel, and we join him insofar as we also "experience this." ("I can / Do all that angels can," he is about to say.)

Coming down to earth, when it happens, is a shock. The conclusion sounds almost gross, though this is not the first time Stevens has turned against his angelic or aspiring self. We recall the second half of I.iii, and an early entry in Stevens' journal is much to the point. It is written immediately after the aspiring lines from Browning, quoted above, and it is one word only, "pumpkin-coach," as if Stevens was on guard against his aspiring self even so early (*SP* 220). Here, Stevens uses the same fairy tale, and the diction is bleak, though Cinderella herself is not a conclusive figure. If we read naively, she is fulfilling herself with the solacing majesty of the prince, whether under her roof or his. If we read reductively, the whole thing is a fairy tale, by Perrault, to be put away with other childish things. If we read archetypally, the whole thing answers some human need for fictions of fulfillment, and will keep being told. If we read decreatively, the whole thing can be rewritten anyway—as, say, in Randall Jarrell's *Cinderella*. All these readings may also be made of the texts of "supreme fictions." Myth down to fairy tale, bliss and majesty down to death. Stevens is wary of the Cinderella in us, who will want to project a prince from that majesty. As he is about to tell us, he has enjoyed himself like and with the angels, including Milton, in the Canon Aspirin and the angel cantos. Now he sets them aside, and prepares for closure:

> Fat girl, terrestrial, my summer, my night,
> How is it I find you in difference, see you there
> In a moving contour, a change not quite completed?
>
> You are familiar yet an aberration.
> Civil, madam, I am, but underneath
> A tree, this unprovoked sensation requires
>
> That I should name you flatly, waste no words,
> Check your evasions, hold you to yourself.
> Even so when I think of you as strong or tired,

Bent over work, anxious, content, alone,
You remain the more than natural figure. You
Become the soft-footed phantom, the irrational

Distortion, however fragrant, however dear.
That's it: the more than rational distortion,
The fiction that results from feeling. Yes, that.

They will get it straight one day at the Sorbonne.
We shall return at twilight from the lecture
Pleased that the irrational is rational,

Until flicked by feeling, in a gildered street,
I call you by name, my green, my fluent mundo.
You will have stopped revolving except in crystal.

If we read this against the opening canto, we can hear how far Stevens makes this a decreated Book of Revelation, just as he made 1.i a decreated Book of Genesis. This canto is not pedagogical and parental but spousal. Not an apparent forbidding of naming, but a hoping to name. Not a beginning but a consummation. We enter another order of language, another dispensation, leaving behind the tutelary voice and hearing a lover's voice, as if we had moved from law into grace. (The law was our schoolmaster, says St. Paul.) Here the only authority is the authority of one lover over another, for the poet has left his father and his mother and is cleaving unto the fat girl. The focus is human and earthly, not angelic and heavenly.

We have listened to Stevens' emerging "I am" throughout this poem. Here "I am" begins by naming himself: "Civil, madam, I am." The word "civil" bears a good deal of weight, coming as it does at the beginning of a line in a reverse word order that recalls a Latinate order of words and things. *Civis Romanus sum* is that Latinate order, and the proud claim of a Roman citizen. (And Stevens knew what it meant to say such a thing, whether with St. Paul or Augustine or Santayana.) "Civil" is a word finely balanced with "sensation" in this poet's and lover's speaking, and it carries the sense of "courteous" as well as "civis." It also bears other senses: "naturally good or virtuous, but unregenerate; moral; good as a citizen but not as a saint" (OED 15.b). And there is a playful echo. This "I am" partly echoes the most famous palindrome of them all, "Madam, I'm Adam," with a difference. Stevens introduced Adam in 1.iv. Here his naming poet recalls Adam's naming in Genesis, a favorite naming figure for the writer. He names, or will name, his fluent mundo, a female figure like an Eve. She is fertile like Eve; hence her fatness and domesticity and general ease of being. She is a mundo at its

261

most fecund or summery, and firmly a mundo, mundane but not fallen. This Adam is not so much man made of dust as he is man as citizen. "Civil," "citizen," and cognate words are strong words in Stevens. Adam, the archetypal ephebe, comes to completion in biblical narrative only in the second Adam, who is Christ, who gives our final names in Revelation. In *Notes toward a Supreme Fiction*, he moves from an ephebe to a citizen, who will walk the streets of his city in a fulfillment.

Biblical narrative ends with the vision of a city and citizens. So does Stevens', though his citizen is civil and not saintly, and his city earthly for all its golden streets. ("Gildered" echoes back against "parcel-gilded" and recalls the streets of gold in the New Jerusalem.) In Stevens' final act of naming, anticipated only, the "I am" moves toward a "you are." Between the "I am" of the poet, and the "it is" of the sun (1.i), lies the possibility of the "you are" of the poem. This mundo becomes fluent in the fullest sense. As with the redeemed who are called by name in Revelation, as with a heavenly muse in Milton, here it is as if an answer may be given by a "fluent mundo," as if, in a Stevensian revelation, for a moment, the impossible possible happens, and one's earth replies to one's imagination.

Stevens' lovely rhetorical gesture in the last line is one we know best from Shakespeare's epilogues. Gently distancing and enfolding his poem, reminding us it is a work of art, handing it to the reader, Stevens also allows his poet and fat girl to take pleasure in its implications. I think that the poem itself is the crystal at the end, this one word containing and closing Stevens' closing gesture. "Crystal" is difficult to read, but the following guidelines may help. The word is commonly used in one of two contexts, either fluid or solid. In the fluid group are all those waters said to be crystalline, often mirroring, often moving, fluent like Stevens' mundo, and sometimes a trope for voice. In the solid group are solid crystals, often globular, and ranging in size from tiny to universal, to Milton's crystal battlements of heaven. In this form, they make a world into which we may peer or inside which we may live, and so also make a figure for a work of art. Insofar as a crystal remains in its natural state, it grows slowly and beautifully, and in this way too, it makes a figure for a work of art, either for its growth in the artist's mind or (as here) for its growth in the audience's mind. To quote Henry Adams, "The form [of a work of art, including autobiography] is never arbitrary, but is a sort of growth like crystallization."[41] Stevens' word "crystal" speaks to current discussions of the act of reading, and it is especially appropriate for a mundo that is both still and moving throughout her

[41] *The Education of Henry Adams* (Boston: Houghton, Mifflin, 1918, 1973), p. 389.

canto. Closure tends by its nature toward stasis. Stevens' closure avoids the "choice between" stasis and movement, end and growth, closed and open. His choice of "crystal" is beautifully apt.

It is likely to be some time before we can read *Notes toward a Supreme Fiction* very fully. Stevens' "irrational rational" will not yield to solely conceptual or logical approaches that ignore the play of dialectic and rhetoric. We may impose orders if we wish, but Stevens' fluent mundo is likely to resist us quite successfully if we do. It is better to hold her to herself in other ways, as in the play "in difference" of rhetoric and dialectic.

IV

* * *

The Auroras

and After

* * * * *

CHAPTER TWELVE

Commonplace Apocalypse:

An Ordinary Evening

in New Haven

I am in the very mire of commonplace common-
place compared with Mr Blake, apo- or rather ana-
calyptic poet and painter. (Coleridge, letter of Feb-
ruary 6, 1818)[1]

FROM THE BEGINNING of this book, I have been speaking of Stevens'
sense of place. The challenge he sets himself in this poem is to see what
remains of the vision that inspired the name and the place, New Haven,
and what vision we can now have of such a place. This is a poem of place
in the fullest sense of the word.

Readers of Stevens have no quarrel with the eucalyptic-apocalytpic
word-play (to which I shall come), but may find themselves frustrated
by what seems a lack of contact with the common corporeal world. (Of
course, "the corporeal world exists as the common denominator of the
incorporeal worlds of its inhabitants," to quote Stevens [*NA* 118, 1948].)
I want to make a case for the poem's close connection with actual place,
with the city of New Haven. Our reading has been inching a little closer
to this view, and I want to encourage this direction. Not, of course, that
Stevens is writing loco-descriptive poetry in ordinary language. Yet log-
ically the poem is centered on New Haven and nowhere else. New Haven
was named by early Christian founders, for whom the name bore a sense

---

[1] *Selected Poetry and Prose*, ed. Stephen Potter (London: Nonesuch, 1933), p. 674.

it has now commonly lost. (To quote Sacvan Berkovitch: "America itself Increase [Mather] describes as 'the desired Haven.' . . . The European Puritans usually reserved such phrases for descriptions of heaven. Here they denote the figural link between New England and New Jerusalem."[2]) New Haven is known as Elm-Tree City ("in the land of the elm-trees," xxix). The climate is often rainy (xiv, xv), and the city is marked by two spectacular rocks, East Rock and West Rock ("the shadow of bare rock," xv). It lies on Long Island Sound ("along the afternoon Sound," xxvi). Yale University is situated in New Haven: its faculty (Professor Eucalyptus, xiv, xxii), its "chapels and . . . schools" (vii), its "statues" (xii), perhaps even its owls (xiii). Stevens' poem is not local in the sense of ordinarily descriptive, but it is not fanciful either. If there are other cities on seacoast sounds, founded by colonists of colonists, with a rainy climate, spectacular rocks, a university, chapels and schools and statues, no other is called New Haven, and the name is necessary for Stevens' poem.

I am proceeding by unabashed referentiality here, reading the poem as meditation on an actual city. I think further that the movements of the meditator can be mapped. Most of the poem is in daylight, with the last few cantos taking place in the evening as night falls. The title suggests that the whole series is under the aegis of such an evening meditation. A visitor may have a room with a mirror (v), may "descend to the street" (viii), may "keep coming back and coming back . . . to the hotel" (ix), may go "walking" in the "streets of the physical town" (xi), and so on until he retires to bed and muses on the day and the place. I do not find such a plot a forced extraction from Stevens' text. The setting and physical action seem quite evident, even if Stevens blocks our ordinary reading of setting and action. But by now, we are used to his strategies of blocking.

One final point about blocking, before some particular reading. Stevens uses a language of substance and the substantial that alters our way of seeing substance. Older loco-descriptive writing assumed a Newtonian physics, and delighted in using Newtonian discoveries to make new figures. ("Newton demands the Muse.") In Einsteinian physics, substantial things are relations. Suppose one tried to write a poem in which things are not substances as solid, inert objects or even substances in a Newtonian sense. Paradoxically, such a poem might remind a reader of the apocalyptic way of seeing things, where their very substantiality was tem-

[2] *The Puritan Origins of the American Self* (New Haven and London: Yale University Press, 1975), p. 124.

pered (though never made unreal) by the sense that it was perpetually upheld by something other.

Much of *An Ordinary Evening in New Haven* is a rich and demanding text, though some is austere and some falters. Much remains unread. Stevens' word-play here is more conceptual and less humorous than elsewhere; he has purged even his own wit. For example, he offers something close to a Spoonerism in the line, "The commonplace became a rumpling of blazons" (xxv). Then, as we are enjoying the play—blazing of rumples? trumpeting of blazons? place blazoned? common rumpled?—Stevens cuts it short, adding: "In isolated moments—isolations / Were false." I want to look at the central "eucalyptic-apocalyptic" word-play, then at Stevens' opening movement (cantos i–v), his apocalyptic canto (xii), his puzzling middle movement, and his extraordinary ending.

Professor Eucalyptus of New Haven began in the form of a tree some thirty years before *An Ordinary Evening in New Haven*, and that is where we should also begin when reading this poem. In 1917, Stevens wrote a short poem, *In the South* (1), which ends thus:

> . . . effects
> Of magenta blooming in the Judas-tree
> And of purple blooming in the eucalyptus—
> Map of yesterday's earth
> And of tomorrow's heaven.
>
> (*OP* 9)

"Eucalyptus" means "well covered," as the flower of the eucalyptus tree is, until its time for uncovering arrives in the ordinary course of things. We need to know this, and we need also to hear the echo from John of Patmos in Stevens' last two lines ("I saw a new heaven and a new earth"). We can then read the implicit word-play: "eucalyptus" as against *apokalypsis* or the sudden, extraordinary uncovering of things. In its implicitness, Stevens' little poem is "well-enveloped," as Whitman calls one of his poems[3]—a eucalyptic and not an apocalyptic poem, we might say.

I argued in 1982 for this pun on the name of Professor Eucalyptus, and so for *An Ordinary Evening in New Haven* as an antiapocalyptic poem.[4]

---

[3] Whitman's anonymous comment on *Out of the Cradle Endlessly Rocking* reads: "The purport of this wild and plaintive song, well-enveloped and eluding definition, is positive and unquestionable, like the effect of music. The piece will bear reading many times—perhaps, indeed, only comes forth, as from recesses, by many repetitions." Cited by Paul Fussell, in *The Presence of Walt Whitman*, ed. R.W.B. Lewis (New York and London: Columbia University Press, 1962), p. 37.

[4] At the conference, Lyric Poetry and the New New Criticism, Toronto, October 1982,

But all remarks I have seen since on this word-play seem to me mistaken in one important way, so that I want to expand my own too-well-covered argument. In his early poem, Stevens works with the simple contraries of eucalyptic and apocalyptic. Not so in 1949, for he does not quite allow Professor Eucalyptus a fulfillment. I take it that he was dissatisfied with this word-play as simple opposition. The word "eucalyptus" implies natural revelation, as a good eighteenth-century botanical invention should, and that is what the word "eucalyptus" is—an eighteenth-century botanical invention. The point is that it implies a law of natural revelation as surely as the flower of the eucalyptus tree unfolds. Thus also one of the important eighteenth-century interpretations of divine, supernatural revelation. (See Newton's argument at the end of his *Optics*, for example.) For Stevens, natural revelation does not come necessarily in the ordinary course of things, on an ordinary evening in New Haven. This is why Professor Eucalyptus is admired but allowed only so far, like his fellow quest figure, Canon Aspirin. It is not that moments of revelation never come. It is that they come fortuitously, in unpredictable moments. In this, they are paradoxically more like the old visitations of grace than like some law of natural revelation. (So also is Derrida's unpredictable word that comes speaking to him out of the Apocalypse, compelled by no system, yet saying *Viens, viens*, Come, come.[5])

One function of Professor Eucalyptus is generic: he points the reader toward the antiapocalyptic mode of *An Ordinary Evening in New Haven*. For here, no "I" sees a new heaven and a new earth; in fact, no first-person "I" enters the poem. Instead, an eye sees or rather tries to see New Haven. We can hear the echoing of the consonantal rhyme, "heaven-haven," in these lines: "The instinct for heaven had its counterpart: / The instinct for earth, for New Haven. . . ." The "New Haven / new heaven" pun began with Hopkins: I surmise that it gave Stevens his title, one of a long list of possible titles, which in turn gave him his poem.[6] If the Apocalypse is an extraordinary dawning in a new heaven, where else could an ordinary evening be for Stevens but in New Haven?

---

in a paper later published as "Directions in Reading Wallace Stevens: Up, Down, Across," in *Lyric Poetry: Beyond New Criticism*, ed. Chaviva Hosek and Patricia Parker (Ithaca: Cornell University Press, 1985), pp. 298–309.

[5] Jacques Derrida, "D'un ton apocalyptique adopté naguère en philosophie," in *Les fins de l'homme: á partir du travail de Jacques Derrida* (Paris: Galilée, 1981), pp. 445–86.

[6] To the question whether Stevens knew that this compound was used by Hopkins, the answer is yes. Stevens copied an extract from a review, which included Hopkins's title (Commonplace Book, I, 16, WAS 70–73, Huntington Library). For the list of titles, see George S. Lensing, "From Pieces of Paper: A Wallace Stevens Notebook," *Southern Review* 15 (1979), 877–920, item 339.

The founders of New Haven, needless to say, would have heard the echo differently.

Once we hear this word-play, other words and phrases take on apocalyptic resonance. Thus, in Revelation 5:5, "behold, the Lion of the tribe of Juda, the Root of David, hath prevailed to open the book." In *An Ordinary Evening*, "In the metaphysical streets of the physical town / We remember the lion of Juda and we save / The phrase" (xi). No book opens, *we* save the phrase, but then "the phrase grows weak" in most unleonine fashion, it being merely a phrase. Something else "contrives the self-same evocations / And Juda becomes New Haven or else must."

Thus also, in the Apocalypse, the Christus Victor, supreme interpreter and final reality of things repeats three times: "I am Alpha and Omega, the beginning and the end" (Rev. 1:8, 21:6, 22:13). Stevens well-known canto vi opens:

> Reality is the beginning not the end,
> Naked Alpha, not the hierophant Omega,
> Of dense investiture, with luminous vassals.

Against the teleology of Eliot's "In my beginning is my end" and "In my end is my beginning," Stevens presents Alpha and Omega. They are called "characters . . . in the scene," look like characters on a page ("seen"), and behave like characters in a drama ("scene"), miming their own functions. Alpha and Omega encompass all texts, even the Apocalypse, being the limit of a spectrum of letters, the alphabet. The versions of our reading are sometimes plain or minimal, and could be represented by Alpha or A. Or they are elaborate, as in the perception of a "mythological form" (i) or in the Apocalypse of St. John; the most elaborate versions could be represented by Omega or Z. Even "naked Alpha" is an interpreter, for reality always comes to us in some version, and Stevens also suggests, as does much current theory, that all turning of language is troping.[7] Alpha has priority but Omega has authority; he is the ultimate trope, aged ("twisted, stooping"), learned ("polymathic"), venerated ("vassals"), knowing priestly mysteries ("hierophant"), yet like Alpha no more than one of the interpreters of life. To the apocalyptic sentence, "I am Alpha and Omega," Stevens' characters implicitly retort,

---

[7] On the existence of texts as versions, see Gerald L. Bruns, "Intention, Authority, and Meaning," *Critical Inquiry* 7 (1980), 297–309. On the difficulty of speaking about "ordinary language," and the hazards of giving priority to "ordinary language," see Paul de Man, "Literature and Language: A Commentary," *New Literary History* 4 (1972), 181–92, and Stanley Fish, "How Ordinary Is Ordinary Language?" *New Literary History* 5 (1973), 41–54. Of course, language often functions in an ordinary way for practical purposes, and for poetic purposes too.

"*We* are Alpha and Omega," overleaping Wordsworth's "characters of the great Apocalypse."

All these echoes, which are strong enough to be allusive echoes, are present in the abbreviated version of *An Ordinary Evening in New Haven*, the eleven cantos that Stevens selected to read in New Haven in November 1949, and later published (*L* 636n, 662n).[8] The shorter version, in fact, emphasizes *An Ordinary Evening* as an antiapocalyptic poem.

The conventions of apocalypse or revelation can be among our most abstruse. How long did Newton work on the riddles of the Book of Revelation? Yet now, as the ontological force of the old language of revelation is vanishing, we are more than ever fascinated by how that language works. Though revelation may be one of *the* logocentric notions par excellence (to quote Barbara Johnson on Derrida),[9] critics of very different persuasions still desire the language of revelation, either general (we unveil or unfold what is implicit in the text) or particular (we variously revise the word "revelation"). Derrida's exploration of the language of revelation is a direct attack on the problem. (He and Borges are the only other punsters on eucalyptus and apocalyptic that I know.[10]) Stevens' antiapocalyptic strategies are rigorous, and they help us to test current antiapocalyptic writing.

Stevens uses traditional apocalyptic literature as a model rather than an appropriation, to follow Joseph Wittreich's distinction. (Models break with apocalyptic conventions; appropriations follow them.) In apocalyptic literature, "the prophet submits others to the process of purgation and purification which, inwardly directed, result in mankind's transformation into a race of visionaries . . . the prophet employs a series of strategies designed to force open the doors of perception, teaching men to see not *with* but *through* the eye."[11] What Stevens desires to purge is precisely the way of seeing that made former visionaries; for him, it is no longer real. In apocalyptic literature, the hero and the reader must learn "to pierce appearances and grasp reality."[12] Stevens' kind of pur-

---

[8] Stevens completed the thirty-one cantos before choosing eleven to read in New Haven; "abbreviated version" is his phrase. See my "Directions in Reading Wallace Stevens," in *Lyric Poetry*, ed. Hosek and Parker, p. 301n.

[9] Translator's Introduction, Jacques Derrida, *Dissemination*, trans. Barbara Johnson (Chicago and London: University of Chicago Press, 1972, 1981), p. x.

[10] Derrida, "D'un ton apocalyptique," in *Les fins de l'homme*, p. 467. My former student, Paul Morrison, pointed out to me the implicit eucalypti-apocalyptic pun in Borges' story, "Death and the Compass."

[11] Joseph Wittreich, Jr., *Visionary Poetics: Milton's Tradition and His Legacy* (San Marino: Huntington, 1979), pp. 43, 26.

[12] Ibid., p. 29.

gation and envisioning does not lead to a "piercing" of appearances. His insistence on "surfaces" in *An Ordinary Evening* works against concepts and tropes of reality as deep or hidden or profound, a veiled or clouded reality that exists under things: "It is a fresh spiritual that he defines, . . . / A thing on the side of a house, not deep in a cloud . . . The difficulty of the visible / To the nations of the clear invisible" (xiii); "this place, / The things around—the alternate romanza / Out of the surfaces, the windows, the walls" (xxi).

My word "purge" is Stevens' own, in a phrase he borrowed from Valéry:[13] "Here my interest is to try to get as close to the ordinary, the commonplace and the ugly as it is possible for a poet to get. It is not a question of grim reality but of plain reality. The object is of course to purge oneself of anything false" (*L* 636, May 3, 1949). Stevens' word "purge" suggests that we test *An Ordinary Evening in New Haven* to see how far it is a purgatorial poem in the antiapocalyptic mode. As with Professor Eucalyptus, we must be careful. The word "antiapocalyptic" is wrong if we visualize Stevens reaching the top point of a hill of purgatory, then turning away from the heaven beyond or the earthly paradise there at the peak, and coming back down. Such a movement (to follow Northrop Frye's mapping) may be seen in Yeats, who "deliberately turns his back on the Logos vision and goes downward again."[14] Eliot makes the upward or Dantean journey of the "poem of the ascent into heaven" (*OP* 193), and both Yeats and Eliot work out paradoxical reversals. Stevens' movement in *An Ordinary Evening in New Haven* is different from upward and downward journeys. He makes a lateral exploration, neither up nor down. This is a poem written against the upness of all heavens and the downness of earth. A simple reversal of apocalyptic conventions would come down to earth. It would eliminate Omega and move toward Alpha art. It would make Professor Eucalyptus central to Stevens' ending, and natural flowering the opposite to supernatural uncovering. It would delete the "habits of saints" (ix) rather than including them as a part of human reality. Instead, Stevens practices a decreation of apocalyptic literature.

Not only does Stevens not journey upward or downward in this poem. He unobtrusively purges his poem of the prepositions "up" and "down." These two words appear only as adverbs, "down" only once and "up" only seven times in 558 lines. Variations of the word "outside" are sim-

---

[13] Valéry, "If our soul purges itself of all falseness [si notre âme se purge de toute fausseté"], from "Dance and the Soul," *Collected Works of Paul Valéry*, ed. Jackson Mathews (New York: Pantheon, Bollingen, 1956), p. 51.

[14] "The Top of the Tower: A Study of the Imagery of Yeats," in his *The Stubborn Structure: Essays on Criticism and Society* (London: Methuen, 1970), pp. 257–77.

ilarly restricted, though not as severely. In its movement, Stevens' poem is a poem of acrossness, as in the beautifully balanced closing tercet, with its repeated verb, "traverse." Up is the direction of the U-shape of comedy, divine or other. Down is the direction of the upside-down-U-shape of tragedy.[15] In canto xvii, both comedy and tragedy are subordinated to what Stevens calls the commonplace: "The serious reflection is composed / Neither of comic nor tragic but of commonplace." Interpretation of *An Ordinary Evening* suffers, I think, from an inadequate reading of the word "commonplace." Too often, "plain reality" slides over into "grim reality." And grim realists may have a passion for a new heaven and a new earth. Plain reality is more radically antiapocalyptic; there is for it no new heaven, Christian, Marxist, or other, just New Haven. That is, while Stevens is wary of simple reversals, we ourselves sometimes are not. We assume that the common place (say, New Haven) is down. Rather, I think we should read the "commonplace" looking for "every latent double in the word" (*CP* 387)—not just the most reductive plain and ordinary, but also places of argument, topoi, the communal, and so on. Stevens' poem includes a complex of cognate, homonymic, and near-homonymic words that suggests such a wide reading: commonplace, communication, composed, coming together, coming on, and coming forth, Incomincia. And I shall suggest one other meaning.

Commonplace as Stevens' "serious reflection" would move neither up like comedy nor down like tragedy, but across in a line, in the shape of wisdom literature. (Canto xxx suggests a curved rather than a straight line.) Wisdom literature is the literature of the commonplace or proverbial, and also of the light of common day. Stevens himself loved wisdom literature—the Adages of Erasmus, for example—and made his own collection of commonplaces. In 1947, he spoke of the effects of the symbols in the Book of Ecclesiastes as pleasurable: "they give us the pleasure of 'lentor and solemnity' in respect to the most commonplace objects" (*NA* 80). In canto xix of *An Ordinary Evening*, the Ecclesiast enters his poem. And Stevens' final tercet speaks with the balance of the voice of wisdom, and in a wisdom formula (no more but also no less). For Stevens' desire is to place his antiapocalyptic poem within the perspective of the line of wisdom literature, of the commonplace, not to contain it within a genesis-to-apocalypse structure.

VISIONS of a new heaven and a new earth are the subject of Stevens' first movement, cantos i to v. Dante's vision, so long pondered by him,

[15] Cf. Northrop Frye, *The Great Code: The Bible and Literature* (Toronto: Academic Press, 1982), pp. 169, 176.

is central, as Stevens engages with key words in Dante and his modern disciple, Eliot. How does radical idealism see the place called New Haven? Canto ii opens like a Euclidean problem, with a hypothesis, and radical idealism is allowed its say: "Suppose these houses are composed of ourselves." And radical idealism is then allowed to see and hear New Haven, and to build a place of argument that corresponds to its kind of argument, just like an old memory-place. Or rather, no more build than argue, for "buildings" here flow in any transition. They cannot fall, stone from stone, "dilapidate" (i), and they cannot touch or be touched, being repeatedly "impalpable." Parodic mimicking is easier to read in a fluency poem on a muddy river (*CP* 78) than a fluency poem on visionary idealism, but the technique is much the same in both. Some kinds of thinking flow readily around or over things and find no "difficult objects" (i). Bridgings and crossings of objects, as of rhetoric, are easy here. This is the only one-sentence canto, and the only canto with no turn whatever in the argument, no form of "and yet, and yet, and yet" (i). The syntax, like some Platonic escalator to heaven, moves easily through sixteen appositive phrases or clauses to leave the language of sensation behind. For the relentless synaesthesia does not heighten sense effects, but dissipates them. If "synaesthetic apperception always bears witness to the idea of world harmony" (by which Leo Spitzer means classical and Christian ideas of world harmony),[16] Stevens has chosen well his language of parody.

Stevens' polemic may function as a warning against any idealist misreading of his own work, but its chief target is a Dante-Eliot point of view: "In the perpetual reference, object / Of the perpetual meditation, point / Of the enduring visionary love, / Obscure. . . ." The "reference" or "object" or "point" of perpetual meditation or enduring visionary love for, say, Berkeley as for Eliot would be God, Dante's *punto* or point. "Obscure," emphasized by enjambment and stanza break, darkens any revelatory, luminous Dantean associations with "enduring visionary love," drawing it toward a "selva oscura." Stevens' polemic is only intermittently effective against particular poems; his open disagreement with a Dante-Eliot perspective in canto iii is more telling.

Canto iii does not "suppose" anything. It asserts, in a sharply antiEliot turn of argument, as Stevens begins to work with the words "point," "vision," "desire," and "love." "The point of vision and desire are the same." Here it is as if two contradictory concepts of "desire"

---

[16] Leo Spitzer, *Classical and Christian Ideas of World Harmony: Prolegomena to an Interpretation of the Word "Stimmung"* (Baltimore: The Johns Hopkins University Press, 1963), p. 24.

constituted a pun, two meanings within one word, depending on our own "point" of view. This statement reads logically in Stevens' view of things, but not in Eliot's. (I am taking "vision" in its "visionary" sense.) For Eliot,

> Desire itself is movement
> Not in itself desirable;
> Love is itself unmoving,
> Only the cause and end of movement,
> Timeless, and undesiring
> Except in the aspect of time.
>
> (*Burnt Norton* v)

Only of paradise could Eliot say, like Dante, that "the point of vision and desire are the same," for there, as in *Paradiso* III.70–87, the blessed desire exactly what they have. Desire possesses: it contains what satisfies it and is itself contained, and "e'n la sua volontade è nostra pace" (85). In Stevens, by definition, desire cannot have:

> But this cannot
> Possess. It is desire, set deep in the eye,
> Behind all actual seeing, in the actual scene,
> In the street, in a room, on a carpet or a wall,
>
> Always in emptiness that would be filled,
> In denial that cannot contain its blood,
> A porcelain, as yet in the bats thereof.

The argument like the imagery is that of *The Poems of Our Climate*. (Implicit incarnation there is explicit blood here.) Stevens' letter of December 1948 is a useful gloss on canto iii, not only because words and sentiments come over into the poetry, but also because one antagonist is named as Eliot and those of like mind.

> The *savage* assailant of life who uses literature as a weapon just does not exist, any more than the *savage lover* of life exists. . . . Here one is in a *fury* to understand and to participate and one realizes that if there is anything to understand and if there is anything in which to participate one will pretty nearly have to make it oneself. Thus José stands up *in his room* at 2 Dickinson (as the clock strikes *midnight* and as Eliot and Blackmur step into their nightshirts and kneel down to say their *prayers*) and he creates by mere *will* a total wakefulness, brilliant in appearance, multi-colored, of which he is the dominant master, and which he *fills* with words of understanding. . . . Bárbaro! Here the word shows its excellence.
>
> (*L* 624, December 1, 1948, italics mine, of words in canto iii or iv)

One repeated phrase in canto iii makes an important distinction we have not noticed. "*Next to* holiness is the will thereto, / And *next to* love is the desire for love" (my italics). In 1951, Stevens would write: "Men feel that the imagination is the *next greatest* power to faith" (*NA* 171, my italics). Stevens refuses the easy assumption that we can simply substitute the human imagination for faith. Rather, it is the next best thing. In *An Ordinary Evening*, he calls without irony on the "ancientest saint" to testify for him, and this means testifying to what is next to holiness and love.

In canto ii, Stevens effects a vague heaven. In iii, he effects an eternal purgatory—Purgatory, formerly Paradise, as Richard Howard's title succinctly puts it. I read that "hill of stones" as decreating countless rocks of salvation or mountains of vision or everlasting hills. Canto iv turns savagely against saccharine or fairy-tale heavens:

> Plain men in plain towns
> Are not precise about the appeasement they need.
>
> They only know a savage assuagement cries
> With a savage voice; and in that cry they hear
> Themselves transposed, muted and comforted. . . .

"The voice said, Cry. And he said, What shall I cry?" We are going to hear this great text from Isaiah in Stevens' own apocalyptic canto xii, but the first cry we hear is a fierce elemental cry, savage with the force of "bárbaro" in his letter. "Savage assuagement" sounds like oxymoron until we remember Orpheus and note the musical tropes here. Or until we read it sexually. It comes together in the ear by internal rhyme before the mind conceives a reason for its coming together—a fine rhetorical device that both is and is about "a matching and mating of surprised accords" four lines later. The internal rhyme is Eliot's in the headnote to *Dry Salvages*: "salvages" rhymes with "assuages," Eliot notes. (The word "salvages" means "savages"; Stevens could not have known that Eliot first offered the more logical rhyme of "rampages."[17]) What Stevens hears in the rhyme is possible paradox, and he turns the paradox against Eliot in a submerged encoding. (Your kind of "savage" assuages? Your music, your eros? Your salvation assuages?)

I take it that Stevens is precise about the appeasement he needs, even if plain men in plain towns are not. Their understandable need ends in a "children's tale of ice," where "cold . . . Seems like a sheen of heat romanticized." Stevens' obvious puns need no comment, but two subtexts should be noted. If we ask, in what children's tale does cold seem like "a

[17] Helen Gardner, *The Composition of "Four Quartets"* (London and Boston: Faber & Faber, 1978), p. 120.

sheen of heat romanticized," one answer is Andersen's "Snow Queen." With its cold-heat, eye-heart imagery, its saccharine allegorical moralizing, and its final biblical sententia, Ye must become as little children, it makes a proper target. Stevens is sixty-nine years old, and such pretty tales do not speak to the cold of approaching death. No more does the second subtext I infer here, Eliot's *Little Gidding*, where midwinter "sun flames the ice . . . In windless cold that is the heart's heat," and so "seems like a sheen of heat romanticized," "a children's tale of ice."

But when we cross the divide between cantos iv and v, we find ourselves caught, it seems, in "inescapable romance." Here is the entire remarkable canto, the climax and close of Stevens' first movement:

> Inescapable romance, inescapable choice
> Of dreams, disillusion as the last illusion,
> Reality as a thing seen by the mind,
>
> Not that which is but that which is apprehended,
> A mirror, a lake of reflections in a room,
> A glassy ocean lying at the door,
>
> A great town hanging pendent in a shade,
> An enormous nation happy in a style,
> Everything as unreal as real can be,
>
> In the inexquisite eye. Why, then, inquire
> Who has divided the world, what entrepreneur?
> No man. The self, the chrysalis of all men
>
> Became divided in the leisure of blue day
> And more, in branchings after day. One part
> Held fast tenaciously in common earth
>
> And one from central earth to central sky
> And in moonlit extensions of them in the mind
> Searched out such majesty as it could find.

The echo of "romanticized" and "illusion" from canto iv might tempt us toward reading simple separation here— romance as illusion versus romance as disillusion. Stevens implicitly warns us that such separation may not be simple. Separation is the precise subject here, in this canto of Latinate "di-vided" and French "entre-preneur." Stevens' own view of the romantic is itself divided, according to context, and the same is true of the words "evasion," "illusion," and "escapism." Three of these four words—all important for Stevens—are in play in this canto. I include "escapism," for the opening line makes us ask whether and how romance

278

itself is escape. And if it is escape, either beneficent or not, is it also inescapable? Is Stevens' first sentence an assertion or a subject to be meditated? Are we inside romance, bound by its concepts, forms, conventions, bound to it even when we reverse its "illusions"? The question of containment, of inside and outside, is evident here in Stevens' insistent encapsulating and reflecting, with the prefix and preposition "in" taking increasing weight.

The "glassy ocean" is referentially Long Island Sound, though allusively it is something else. It is that sea of glass in the New Jerusalem of Revelation, an ocean both seen and seen by and through. And if "hanging pendent" sounds Miltonic to our ears, because of the etymological doubleness, we are right. The phrase itself encapsulates Milton: "And fast by hanging in a golden chain / This pendant world" (*PL* ii.1051–52). Milton is Christianizing Homer, for Homer's golden chain (seire chryseie, *Iliad* viii.19) was itself a figure pendent on an old cosmology. Stevens elides Milton's phrase, and hangs New Haven, not in a golden chain, but in a shade—whether in shadowy darkness or in the shade of St. John or Milton, or in the shade of a lamp. The Miltonic echoes continue more faintly. "What makes a Nation happy," Milton asserts, may be known through the Old Testament's "majestic unaffected style" (*Paradise Regained* iv.362, 359). "An enormous nation happy in a style," Stevens writes. He is musing on how we enclose our views within something. The canto repeats "in" eleven times in twenty-one lines, beginning with "inescapable romance," and it plays with inside-outside metaphors throughout. Milton's phrase about the earth hanging pendent in a golden chain is part of a sentence about Satan at the end of Book ii, just before the superb Invocation to Light at the beginning of Book iii. Satan floats, "at leisure to behold" the world that he has come to divide. Thus Stevens' phrase, "leisure of blue day," echoing the Satanic "leisure." Thus one answer to Stevens' question, "Who has divided the world?" Thus Stevens' "chrysalis," punning on Homer's "seire chryseie." Thus the self "searched out such majesty as it could find"—find in Milton and his majestic style, and in Revelation. Thus Stevens' grammatical free-floating of Milton's pendent world, which depends on no verb in this canto.

Stevens' strategy is to encapsulate Milton's cosmos within an eye or viewpoint, an "inexquisite" or not-out-searching eye, and then to move on to Wordsworth. Wordsworth, revising Milton, draws Milton's great cosmos within his own eye, in a chain, he says, though not a golden chain. Stevens' verb "search out" is Wordsworth's: "the bodily eye . . . Was searching out the lines of difference . . . And . . . Did bind my feelings even as in a chain" (*Prelude* iii.158–69). As in 1944, Stevens restores Milton and also limits him. As in 1942, he makes us hear Milton through Wordsworth as the canto proceeds, as if we were hearing literary history freshly. (And so we are, for standard editions of Wordsworth hear little of what Stevens heard.) Do we end, then, essentially with Wordsworth and Wordsworth's Milton?

We need to go on. What about romance, a matter of much interest for both Milton and Wordsworth? What did they think of romance? Not very highly, is one answer. Though Wordsworth wishes to distance himself from Milton's transcendence, he agrees fully about romance. It is important that *The Prelude* be read as epic, not as romance, he insists. He will not treat "some old / Romantic tale by Milton left unsung" (I.168–69). I hear Stevens replying to both Milton and Wordsworth in his opening lines: "Inescapable romance, inescapable choice / Of dreams." Yet we want to take care with this play of echo, for it is all too easy to collapse myth into romance. Stevens sounds as if he is collapsing both Milton's and Wordsworth's epics into romance, but he does not end this way.

"Who has divided the world, what entrepreneur?" Satan? Descartes? Freud? "No man," answers this canto. A god or devil, then? No, "the self, the chrysalis of all men." Like original sin, our dividing self is human and now unavoidable. Stevens' formulation sounds abrupt, but once more, in this echoing canto, we hear a faint echo. This is the same line in which Stevens puns on Homer's golden chain, and I wonder if he did not mean us to hear the most famous answer of "No man" in Western literature. This is the answer given to the Cyclops by one of Stevens' recurring figures, Ulysses. "No man" is, in fact, someone: it is Noman (the difference is in the Greek accent). Do we then hear "No man" as the Cyclops's agonized roar? This makes Stevens' preceding question sound quite different. (Why are you roaring and howling if this affliction is sent from Zeus? Say your prayers. Why are you roaring and howling if this Satanic or Cartesian or Freudian divided world is sent by God? Say your prayers.) But it was not Zeus. It was Ulysses who blinded the Cyclops, and so escaped. We should also hear "No man" as the word-play by which Ulysses escapes the various containments of a giant, one-eyed questioner with single vision. Ulysses is Stevens' archetypal quester or inquirer. And Ulysses is an escaper par excellence from romances, whether sinister or erotic, though he is also within our great archetypal romance, the *Odyssey*. Or is he? He seems to get out of it and into us. He is also one figure who follows the pattern of Stevens' last lines. He "held fast tenaciously in common earth," his common earth being Ithaca and Penelope. He also "searched out such majesty as [he] could find,"

280

"from central earth to central sky." A chrysalis, though etymologically a golden thing, is referentially a torpid thing, and is a standard symbol of a temporary human state (cf. *In Memoriam* LXXXII). But Stevens' syntax prevents it and us from discarding "common earth" for "central earth" and "central sky," as this favorite Platonic symbol of the soul always does. The "chrysalis of all men" gives us a typic pattern of metamorphosis that does not leave common earth behind, any more than Ulysses did. Canto v is a brilliant meditation on ideas of "in," including Homer's, Milton's, and Wordsworth's. Stevens goes beyond our common readings in revising them all.

Nor does metamorphosis in canto vi leave earth behind. One hazard in antiapocalyptic writing is that heaven may be too easily cut off. Alpha sounds so fresh and energetic, and Omega so old and tired. And Stevens' canto does pull toward new Alpha tropes, while it tries as by fire the old Omega tropes. Yet the canto makes clear that both have due place, and neither should necessarily prevail. Only when we are clear about this can we see why Stevens includes within reality the "habits of saints" (their customs and their clothes), the spirit's "alchemicana" (all-alchemy-can, all-chemistry-can, all-chem-and-I-can), and so on (canto ix). For these *are* a part of our reality, a part that we try to ignore at our peril. Canto vi marks a new beginning, and canto vii introduces the language of actuality, as if we were only now walking the streets of New Haven.

Once Stevens has included "everything" (ix), he makes possible what his word-play invites: his own kind of apocalypse. It does not come at the end, for there it would effect formal if not teleological closure. It comes in the powerful canto xii:

> The poem is the cry of its occasion,
> Part of the res itself and not about it.
> The poet speaks the poem as it is,
>
> Not as it was: part of the reverberation
> Of a windy night as it is, when the marble statues
> Are like newspapers blown by the wind. He speaks
>
> By sight and insight as they are. There is no
> Tomorrow for him. The wind will have passed by,
> The statues will have gone back to be things about.
>
> The mobile and the immobile flickering
> In the area between is and was are leaves,
> Leaves burnished in autumnal burnished trees

And leaves in whirlings in the gutters, whirlings
Around and away, resembling the presence of thought,
Resembling the presences of thoughts, as if,

In the end, in the whole psychology, the self,
The town, the weather, in a casual litter,
Together, said words of the world are the life of the world.

No matter how we read "res," whether as Ciceronian subject matter or Baconian objects-out-there, I do not think Stevens is primarily concerned with the old res-verba or realist-nominalist debate. He is interested in making us hear the metaphor in that preposition "about," the metaphor that automatically makes a poem (or any work of art) surround its subject, the subject being central and the poem peripheral. (If this wording sounds familiar, it is meant to, for *Anecdote of the Jar* is precisely about this question of aboutness or aroundness ["round . . . surround . . . around . . . round"]: "It made the slovenly wilderness / Surround that hill.") The metaphor of "about," useful as it is, has the movement of a metaphor rather than the status of a definition. Poems are not necessarily and always outside because they are "about" something. Stevens' "part of" formula, so resonant in his mature work, reappears as itself part of the whole question of what belongs where.

Throughout canto xii, things lose their normal stability. Statues are etymologically standing things, but they no longer stand still. At least, things are so described, though the describing words themselves function in a reasonably stable way, with comprehensible syntax and word-play. Though artfully varying, the syntax may be mapped, as it is by Helen Vendler.[18] The troping on the leaves is very rich, even for Stevens, but it is not abstruse, and most readers will hear at least some of it.

The canto's first half appears to be more "about" its subject than the second half, which is one long sentence of cunning syntax with a core metaphor. "Immobile flickering" is so odd a notion that the syntax itself momentarily flickers between "flickering" as participle and "flickering" as gerund. Still, the "area between is and was" is conceptually familiar if impossible to pin down. It is that flicker or moving point of the present that we can grasp only after it has passed. This is true of perception as well as reading. (The phenomenon fascinated Stevens, who called it poetic.[19]) That flickering moment is for Eliot unreal if it is only in time

---

[18] Helen Vendler, *On Extended Wings: Wallace Stevens' Longer Poems* (Cambridge, Mass.: Harvard University Press, 1969), p. 277.

[19] "For instance, the idea that because perception is sensory we never see reality immediately but always the moment after is a poetic idea" (L 722, July 25, 1951), and cf. OP 190–91.

(*Burnt Norton* I). But Stevens locates his apocalyptic moment fully in time, all the while echoing some of Eliot's apocalyptic language. "Flickering" is not here the pentecostal, transcendent tongues of flame or its terrible contrary, gunfire. The "windy night" of Eliot's early rhapsody echoes oddly, and I think deliberately, against the wind and leaves of *Little Gidding*. Stevens' sequence of "whirlings, whirlings, words, world, world" plays against Eliot's "whirled, world, word" sequence. Stevens' "as if," unlike Eliot's, governs the whole scene of speaking. He wants us to hear Eliot's apocalyptpic 1942 meeting as the same in kind as his 1917 windy night. Eliot's poetry in this episode of *Little Gidding* is too powerful to be undone this way, though this canto can modify the way we hear it.

"Leaves" are first of all what the logic of the syntax tells us: what is left, the leavings of our lives and times. They become tree leaves, in apposition and enjambment, autumnal because fallen (this is an "occasion" or etymological falling). They are ghosts of this ancient topos itself, known to us through leaves in a third sense, the leaves of a book. "Flickering" suggests not so much a turning of leaves, as in *Domination of Black*, as a riffling of pages by the wind. Stevens' lines give us a paradox of ordinary reading, and also, as the meaning of "leaves" shifts or flickers, a speeded-up reading, with the wind blowing as it listeth, and thoughts like leaves whirling, not just around (as if centered on a word) but away.

Stevens last and much-quoted line does not imply solipsism. Even when leaves tell us to go away and leave reading (leave leaves), they have to say so in words. The older form of this is the Word who says "I am the Life of the world" (more precisely, I am the way, the truth and the life). Stevens' use of the plural "words" is the true revision here, as he changes the ancient prophetic voice. Our readings have been too exclusively, and so weakly, Shelleyan. Stevens hears what it is that Shelley challenged with his apocalyptic voice in *Ode to the West Wind*: it is the ancient prophetic Word of God. Just such a challenge is Stevens' also. Isaiah gives Stevens the beginning and the end of his canto, together with the figures of wind and vegetation, and the theme of mutability: "The voice said, Cry. And he said, What shall I cry? All flesh is grass, and all the goodliness thereof is as the flower of the field: the grass withereth, the flower fadeth: because the spirit of the Lord bloweth upon it: surely the people is grass. The grass withereth, the flower fadeth: but the word of our God shall stand for ever" (Isa. 40:6–8). Shelley's prophetic stance ends with hope: "If Winter comes, can Spring be far behind?" Stevens remains autumnal. His leaves become "litter" as the voices of the dead on the leaves of books also become litter, as even this poem which is his voice or cry may become litter in its time. The association of "leaves-litter-obliteration" goes back to *Sunday Morning*, but in *An Ordinary Evening in New Haven*, Stevens works with the sequence "gutter-litter"—a surer and bleaker kind of obliteration than under the feet of impassioned maidens. Stevens accepts simply a common fate: that even his own best poems may in their time be left. What he affirms is the enduring power of human words.

We are as yet some way from reading the Professor Eucalyptus cantos, with their insistent rain and noisy spout, so repugnant to professorial ears. The repeated spout is "ramshackle" and produces only a drip that says "tink-tonk"—a far cry from canto i's watery words, "down-pouring, up-springing and inevitable." Stevens' "tink-tonk" is a variation on his favorite watery image of voice (spouting new orations of the cold, and so on). This spout only drips in onomatopoeia. Stevens once wrote a love letter in the form of a prose-poem on rain, a letter he remembered in 1949:

My Lady:
  The sweet sound of the down-right rain changes the city into something very much like the country—for rain falls on roofs, pavements etc. with pretty much the same sound with which it falls on trees or fields: no, trees; for surely it falls on fields (and the grass of them) with a softer sound than this.—So much for the sweet sound of the down-right rain! . . . One long, unbroken, constant sound—the sound of the falling of water. —A sound not dependent on breath. . . . A sound native to the mind, remembered by the mind. —Therefore, the ancient and immemorial sweet sound of the down-right rain . . . surely there never was a more melodious fall of rain than this . . . bare existence . . . similar revelations . . . things actual. . . . It is all a grotesque puzzle. But the heart is the most obstinate thing in the world—and will never pour itself out in ink, as it should, and when it should—for which the Heavens be praised. —"Old Dry-as-Dust!" cries the crowd. No: only Harlequin, in a poor light. —Perhaps this is not clear. A little mystery, then—deluged with a sound that, all the while, has never stopped— to say it again, the constant murmur of down-falling rain. Only now it seems to grow a little lighter, a little softer—so that there is a path through the weather to the letter-box. Let this bring with it a little of a whole evening's leafy noise—and always the same delight in it.

Your
W.
(*L* 145–46, June 17, 1909)

At the end of the letter, the rain grows softer and lighter, two adjectives Stevens will use forty years later at the end of canto xv, where he also turns toward the gently erotic. That "actual hand" takes some force from memories of his courtship (*L 78*), such memories helping to account for his sensitivity to Milton's lines on the hands of Adam and Eve:

> The heaviness we lighten by light will,
> By the hand of desire, faint, sensitive, the soft
> Touch and trouble of the touch of the actual hand.

Here is Milton, in a passage echoed more than once in Stevens: "with voice / Mild, as when *Zephyrus* on *Flora* breathes, / Her hand soft touching, whisper'd there" (*PL* v.15–17). "Trouble" is part of Eve's dream (v.34, 96), and Stevens brings together touch and trouble in his stanza so that we will not just hear the paradisal bliss of "soft / Touch." We will also hear trouble, though soft, in the troubling touch itself. The line softly touches an area of trouble in Stevens' earlier erotic poetry: the area of actual touch.

Canto xvi declines tragedy as a pattern for this poem, and canto xvii declines comedy. Stevens is moving toward the "serious reflection" of the "commonplace." The last stanza of xvi is especially moving though it has caused some problems:

> It is a bough in the electric light
> And exhalations in the eaves, so little
> To indicate the total leaflessness.

Stevens cannot find an image of time to suit him, and so he sets about making one of his own. If eaves are sometimes flowing with water, or dripping tink-tonk, they also may be empty without being bone-dry. They may be damp and steaming, like a mist rising. As a trope of voice, they would neither flow nor drip but exhale, breathe out, like the rising mists that we may call exhalations. ("Ye Mists and Exhalations that now rise / From Hill or steaming Lake, dusky or grey, / Till the Sun paint your fleecy skirts with Gold" [*PL* v.185–87].) There is much breathing in this evening poem, and eaves in an evening poem invite thoughts of word-play. (Keats misspelled "eves" as "eaves" in *To Autumn*, and Joyce defined "eavesdrip" exuberantly: " = would listen to the dripping drops of his house's e(a)ve Δ water."[20]) Stevens' exhalations are like a voiceless sigh, and quite unlike the vigor of "inhale a health of air" (viii). If inhaling takes in health, exhaling marks its going, in each outward-bound breath of an aging man.

[20] James Joyce, *Selected Letters*, ed. Richard Ellmann (New York: Viking, 1975), May 13, 1927, p. 322.

If we also listen to the assonantal rhyme, eaves-leaflessness, remembering how "leaves" in xii meant "leavings," we will hear the missing middle term. That term is "leaves" in a sequence of eaves, [leaves], leaflessness. Stevens' earlier troping makes us hear "exhalations in the leaves," but there are no leaves here, only eaves. A leafless branch, lit by electric light, has shed its leaves, cluttering the eaves so that they neither rain nor drip (a standard household nuisance is what they are, in fact). Stevens remembers all poets' leaves, all his earlier watery tropes for voice, the eaves of Milton and Coleridge, and one paradisal morning with exhalations. His e(a)ves sigh faintly, breathing "leaves, eves, eaves" and "indicate the total leaflessness," not yet here, but coming.

I said "branch," but Stevens does not use this ordinary term, and we need to listen also to the faint echo in his deliberately poetic word "bough." Why "bough"? Vendler reads it as an analogue for what is "altogether drier and more brittle," while also hearing a "concealed allusiveness." Bloom reads it naturalistically: "A bough in artificial light makes a very different and doubtless more qualified impression than a bough in sunlight, yet it is a bough."[21] I want to pursue a reading informed by one echo Vendler hears, the echo of what must be the best-known bough in English literature, and one that haunted Stevens.

> That time of year thou mayst in me behold,
> When yellow leaves, or none, or few, do hang
> Upon those boughs which shake against the cold,
> Bare ruin'd choirs, where late the sweet birds sang.
> In me thou seest the twilight of such day,
> As after sunset fadeth in the west,
> Which by and by black night doth take away,
> Death's second self, that seals up all in rest.
> In me thou seest the glowing of such fire,
> That on the ashes of his youth doth lie,
> As the death-bed whereon it must expire,
> Consumed with that which it was nourished by.
> This thou perceiv'st, which makes thy love more strong,
> To love that well which thou must leave ere long.

We can hear Shakespeare punning on "leaves-leave" and we easily read his allegory of evening twilight. Stevens' "electric light" speaks to Shakespeare's two dying lights, the light of day and the firelight (by analogy, lost song). Shakespeare modulates from global dying light to

---

[21] Vendler, *On Extended Wings*, pp. 273–74; Harold Bloom, *Wallace Stevens: The Poems of Our Climate* (Ithaca: Cornell University Press, 1977), p. 325.

domestic dying light, that is, firelight, the common domestic light of the sixteenth century. For Stevens to use firelight would be inappropriate, and he rightly turns to the twentieth-century equivalent, electric light. Nor does he follow a "leaves-leave-love" movement like Shakespeare's. Instead, love is left behind with youth, and with words that belong with youth, the "young palaver of lips." Even Shakespeare's beautiful sonnet does not satisfy Stevens among time's images, and he offers a new one that is also a tribute. He has already warned us not to make this into tragedy, so that the absence of all tropes of leaves here should not be misconstrued. Stevens omits leaves deliberately, as we realize near the end, in canto xxx: "The last leaf that is going to fall has fallen." And against the thought of total leaflessness halfway through his poem, Stevens writes:

> The barrenness that appears is an exposing.
> It is not part of what is absent, a halt
> For farewells, a sad hanging on for remembrances.

There are some kinds of elegiac reading that are an insult to the aged.

The cantos from here until the four climactic end cantos are particularly hard to read for at least two reasons. One is that Stevens is avoiding the familiar shapes of comedy or tragedy, upward or downward. The second reason is Stevens' experimental work, as he tries different "models" (his own word, in the carpenter's canto, xviii). These are not mapped as a progression, as far as I can see. They may be attempting to find a "radial aspect of this place" (xix). Throughout this ascetic part of the series, we are conscious of placing and being placed: of dwelling places (rooms, windows), of land (isles, Long Island Sound), of the sea, of the horizon, of space, of stars, of night.

In canto xxvi, we may hear Stevens gathering up his earlier language of creation, revising Milton as he proceeds:

> Away from them, capes, along the afternoon Sound,
> Shook off their dark marine in lapis light.
> The sea shivered in transcendent change, rose up
>
> As rain and booming, gleaming, blowing, swept
> The wateriness of green wet in the sky.

The puns on "cape" and "sound" are obvious, as is the double sense of "shook off," applied to weather and to clothing, and the contraries of light-dark and light-heavy. Descriptively, this is rain become lighter, and light appearing, as at the end of Stevens' early letter on rain. "When the Sea threw off his evening shade," writes Wordsworth, and Stevens literalizes the trope. The punning sounds pointless until we hear its origin in Milton: "at the voice / Of God, as with a Mantle, didst invest / The rising world of waters dark and deep" (*PL* iii.9–11). There is much falling in *An Ordinary Evening in New Haven* and there is much rising too, both being limited or equivocal in their upness and downness. Stevens is fully aware of Milton's powerful rhetoric and dialectic of rising and falling; he was aware of it in *Sunday Morning* and played with it in *Autumn Refrain*. He approaches Milton's lines more closely in 1952:

> Or we put mantles on our words because
> The same wind, rising and rising, makes a sound
> Like the last muting of winter as it ends.
>
> (*CP* 519)

Capes are not quite mantles, for mantles are prophetic and can descend from one prophet to another. Perhaps Stevens' cape is more like some Spanish hidalgo's cloak than a Miltonic mantle. In *An Ordinary Evening*, Stevens makes changes of weather vivid; he makes his own word-changes evident; he notes unobtrusively that our usual metaphors for voicing sea and weather are of clothing (the voice of God invests, says Milton). That word "transcendent" is a bold stroke, but Stevens is sure enough of his placings that he can use it without fear of being misunderstood. (This is also true of Stevens' use of "transcends" and "transcendence" at the end of "Effects of Analogy" [*NA* 130].)

Milton's ghostly presence here is confirmed by Stevens' return to Milton's touching hands, the echo now attenuated. It is not now the soft touch of unfallen Adam awakening dreaming Eve, but an earthly touch, with a touching voice too. The voice speaks "without form," which we read as "without words," but Stevens is also echoing the English Bible, where "the earth was without form and void." (Milton's version is "the void and formless infinite" [iii.12].) In Stevens, the poor and ragged earth nonetheless has a voice and movingly "whispers humane repose," "gritting the ear." Though the last phrase sounds rough and poor, it is a beautiful turning of Miltonic language, as I noted earlier. Milton's transcendent language is lost to Stevens, but he does not mourn or parody a failed pipe or a lost prophetic mantle here. Instead, those parodic noises in Stevens (grate, grackle, crackle, skreak, skritter) are themselves ingathered in a voice that, though gritting the ear, whispers humane repose. Yet even this is not quite right, for Stevens does not say *"though* gritting the ear." The gritting is accepted without comment.

"Her hand soft touching, whisper'd thus. . . ." But Adam's whisper brings no repose, nor will Adam and Eve ever sleep again in repose. "Noontide repast, or Afternoon's Repose . . . O much deceiv'd . . .

Thou never from that hour in Paradise / Found'st either sweet repast, or sound repose" (ix.403–407). We may hear Stevens very quietly replying to this: "The afternoon Sound . . . the inamorata . . . lost . . . Touches, as . . . a voice . . . whispers humane repose." Stevens' Long Island Sound repose is not Milton's "sound repose." The canto comes to rest on "humane repose," with nothing of Stevens' sometimes restless word-play on "re-pose." Then he turns abruptly to a detached mode in canto xxvii, a mode he called the mask of "Old Dry-as-Dust" in his rain letter. The Miltonic lines have almost too great a personal force for him, and he moves to dry allegory in something close to a parody of the apocalyptic marriage.

All four of Stevens' closing cantos also close the shorter version of his poem, though in a different order. In the short version, canto xxix ends the series; in the long, canonical version, canto xxxi ends it. It is to these two cantos I want to turn now, in a close reading of some of Stevens' most remarkable poetry.

In canto xxix, as we might expect at the end of a purgatorial poem, Stevens brings the reader to the earthly paradise, the land of the lemon trees, Goethe's *Land, wo die Zitronen blühn*. Or rather, not us, but mariners, and mariners not in the present tense of most of *An Ordinary Evening*, but in the past. Once entered, the earthly paradise proves to be the common place turned inside out, a stark and simple reversal. Or is it? Here is the fable, preceded by the last line of canto xviii:

The heavens, the hells, the worlds, the longed-for lands.

In the land of the lemon trees, yellow and yellow were
Yellow-blue, yellow-green, pungent with citron-sap,
Dangling and spangling, the mic-mac of mocking birds.

In the land of the elm trees, wandering mariners
Looked on big women, whose ruddy-ripe images
Wreathed round and round the round wreath of autumn.

They rolled their r's, there, in the land of the citrons.
In the land of big mariners, the words they spoke
Were mere brown clods, mere catching weeds of talk.

When the mariners came to the land of the lemon trees,
At last, in that blond atmosphere, bronzed hard,
They said, "We are back once more in the land of the elm trees,

But folded over, turned round." It was the same,
Except for the adjectives, an alteration
Of words that was a change of nature, more

Than the difference that clouds make over a town.
The countrymen were changed and each constant thing.
Their dark-colored words had redescribed the citrons.

A competent close reading will easily find contrasts of light against dark;
Impressionist, Mediterranean painting against Dutch, northerly paint-
ing; the flowers and fruit of language against weeds of language; tasting
language or "rolling" it on the tongue against having it "catch" like
burrs. (Stanley Burnshaw said of Stevens' language that "one rolls [it]
on the tongue";[22] Mediterranean Romance languages roll their r's; roll-
ing words means being voluble.) We might also observe the self-con-
sciousness of the land of the elm trees, which, in a post-Cartesian view,
marks it as fallen. (Stevens notes not just color but the act of looking;
not just rolling r's, but the act of speaking.) We note also the presence of
desire in the land of the elm trees in the biblical verb, "looked on." Many
a land of lemon trees has memorable women but not Stevens' land here.

The mariners are swiftly translated to the land of the lemon trees,
Stevens here having no interest in the struggles of a quest. They say:
"We are back once more in the land of the elm trees, / But folded over,
turned round." "Folded over, turned round"? 1) On a piece of paper,
folded over in a circle, with the letters turned round, elm becomes lemon
becomes elm becomes lemon. 2) Folded over: implicit. Turned round:
troped. And perhaps, 3) "folded over": *in aenigmate* (enigmatical, folded
language, says Francis Bacon); turned round: reversed, as in a mirror
image, per speculum. "Videmus nunc per speculum in aenigmate," reads
St. Paul's famous text. In the land of the lemon trees, the mariners pass
beyond the mirroring symmetry of the first half of their canto, and meet
face to face—themselves and the land of the elm trees. The land of the
lemon trees is no enlightening Eden, no place of revelation.

But the first tercet warned us that the earthly paradise is itself a topos,
not necessarily transforming. Stevens is again remembering Goethe but
more loudly than in *Notes*. His movement between the words "lemon"
and "citron" corresponds to the double meaning of Goethe's *Zitronen*:
first, lemon trees, pointing in part to Goethe's paradisal Italy and Ste-
vens' once-loved American South, home of the New World mockingbird;
second, citrons, the *citrus medica* or *malus medica* used generically in
Thomson's *Spring*, specifically in Milton, and the tree Carlyle had in
mind when he translated Goethe's *Zitronen* not as citrons but as "citron-
apples." This is the tree of Virgil's *Georgics*, whose phrase "tristis sucos

---

[22] Burnshaw: "words and phrases that one rolls on the tongue . . . [but] can hardly
swallow today" (*New Masses* 17 [1935], cited in *Wallace Stevens: A Critical Anthology*,
ed. Irvin Ehrenpreis [London: Penguin, 1972], p. 101).

tardumque saporem / felicis mali" (II.126–27) Stevens may be translating and condensing in his "pungent with citron-sap." In that compound word, we may also hear a faint echo of Milton's famous punning on fallen *sapor*, itself perhaps originating in Virgil's word-play, "saporem / felicis mali." We shall not miss the echo of Stevens' own earthly paradises, in *Sunday Morning* and in *Notes* II.v. I cannot solve the problem of tone here. Stevens' echoes open back out into the topos of the earthly paradise. It seems to me he presents it, remembers its beauty, tries it, purges it.

Perhaps it is Long Island in any case. The reader who delights in toponymy and paronomasia will recall that Long Island lies (as we say) not far from New Haven; will remember Stevens' phrases, "the longed-for lands" (xxviii), "the afternoon Sound" (xxvi), "a long, inevitable sound, / A kind of cozening and coaxing sound / And the goodness of lying in a maternal sound" (xxiii); and, listening to the sound of Long Island sound, will hear therein an invitation to a literary voyage as beguiling as any in the ample pages of Curtius.

As for the birds in this earthly paradise, they set up the most extraordinary song. "Mic-mac" may be read five different ways. 1) Indian Mic-Mac or "allies." 2) Mic-mac as a nonsense effect, emphasizing the arbitrariness of representation. 3) Mic-mac-mock, questioning whether mimesis is ironic imitation or not. 4) Syntactic mic-mac, implying a snack or fruit. 5) Syntactic mic-mac, implying mockingbird song, playing also with the first syntactic meaning of "fruit," just as the word "philomel," meaning "lover of fruit," is sometimes played against the incorrect meaning, "lover of song." Why all this play? Partly to address perennial questions of mimesis and mimicking, and partly to address other birds, like any good mockingbird (more precisely, "mocking bird"). I mentioned Milton and Goethe and hinted at Whitman in my Long Island remarks. Here is part of an old line of inheritance we have heard before in *Autumn Refrain* and *Notes* II. To read historically, we may hear Goethe as heir to Milton.[23] But what of Whitman and his great mockingbird?

Suppose we ask a different question. What mimic (or mic-mac-mock, so to speak) do we find in the greatest earthly paradise in English writing, Milton's Eden? The answer is startling, for there is one mimic only, and it comes where it ought to come, in Milton's scene of the citron trees, which is the scene of Eve's dream. I have been tracing echoes of this scene in *An Ordinary Evening in New Haven* and here is another submerged one. But Milton's mimic is, in fact, no bird; it is fancy, "mimic fancy."

[23] Ronald Gray's edition, *Poems of Goethe* (Cambridge: Cambridge University Press, 1966), notes Thomson's lines, "which Goethe could have known" (p. 119).

This echo sounds unhelpful until we think of Milton's one rival singer of birdsong in an earthly paradise, Keats. Then we may hear Stevens once more writing literary history: listening to the bird of paradise descend from Milton's various nightingales, including the false nightingale of mimic fancy—descend to Keats's nightingale and his cheating fancy— descend finally to Whitman's New World nightingale, which is the mockingbird. (It is sometimes called the American nightingale, the songs are often compared, and Whitman's "musical shuttle" in line 2 of *Out of the Cradle Endlessly Rocking* surely echoes Sophocles' metonymy for Philomel, "the voice of the shuttle.") Stevens has heard what Keats did with Eve's dream in the nightingale ode, and how Whitman made use of both Milton and Keats. It is a way of proceeding. Stevens has pondered it well and he presents it here.[24]

This extraordinarily rich canto is a small history of the earthly paradise, both general and personal. It is personal in its allusion to Goethe, its allusive echoing of Whitman, and its fainter echoing of Milton—a compound farewell tribute to Stevens' masters, appropriately offered at the threshold of the earthly paradise, where Dante offered his tribute.[25] Keats was also a master for Stevens, and it will not have escaped the observant reader that Stevens leaps over Keats himself in stanza i. I followed the logic of Stevens' metaleptic echoing in order to recover Keats's place in a line of succession, but Keats is transumed, not echoed, in stanza i. It is in stanza ii that we hear Keats. For in stanza ii Stevens sees and hears our ordinary earthly places, the here and now—say, New Haven or "Elm-Tree City"—through a Spenser-Keats line of succession. The "wreath of autumn" is a conventional metonymy, beautifully presented in a chiastic scheme of echo. We hear how the topos of autumn so often has to do with the rounding of the seasons, and so of human life. We hear a history of tropes of autumn, themselves wreathing an undefined center. We remember also the fruit of Eden, and its association with the first and archetypal woman. It is Spenser that gives us an early and memorable example of Stevens' topos: "Then came Autumne . . . Upon his head a wreathe that was enroll / With ears of corn . . . And in his hand a sickle he did holde / To reape the ripened fruits the which the earth had yold" (*Mutability Cantos* VII.xxx.1–9). But it is Keats who is unavoidable when this topos is used, and we know how Stevens reechoed *To Autumn* all through his work. Stevens' land of the elm trees, if mutable and lumpish in language, is a land whose images are ruddy-ripe and alive

[24] For a full discussion of this line of inheritance, and this strategy, see my "Birds in Paradise: Uses of Allusion in Milton, Keats, Whitman, Stevens, and Ammons," *Studies in Romanticism* 26 (1987), 421–43.

[25] This parallel was suggested to me by Lee Patterson.

with desire. The two lands are one and the same, "except for the adjectives." The two lands are not separated by the Fall, as in Milton. The Miltonic dialectic is not encompassed with little sense of separation, as in Whitman. Stevens is closest to Keats in this canto, which assumes Keats's *Ode to a Nightingale* and evokes Keats's *To Autumn*. Are not Stevens' mariners themselves poets, desiring to cross to a paradise of immortal song? "Sings darkling . . . Kennst du das Land wo die Zitronen blühn, / Im dunkeln . . . Darkling I listen . . . I listen . . . the song of my dusky demon and brother . . . Their dark-colored words had redescribed the citrons."

How can Stevens end a poem that has undone so many patterns of ending, including the end of the world? What will this master of endings do at this ending? He cannot celebrate earth, as at the end of *Notes toward a Supreme Fiction*, for this is not a celebratory poem. Yet a closure too inconclusive would belie his own fierceness for purgation. "I leave my poem open-ended because reality is open-ended" is far too crude a formula for Stevens.

He ends with two hypotheses, the first a dark one.

> It is not in the premise that reality
> Is a solid. It may be a shade that traverses
> A dust, a force that traverses a shade.

"Dust" is metonymically a place in many a biblical text, and shade that traverses a dust evokes a human or ghostly or sundial crossing of time across place. "Dust thou art and unto dust shalt thou return" is the text for Ash Wednesday, the day that gave its title to the best-known modern poem of purgation. Older troping might speak of a breath that traverses a dust, or a soul that traverses a dust. And Stevens himself has troped finely on "dust" and "shade" for some thirty years. Stevens provides a double for his first, dark hypothesis, an "and yet, and yet, and yet" (i). Shade itself may be traversed by a force. So also, the water of the sea may be traversed by a force. Stevens used the analogy for the force of the sublime, or "nobility": "as a wave is a force and not the water of which it is composed, which is never the same, so nobility is a force and not the manifestations of which it is composed, which are never the same" (*NA* 35–36, 1942). Reality may be the force that traverses the shade that traverses the dust that is New Haven. Or the dust that is Wallace Stevens, or the dust that is his reader, or the dust that is this poem. The force that traverses a shade may serve as a trope for a brain wave, a trope for the power of troping. Stevens' first hypothesis concentrates on what is dark and traditionally most mutable; his second hypothesis changes all that by one word, "force." Stevens does not move toward any kind of light. The least move toward light would defeat his purpose here, and he rightly ends on the word "shade," allowing nothing to break the fine gravity. His last stanza is his final balance in this poem in which so much depends on right balancing.

Yet it is not quite right to say that reality may be a shade or may be a force. It is more correct to say that reality may be a shade-that-traverses or a force-that-traverses. The noun clause gives a fuller definition and keeps us aware that Stevens may be playing with a definition of reality as energy. Reality is not a solid or an inert mass, and there is no "may be" in Stevens' negative. Reality is something closer to Einstein's physics than to Newton's. Stevens works to keep the reader from saying that reality "is" this or that, and even more to keep the reader from saying that reality "is" here or there. Reality is not, in this premise, a solid. Reality is not, in this premise, a realm of light, not a heaven, not a topos beyond the heavens, in Pindar's phrase that Plato borrowed and made live.[26] Nor should our reading assume that words are a solid. As in Einsteinian physics, a force may flow through actuality and through words. Energy is mass crossed by the speed of light, squared. It is not in the premise that reality is a solid. It may be a shade that crosses a mass, a force that crosses a shade.

The fine balance of Stevens' conclusion is seen in other ways too. A "premise" about "reality" leads us to expect a firm concluding argument, but "may be" keeps Stevens' poem in the realm of possibility. The repetition of a formula gives a sense of closure, but the word "traverses" keeps a sense of something ongoing. "Shade" and "dust" have strong associations with the end of things, but "force" suggests something not easily stopped. It is as if Stevens had presented a Ptolemaic pattern of the universe, and then added, "And yet it moves."

[26] Thomas McFarland uses the phrase, "beyond the heavens," to characterize "meontic poetry," which he contrasts with mimetic poetry. His stimulating discussion suggests indirectly why Stevens wanted to avoid such a division. See "The Place beyond the Heavens: True Being, Transcendence, and the Symbolic Indication of Wholeness," *Boundary 2*, 7 (1979), 282–317.

* * * * *

CHAPTER THIRTEEN

Late Poems:

Places, Common and Other

> One turns with something like ferocity toward a
> land that one loves, to which one is really and es-
> sentially native, to demand that it surrender, reveal,
> that in itself which one loves. This is a vital affair,
> not an affair of the heart (as it may be in one's first
> poems), but an affair of the whole being (as in one's
> last poems), a fundamental affair of life, or, rather,
> an affair of fundamental life; so that one's cry of O
> Jerusalem becomes little by little a cry to something
> a little nearer and nearer until at last one cries out
> to a living name, a living place, a living thing, and
> in crying out confesses openly all the bitter secre-
> tions of experience. (*OP* 260, 1948)

I HAVE moved from the end of *Transport to Summer* to *An Ordinary Evening in New Haven*, the major long poem of Stevens' next volume. That poem, and the volume's title poem, *Auroras of Autumn* explore ways of saying farewell. At the same time, Stevens increasingly writes short poems of peculiar force and intensity that do not give the effect of meditating on farewells, except by indirection. Randall Jarrell describes them as the work of a man "at once very old and beyond the dominion of age; such men seem to have entered into (or are able to create for us) a new existence, a world in which everything is enlarged and yet no more than itself, transfigured and yet beyond the need of transfiguration."[1]

[1] Jarrell, *The Third Book of Criticism* (New York: Farrar, Straus, & Giroux, 1979), p. 60.

It is hard to find a language in which to speak well of these extraordinary late lyrics. We speak again and again of a sense of doubleness in them, of the strange and right combining of the everyday and the visionary. The everyday and the visionary come together yet are held apart, before us; or, to change the metaphor, we cross easily back and forth from one area to the other. Things familiar and ordinary live in tension with their own unfamiliarity and extraordinariness. There is no sense of blocking, and this is one difference from the early poems. It is not at all that outside place and the order of words are made to sound stable. It is that the word "stable" and the inside-outside metaphor seem insufficient, even wrong. In *Things of August*, for example, are we inside or outside the egg?

> Spread sail, we say, spread white, spread way.
> The shell is a shore. . . .
> Spread outward. Crack the round dome. Break through. . . .

Outside if we are cracking a breakfast egg, and inside if we are cracking the old egg of the world. The egg turns inside out and outside in (and we all began in or as an egg), like words themselves: "It is a world of words to the end of it" (which we usually misread through insufficient attention to the word "it"). In the opening poems, the figures seemed to belong properly to neither mimetic nor legendary nor allegorical worlds. The figures in these late poems seem to belong properly to different worlds at the same time. Stevens admits what he can of older tropes, legends, beliefs, ideas, and even some old ghosts. He has tried them as by fire, and he knows to the last syllable what he can allow into his poetic world.

Thematically, these are poems of last things, of memories, of repetitions, of attentuations, yet also of a fierce will to live and a love of this earth. They are poems of being at home yet also of seeking home. (It is little wonder that the Ulysses figure reappears in force.) Generically, we may usefully think of some as tombeau or epitaph poems, as Charles Berger suggests,[2] or as testamentary poems. There is a high proportion of fluency poems, this subgenre being appropriate for a man musing on the river of time.

Much of Stevens' familiar word-play is here, with his tactics often foregrounded. From the beginning, Stevens' lines could do what they described. From the beginning, Stevens could find language for his methods of doing and describing. These late poems are different in the sim-

---

[2] Berger, *Forms of Farewell: The Late Poems of Wallace Stevens* (Madison: University of Wisconsin Press, 1985), pp. 143–45.

plicity and obviousness of Stevens' language for his methods. Here Stevens achieves the seemingly impossible, as he did also in *An Ordinary Evening in New Haven*: to look through and at language at the same time. He opens his 1950 volume, *The Rock*, with a poem ending on the line, "The river motion, the drowsy motion of the river R." The word-play is presented to the reader as if in a Shakespearean epilogue. Reader, the poem says, we all know of that old trope and allegory, the river of time, the river of being, the capital-R River of Are. Once more, here it is, repeated yet new, simple and evident, like this cadence. It is as if the river began to say its own proper name, then fell asleep like an old man, for this is a poem titled *An Old Man Asleep*. Stevens is writing of an old man's river, and Old Man River too—not the Mississippi but the typic River.

I have isolated this one line, though my reading depends on the rest of this short poem, and it is instructive to consider how:

> The two worlds are asleep, are sleeping, now.
> A dumb sense possesses them in a kind of solemnity.
>
> The self and the earth—your thoughts, your feelings,
> Your beliefs and disbeliefs, your whole peculiar plot;
>
> The redness of your reddish chestnut trees,
> The river motion, the drowsy motion of the river R.

We hear behind this poem Stevens' earlier fluency poems and somnambulist poems: *Hibiscus on the Sleeping Shore, Frogs Eat Butterflies*, and especially the powerful poem, *Somnambulisma*.[3] What keeps this late lyric from sliding back into a pleasing exercise like the first two poems? Two things, I think, that are largely present in the late lyrics: a sense of dialectic, and the universal human subject of the way things look and feel when one is old. Stevens' dialectic in the late poems may be muted but it is clearly present. His subject matter is strongly human, and his "I" or "he" emerges as acting, willing, desiring. Word-play can afford to be as obvious as "the river R" when it plays against a tough dialectic and on a human subject. The danger for a lesser poet would be portentousness, but Stevens' touch is sure.

Stevens' familiar play with grammar goes on, for example with prepositions, a play I have noted from the start. *The Woman in Sunshine* turns on an unexpected use of "in"; the effect is obvious. In *The Plain Sense of Things*, the play with "in" is unobtrusive. The last stanza of

---

[3] See Helen Vendler's fine commentary in her *Wallace Stevens: Words Chosen Out of Desire* (Knoxville: University of Tennesse Press, 1984), pp. 69–72.

Stevens' ten-part elegy, *Auroras of Autumn*, sounds baroque in its prepositions; it has more play of prepositions than any three lines I know. They challenge and establish different senses of place:

> As if he lived all lives, that he might know,

> In hall harridan, not hushful paradise,
> To a haggling of wind and weather, by these lights
> Like a blaze of summer straw, in winter's nick.

One grammatical-rhetorical punning is especially fine, a pun on apostrophe, to which I shall return. As for play with figures, I hear less of this, though it includes one example that is especially remarkable because Stevens admits anagogic metaphor. This is *Of Mere Being*, to which I shall also return.

The etymological play continues, and we need it in order to read well such a poem as *This Solitude of Cataracts*. In *The River of Rivers in Connecticut*, "there is no ferryman. / He could not bend against its propelling force." The ferryman would be Charon if he were there, just as the preceding "shadow" would be a shade of the dead if it were present. "Bend against" is so nearly, and yet not quite, the literal, etymological meaning of "reflect" ("bend again"). Stevens is punning richly and beautifully and fiercely, punning his life-force against all the pull of the dead.

Tropes continue to be literalized, dead metaphors revived, idioms punned upon. "Fixed one for good" (*CP* 529) can be deadly (good = forever) or excellent (good = the cause of goodness). In *July Mountain* (*OP* 114–15),

> We live in a constellation
> Of patches and of pitches . . .
> In an always incipient cosmos,
> The way, when we climb a mountain,
> Vermont throws itself together.

"Ver" and "mont" do combine to make the green mountain, Vermont. And Greek *symballein*, whence our "symbol," means "throw together." When we climb a mountain, then, word and state and the etymological "mountain" of Vermont self-symbolize. It is not that they "are symbolized." This is not Coleridgean symbolism, but a composing like "piece the world together, boys" or "patches the moon together."

One late poem that is close to a riddle poem literalizes a common trope. This is *The Desire To Make Love in a Pagoda* (*OP* 91).

Among the second selves, sailor, observe
The rioter that appears when things are changed,

Asserting itself in an element that is free,
In the alien freedom that such selves degustate:

In the first inch of night, the stellar summering
At three-quarters gone, the morning's prescience,

As if, alone on a mountain, it saw far-off
An innocence approaching toward its peak.

Stevens' title plays with the preposition "in," for this is both the desire felt by a human to make love in a pagoda, and the desire felt by a pagoda to make love. Stevens also plays with the different senses of "peak," for the act of making love has a peak both physiologically and emotionally. (And pagodas are "strange buildings that come to a point at the end," as Ruskin says.) We recall the old trope of the body as a temple of the Lord, and remember that for most of Stevens' readers, a pagoda is a foreign or "alien" temple. If we read the noun clause in the second line as describing itself, we note also that a "rioter," "when things are changed," is anagrammatically a near-complete erotic, an appropriate enough change in a poem about a desire to make love. The poem is a gently witty, erotic, multilayered verse on overlapping subjects: on desires of the body and of feelings; on primal desires for morning, which a temple might desire, as in love; on the desire to make riots, or anagrams, of letters, and to trope. The poem is close to a riddle poem. (Query: Is the body a temple? A temple of the Lord? Answer: Sometimes it is a pagoda.)

After I argued this case in 1983, two people mentioned the existence of an actual pagoda that Stevens knew, the one overlooking Reading.[4] On reflection, this made perfect sense. Once more, Stevens' word-play is connected with an actual place, even as he sums up over a history of troping, and brings it and an actual place alive for us. We read freshly Shakespeare's "heaven-kissing hill" or Wordsworth's more neutral verb: "these steep and lofty hills . . . connect / The landscape with the quiet of the sky" (*Tintern Abbey*). Other writers can use tropes that are rude and funny. We look more closely at the way tall buildings or trees or hills "meet" the sky, and see them more fully in the act of considering our words.

---

[4] See my "Riddles, Charms, and Fictions in Wallace Stevens," *Centre and Labyrinth: Essays in Honour of Northrop Frye* ed. Eleanor Cook et al. (Toronto: University of Toronto Press, 1983), p. 228. See also Joan Richardson, *Wallace Stevens: A Biography* (New York: Beech Tree Books, 1986), vol. 1, p. 349. "Look for me in Sacred Pagodas," Stevens wrote when young (ibid., p. 340).

The crowded style and self-lacerating wit of *The Comedian as the Letter C* have gone. There is little irony left, and it tends to be simple and clear, as in "St. Armorer's was once an immense success, / It rose loftily and stood massively" (*CP* 529). The tone makes us supply quotation marks: "St. Armorer's was once an 'immense success,' " etc. The attack here will offend no one. In fact, it is Stevens' retrievals from Christianity rather than his attacks that sometimes cause offense. Such retrievals as "God and the imagination are one" or the end of *St. Armorer's Church from the Outside* are variously read. The orthodox are sometimes angered, while those more accommodating sometimes assimilate Stevens a shade too easily into the Christian fold.[5] (He did say, after all, that his aim was to make the Archbishop of Canterbury jump off the end of the dock.) Geoffrey Hill's phrase is both generous and rightly placed: "magnificent agnostic faith."[6]

Stevens' echoing in the late lyrics is very quiet for the most part. We are unlikely to hear it unless we have attended to the earlier, louder, combative echoes. It is as if he were smiling to himself at the old battles, remembering them clearly but softly, now past combat. When he does send echoes to war, he signals his procedure very clearly. Thus in *In the Element of Antagonisms*: "Birds twitter pandemoniums around / The idea of the chevalier of chevaliers" (*CP* 426). Keats and Milton and Hopkins are once more recalled, though not as in the quiet closing of *Sunday Morning* but "in the element of antagonisms." Stevens uses a different verb from *To Autumn* ("twitter," not "whistle") and a discordant noise from *Paradise Lost* (though without a capital) in order to attack a "chevalier of chevaliers" ("O my chevalier," said Hopkins of a bird). Or rather, to attack such an "idea." Medieval bird debate could hardly do better.

I hear little of Stevens' extraordinary metaleptic or leaping-over echoes, as for example the leap of the mockingbirds over Keats. I hear little of his extraordinary hearing-through echoes, as for example we gradually hear Milton's serene angelic gaze through Wordsworth. In *This Solitude of Cataracts*, the echoing takes disagreement for granted, and goes back from Wordsworth to end with Milton and the unusual wish to possess a Miltonic or biblical sense of the world. Other old echoes are reechoed: Theseus on the lover, the lunatic, and the poet: "The lover, the believer and the poet. / Their words are chosen out of their desire . . . The lover writes, the believer hears, / The poet mumbles" (*CP* 441–43). Or the Exodus journey: "These locusts by day, these crickets by

---

[5] I find both Adelaide Kirby Morris and Milton Bates a shade accommodating in their assimilation of Stevens.

[6] Geoffrey Hill, *The Lords of Limit: Essays on Literature and Ideas* (New York: Oxford University Press, 1984), pp. 16–17.

night" (*CP* 489). And Stevens reechoes his own work, time and again. "Oto-otu-bre" from *Metamorphosis* comes back: "Otu-bre's lion-roses have turned to paper / And the shadows of trees / Are liked wrecked umbrellas" (*CP* 506).

Among other old subjects, we might note the late form of Florida as Madame la Fleurie, a wicked fairy-tale earth mother whose reality awaits us all. Venus has mostly vanished, though there is "a mother with vague severed arms" (*CP* 438). As a force, she has become Penelope, the longed-for and longing woman of this earth. As with old subjects and arguments, so with old topoi. The leaves, birdsong, light, evening, flowers, fire, ghosts, dwelling places: Stevens sums up over these familiar topoi. Some old figues reappear though not others: the ghosts, the angel, the reader, but not the scholar or rabbi or mentor. Of his old selves, the Spaniard remains (I shall come to him), and a new name comes forward, retrieved from the early letters, Ariel. Not Prospero, commanding then leaving a world, but Ariel, also leaving a world, about to be released into his own element, air: "Ariel was glad he had written his poems." Stevens' memory is going back forty-four years. "I like to write most when the young Ariel sits, as you know how, at the head of my pen and whispers to me—many things; for I like his fancies, and his occasional music. . . . Now, Ariel, rescue me. . . . Ariel was wrong, I see" (*L* 123, 124, June 17 and 19, 1909; *CP* 532).

I mentioned the reappearance of Ulysses in these late poems, reappearance because Ulysses like Virgil was there at the start. Crispin's journey is an "Odyssey"; du Bellay's sonnet on Ulysses is mentioned more than once. Among the gods, Vulcan is closest to Stevens. Among legendary mortals, Ulysses is his alter ego, just as *pius* Aeneas is Eliot's. Many-sided Odysseus, wily, resourceful, gifted with words and so loved by Athena, is nonetheless simple in feeling and desire. I think Stevens liked him especially because he journeyed to earthly paradises, cohabited with goddesses, was promised immortality if he would stay, and always refused. "The nymph Calypso . . . yearning that he should be her husband . . . tended him, and said that she would make him immortal and ageless all his days; yet she could never persuade the heart in his breast" (*Odyssey* xxiii.333–36, repeating vii.256–57, Loeb). Penelope and Ithaca, that poor land and that rich woman, make a home for Ulysses that no heaven can provide. It is that sense of home, which is also du Bellay's sense, that makes Ulysses a potent figure in Stevens' late poetry. Du Bellay also reppears in the late work (*OP* 198, 1951).

Stevens' old genius for borrowing and inventing proper names continues. Throughout his work, there are a surprising number of actual names, surprising because our memory may tell us that there are not many. Actual names sometimes act as a metonymy for a system of belief or ideas, or for the spirit of an age, or for a tradition of thought: "In the John-begat-Jacob of what we know . . . In the generations of thought" (*OP* 103). Thus also in *Description without Place*, with Calvin or Queen Anne of England or Lenin: "Things are as they seemed to Calvin. . . ." Stevens occasionally uses the names of friends and acquaintances, as well as family names like John Zeller. Châtillon is, I think, a family name, or at least a desired family name, for Stevens liked the thought that this Protestant reformer was among his ancestors.[7] Some random names give a flavor in themselves; their function is generic (Bonnie and Josie, Mrs. Dooley, Swenson, Solange).[8] Stevens can play with the authority of names and titles, as we know from his Canon and Professor and Herr Doktor. As for the name of greatest authority, the name of God, Stevens sometimes treats it with humor, genial and other ("the Got whome we serve," "Herr Gott"). God's name for himself, "I am that I am," echoes through *Notes toward a Supreme Fiction*, together with some of our human echoes of "I am" (those of Coleridge and Descartes). In the late poetry, he returns to it in *The Sail of Ulysses* (*OP* 99): "As I know, I am and have / The right to be." (He is punning on "as," revising Descartes's "ergo," and using enjambment to play on the verb "have.") He was always as interested in American place names as Milton was in English or Latin ones.[9] And he always enjoyed inventing place names, including typic place names like Indyterranean, on the model of Mediterranean. He invents allegorical and onomatopoeic rivers in the late poetry, with no loss of the sense of actual flowing water: the z sounds of a river in Brazil, "the river R."

It is Stevens' invented personal names that especially surprise and delight us as we look back over his poetry: Chief Iffucan, Bawda, Nanzia Nunzio, Mr. Blank, Madame la Fleurie, Mac Mort, Mr. Homburg, Hoon, Flora Lowzen, General du Puy, Mrs. Alfred Uruguay, Berserk,

[7] Stevens speaks of his ancestor, Gaspard de Châtillon, grandson of Coligny, "one of the great Protestant figures of his time," in a letter to Paule Vidal, May 21, 1945 (WAS 2887, Huntington Library, quoted by permission of Holly Stevens and the Huntington Library).

[8] Cf. Alastair Fowler, *Kinds of Literature: An Introduction to the Theory of Genres and Modes* (Cambridge, Mass.: Harvard University Press, 1982), "Generic Names," pp. 75–87.

[9] Cf. T. S. Eliot: "It remained for Marlowe to discover, and Milton to perfect, the musical possibilities of classical names almost to a point of incantation" (*Selected Essays*, 3d ed. [London: Faber & Faber, 1951], p. 103). Or cf. Ezra Pound: "I have read a reasonable amount of bad American magazine verse, pseudo-Masefieldian false pastoral and so on. Not one of the writers had the sense, which Mr Ford shows here, in calling up the reality of the Middle West by the very simple device of names" (*Egoist* 2:1 [January 1, 1915], 12).

Augusta Moon and Alpha and Omega. Lulu Gay and Lulu Morose are wonderfully funny, though their poems are strained (*OP* 26–27). Stevens invented them after he received from Harriet Monroe a book called *Lillygay: An Anthology of Anonymous Poems* (*L* 221, March 14, 1921). Lulu Gay is l'Allegro, 1921 style, female version, with a refrain of ululate, sung by eunuchs. Lulu Morose is Il Penseroso, 1921 style, female version. Stevens' "diva-dame" (*CP* 353) is presumably a late form of the sybil—Dryden's "mad divining dame" (*Aeneid* vi.54) in operatic mood. Phoebus Apothicaire (*CP* 105) should be Phoebus Apollo—or Apollinaire, but what the connection is with Guillaume, I must leave to others.

Stevens is especially inventive in names for his (and our) various public and private selves, as well as his poetic selves. His early poetic selves are like Chaplin characters: the bumbler, the modest poet, the clown. They come out of Shakespeare or Dickens or old comedy, and they come with c-sounds, on which Stevens commented, and with p-sounds, on which he did not: Peter Quince, Pecksniff, Crispin. Later, Stevens invents names, still with c- and p-sounds: a clerical figure for an aspiring self, Canon Aspirin; a professor for an earnest self, Professor Eucalyptus. Stevens figures as Pierrot in letters to his future wife,[10] and also as Ariel, a figure who enters his poetry only late in life. Comic in sound (said Stevens), bumbling and so part of a modesty topos, these early masks are mostly drawn from other worlds. Milton Bates has provided a fine account of them.[11] Their function is not simple, as witness our disputes over Peter Quince's role in his poem. Sometimes they approach a dramatic character, for example, Crispin. Sometimes they seem something like dramatic masks, or characters who speak the prologue or epilogue, presenters under whose aegis a poem goes forward. Michael Hamburger's term, a "mask of style," fits them well.[12] They are at once part of the action yet detached from it, mediators of a kind between audience and poem. Sometimes they seem defensive. Stevens remarked on the different characters present within all of us, and imagined a trunkful of

[10] Jacques Derrida offers a "library of Pierrots" in "The Double Session," *Dissemination*, trans. Barbara Johnson (Chicago and London: University of Chicago Press, 1972, 1981), p. 205n 23. The question of "specular doubling" is of interest for Stevens.

[11] *Wallace Stevens: A Mythology of Self* (Berkeley and London: University of California Press, 1985), pp. 55–60 and *passim*.

[12] Hamburger, *The Truth of Poetry: Tensions in Modern Poetry from Baudelaire to the 1960s* (London and New York: Methuen, 1969, 1982), p. 110. David Walker distinguishes between poems written in the traditions of the dramatic monologue and dramatic lyric and those written as "transparent lyrics," which replace "the lyric speaker with the reader as the center of dramatic attention" (*The Transparent Lyric: Reading and Meaning in the Poetry of Stevens and Williams* [Princeton: Princeton University Press, 1984], p. xii).

costumes in our mental makeup: "There is a perfect rout of characters in every man—and every man is like an actor's trunk, full of strange creatures, new & old. But an actor and his trunk are two different things" (*SP* 166). Stevens does not write dramatic monologues proper, but his word-play with names, and with the word "mask," make his interest in dramatic functions clear. Our discussions of the changing dramatic monologue, of dramatis personae, and of theories of the mask should look again at Stevens' names.

One series of characters has not been remarked on, and that is the Spanish series of figures that appear all through Stevens' work. They run from Don Joost in 1921 to the demanding hidalgo in 1949 (*CP* 483), a tutelary spirit and poetic conscience in one. "Don Joost is a jovial Don Quixote," said Stevens (*L* 464), a remark that makes no sense of his unjovial poem, *From the Misery of Don Joost.* (It follows *The Comedian as the Letter C,* also a very uncomfortable mixture of joviality and misery.) Sometimes the Spaniard plays a guitar, as Stevens himself did literally and also poetically. He may be Don John (*CP* 49) or Don Juan (*OP* 64) or simply Don Don (*CP* 104). Stevens does not especially like him in these last manifestations, nor as the "moralist hidalgo" (*CP* 186). It is in the mature verse that the hidalgo comes into his own: "The knowledge of Spain and of the hidalgo's hat— / A seeming of the Spaniard, a style of life, / The invention of a nation in a phrase (*CP* 345) . . . This was / Who watched him, always, for unfaithful thought. / This sat beside his bed, with its guitar . . . Nothing about him ever stayed the same, / Except this hidalgo and his eye and tune" (*CP* 483). The Spaniard is a singer and a lover and a fighter. In one desperately bitter, uncollected poem, he considers mock-fighting like mon oncle's, and gives it up (*The Woman Who Blamed Life on a Spaniard* [*OP* 34]).

Once we hear this Spanish figure through Stevens' work, we begin to discover other appearances. The "Spaniard of the rose" (*CP* 316) is still unidentified but he is related, and somehow through the Order of the Knights of the Rose. The Pastor Caballero (another c-plus-p name) follows the Pastoral Nun to end the short poems of *Transport to Summer.* Christian "pastoral" is not quite the same as a pastor that goes with a caballero (a knight), whose poem opens thus:

> The importance of a hat to a form becomes
> More definite. The sweeping brim of the hat
> Makes of the form Most Merciful Capitan,

> If the observer says so: grandiloquent
> Locution of a hand in a rhapsody.
> Its line moves quickly with the genius

Of its improvisation until, at length,
It enfolds the head in a vital ambiance,
A vital, linear ambiance. The flare

In the sweeping brim becomes the origin
Of a human evocation, so disclosed
That, nameless, it creates an affectionate name,

Derived from adjectives of deepest mine.

"Mine" indeed, we murmur, thinking of Stevens' affection for his Span-
ish self. This poem sweeps (not strides) in enjambment, and makes "a
human evocation." (It reminds, it calls forth.) The pastor is nameless,
and which word of "pastor caballero" is adjective, I do not know, yet the
lines also create "an affectionate name." We speak of donning this or
that hat, when we take on certain jobs or roles. This is a Spanish hat,
become a role through idiom and through analogy.

The Spaniard is a compound figure whose clearest ancestor is Don
Quixote. His immediate relatives are Stevens' mentor at Harvard,
George Santayana, and his contemporary, Picasso. Santayana is obvious
but Picasso may not be, especially if we recall Stevens' phrase about the
"dilapidations of Picasso." A notebook entry makes Picasso's presence—
or at least, the presence of his Spanishness—in Stevens' imagination
clearer: "In a review of *Middle Spain* by George Santayana, in *The New
Statesman* June 26, 1948, Raymond Mortimer joined him with Picasso
as the two living Spaniards most conspicuous for genius and said . . they
have both chosen to be expatriates yet retain under their cosmopolitan-
ism a deep Spanishness—the sense 'that in the service of love and imag-
ination nothing can be too lavish, too sublime or too festive; yet that all
this passion is a caprice, a farce, a contortion, a comedy of illusions.' "[13]
The passage is especially interesting because of the combination, some-
times strange to an Anglo-Saxon mode of behavior, of entire devotion
and seriousness with complete comic grace. It is serious play, Spanish
style, and Stevens, from the beginning, liked to take on what Cervantes
calls "the syle of a Don."

The Spaniard's last appearance is in 1954 in *Farewell without a Guitar*
(*OP* 98):

Spring's bright paradise has come to this.
Now the thousand-leaved green falls to the ground.
Farewell, my days.

---

[13] Commonplace Book, II, 12, WAS 70–73, Huntington Library, quoted by permission
of Holly Stevens and the Huntington Library.

This short poem, of great poignancy, speaks quietly back over Stevens' whole life.

Some of Stevens' late poems become clearer from a knowledge of his earlier work, for example, *Study of Images II*:

> The frequency of images of the moon
> Is more or less. The pearly women that drop
> From heaven and float in air, like animals
>
> Of ether, exceed the excelling witches, whence
> They came. But, brown, the ice-bear sleeping in ice-month
> In his cave, remains dismissed without a dream,
>
> As if the centre of images had its
> Congenial mannequins, alert to please,
> Beings of other beings manifold—
>
> The shadowless moon wholly composed of shade,
> Women with other lives in their live hair,
> Rose—women as half-fishes of salt shine,
>
> As if, as if, as if the disparate halves
> Of things were waiting in a betrothal known
> To none, awaiting espousal to the sound
>
> Of right joining, a music of ideas, the burning
> And breeding and bearing birth of harmony,
> The final relation, the marriage of the rest.

We may start with the title, taking it as a directive, and follow the old-fashioned method of image study. Moon images as a series of "pearly women" are not hard to read, though we may quarrel about their "witchy origins." The moon as brown bear in a cave is an image that "remains dismissed," as Stevens says. When we recall his own "brown moon" that opens *Transport to Summer*, the two antithetical moon types come clear. Stevens is inventing a land of images, like the *pays de la métaphore*, a place inhabited by images who are "congenial mannequins, alert to please"—model models, so to speak. He devises moon images drawn from the sea, for half- or quarter-moons may be reflected as shiny mermaids, "women as half-fashion of salt shine." (The acoustic effects are very fine here.) And he reads a fable from the light and dark halves of the moon, in which the two halves yearn for each other, are betrothed, and await marriage, consummation, and the birth of harmony. *The Motive for Metaphor* helps us read this fable, as does Harmony, daughter of contraries, of Venus and Mars, allegorically Love and

306

Strife, and one presiding genius of Stevens' volume *Harmonium*. Many of Stevens' late poems are like this; they play back over his own work, echoing it, reshaping it, enlightening it. Here, for example, we might ask if *The Motive for Metaphor* is also a fable of moon and sun. (We recall that its land of the moon is half- and quarter- and mutable. Its land of the sun is full, and fixes, as with the classical sun, "He Who Smites from Afar.") Stevens' vision of union and harmony here is a metaphor, resting grammatically on a repeated "as if." Yet his tercet of appositive phrases sounds like positive affirmation. The poem is a remarkable summing-up.

This Solitude of Cataracts (CP 424) is a fluency poem of sorts, and a rich one. It is a poem of desire, not so much the desire to stop time as the desire to make it keep on flowing in the same way. The tension is between familiar change and unfamiliar change. Stevens opens with a variation on Heraclitus: "He never felt twice the same about the flecked river, / Which kept flowing and never the same way twice, flowing. . . ." The poem is full of doublenesses that are near but not complete, whether syntactical or mimetic. The reflections in the water are like the reflections of thought, "thought-like Monadnocks" (with a ghost of Leibniz rendering that Indian name and actual mountain "thought-like"). Yet they are not the same, not even a mirror image, for on the surface, "wild ducks fluttered, / Ruffling its common reflections." (Auden also uses the word "ruffled" in a poem of doubleness and reflection to imply that we only see on or into water when it is still: "Fish in the unruffled lake.") Common reflections in both senses of the word are ruffled when their surface is fluttered. The poem also "flows through many places, as if it stood still in one" (representations of actual places like Mount Monadnock and also the topoi of poetry). As in many late poems, Stevens moves from wit to intense desire:

> He wanted to feel the same way over and over.

> He wanted the river to go on flowing the same way,
> To keep on flowing.

"Feel," rhyming with both "real" and "not real" in the preceding line, alters the tone of the opening line. Something is suppressed here, like a lament—or in Stevens' unexpected metaphor, like an apostrophe: "There seemed to be an apostrophe that was not spoken." What is this apostrophe? Like the one forbidden on the funicular, as we travel up a nonvisionary mountain? Like the spouting "volcano Apostrophe"? We may hear a suppressed "O" flowing through the poem, as if Stevens thought something like "O wild West Wind," but would not speak it. His negative, "not spoken," plays on a paradox of absence and presence.

This line is especially fine because of the pun on apostrophe, a pun that current theories of apostrophe have not thought of. An apostrophe is also a mark of elision. In this sense, apostrophe is *defined* as something "not spoken," so that "there seemed to be" an elision, a contraction, something omitted but understood. This is a secondary meaning that limits the sense of loss or suppression in something "not spoken." It is as if Stevens said: I could write an apostrophe but will only evoke the thought of one, eliding it like apostrophe in another sense; that little mark stands for, or evokes, the "O," etc., of appropriate apostrophe. As it happens, there are no apostrophes of either kind in the poem; the grammatical and rhetorical pun is "not spoken."

Thematically, this is a poem of solitude, recalling other solitudes in Stevens' poetry. It closes on a most unusual desire for him, a desire to feel oneness, unity, paradisal vision—or to feel what it would be like to feel that way. It remains only a passing desire. Stevens' poem begins with paradox, and goes on to meditation on the fact that some things, though changed, look and feel so nearly the same. This is as true of nature as of the self, and the two may be connected. Wordsworth is our most familiar writer on this theme. "Though changed," he comes again for restoration to the river Wye. The question of its change is not raised, and its restorative power seems constant. Doubleness that is not quite the same is felt differently by a twenty-eight-year-old looking back five years and a sixty-nine-year-old.

Stevens' word "cataracts" is surprising if read descriptively, for there is no reference to cataracts in the body of the poem. (This quiet riddling device is one he likes, as we know from *Invective against Swans* and *Ghosts as Cocoons*.) Allegorically, the word implies a turbulence of feeling that is not spoken. Allusively, the word recalls some of Wordsworth's most memorable lines: "I cannot paint / What then I was. The sounding cataract / Haunted me like a passion." Stevens works against Wordsworth's sense of how memory may refresh us and become "the bliss of solitude." His title responds to Wordsworth *sotto voce* when we emphasize its first word: *This Solitude of Cataracts*. His desire is not just for what he has had, but for what he never had—that biblical and Miltonic sense of being at the center:

> He wanted the river to go on flowing the same way,
> To keep on flowing. He wanted to walk beside it,
>
> Under the buttonwoods, beneath a moon nailed fast. . . .
>
> Just to know how it would feel, released from destruction,
> To be a bronze man breathing under archaic lapis,

Without the oscillations of planetary pass-pass,
Breathing his bronzen breath at the azury centre of time.

This is desire for an earthly paradise, American version, as the "button-wood" tells us. (The tree is the *Platanis occidentalis*, the American plane-tree, another species of the genus under which Eve first saw Adam, a tree of felicitous associations.) The diction, beautifully ordinary and clear, comes with the resonance of associative sound. The moon of mutability is stopped here, nailed as if on some stage set. If Stevens could "be a bronze man breathing under archaic lapis," he would be under the archaic lapis of the biblical heavens, like Milton's steps "on Heavens azure" (*PL*i.297). Stevens' word "archaic" is pointing us toward archaic usage. "Breathing his bronzen breath at the azury centre of time" links "azury" and "archaic lapis" in an implied lapis lazuli, which is the Arabian origin of the word "azure." The two words are quite separate in modern usage, but once were nearly the same like so many other near-doubles in this poem.

The "planetary pass-pass," punning finely on French *passe-passe* or sleight of hand, suggests the illusion in our reading of the passing planets. They do seem to return to the same orbits as they pass and then pass again, with "pass-pass" accelerating the pace. Yet they do not: that seeming sameness by which "pass" reduplicates "pass" is itself a passe-passe or illusion, with the eye deceived by a motion. The second word "pass" is not the same as the first, because it comes after itself and so sets up an echoing compound. The planets, once assumed to be beyond change, follow the same pattern of near-sameness, for their orbits vary slightly each time.

With these senses of "pass-pass" and "azure" in mind, we return to the word "cataracts" and consider it diachronically or in its "pass-pass" aspect. Like "azure," "cataracts" has an archaic meaning (OED 1). It once meant the floodgates of heaven, which in the old cosmography were thought to keep back the rains. When they go, the deluge comes. (*Cataractae*, says the Vulgate.) Either as something dashing down or something holding back complete inundation, the word is a powerful figure for an aging human being. The ghost of an old cosmography hovers in "cataracts" and "lapis" and "azury." But in the end, Stevens' desire to be part of an old scheme is unreal for him.

Stevens returns to his earlier vexed subject of birdsong. *Song of Fixed Accord* evokes the maddeningly insistent cooing of mourning doves on spring mornings. Poets see various suns at five and six and seven of a spring morning, but this dove accepts them, "Like a fixed heaven, / Not subject to change." "Fixed accord" of the title implies a song about fixed

accord or a song made by fixed accord. The various sound patterns won-
derfully imitate the dove, and one repetition imitates it visually: "hail-
bow, hail-bow, / To this morrow" and we see the bobbing head of the
dove. One small sound, "a little wet of wing," evokes an early line from
Le Monocle, "Among the choirs of wind and wet and wing," a farewell
to torrents of erotic song. "Softly she piped" also allows back into Ste-
vens' work the much-abused trope of pipes.

Yet the poem comes with a caveat, gentle and insistent like the song of
a mourning dove. This is *her* song of fixed accord; we are free to hear
something more. There is a fine unobtrusive movement from simile to
metaphor over the ellipsis. The dove speaks "like the sooth lord of sor-
row" in line 2, and "the lord of love and of sooth sorrow" arrives at the
end. This is day's "invisible beginner" as against the visible beginner,
the sun. "The lord of love and of sooth sorrow, / Lay on the roof / And
made much within her." She appears to have summoned her lord, muse,
and male all at once. Stevens' play with archaic and religious diction
makes this an earthly version of the bird of the Holy Ghost. Milton's
inspiring Holy Spirit has, dovelike, satst brooding, not on the vast abyss
and made it pregnant, but on one female dove and made her pregnant,
whether with song or more, Stevens keeps unclear. The play with the
dove is like Joyce but the effects are Stevens' own, and finely controlled
as they must be.

"Part of the res itself and not about it," Stevens said in *An Ordinary
Evening in New Haven*, in the canto beginning "The poem is the cry of
its occasion." In *Not Ideas about the Thing but the Thing Itself*, the cry
is "a bird's cry." Not birdsong but a call. (The call and the song of birds
differ for many species.) This is an Alpha cry, so to speak, as Stevens
catches the strange predawn effect of the first bird-sound. And the first
strange predawn effect of March, a very early beginning to birdsong at
dawn. It will become loud enough to interrupt sleep by May, and a little
louder on this March morning as other birds join in. Hence:

> That scrawny cry—it was
> A chorister whose c preceded the choir.
> It was part of the colossal sun,
>
> Surrounded by its choral rings,
> Still far away. It was like
> A new knowledge of reality.

The tentative, then surer, placing of that bird-cry imitates the mind and
ear coming to consciousness, at first hearing as in a dream, then realizing
actual sound, outside. The sound of the predawn that Stevens loves

comes as a kind of gift. He plays easily with old arguments of inside and outside, with a sense of place, with puns and echoes, as he closes his poem and his volume on these stanzas. He repeats "scrawny cry" three times, a repetition and mimesis enriched by memory. For "scrawny" is our modern form of the word "scrannel," Milton's word in "Grate on their scrannel pipes of wretched straw." Stevens here writes of neither night-ingale nor grackle nor any named bird. This March sound recalls his autumn refrain of "skreak and skritter" and "grackles" and "grates"—recalls and rewrites it, turning thin, false-piped scr-sounds into thin, ear-liest sounds like "scrawny." The old play with the letter c is here too, placed before the reader with simple charm. The bird-cry lines are full of c-sounds; the old wintry and sleepy worlds sound out "sh" ("panache," "papier-mâché"); c-sounds intrude slowly into non-c "knowledge" in stanza ii and make a firm non-c simile at the end. Here is a "nota," c, that pre-cedes the sound of the choir, and, as a letter, is "part of the colossal sun." Like some precentor with a tuning fork, the bird sounds out his note. Stevens moves among different senses in his old c-see pun, which makes "choral rings" seen as well as heard.

The series "chorister," "choir," "choral," is a little insistent, again be-cause of memory, I think. At least two memories are at work here, one of song and eros, and one of song and the divine. One memory is Shake-speare's Sonnet 73 and its "bare ruin'd choirs where late the sweet birds sang," repudiated in *Le Monocle de Mon Oncle* and attenuated in the bough of *An Ordinary Evening in New Haven*. Choirs have ceased vex-ing Stevens, and a scrawny cry can be much. He centers things on the sun, not on the light of God, like Dante's choral rings at the end of the *Paradiso*. He makes choral rings, not perfect rounds. "Item: The wind is never rounding O," he wrote in 1942 (*CP* 263). Item, we add: the choir is never rounding O but only C.[14] Coleridge's great "choral echo" at the end of the *Biographia Literaria* echoes the great "I am." Stevens' bird-cry is "part of" something, where "part of" implies no transcendence, no sacramental symbolism, no associative analogy. Recalling complex rhetorical and dialectical matters for some readers, the poem remains simple and moving, scrupulously placed, a hymn.

Of Mere Being (*Palm* 398) allows what Stevens has not allowed before, anagogic metaphor, which we may hear in his explicit and implicit word-play:

> The palm at the end of the mind,
> Beyond the last thought, rises
> In the bronze decor,

[14] I am indebted for this point to Carolyn Masel.

A gold-feathered bird
Sings in the palm, without human meaning,
Without human feeling, a foreign song.

You know then that it is not the reason
That makes us happy or unhappy.
The bird sings. Its feathers shine.

The palm stands on the edge of space.
The wind moves slowly in the branches.
The bird's fire-fangled feathers dangle down.

This slowly moving play of exaltation begins with the title and its ob-
vious double sense of "mere." This is mere (bare, only) being and also
mere (utter, very) being. On the edge of things, including life, this is
how being may be. The implicit pun is on the word "phoenix," which is
what this fiery bird is. The Greek word for this fabulous sacred bird is
also used for a date-palm. The bird "sings in the palm" and through a
pun *is* the palm. So also the poem is contained in its words or its leaves,
and vice versa; it also *is* its words or leaves. So also space is contained in
the mind, and vice versa; it also *is* the mind.

This use of "is" sounds like the merest play of the verb "to be" or of
"being." Yet such a visionary sense "at the end of the mind" is also of
utter and very being. These are no longer the "intricate evasions of as";
here "as and is are one" (*CP* 476, 486). This is being as in the A *is* B of
anagogic metaphor. And we recall Stevens' old play with "B," "be," "to
be"—of mere being, so to speak. Anagogic metaphor is paradisal: this is
as close to paradisal language as Stevens will allow himself. He echoes
the bird of the earthly paradise from the lemon-tree land of *An Ordinary
Evening* in "dangle down," also rhymed on. He evokes the sun once
more, for the phoenix lives in the City of the Sun (Ovid, *Met.* xv.391–
407). He uses no language of upwardness and no language of home. The
poem is of mortality yet with a sense of immortality, though not per-
sonal immortality. It is a kind of will and testament of song. Thus, I
think, the touching on Yeats; this is a Byzantium poem of sorts, a land
of gold and kinds of transmutation. The "last thought" is the last
thought possible before we move beyond reason, whether toward imag-
ination or toward death.

I began by looking for the point at which Stevens' poems break with
our expectations. More and more, his poetry ceases to have one or two
or three such points. They multiply, and the language "flitters," to use
a word from *Notes*. If the late poetry displaces the reader at all, it is in a
very different way from the early work. And it also attaches, for it makes

this too loved earth lovelier still. These are poems of a man who loves this earth and does not want to leave it. Nothing of this passion sounds in the early poems for all their wit and pleasure. And paradoxically, for all their sensuousness. The early poems may have been poems of Stevens' heart. The late poems, some of deprivation, are often poems of Stevens' whole being.

Index to Works by Wallace Stevens

General Index

abstraction, 228–31
Adams, Henry, 35–36, 214n, 262
Aeschylus, 37
allusiveness (allusion, echo, quotation), 9,
    87–98; allusion, 65–66, 129, 155–57; al-
    lusive echo, 38–39, 45–46, 79, 81, 122,
    125–30, 140, 143, 200–203, 256, 258–60,
    279–81; echo, 63, 77n, 106–10, 157–59,
    197–98, 252–53, 300–301; faint echo,
    50, 83, 122, 129, 249, 286, 311; meta-
    leptic echo, 292, 300; schematic echo,
    31, 80, 82, 106, 113, 180, 202, 270, 309;
    terms defined, 87–88
Altieri, Charles, 176n, 229
analogy, 62, 65, 121–23, 162, 175, 311
Andersen, Hans Christian, 278
anecdote. See genre, kinds
Anne, of England, 302
apocalypse, 13, 267–94 passim. See also
    Bible, books of: Revelation; genre,
    kinds: apocalyptic writing
Apollinaire, Guillaume, 119, 303
argument. See dialectic
Ariosto, Ludovico, 67, 74
Aristophanes, 37
Aristotle, 5, 44, 62, 174, 194
Arnold, Matthew, 132
Ashbery, John, 59, 110
Auctor ad Herrennium, 34n
Auden, W. H., 16, 209, 307

Bach, J. S., 201
Bacon, Francis, 281, 290
Balzac, Honoré de, 190
Barfield, Owen, 253n
Barrett, Elizabeth, 199
Bates, Milton, 9, 142n, 251n, 300n, 303
Baudelaire, Charles, 15, 89, 138, 189–91,
    205, 220
Beardsley, Monroe, 175
Beckett, Samuel, 217

Beerbohm, Max, 60n
beginnings, 25–51, 38–39, 76–79, 84, 113,
    117–34 passim, 172, 215–19, 224, 235,
    310–11
Benveniste, Emile, 176n
Berger, Charles, 212n, 296
Berkeley, George, 195, 275
Berkovitch, Sacvan, 268
Bible: Belshazzar's Feast, 15–16; biblical
    tradition, 12, 106–11, 214–63 passim;
    Holy Spirit, 107–8; language of, 71, 90,
    125, 133, 143–44, 149–50, 227, 230,
    293; marriage at Cana, 253; translations
    of, 241, 244–45, 248, 309
Bible, books of: Genesis, 12, 62, 71, 215,
    217–18, 288; Exodus, 108, 221, 251,
    301–2; Deuteronomy, 204; II Samuel,
    221; II Chronicles, 241; Job, 90; Psalms,
    134, 143, 157, 158, 210, 216; Proverbs,
    20, 22, 218; Ecclesiastes, 274; Song of
    Solomon (Song of Songs, Canticles), 35,
    180, 241–42, 243, 249–50; Isaiah, 283;
    Daniel, 204; Joel, 173; Gospel of John,
    155–56; Gospels, 221, 257; Acts, 103n;
    Romans, 227; I Corinthians, 16, 223–25,
    227, 246, 253–54, 290; Hebrews, 249; II
    Peter, 81–82; Revelation (Apocalypse),
    13, 46n, 81–82, 241, 261–62, 269–73,
    279; Old Testament, 33, 253; New Tes-
    tament, 104, 251
Bible, persons in: Adam, 260–61, 285,
    288; Bathsheba, 65–66; Belshazzar,
    157–58; David, 157; Eve, 59, 61, 62,
    179, 261, 285, 288, 291; Hosea, 65;
    Isaiah, 235; Jacob, 150; Moses, 217–18,
    251; Nathan, 15, 65–66; Potiphar's
    wife, 65; St. Paul, 196, 228, 261; St. Pe-
    ter, 128; Samuel, 243; Sheba, Queen of,
    214; Solomon, 241
Blackmur, R. P., 151, 190, 276
Blake, N. F., 30n